To the

Blessed Virgin Mary

and my

own mother

GUIDE

TO THE

CATHOLIC SISTERHOODS

IN THE

UNITED STATES

Edited by

THOMAS P. McCARTHY, C. S. V.

With foreword by
THE MOST REVEREND AMLETO GIOVANNI
CARDINAL CICOGNANI
Secretary of State, Holy See

and

introduction by
THE MOST REVEREND EGIDIO VAGNOZZI
Apostolic Delegate to the United States

Revised and Enlarged

THE CATHOLIC UNIVERSITY OF AMERICA PRESS
WASHINGTON D.C.

First edition, 1952
Second edition, 1953
Third edition, 1955
Fourth edition, 1958
Fifth Edition, 1964
Reprinted, 2002

Imprimi Potest
    John W. Stafford, C.S.V.
        Provincial

Nihil Obstat
    Peter J. Rahill
        Censor Deputatus

Imprimatur
   ✠ Patrick A. O'Boyle
        Archbishop of Washington
    April 25, 1963

The *nihil obstat* and *imprimatur* are official declarations that a book or pamphlet is free of doctrinal or moral error. No implication is contained therein that those who have granted the *nihil obstat* and the *imprimatur* agree with the content, opinions, or statements expressed.

Copyright © 1964
The Catholic University of America Press, Inc.
All Rights Reserved

Library of Congress Catalog Number: 64-15336
ISBN 0-8132-1312-6

CONTENTS

FOREWORD

by

The Most Reverend Amleto Giovanni Cardinal Cicognani

From all sections of the country, metropolitan, rural, and missionary, and from beyond the borders of this land, the constant appeal of bishops can be heard: "Where can we find more Sisters to staff our schools, our hospitals, our institutions, our missionary projects?" If this *Guide to the Catholic Sisterhoods in the United States* serves young women blessed with a vocation, encourages others to consider a religious calling or even prompts others to take the step sooner, its publications will be more than justified and the efforts of its author, the Reverend Thomas P. McCarthy, C.S.V., will be amply rewarded.

The words of Martha to Mary, "The Master is here and calls thee," have been quoted frequently in connection with the vocation of religious women. It must be remembered that these words were spoken on the occasion of the resurrection of Lazarus from the dead. This seems to emphasize the truly great privilege that comes with a religious vocation, for time and again those who embrace the religious life have opportunities to be cooperators with divine grace by taking an active part in the spiritual resurrection of souls.

May all who glance through the pages of this volume in search of vocational guidance find inspiration and that direction which is divine.

INTRODUCTION

The Church, the Body of Christ, is in our day sorely afflicted. Christians of this generation can easily perceive how true it is that Christ, the Head of the Mystical Body, has need of his members. The welfare of His Body the Church requires, in the words of St. Paul, "the functioning in due measure of each single part" (Eph. 4, 16). Because "we have gifts differing according to the grace that has been given us" (Rom. 12, 6), the health of the Mystical Body is most effectively fostered when each member is using his gifts to best advantage within the wide range of the Church's apostolic activity.

For almost ten years now, Father McCarthy's *Guide to the Catholic Sisterhoods in the United States* has been assisting young women in determining where among the many institutes they may most effectively labor in "building up the body of Christ" (Eph. 4, 13). In so doing, it has been providing a valuable service. So great is the need for sisters, both here in the United States and in the missions throughout the world, that it would certainly be tragic if the Church were deprived of laborers because young women could not find a suitable outlet for the gifts with which God has endowed them.

Within this book Catholic young women have spread before them, as so many precious jewels, the Religious and Secular Institutes within the Church. Every one who feels within herself the stirrings of a divine call should be able to find among them that institute within which she can best serve the interests of God's glory, her own perfection, and the good of souls.

May this book, in the years ahead, continue to give guidance to those who respond generously to the voice of Our Lord calling them to service in his vineyard. May it serve to increase the numbers of those dedicated and self-sacrificing women who have brought so much benefit to the Body of Christ.

Washington, D. C.
January 16, 1962

✠ Egidio Vagnozzi
Titular Archbishop of Myra
Apostolic Delegate to the United States

PREFACE TO THE FIFTH EDITION

THE GUIDE TO THE CATHOLIC SISTERHOODS IN THE UNITED STATES has a threefold purpose. Its primary objective is to place in the hands of young women interested in entering the religious life a manual briefly describing the history, mode of life, nature of the work or works carried on, the spiritual life, training program, general qualifications for admission, and the descriptions of the habit with photographs, of three hundred and fifty-two congregations of women in the United States. This information should prove of great value to girls in the selection of a community whose rules and apostolate are most suitable to their talents, desires, and aptitudes.

A secondary purpose is to provide a compact informational directory for priests, sisters, parents, teachers, and others who are employed in the vocational guidance of young women.

The volume is also intended as a reference for the general public. More than six hundred sisterhoods with foundations in the United States are included. Also included are pictures of professed members of the respective congregations in the habits distinctive to each. This should not only serve to make each community better known to the general public but it should also result in a better understanding of the ideals of the religious life and a greater appreciation for the noble work being carried on by the sisters, not only in the United States but throughout the entire world.

The *Guide* has well defined limitations. It is not intended as a complete historical or statistical account of the communities of women with foundations in the United States. Moreover, to keep such an extensive undertaking within the confines of a convenient manual, each congregation, with a few exceptions, has been given a single page.

In every instance a young woman interested in a particular community of sisters is provided with an address to which she may apply for more detailed information.

In this edition, the communities of sisters have been arranged according to their general apostolic work, viz., contemplative, domestic, foreign and home missions, nursing, retreat and social work, teaching, and writing and publications. Such an arrangement will prove beneficial to the reader. By arranging the congregations according to their main apostolate, it is hoped that the *Guide* will become a definite aid in fostering vocations to the sisterhoods. It will be helpful not only for girls who are interested in a particular apostolate but especially for those who are unaware of the many works of the religious life.

Another feature of this edition is the inclusion of community addresses by city and state. Since many girls are interested in entering a congregation which is close to their homes, a special index has been added which lists the location of every principal house alphabetically arranged by city and state.

To further aid the reader in interpreting the various names and nomenclature of the religious life used throughout this book, a special glossary of terms has been added.

Special consideration has been given to over-age and under-age candidates to the religious life. Most congregations will not accept girls who are over thirty years of age. Some religious communities will receive late-vocations if they have sufficient intelligence and possess those qualities which will make them good religious. The communities that will accept candidates over the age of thirty have been noted in the section under QUALIFICATIONS.

While a greater number of communities are reluctant to accept non-high school graduates, there are a few that will receive teen-age girls who have not yet graduated from high school as candidates for the religious life. Such religious groups conduct what are known as aspirancies. These are community-supervised secondary schools, where girls may complete their high school studies while living and enjoying the spiritual benefits of convent life. Girls who desire to enter the religious life, although they have not completed their secondary school training, are asked to take special notice of the section on TRAINING PROGRAM where congregations conducting aspirancies may be found.

This edition also contains a section on the SECULAR INSTITUTES. There has been a notable increase in these societies in our own country. The last edition recorded eleven. Today there are twenty-three such organizations in the United States. Young women interested in the lay-apostolate, under vows, are advised to investigate the SECULAR INSTITUTES located at the end of the book.

Prospective candidates to the religious life should seek vocational guidance and direction from their pastor, parish priest, religious priest, sister-friend, or counselor because a vocation to the sisterhood is one of total dedication to God and should be made only after sufficient reflection and proper guidance.

The author makes grateful acknowledgement to His Excellency, The Most Reverend Amleto G. Cardinal Cicognani for permission to include his Foreword; to His Excellency, The Most Reverend Egidio Vagnozzi, for his kindness in writing the Introduction for this edition; to the Very Reverend John W. Stafford, C.S.V., for permission to undertake this work: to the Very Reverend John F. Brown, C.S.V., for providing the time to engage in this book; to Monsignor James A. Magner, Manager of the Catholic University of America Press for sponsoring the book; to Father Peter J. Rahill, Mr. John Graninger, and Miss Betty Goode for their assistance; to Father James P. Sweeney, C.S.V., for reading the original manuscripts and offering valuable suggestions; to Sister Mary Carmen, C.S.J., and Sister Gerard Joseph, C.S.J., for not only reading and correcting the manuscripts but also for arranging to have the manuscripts typed; to Sisters Louise, O.S.B., and Mary Amata, O.S.F., and to Fathers Leo Weiland, C.S.V., Robert Foster, C.S.V., John Lane, C.S.V., Edward Heitjan, C.S.V., and Brother Donald Houde, C.S.V., all of Spalding Institute, for their kind help and thoughtful suggestions.

Spalding Institute
Peoria, Illinois
June 10, 1963

I

CONTEMPLATIVES:

STRICTLY-CLOISTERED (Major Enclosure)

and

SEMI-CLOISTERED (Minor Enclosure)

also Teaching . . .

Retreat and Social Work . . .

Catechetics . . .

BENEDICTINE NUNS (O.S.B.)

History: The Regina Laudis Monastery was founded by Mother Benedict Duss, an American nun of the Benedictine Abbey of Jouarre, France. The Archbishop of Hartford graciously accepted the foundation and enclosed the community of eight nuns in September, 1948.

Purpose: The apostolate consists chiefly in the solemn celebration of the liturgy. The nuns offer the official prayer of the Church for the needs of the entire world. Day and night they prolong the praise which Christ, during His earthly life, offered to His Eternal Father. That lay-women may participate in their liturgical life, the nuns maintain a guest house where Benedictine hospitality is dispensed. They also endeavor to foster interest in pure Christian art by their own work and the display of religious objects.

Spiritual Life: The entire day receives a recollected character from the recurring hours of the Divine Office, which are chanted according to the monastic breviary in Latin. The nuns rise for Matins at 2 a.m. The focal point of monastic life is the Conventual Mass, the supreme act of loving worship. Time is also devoted to mental prayer and spiritual reading.

Training Program: The training for the Benedictine contemplative life is given in the novitiate to postulants, novices, and junior professed over a period of four and one-half years.

Qualifications:
* The maximum age for choir religious is 30. Those between 30 and 45 will be accepted as Oblate Sisters.
* Completion of high school for the choir religious.

Habit: The sisters wear a black habit and scapular and a white linen wimple.

> *Write to:* Regina Laudis
> Bethlehem,
> Connecticut

BENEDICTINE SISTERS OF PERPETUAL ADORATION (O.S.B.)

History: This community of sisters was founded in 1875 by a group of sisters from Maria Rickenbach in Switzerland. It consists of one motherhouse foundation in Clyde, Missouri, and four dependent monasteries. A sixth foundation is in the process of being erected in St. Louis, Missouri. Perpetual adoration has been maintained at the motherhouse since 1878 with continuous exposition of the Blessed Sacrament from 1920. The same privileges are enjoyed by the other priories.

Purpose: The primary apostolate is perpetual adoration of the Blessed Sacrament and the spreading of the Eucharistic devotion through apostolic works. They make altar breads, church vestments, operate an art department and ceramic shop, and staff a print shop in which the sisters print and publish prayer pamphlets, booklets, and a monthly magazine.

Spiritual Life: The religious exercises include Holy Mass, choral recitation of the Divine Office in Latin, meditation, spiritual reading, and the rosary. Each sister spends one-half hour a day and one hour at night in adoration.

Training Program: The six-month postulancy is followed by a two-year novitiate. The novices then make their temporary vows. For another two and one-half years the sisters receive special instruction from the junior-mistress before perpetual profession is made.

Qualifications:
* Age: 16 to 30.
* Completion of high school is preferred.

Habit: The sisters wear a black habit, scapular, and veil, and a white pleated collar and starched band.

Write to: Mother Prioress
Benedictine Convent of Perpetual Adoration
Clyde, Missouri

CARMELITE NUNS OF THE ANCIENT OBSERVANCE (O. CARM.)

History: Mother M. Therese of Jesus and Mother M. Clement Mary of the Guardian Angel founded the first primitive or calced monastery in the United States in 1931. These two nuns from the monastery in Naples, Italy (founded in 1536), were delegated to establish the American foundation in Allentown, Pennsylvania.

Purpose: The nuns of this strictly cloistered congregation make special supplication for priests and religious and for all who are engaged in the task of saving souls. Moreover they pray and do penance for those who will not pray or do penance for themselves. The sisters maintain their own orchards, bake altar breads, and are engaged in needlecraft, art work, and the making of vestments.

Spiritual Life: The religious exercises include Holy Mass, the chanting of the Divine Office in Latin, perpetual adoration of Our Lord in the Most Holy Sacrament, the rosary, meditation, spiritual reading, and other community prayers and devotions.

Training Program: The postulancy is followed by a two-year novitiate. The novices then make their temporary profession of vows. During the juniorate, the sisters continue their spiritual formation while taking courses toward their academic degrees. They also assist in the spreading of the Carmelite apostolate of the devotion to the brown scapular and the Third Order Movement.

Qualifications:
* Age: 15 to 30.
* Average intelligence.

Habit: The sisters wear a brown tunic and scapular, white mantle, and a black veil.

> *Write to:* Carmel of the Little Flower
> Saint Therese's Valley
> Allentown, Pennsylvania

DISCALCED CARMELITE NUNS
(O.C.D.) Cloistered

History: This ancient order originated on Mount Carmel. In 1562 in Avila, Spain, St. Teresa initiated a reform among the Carmelites, a return to the primitive rule given to the hermits of Mount Carmel by Albert of Jerusalem in 1207. St. Teresa directed the foundation of thirty-two convents herself. Her reform spread throughout the world reaching Maryland in 1790, the first of sixty-two foundations now existing in the United States.

Purpose: The Carmelite nuns are called to a life of love demanding total dedication to God. Retaining the spirit of her desert heritage, the Carmelite pursues the contemplative ideal, divine intimacy, while embracing the world with her apostolate of prayer and penance. It is intimate friendship with God which gives power to her prayer and effectiveness to her self-sacrifice, making her a collaborator in the redeeming work of Christ.

Spiritual Life: Each Carmelite chooses a life of renunciation and prayer. The Divine Office recited or chanted in Latin, two hours of mental prayer, spiritual reading, a variety of manual work, a strict fast, perpetual abstinence, and brief recreations comprise the religious exercises in the life of a Carmelite nun.

Training Program: The candidate is a postulant for six months before receiving the Carmelite habit and beginning the canonical year of novitiate. During this time the novice is trained by formal instructions and actual experience to live the contemplative life according to the primitive rule and St. Teresa's Constitutions. The novice makes her temporary vows after completing the novitiate. Profession of solemn vows consecrates the Carmelite nun to God forever.

Qualifications:
* Age: at least 17.
* An attraction for and understanding of contemplative life.

Habit: The sisters wear the brown habit and scapular of Our Lady of Mount Carmel, a black veil, white guimpe, and a white choir mantle.

Write to the Mother Prioress at the nearest Carmelite Monastery.

Alabama—716 Fulton Rd., Mobile 18, Alabama; *Arkansas*—721 W. 32nd St., Little Rock, Arkansas; *California*—215 E. Alhambra Rd.; Alhambra, California; 68 Rincon Rd., Berkeley 7, California; Carmel-by-the-Sea, (Box 17), California; 3361 E. Ocean Blvd., Long Beach 3, California; 2110 Stockton Blvd., Sacramento 17, California; 5158 Hawley Blvd., San Diego 16, California; 721 Parker Ave., San Francisco 18, California; 1000 Lincoln St., Santa Clara, California; *Colorado*—6138 S. Gallup Ave., Littleton, Colorado; *Georgia*—Route 5, Box 256, Coffee Bluff, Savannah, Georgia; *Illinois*—River Road and Central, Des Plaines, Illinois; *Indiana*—2500 Cold Springs Rd., Indianapolis 22, Indiana; 63 Allendale Rd., Terre Haute, Indiana; *Iowa*—14th St. and Central Ave., Bettendorf, Iowa; *Kansas*—3535 Wood Ave., Kansas City 2, Kansas; *Kentucky*—1740 Newburg Rd., Louisville 5, Kentucky; *Louisiana*—Breaux Bridge Rd. and Carmel Ave., Lafayette, Louisiana; 1236 N. Rampart St., New Orleans 16, Louisiana; *Maryland*—1318 Dulaney Valley Rd., Baltimore 4, Maryland; *Massachusetts*—61 Mt. Pleasant Ave., Roxbury, Boston 19, Massachusetts; Mt. Carmel Rd., Danvers, Massachusetts; *Michigan*—16630 Wyoming Ave., Detroit 21, Michigan; 1036 Valley Ave., N.W., Grand Rapids 4, Michigan; 317 E. B St., Iron Mountain, Michigan; Silver Lake Rd., Traverse City, Michigan; *Minnesota*—3890 deMontreville Rd., St. Paul 9, Minnesota; *Mississippi*—2155 Terry Rd., Jackson 4, Mississippi; *Missouri*—2521 W. Main St., Jefferson City, Missouri; 9150 Clayton Rd., Clayton 17, St. Louis, Missouri; *Nevada*—2750 Thomas Jefferson Dr., Reno, Nevada; *New Hampshire*—275 Pleasant St., Concord, New Hampshire; *New Jersey*—Carmel Rd., Mt. Carmel, Flemington P. O., New Jersey; 189 Madison Ave., Morristown, New Jersey; *New Mexico*—185 Sunset Rd. S.W., Albuquerque, New Mexico; Mount Carmel Rd., Sante Fe, New Mexico; *New York*—745 St. John's Pl., Brooklyn, New York; 75 Carmel Rd., Buffalo 14, New York; 1381 University Ave., New York 52, New York; 1931 West Jefferson Rd., Pittsford, New York; 68 Franklin Ave., Saranac Lake, New York; 428 Duane Ave., Schenectady 4, New York; *North Carolina*—Mason Rd., R. D. 2, Durham, North Carolina; *Ohio* —3176 Fairmont Blvd., Cleveland Heights 18, Ohio; 2065 Barton Pl., Columbus 9, Ohio; *Oklahoma*—4200 N. Meridan Ave., Oklahoma City 12, Oklahoma; *Oregon*—Route 5, Box 1209, Eugene, Oregon; *Pennsylvania*—Thornbrow, Elysburg, Pennsylvania; 510 E. Gorre St., Erie, Pennsylvania; Mount Carmel, Pennsylvania; Loretto, Pennsylvania; 66th Ave. and York Rd., Philadelphia 26, Pennsylvania; *Rhode Island*—Watson at Nyatt, Barrington, Rhode Island; *Texas*—P. O. Box 2903, Dallas, Texas; 1600 Sunset Terrace, Fort Worth, Texas; Old Katy Rd., and Upland Dr., Houston 24, Texas; 1104 Kentucky Ave., San Antonio 1, Texas; *Utah*—5714 Holladay Blvd., Salt Lake City 17, Utah; *Vermont*—Williston, Vermont; *Washington*—1808 18th Ave., Seattle, Washington; *West Virginia*—Pleasant Valley, Wheeling, West Virginia; *Wisconsin*—Route #4, Pewaukee, Wisconsin.

SERVANTS OF THE BLESSED SACRAMENT (S.S.) Cloistered

History: Blessed Peter-Julian Eymard founded this contemplative community in France in 1859. It was canonically erected as a religious congregation by Pope Pius IX in 1871 and received approval from Pope Leo XIII in 1885. The monastery in Maine was founded in 1947; the monastery in Colorado was established ten years later.

Purpose: The nuns of this congregation, who are divided into choir and co-adjutrix sisters, have for their exclusive occupation the motto of their founder, "All for the service of Jesus in the Blessed Sacrament." By means of a Guard of Honor, Holy Hours, and Triduums, the nuns promote adoration of the Blessed Sacrament and love of the Holy Eucharist.

Spiritual Life: The religious exercises include Holy Mass, the recitation of the Divine Office in Latin —the co-adjutrix sisters are excused from this exercise—perpetual adoration in which each nun takes her turn in adoration of Our Lord in the Blessed Sacrament, the rosary, spiritual reading, and other community prayers and devotions.

Training Program: The six-month postulancy is followed by a two-year novitiate. Temporary vows are made for three years after which perpetual vows are pronounced.

Qualifications:
* Age: 16 to 25. Exceptions are sometimes made.
* Completion of high school is preferred.
* Entrance dates: May 2 and November 4.

Habit: The sisters wear a white habit and veil.

Write to: Mother Superior   Mother Superior
101 Silver Street   2116 Oakland Street
Waterville, Maine   Pueblo, Colorado

DOMINICAN NUNS OF THE SECOND ORDER OF PERPETUAL ADORATION (O.P.) Cloistered

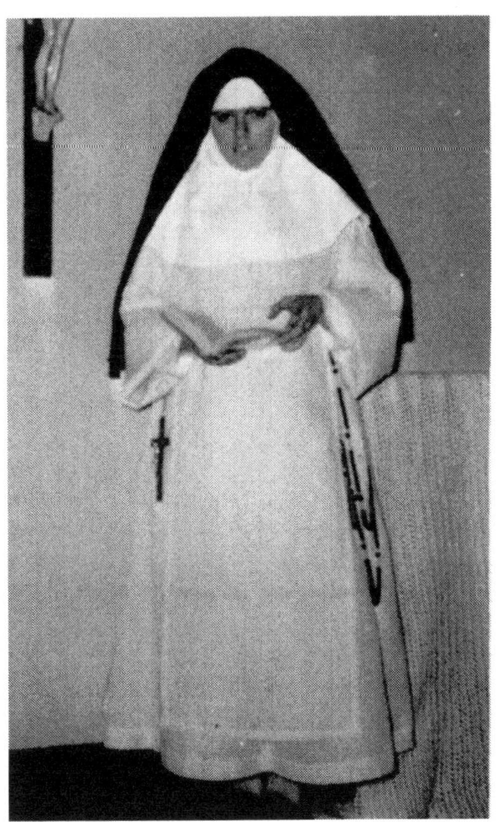

History: This order of Dominican nuns traces its origin directly to St. Dominic through the Monastery of the Blessed Sacrament at Ouillins, near Lyons, France, which descends directly from the first Dominican monastery established by St. Dominic himself, at Prouille, France, in 1206. After founding his cloistered daughters, St. Dominic established their enclosure and rules, which today are still observed and unchanged. In 1880 upon the invitation of Bishop Michael A. Corrigan of Newark, New Jersey, a colony of sisters left the monastery at Ouillins and with Mother Mary of Jesus founded the first monastery in the United States. Presently there are thirteen monasteries in the United States.

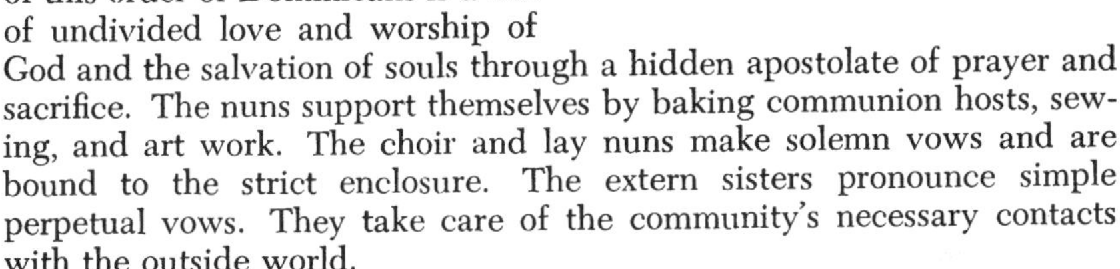

Purpose: The primary objective of this order of Dominicans is a life of undivided love and worship of God and the salvation of souls through a hidden apostolate of prayer and sacrifice. The nuns support themselves by baking communion hosts, sewing, and art work. The choir and lay nuns make solemn vows and are bound to the strict enclosure. The extern sisters pronounce simple perpetual vows. They take care of the community's necessary contacts with the outside world.

Spiritual Life: The religious exercises include Holy Mass, the chanting of the Divine Office in Latin, the rosary, spiritual reading, and other community prayers. Each night the nuns rise for two hours of prayer.

Training Program: The one-year postulancy is followed by a one-year novitiate. Temporary vows are made for three years. During this time the novice is under the direction of the Novice Mistress. Perpetual vows are then pronounced.

Qualifications:
* The maximum age is 30.
* Completion of high school is preferred.

Habit: The sisters wear a white tunic, scapular, guimpe, and forehead band, a black veil, and a leathern belt with a rosary and crucifix attached.

See page 377 for address of nearest monastery.

DOMINICAN SISTERS OF BETHANY (O.P.)

History: A French Dominican priest, Father Lataste, founded this community in 1866 to pray for women in prison and to offer those women who had fallen in the past and who desired to make amends for their former mistakes a spiritual haven of prayer and contemplation. The congregation has foundations in Europe.

Purpose: The apostolic activity of this community is to accept women who have incurred public disgrace, especially those who have been placed in penal institutions, provided that they have a true spirit of repentance and a sound desire for the religious life. Other congregations rarely accept women who have sinned publicly. In this community they are received with open arms. Two or three sisters are assigned to visit prisons to bring hope and courage to the women prisoners and to offer them a place of spiritual sanctuary at Bethany upon their release.

Spiritual Life: A contemplative community, these sisters live a life of silence, manual work, prayer, community life, and recite the Divine Office in choir.

Training Program: There are two groups of sisters in this congregation, the choir religious who enter the canonical novitiate leading to religious profession for life with simple vows, and the tertiary religious who enter the tertiary novitiate which leads to profession in the third order of Bethany. They all wear the same habit and live the community life together. The formation and obligations are less exacting for the tertiary sisters. The tertiaries may continue all their life in the third order or, upon the approval of the superiors, they may be accepted as choir religious.

Qualifications:
* Girls who are interested in rehabilitating fallen members of the Mystical Body.
* Penitents who wish to spend the rest of their lives in prayer.

Habit: The sisters wear the traditional white Dominican habit and black veil.

Write to: Dominican Sisters of Bethany
19 Dartmouth Street
West Newton 65, Massachusetts

DOMINICAN SISTERS OF THE PERPETUAL ROSARY (O.P.)
Cloistered

History: Father Damien M. Santourens, O.P., founded this community in France in 1880. The first American foundation was made on December 21, 1891. There are eight monasteries in the United States. Each is completely independent.

Purpose: The primary objective of this congregation is the personal sanctification of its members through a cloistered life of contemplation, prayer, and sacrifice. Each monastery is self-supporting. The principal means of income consists in the making of altar breads, rosaries, and vestments, and in fancy needle work.

Spiritual Life: The religious exercises include Holy Mass, the recitation of the Divine Office in Latin —Compline is sung every evening— two half-hour periods of mental prayer, the uninterrupted recitation of the perpetual rosary, and other community prayers and devotions.

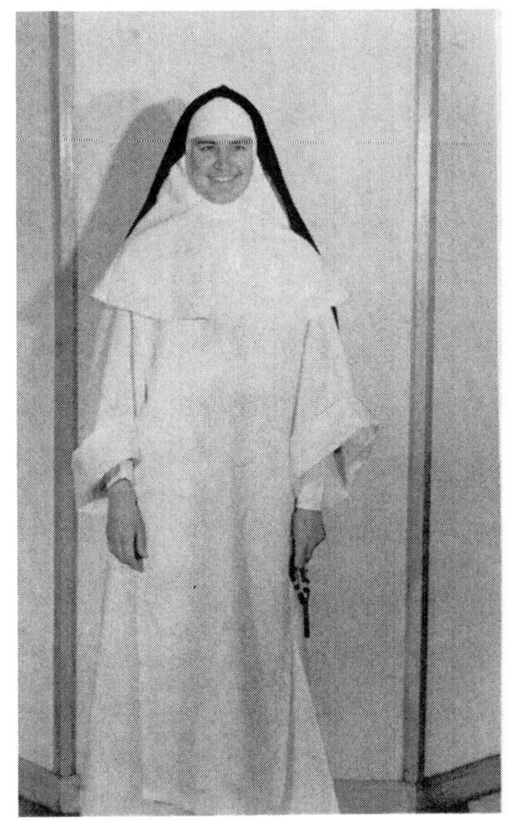

Training Program: The postulancy of six months to one year is followed by a five-year novitiate. The postulant is a simple novice for one year. At the completion of the canonical year, the novice makes temporary vows for three years, during which time she remains in the novitiate for further training. The sister becomes a fully professed member of the community when she makes her profession of perpetual vows.

Qualifications:
* The maximum age is 30.
* Completion of high school for the choir religious. There are no educational requirements for the lay or extern sisters.

Habit: The sisters wear the traditional white Dominican tunic and scapular.

See page 377 for address of nearest monastery.

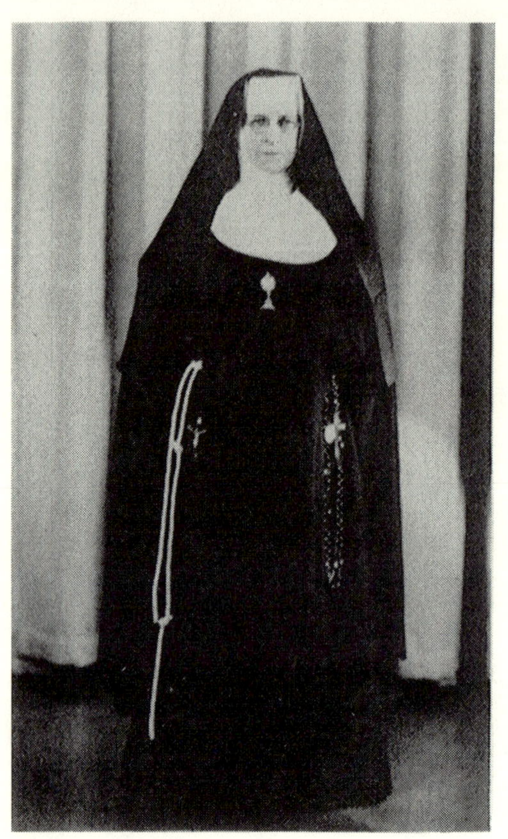

FRANCISCAN NUNS OF THE MOST BLESSED SACRAMENT (F.SS.S.)
Cloistered

History: Mother Mary Claire Bouillevaux founded this order in Paris, France, in 1854. The first foundation in the United States was made in 1921 at Cleveland, Ohio. In 1931 the noted Old St. Paul's Episcopal Cathedral was converted into a magnificent shrine of perpetual adoration. From this spiritual source the blessings of God have been emanating into the city of Cleveland and into the entire world.

Purpose: The apostolate of this cloistered contemplative order is the perpetual adoration of the Most Blessed Sacrament solemnly exposed day and night. In their monasteries the nuns pray for the church, the sanctification of priests, and for the world. The time not given to prayer is devoted to art and music and the making of altar breads.

Spiritual Life: The religious exercises include Holy Mass, mental prayer, the rosary, and spiritual reading. The choir nuns chant the Divine Office in Latin. The lay and extern sisters also recite Office. The extern sisters care for the public shrine and handle the secular business of the monastery.

Training Program: The six-month postulancy is followed by a one-year novitiate. After six years in temporary vows, the nuns make solemn perpetual vows.

Qualifications:
* Age: 18 to 30. Exceptions are sometimes made.
* Completion of high school for choir nuns.
* A desire to live a hidden life of contemplation.

Habit: The sisters wear a dark brown habit, white cord, the seven decade Franciscan Rosary, a small metal monstrance, and a silver ring.

Write to: Adoration Monastery
4108 Euclid Avenue
Cleveland 3, Ohio

INSTITUTE OF PERPETUAL ADORATION

History: Mother Anna de Meeus founded this congregation in Brussels, Belgium, in 1857. Full papal approbation was granted to the constitutions and rules fifteen years later. Foundations have been established in Belgium, Italy, Holland, England, and in the United States. The chapels of these houses are open to the public and the Blessed Sacrament is exposed daily after Mass until Benediction.

Purpose: The primary apostolic activity is to promote the glory of God in the Blessed Sacrament chiefly by means of the arch-association of Perpetual Adoration and work for poor churches. Members must spend one hour monthly in adoration and contribute financially to the work. The religious teach religion, hold spiritual retreats, and devote themselves to other works which are compatible with their life as adorers, such as conducting kindergartens and nursery schools.

Spiritual Life: The religious exercises include Holy Mass, the recitation of the Office of the Feast of Corpus Christi, mental prayer, the rosary, spiritual reading, an hour of adoration before the Blessed Sacrament exposed, and other community prayers and devotions.

Training Program: The six-month postulancy is followed by a two-year novitiate. Temporary vows are made for three years after which perpetual vows are pronounced. After first profession, the sisters continue their spiritual formation while being trained in the active works of the apostolate or by taking courses toward their academic degrees.

Qualifications:
* Age: 16 to 35. Exceptions are sometimes made.
* Completion of high school.

Habit: The sisters wear a black habit and veil, a white guimpe and head band, and a silver cross.

Write to: Convent of Perpetual Adoration
2907 Ellicott Terrace, N.W.,
Washington 8, D.C.

INSTITUTE OF PERPETUAL ADORATION (A.P.)

History: Mother Maria Loretto del Santisimo Sacramento, a professed nun of the Brigettine Order, founded this congregation in Mexico City, Mexico, in 1879. Mother Maria de las Mercedas de la Santisima Trinidad was named the first superior.

Purpose: As contemplatives, the sisters give glory to God through the adoration of the Blessed Sacrament exposed and the recitation of the Divine Office in Latin. In the active apostolate, the sisters teach college, conduct retreats, give catechetical instructions, and make altar breads and altar vestments.

Training Program: The twelve-month postulancy is followed by a two-year novitiate. The novices then make their temporary vows. Profession of perpetual vows is made after three years in temporary vows. Following the reception of first vows, the sisters continue their spiritual formation while taking college courses required for their teaching degrees.

Qualifications:
* Age: 18 to 30. Exceptions will be made up to 35.
* Completion of high school.
* Entrance dates: December, January, June, and July.

Habit: The sisters wear a dark red habit and a black veil. A white habit and red cape are worn on principal feasts.

Write to: Perpetual Adoration Convent
2701 Travis Street
San Antonio, Texas

ORDER OF THE MOST HOLY REDEEMER (O.Ss.R.)

History: The Redemptoristine nuns were founded in Scala, Italy, one year before the Redemptorist Fathers. The idea for the order was revealed by God to the foundress Mother Mary Celeste in 1726. The rule was written by St. Alphonsus Liguori in 1731. It was approved by Benedict XIV in 1750. Two monasteries have been established in the United States.

Purpose: This strictly cloistered order is dedicated to praying for the most abandoned souls, especially those in the care of the Redemptorist missionaries. Their life is essentially Christo-centric. Each exercise of the day is in memory of some mystery in the life of Christ. They seek to spread the graces of the redemption by a life of perfect imitation of Jesus Christ.

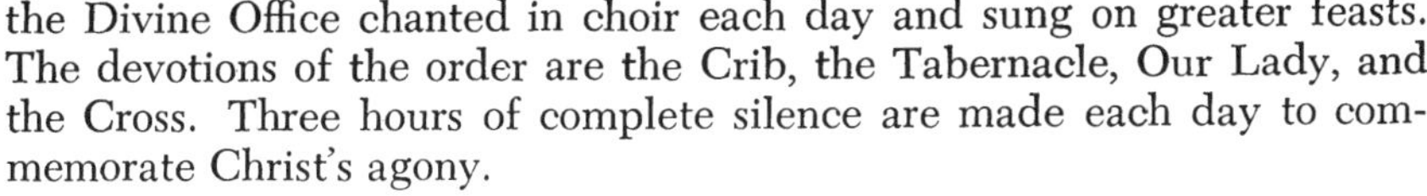

Spiritual Life: The most cherished spiritual exercise of these nuns is the Divine Office chanted in choir each day and sung on greater feasts. The devotions of the order are the Crib, the Tabernacle, Our Lady, and the Cross. Three hours of complete silence are made each day to commemorate Christ's agony.

Training Program: Candidates are postulants for one year. Simple vows are made for three years after the first year of novitiate. Besides learning the essentials of the spiritual life of a Redemptoristine, the sisters also learn how to sew, paint, and take part in the household tasks of the community. Solemn vows are made at the end of this three-year period.

Qualifications:
* The maximum age is 30.
* Completion of high school.

Habit: The sisters wear a deep red tunic, a sky blue scapular and choir mantle, a white coif, and a black veil.

Write to: Mother of Perpetual Help
              Monastery   Monastery of St. Alphonsus
              Esopus,   Liguori,
              New York   Missouri

ORDER OF PERPETUAL ADORATION NUNS (A.P.)

History: Mother Mary Magdalen of the Incarnation, a professed nun of the Franciscan Convent in Ischia, Italy, founded this community in Rome, Italy, on July 8, 1807. There are forty-four independent monasteries: twelve in Italy; one in Austria; three in Spain; two in South America; twenty-four in Mexico, and two in the United States.

Purpose: Each hour, in turn, day and night, the sisters are summoned to their noble mission of holy adoration before the altar in holy solitude. Unknown, these nuns re-enact the role of Mary, continually praying God's blessings on His church and members. The sisters make vestments, altar linens, altar breads, and paint spiritual bouquets.

Spiritual Life: The religious exercises include Holy Mass, mental prayer, the rosary, and spiritual reading. The choir nuns make solemn vows and are obliged to recite the whole breviary in Latin. The lay-sisters who make simple vows do not recite the Office nor engage in adoration. They are employed in the household tasks.

Qualifications
* Age: 18 to 30.
* The El Paso monastery requires a little understanding of Spanish.
* A dowry is required of choir nuns. Exceptions will sometimes be made.
* The lay-sisters do not have to provide a dowry.

Habit: The sisters wear a white habit, a black veil, and a red scapular. A red sash is worn on feast days.

Write to: Monastery of Perpetual Adoration
145 North Cotton Avenue
El Paso, Texas

Monastery of Perpetual Adoration
771 Ashbury Street
San Francisco 17, California

THE ORDER OF ST. BRIDGET (O.SS.S.)

History: Saint Bridget, the re-nowned mystic, founded this con-gregation in Sweden in the four-teenth century. The "Brigittines" strove to reform the monastic life in Sweden and to make their order a new vineyard of the Lord. They grew and prospered until the Prot-estant Reformation when the order was expelled from Sweden. The revival of the order did not come until early in the twentieth century through the labors of Mother Mary Elizabeth, who made foundations in Europe, India, and the United States.

Purpose: The nuns lead a mo-nastic life of prayer and adoration, in reparation for the outrages com-mitted against God and for the salvation of souls. They make it their special duty to pray for priests everywhere and especially for the Holy Father.

Spiritual Life: The religious exercises include Holy Mass, the recitation in choir of the Divine Office in Latin, one-half hour of meditation before Lauds and Prime of the Holy Office, another half-hour in the afternoon before Vespers, one-half hour of spiritual reading, and other community prayers and devotions.

Training Program: The six-month postulancy is followed by a one-year novitiate. The novice then makes her profession of temporary vows. At the expiration of her three years as a junior professed, the sister is allowed to make her profession of perpetual vows.

Qualifications:
* Age: 16 to 30. Exceptions are sometimes made.
* Completion of high school is preferred.

Habit: The six-hundred year old Brigittine habit is grey in color, with a black veil and a white wimple.

Write to: Mother Abbess
Convent of St. Birgitta
Vikingsborg
Darien, Connecticut

PASSIONIST NUNS (C.P.)

History: St. Paul of the Cross and Mother Mary of Jesus Crucified founded this congregation in Tarquinia, Italy, in 1770. The community has established monasteries in France, Belgium, Holland, South America, and the United States. The first monastery in America was opened in Pittsburgh, Pennsylvania, in 1910. Since then four other independent monasteries have been founded in the United States.

Purpose: The Passionist Nuns devote themselves to the practices of the contemplative life, prayer, and penance. The members of this cloistered congregation live in complete retirement from the world and never leave their convent grounds except for hospitalization. They conduct retreats for women.

Spiritual Life: The religious exercises include Holy Mass, the chanting of Matins and Lauds of the Divine Office at 1:30 a.m.—the other hours are said at designated times—three hours of mental prayer divided into three different intervals, the rosary, spiritual reading, and other community prayers and devotions.

Training Program: The one-year postulancy is followed by a year novitiate. Temporary vows are then made for three years. At the expiration of this time, the nuns pronounce their perpetual vows. In addition to the three religious vows, the nuns also make the Passionist vow to promote devotion to the Passion of Jesus Christ and the vow of strict enclosure.

Qualifications:

* Age: 18 to 25. Exceptions are sometimes made.
* Completion of high school for the choir religious. This is not necessary for the lay-sisters.

Habit: The sisters wear a black habit, veil, and belt, a rosary, and sandals.

See page 378 for address of nearest monastery.

RECLUSE MISSIONARIES OF JESUS AND MARY (R.M.J.M.)

History: This diocesan congregation originated in Montreal, Canada, in 1941. It was granted episcopal approval in 1946. The sisters arrived and established their first foundation in the United States in Louisiana in 1951, which now serves as the American novitiate.

Purpose: The sisters are cloistered except for a few missionaries in each convent who are allowed to leave the cloister. The main apostolic activity is perpetual adoration and the rosary. The missionary work includes teaching religion, and conducting parish census and retreats.

Spiritual Life: The religious exercises include Holy Mass, one-half hour of meditation, the recitation of the Roman breviary in English, the short Office of the Blessed Virgin, an hour of adoration, spiritual reading, and other community prayers and devotions.

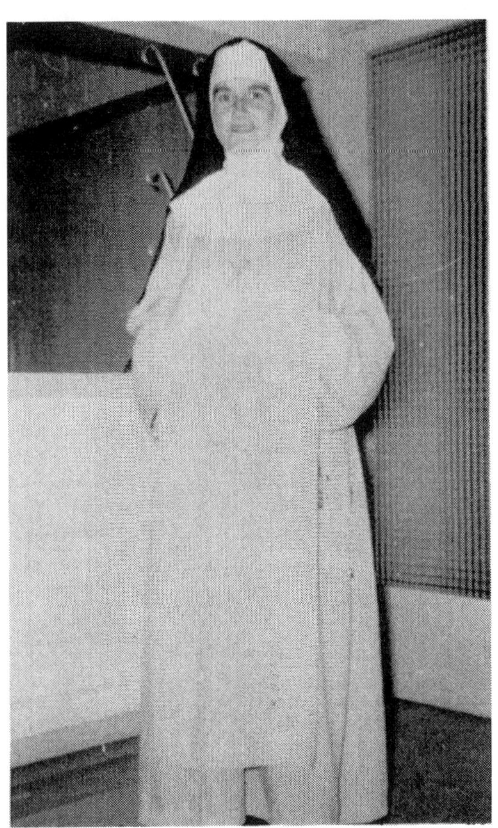

Training Program: The six to twelve-month postulancy is followed by a two-year novitiate. The novice then pronounces her temporary profession of vows. These are renewed annually for five years. At the expiration of the temporary vows, profession of perpetual vows is made. During this time, the sisters continue their spiritual formation while preparing for their duties either in the cloister or in the missions.

Qualifications:

* Age: 16 to 35.
* Completion of high school is preferred.

Habit: The sisters wear an ash-grey tunic and scapular which has a monogram of Christ embroidered on it, a fifteen decade rosary, white headdress, and black veil.

> *Write to:* Recluse Missionaries of Jesus and Mary
> Route 1
> Box 170
> Lafayette, Louisiana

POOR CLARE NUNS
(O.S.C.) (P.C.C.)

History: This order originated on March 19, 1212, when St. Clare of Assisi received the religious habit from her spiritual father, St. Francis. During the fifteenth century, one of her daughters, St. Colette of France, founded monasteries renewed in the strict observance. There are two branches of Poor Clares, the Colettines and the Franciscan Poor Clares. The former observe the constitutions of St. Colette, the latter follow the general rules for contemplative nuns. Each of the twenty-three monasteries in the United States is a separate and autonomous unit.

Purpose: The Poor Clares are a contemplative group of cloistered nuns and extern sisters. Their aim is to arrive at a complete union with God through a life of mortification and the discipline of the common life. The nuns also make vestments, sew altar linens, bake altar breads, and do art and other similar work. The extern sisters are not bound by the strict enclosure. They attend to the outside business of the monastery.

Spiritual Life: About seven hours of the day are spent in prayer, the foremost place being given to their obligatory recitation of the Divine Office in Latin. The liturgical day begins with the chanting of Matins, the first canonical hour, at midnight. The rest of the daily schedule is centered around the remaining canonical hours. Most of the monasteries have exposition of the Blessed Sacrament during part of each day, or all day. The horarium includes meditation and other religious exercises.

Training Program: The training period for extern sisters consists of one year as postulants, two years as novices, and six years in temporary vows. The canonical year is spent in the enclosure. The cloistered sisters have a postulancy of one year and the canonical year as a novice, then simple vows for three years, and finally solemn perpetual vows. The postulants and novices are introduced gradually to the monastic life. Perpetual fast and abstinence, walking barefoot, nocturnal rising, and other aspects of the life become a joy for all Poor Clares.

Qualifications:
* Age: 17 to 25 for cloistered nuns. Thirty is the maximum age for the extern sisters.
* Completion of high school for cloistered nuns only.

Habit: The sisters wear a mixed brown and grey habit and mantle, with a black veil, and a plain white linen headcover. The nuns go barefoot in the spirit of humility and poverty.

Write to the Mother Abbess at the nearest Monastery of Poor Clares listed below:

California
280 State Park Drive
Aptos, California

28210 Natoma Road
Los Altos, California

215 Los Olivos Street
Santa Barbara, California

Illinois
5245 So. Laflin Street
Chicago 9, Illinois

2111 So. Main Street
Rockford, Illinois

Indiana
809 W. Sycamore Street
Kokomo, Indiana

509 Kentucky Avenue
Evansville 14, Indiana

Louisiana
720 Henry Clay Avenue
New Orleans 18, Louisiana

Massachusetts
920 Center Street
Jamaica Plain, Massachusetts

236 Westford Street
Lowell, Massachusetts

Minnesota
86th and Russell Avenue
Minneapolis 31, Minnesota

St. Clare Monastery
Sauk Rapids, Minnesota

Missouri
200 Marycrest Drive
St. Louis 29, Missouri

Nebraska
1310 N. 29th Street
Omaha, Nebraska

New Jersey
Crosswicks Street
Bordentown, New Jersey

New Mexico
Route 1, Box 285-C
Roswell, New Mexico

New York
142 Hollywood Avenue
New York 65, New York

Ohio
3501 Rocky River Drive
Cleveland 11, Ohio

Pennsylvania
2028 W. Girard Avenue
Philadelphia 30, Pennsylvania

So. Carolina
North Pleasantburg Drive
Greenville, So. Carolina

Tennessee
1310 Dellwood Avenue
Memphis 7, Tennessee

Virginia
28 Harpersville Road
Newport News, Virginia

Washington
4419 N. Hawthorne Street
Spokane 18, Washington

RELIGIOUS OF THE ASSUMPTION (R.A.)

History: Mother Marie-Eugenie of Jesus and Mother Therese Emmanuel founded this congregation in Paris, France, in 1839. The community spread rapidly throughout Europe. The first foundation in the United States was made in 1919.

Purpose: The apostolate of this community embraces all branches of Christian education of girls and women. This includes day and boarding schools, colleges, orphanages, retreats, and religious instruction. The congregation will undertake any social work that is compatible with their rule of semi-enclosure. Several mission houses have been founded in Africa, Japan, and among the Indians of Guatemala. The sisters have two colleges in the Philippines and a training college for African teachers in Tanganyika.

Spiritual Life: The religious exercises include Holy Mass, the recitation of the Divine Office in Latin, forty-five minutes of mental prayer divided into two periods in the day, exposition of the Blessed Sacrament daily, the rosary, spiritual reading, and other community prayers and devotions.

Training Program: The one-year postulancy is followed by the canonical year of novitiate. The co-adjutrix sisters have a two-year novitiate. Temporary vows are made for five years, after which perpetual vows are pronounced. During the scholasticate period, the sisters pursue courses leading to their academic degrees. After ten years of profession, it is customary for the religious to return to the motherhouse in Paris for further religious formation.

Qualifications:
* Age: 15 to 30. Exceptions will sometimes be made.
* Completion of high school for the choir religious; graduation from elementary school for the coadjutrix sisters.
* Entrance date: There is no specified time.

Habit: The sisters wear a purple habit and cincture, with a white veil, guimpe, and rosary.

> *Write to:* Ravenhill
> 3480 West Schoolhouse Lane
> Philadelphia 44, Pennsylvania

SACRAMENTINE NUNS (O.S.S.)

History: Venerable Antoine Le Quieu, O.P., founded this congregation in Marseille, France, in 1639. The order was canonically erected with solemn vows and papal enclosure in 1693. There are two foundations in the United States. The first monastery was established in Yonkers, New York, in 1912, and the other was opened in Conway, Michigan, in 1951.

Purpose: The principal occupation of the Sacramentine Nuns is perpetual adoration of the Blessed Sacrament. The Yonkers monastery conducts an academy for girls while the monastery at Conway maintains retreats for women. The nuns also make altar breads and liturgical vestments.

Spiritual Life: The religious exercises include Holy Mass, the chanting of the Divine Office in English, two hours of mental prayer, the rosary, spiritual reading, and other community prayers and devotions.

Training Program: The six-month postulancy is followed by a one-year novitiate. Temporary vows are made for three years. Perpetual solemn vows are pronounced at the end of this period. Those selected for teaching acquire their professional degrees by attending nearby Catholic colleges and universities.

Qualifications:
* Age: 16 to 30.
* Completion of high school for the choir religious.
* The extern sisters lead the same life as the choir nuns except for the law of enclosure and solemn vows. They recite the Little Office of the Blessed Virgin in English.

Habit: The sisters wear a black habit, a white veil, scapular, guimpe, bandeau and mantle, and two silver medals.

Write to: Blessed Sacrament Monastery
23 Park Avenue
Yonkers 3, New York

Sacramentine Monastery of
Perpetual Adoration
Conway, Michigan

SISTERS OF JESUS CRUCIFIED (J.C.)

History: Mother Marie des Douleurs and Father Maurice Gaucheron founded this congregation in France in 1930. It became a papal institute in 1950. Ten years later the community was given papal approbation by the Holy See. Priories are located in France, England, Holland, Germany, and in the United States.

Purpose: The primary objective of this congregation is to make the religious monastic life possible for the sick and the physically handicapped. The choir sisters are cloistered under the rule of minor pontifical enclosure. The active apostolate of devotion to the spiritual and material needs of the sick is carried on by the Regular Oblate Sisters. They live with the community but are not bound by the rule of enclosure. Each priory may also undertake other apostolic works according to the needs of the area. The sisters in the United States conduct Cytology Laboratories for the early detection of cancer.

Spiritual Life: The religious exercises include Holy Mass, the recitation of the Divine Office in Latin, and two half-hour periods of mental prayer each day. The sisters strive to welcome joyfully the sufferings, limitations, and humiliations resulting from their illnesses and unite them with those of Christ so as to continue the work of redemption and help others understand the mystery of the Cross.

Training Program: The postulancy of six months is followed by a two-year novitiate. The candidates make their temporary vows and the promise of fidelity to the will of God in the state of illness. These vows are renewed for five years. Perpetual profession is then made. Candidates must make a retreat in one of the houses before being accepted.

Qualifications:
* Age: choir sisters—20 to 30.
* There is no age limit for the Regular Oblate Sisters.
* Poor health or a physical handicap is not an impediment.

Habit: The sisters wear a white habit, scapular, black veil, and a crucifix. The Oblate Sisters wear grey.

Write to: Mother Prioress
Regina Mundi Priory
Devon, Pennsylvania

SISTERS OF ORDER OF
ST. BASIL THE GREAT (O.S.B.M.)

History: St. Basil in 358 A.D., resolving to lead a life of asceticism, set out to a place located on the River Iris, opposite Amnesi, in Asia Minor, and there laid the nucleus of the religious family which bears his name today. St. Macrina, his sister, founded a monastery for women at Pontus adapting the pattern of his rule. From Asia Minor the order spread to Europe and to the United States in 1911.

Purpose: It is the special task of the sisters of this congregation to impart Christian education and instruction in orphanages and schools, to foster religious art according to the Eastern Rite by making vestments and other ecclesiastical supplies, and also to promote Catholic publications.

Spiritual Life: All the nuns attend Holy Mass, make a half-hour of meditation, examination of conscience, spend one half-hour in spiritual reading, and recite the entire Divine Office in the liturgical Slavonic language.

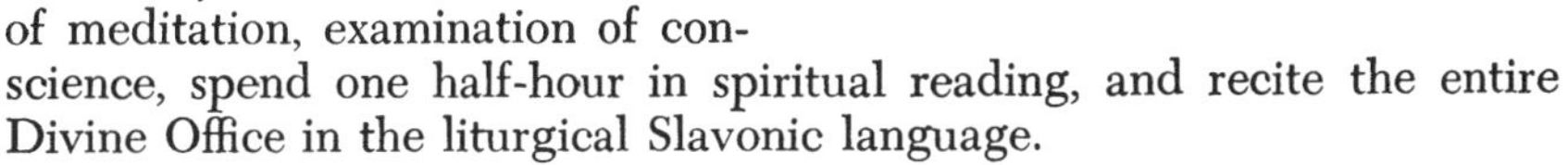

Training Program: The Order conducts an aspirancy program for young girls of high school age who desire to become religious in this community. The six-month postulancy is followed by a two-year novitiate. During the novitiate the novice is occupied with her spiritual training in the monastic life especially in those matters which pertain to the rule, constitutions, vows, virtues, and Christian doctrine. During the second year the novices and professed nuns pursue courses leading toward their academic degrees.

Qualifications:
- * Age: 15 to 30. Exceptions are sometimes made.
- * Average intelligence.

Habit: The sisters wear a black habit, veil, scapular, and cincture, a white wimple and band, a rosary, and a crucifix.

Write to: Mother Superior
710 Fox Chase Road
Philadelphia 11, Pennsylvania

SISTERS ADORERS OF THE PRECIOUS BLOOD (A.P.B.)

History: Aurelia Caouette and three companions formed the nucleus of the first cloistered contemplative community founded on North American soil. These four women, with the approval of Bishop LaRocque of St. Hyacinthe, founded this congregation at St. Hyacinthe, Quebec, Canada, September 14, 1861. Mother Catherine Aurelia became its foundress and first superior. With the exception of the monastery in Ohio, all are independent conforming to the wishes of the bishop of the diocese in which they are located.

Purpose: The characteristic spirit is resumed in a fervent and habitual devotedness to glorifying the Most Precious Blood by a life of contemplation and penance and by the spreading of this devotion. The sisters make altar breads, church vestments, paint, and some monasteries have accommodations for private retreats.

Spiritual Life: The religious exercises include Holy Mass, the Divine Office—they rise at midnight to chant Matins and Lauds—perpetual daily adoration, grand silence except at the prescribed times, meditation, rosary, spiritual reading, and other community prayers and devotions.

Training Program: The postulants and novices are completely dependent upon the Mother Superior and Mistress of Novices. They live apart from the professed sisters but participate in certain community activities. Temporary vows are made for three years. During this time, the novices help with the household tasks and are engaged in sewing, secretarial work, in art, music, and other community works. The third year is spent with the sisters in perpetual vows. The extern sisters attend to the duties outside the cloister.

Qualifications:
* Age: not before 18 and not after 30.
* Completion of high school.
* Entrance dates: April and October.

Habit: The sisters wear a white habit, black veil, red scapular, and a cincture. A red habit is worn during the midnight hour of reparation.

See page 378 for nearest monastery.

SISTERS SERVANTS OF THE HOLY GHOST OF PERPETUAL ADORATION (S.Sp.S. de A.P.)

History: Arnold Janssen and Mother Mary Michaele founded this congregation in Steyl, Holland, December 8, 1896. Eighteen years later Archbishop Prendergast asked the sisters to staff the newly erected chapel and Convent of Divine Love in Philadelphia, Pennsylvania. Perpetual adoration convents have been founded in St. Louis, Missouri, Austin, Texas, the Philippines, Argentina, South America, and until the communist invasion, in China.

Purpose: The chief apostolic activity is perpetual adoration of the Most Blessed Sacrament exposed in the monstrance. Here the nuns offer their prayers and perform their sacrifices for the propagation of the Faith and the sanctification of the priesthood.

Spiritual Life: The religious exercises include Holy Mass, the Divine Office, mental prayer, the rosary, spiritual reading, and other community prayers and devotions.

Training Program: The six to twelve-month postulancy is followed by a two-year novitiate. Temporary vows are made annually for three years and then for two years. After this five-year period perpetual vows are pronounced.

Qualifications:
* Age: 16 to 30.
* Completion of high school or its equivalent.
* Inclination for a cloistered life of prayer and sacrifice.

Habit: The sisters wear a subdued pink habit, a white cincture, scapular, veil and mantle, profession cross, and a silver ring.

> *Write to:* Mistress of Novices
> Convent of Divine Love
> 2212 Green Street
> Philadelphia 30, Pennsylvania

VISITATION NUNS (V.H.M.)

History: Saint Francis de Sales and Saint Jane Frances de Chantal founded this order in Annecy, France, in 1610. Sixteen years later it received official approbation from Pope Urban VIII as a congregation of contemplatives bound by solemn vows and strict enclosure. The first monastery in the United States was founded at Georgetown, Washington, D.C., in 1799. Each house functions as an independent foundation under the immediate jurisdiction of the ordinary of the diocese in which it is located. In 1952, Pope Pius XII formed the order into a confederation comprising nineteen different federations headed by a mother general. A regional superior guides each federation. There are two federations in the United States.

Purpose: The aim of the holy founders was to secure the benefit of the religious life for women who had neither the physical strength nor the attraction for the corporeal austerities at that time general in religious communities. While holding fast to the monastic traditions of the cloistered life, the Visitandines, with the exception of the monasteries in Wilmington, New York, Richmond, Philadelphia, and Bethesda, Maryland, all are engaged in teaching in educational institutions in their convents.

Spiritual Life: The religious exercises include Holy Mass, the chanting of the Little Office of the Blessed Virgin in Latin, two periods of mental prayer, spiritual reading, and other community prayers and devotions.

Training Program: The six-month postulancy is followed by a one-year novitiate. Temporary vows are made for three years. The choir religious make solemn perpetual vows. The other religious make simple perpetual vows. After first vows, the sisters continue their spiritual formation and those who are qualified take college courses toward their teaching and professional degrees.

Qualifications:
* Age: there is no specific age limit.
* There are no educational requirements. Those without formal education may become either associate, domestic, or out-sisters.
* St. Francis wished his order to be primarily a haven for those desirous of devoting themselves to God in the religious life.

Habit: The sisters wear a black habit and veil, a white linen guimpe, rosary, and a silver cross.

Write to the Mother Superior of the nearest Visitation Monastery listed below:

FIRST FEDERATION OF NORTH AMERICA
(Major Papal Enclosure)

Delaware
2002 Bancroft Parkway
Wilmington 6, Delaware

Georgia
1820 Ponce de Leon Avenue, N.E.,
Atlanta 7, Georgia

Maryland
9001 Old Georgetown Road
Bethesda 14, Maryland

New York
256th Street & Arlington Avenue
Riverdale-on-Hudson
New York 71, New York

Ohio
1745 Parkside Boulevard
Toledo 7, Ohio

Pennsylvania
5820 City Line Avenue
Philadelphia 31, Pennsylvania

Virginia
2209 E. Grace Street
Richmond 23, Virginia

SECOND FEDERATION OF NORTH AMERICA
(Minor Papal Enclosure with the exception of the Monastery at Alabama.)

Alabama
2300 Spring Hall Avenue
Mobile 17, Alabama

District of Columbia
1500 35th Street
Washington 7, D.C.

Illinois
2000 Sixteenth Avenue
Rock Island, Illinois

Kentucky
Georgetown, Kentucky

Maryland
5712 Roland Avenue
Baltimore 10, Maryland

Visitation Monastery
Catonsville 28, Maryland

200 East Second Street
Frederick, Maryland

Minnesota
720 Fairmount Avenue
St. Paul 5, Minnesota

Missouri
Visitation Monastery
Elfindale
Springfield, Missouri

3020 N. Ballas Rd.,
St. Louis 31, Missouri

New York
Ridge Blvd. & 89th Streets
Brooklyn 9, New York

Washington
Route 5
Box 1370
Tacoma 22, Washington

West Virginia
1600 Murdock Avenue
De Sales Heights
Parkersburg, W. Virginia

Visitation Monastery
Wheeling, W. Virginia

SISTERS, SERVANTS OF MARY, NURSES OF THE SICK (S.deM.)

History: The congregation was founded in Madrid, Spain, on August 15, 1851 under the initiative of Father Michael Martinez who wished to found a religious community of sisters who would dedicate themselves to the care of the sick in their own homes. The foundress, Blessed Soledad Torres, was beatified on February 5, 1950. The community numbers about three thousand members in Europe, and North and South America.

Purpose: The two-fold objective of this active-contemplative congregation living under minor pontifical enclosure is the sanctification of its own members and the carrying of Christ to others through the care of sick in their own homes, or through the hidden life of the lay-sisters. Both nursing and lay-sisters enjoy the same privileges and make the same evangelical vows. In the United States their foundations are located in New York, Louisiana, Kansas, and California.

Spiritual Life: The religious exercises include Mass, the recitation of the Little Office of the Blessed Virgin in Latin, the Trisagion to the Blessed Trinity, the rosary, one half-hour spent in mental prayer, and other community prayers and devotions.

Training Program: The six-month postulancy is followed by a two-year novitiate. The novice then pronounces her temporary vows. These are renewed annually for six years. Profession of perpetual vows is then made. This is preceded by a tertianship of eight months, a time of intensive preparation for perpetual consecration to God.

Qualifications:
* Age: 16 to 30.
* Completion of high school.

Habit: The sisters wear a black serge habit, veil, cape and belt, and a large rosary.

> *Write to:* Provincial House
> 800 North 18th Street
> Kansas City 2, Kansas

SOCIETY OF MARY REPARATRIX
(S.M.R.)

History: Baroness Emilie d'Hoogvoorst founded this society on December 8, 1854, in Belgium, the day when the dogma of the Immaculate Conception was proclaimed in Rome. This semi-cloistered congregation numbers over three thousand members located in Europe, Africa, North and South America. The United States province which was founded in 1908 is comprised of three houses situated in New York, Ohio, and Michigan.

Purpose: Intimately united with Jesus in the Blessed Sacrament, the sisters' aim is to make reparation to God for the sins of men and for the sacrileges committed against the name of Christ. It is chiefly by the adoration of the Blessed Sacrament exposed every day, and by prayer united to a life of sacrifice that they attempt to achieve this two-fold goal. They also conduct retreats for laywomen and are engaged in catechetical instruction.

Training Program: The society is comprised of choir religious and co-adjutrix sisters. The postulancy of six months is followed by a two-year novitiate. Temporary vows are then made for three years and again renewed for two more years. A period of final preparation, the tertianship, which includes a long retreat, is given to the religious before perpetual vows.

Qualifications:
* The choir religious who recite the Office and help with retreats and catechetical instructions need at least a high school education.
* There are no educational requirements for the co-adjutrix sisters.

Habit: The sisters wear a white habit and a sky blue scapular.

Write to: Convent of Mary Reparatrix
14 East 29th St.,
New York 16, N.Y.

Convent of Mary Reparatrix
17330 Quincy Avenue
Detroit 21, Michigan

II

DOMESTIC WORK

ANTONIAN SISTERS OF MARY QUEEN OF THE CLERGY (A.M.)

History: Father Elzear Delamarre founded this congregation in Chicoutimi, Canada, July 2, 1904. The first foundation was established in the United States in 1932. Today the sisters are located at Assumption College, Worcester, Massachusetts; Maryknoll Junior Seminary, Clarks Summit, Pennsylvania; Maryknoll Seminary, Glen Ellyn, Illinois, and at Notre Dame Rectory, Springvale, Maine.

Purpose: The primary objective of the Antonian Sisters is twofold: to help the clergy in any capacity and to encourage vocations to the priesthood. This assistance is fulfilled in the following ways: by taking charge of culinary departments of seminaries and colleges whose students are preparing for the priesthood; by assisting in the direction of preparatory schools and orphanages for young boys; and by offering to God their prayers, actions, and sacrifices to foster vocations to the priesthood and to preserve priests in their holy vocations.

Spiritual Life: The religious exercises include Holy Mass, the recitation of the Office of the Blessed Virgin, two periods of meditation, the rosary, spiritual reading, and other community prayers and devotions.

Training Program: The six to twelve-month postulancy is followed by an eighteen-month novitiate. Temporary vows are made for three years. At the expiration of this time, perpetual vows are pronounced. The sisters are trained to accept their role in the active works of the apostolate, or those who are to teach take courses toward their academic degrees.

Qualifications:
* Age: 16 to 30.
* Average intelligence.

Habit: The sisters wear a white habit, a black veil and scapular, a rosary, and a silver cross.

Write to: Mother Superior
Maryknoll Seminary,
Glen Ellyn, Illinois

CONGREGATION OF THE LITTLE DAUGHTERS OF SAINT JOSEPH (L.D.S.J.)

History: Father Antoine Mercier, a Sulpician priest stationed in Montreal, Canada, who desired to establish a congregation of nuns who would consecrate themselves to the spiritual and material welfare of the clergy and seminarians, founded this community with the assistance of Miss de Lima Dauth, the co-foundress. On April 26, 1857, both began this eminently apostolic work of helping priests and seminarians by means of a life of prayer, self-denial, and manual labor. Papal approbation was granted by the Holy See, March 8, 1938. The first foundation of the congregation in the United States was made in Seattle, Washington, in 1931.

Purpose: The congregation is exclusively dedicated to the temporal needs of religious and diocesan clergy and seminarians. This apostolate includes not only domestic work but also such tasks as tailoring ecclesiastical clothing and church vestments and the care of sacristies and altar linens.

Qualifications:
* The maximum age is 30. Exceptions are sometimes made.
* Average intelligence.

Habit: The religious habit, excepting the headdress, is entirely black. The professed sisters wear a silver crucifix suspended from the neck by a black woolen cord. Those in perpetual vows wear a silver ring.

Write to: Convent of St. Thomas the Apostle Seminary
Kenmore,
Washington

MISSIONARY SISTERS OF THE SACRED HEART AND OUR LADY OF GUADALUPE (M.S.C.)

History: Mother Maria Amada Sanchez founded this congregation in Guadalajara, Mexico, in 1926 during the bloody religious persecution taking place at that time in Mexico. The more than four hundred professed sisters are working in Mexico, Cuba, and in the United States since 1956.

Purpose: The sisters teach in secondary and elementary schools, conduct hospitals, homes for the aged, and sanitariums for the mentally ill, and are engaged in catechetical and social work among the Indians in Mexico. In the United States, chiefly in Illinois, they perform the domestic duties in several seminaries and religious houses.

Spiritual Life: The religious exercises include Holy Mass, the recitation of the Little Office of the Blessed Virgin in Latin, one-half hour of mental prayer, the rosary, spiritual reading, and other community prayers and devotions.

Training Program: The community conducts an aspirancy for teen-age girls interested in the religious life. The six-month postulancy is followed by a two-year novitiate. Temporary vows are made annually for three years and are renewed for another three years. At the end of six years, profession of perpetual vows is made. The choir sisters continue their spiritual formation while taking college courses toward their professional degrees. The lay sisters perform the other necessary duties.

Qualifications:
* Age: under 31. Exceptions are sometimes made.
* Average intelligence.
* Entrance dates: January and June.

Habit: The sisters wear a white habit, scapular and veil, and a rosary.

> *Write to:* Mother Superior
> 401 N.E. Madison
> Peoria, Illinois

SISTERS OF ST. MARTHA (S.M.S.H.)

History: Canon Jean-Remi Ouellette, and Eleanore Charron, known in religion as Mother St. Martha, founded this congregation with the approval of His Excellency, Louis Moreau, Bishop of Hyacinthe, Quebec, on the Feast of the Assumption in 1883.

Purpose: The distinguishing mark of the members of this congregation is their great love of God which urges them to immolate themselves obscurely as their holy patron, in the service of God. They devote themselves especially to the service of priests and religious by doing domestic work in colleges, seminaries, and ecclesiastical houses.

Spiritual Life: The religious exercises include Holy Mass, meditation, the rosary, spiritual reading, and other community devotions.

Training Program: The six-month postulancy is followed by a two-year novitiate. The novices then make their temporary profession of vows. These are taken for three years. Profession of perpetual vows is then made.

Qualifications:
* Age: minimum is 17.
* Completion of elementary school.
* Entrance dates: February and August.

Habit: The sisters wear a black habit, veil, and cincture, a white linen coif and guimpe, and a rosary.

> *Write to:* Sisters of St. Martha
> St. Michael's College
> Winooski, Vermont
>
> Sisters of St. Martha
> La Salette Seminary
> Enfield, New Hampshire

III

FOREIGN MISSIONS

CONSOLATA MISSIONARY SISTERS
(M.C.)

History: Father Joseph Allamano, the founder of the Consolata Fathers for Foreign Missions in 1901, and nephew of St. Joseph Cafasso, founded this congregation in Turin, Italy, in 1910. The sisters opened their first foundation in the United States in Grand Rapids, Michigan, in 1954.

Purpose: The aim of the society is the sanctification of its members by means of the propagation and conservation of the Faith in mission lands. Since 1913 they have established mission foundations in Kenya, Somaliland, Tanganyika, and Mozambique, Africa, and in Argentina, Brazil, and Colombia, South America.

Spiritual Life: The religious exercises include Holy Mass, recitation of the Office of Our Lady of Consolata in Latin weekly (it is recited every day in the houses of formation), the recitation of the fifteen decades of the rosary, and other community prayers and devotions.

Training Program: The one-year postulancy is followed by a two-year novitiate. Temporary vows are then taken. During the following years the sisters continue their spiritual formation while taking courses toward their active apostolate on the missions as teachers, doctors, dentists, nurses, or social workers.

Qualifications:
* The maximum age is 30. Exceptions are sometimes made.
* Completion of high school.
* Entrance date: end of August.

Habit: The sisters wear a grey pleated habit, cape, sash, and veil.

Write to: Consolata Missionary Sisters
Belmont,
Michigan

DAUGHTERS OF MARY, HEALTH OF THE SICK (F.M.S.I.)

History: The community was founded in 1935 by Father Edward F. Garesche, S.J., with the authorization of His Eminence, Patrick Cardinal Hayes. One year later the motherhouse was established at Cragsmoor, New York. In 1953 the first foreign mission was opened on the Pacific island of Okinawa.

Purpose: The apostolate of the congregation is exclusively missionary at home and on the foreign missions. The sisters care for the sick, needy, and abandoned through medical ministrations and catechetical instructions. They also train lay-catechists in these apostolates. The work is carried on, not only on the island of Okinawa, but also in the state of New York.

Spiritual Life: The religious exercises include Holy Mass, recitation of the Office of the Blessed Virgin in English, the rosary, one-half hour of mental prayer, spiritual reading, and other community prayers and devotions.

Training Program: During the six-month postulancy and the two-year novitiate, the candidates are trained and instructed in the principal duties of the religious life, the essentials of Christian perfection, and in the spirit and works of the congregation.

Qualifications:
* Age: 17 to 30.
* Completion of high school is preferred.

Habit: The sisters wear a dark blue habit, veil, cincture, and a white rosary. Those attending the sick and on the missions wear white.

Write to: Mother Superior
Vista Maria
Cragsmoor, New York

DOMINICAN SISTERS OF OAKFORD, NATAL, SOUTH AFRICA (O.P.)

History: This pontifical congregation originated in Oakford, Natal, South Africa, in 1889. The sisters expanded their houses into Europe and in 1955 came to the United States where they opened their first foundation in California.

Purpose: This missionary congregation is most widely represented in South Africa where it is engaged in teaching in kindergartens and high schools, nursing in hospitals, maternity homes, and ambulant stations. The sisters also conduct homes for working girls and the aged. In California they teach and perform domestic work.

Spiritual Life: The religious exercises include conventual Mass, the abbreviated Divine Office in English, spiritual reading, rosary, and other community prayers and devotions.

Training Program: The six-month postulancy is followed by a two-year novitiate. Temporary vows are taken for three years after which perpetual vows are made. During these years the sisters continue their spiritual formation while taking courses toward their professional degrees.

Qualifications:
* Age: 16 to 30.
* Completion of high school is desired.
* Entrance dates: January and July.

Habit: The sisters wear a white tunic, scapular and cape, a black veil, mantle, and a rosary.

> *Write to:* Mother Superior
> 2659 Homestead Road
> Santa Clara, California

FRANCISCAN MISSIONARIES
OF MARY (F.M.M.)

History: This international congregation founded by Mother Mary of the Passion, was the first community of sisters dedicated exclusively to the missionary apostolate. Since its foundation in India in 1877, the institute has increased to over ten thousand sisters in sixty-three different countries. Eight sisters have received the honors of beatification. Marie Hermine and six companions were martyred for the Faith in China in 1900 and beatified in 1946. The congregation has twenty-four provinces on five continents.

Purpose: The major categories of apostolic works are catechetics, social service, education, medicine, and nursing. The fourteen establishments in the United States from Rhode Island to California, include child care centers, hospitals, schools, Eucharistic shrines, and the Navajo Indian Reservation in Arizona.

Spiritual Life: The religious exercises include Holy Mass, mental prayer, the chanting of the Office of the Blessed Virgin in Latin, the rosary, spiritual reading, and other community prayers and devotions.

Training Program: The six-month postulancy is followed by a two-year novitiate. During the novitiate, the novices are instructed in the fundamentals of Franciscan spirituality and the religious and missionary life. Upon completing the novitiate the novices make temporary vows for three years. As junior professed, they receive professional and technical training necessary for their missionary work. Profession of perpetual vows is made at the expiration of temporary vows.

Qualifications:
* Age: 17 to 30.
* Applicants between 31 and 40 may be accepted as associate members.

Habit: The habit is entirely white. The sisters wear a black veil and a grey cape when traveling.

Write to: Provincial House
225 East 45th Street
New York 17, New York

FRANCISCAN MISSIONARY SISTERS FOR AFRICA (O.S.F.)

History: Mother Mary Kevin, with a group of six sisters, went in 1903 to Uganda, Africa, from Mill Hill, London, England. Convents were opened throughout Uganda, and later in Kenya, Rhodesia, and South Africa. This missionary branch was erected as a separate congregation in 1952 with Mother Mary Kevin as Superior General. The motherhouse is in Ireland. A novitiate was established in Brighton, Massachusetts, in 1953.

Purpose: The primary aim of this congregation is missionary work among the people of Africa. Here they teach in primary, secondary, normal, and economic schools, care for the homeless, the orphaned, aged, the incurable, including lepers, and nurse in maternity hospitals, clinics, and dispensaries.

Spiritual Life: The religious exercises include Holy Mass, the Office of the Blessed Virgin in Latin, two half-hour periods of mental prayer, spiritual reading, and other community prayers.

Training Program: The six-month postulancy is followed by a two-year novitiate. Temporary vows are made for three years. Perpetual vows are pronounced at the end of this triennium. During these years the sister continues her spiritual formation while acquiring professional or nursing training in preparation for her future work in the missions.

Qualifications:
* The maximum age is 30.
* Completion of high school.
* Entrance dates: October and February.

Habit: The sisters wear a brown habit and scapular, a veil with a soft white linen kerchief, and a Franciscan Crown rosary.

> *Write to:* Mother Superior
> 172 Foster Street
> Brighton 35, Massachusetts

FRANCISCAN MISSIONARY SISTERS OF OUR LADY OF SORROWS (O.S.F.)

History: This congregation of Franciscans resulted from the merging in 1949 of the diocesan community founded by Bishop Raphael Palazzi at Hengyang, Hunan, China, and the Sisters of St. Francis of the Holy Family, who were forced to leave their mission in China, due to Communist occupation. Archbishop Anthony Riberi, Apostolic Nuncio to China, requested the merger and obtained the permission from the Society of the Propagation of the Faith.

Purpose: The apostolate of this community is centered principally in foreign mission lands. The work includes teaching, catechizing, and caring for the sick, poor, and neglected children. Their work at present is centered in the Orient: Hong Kong; Chinju, South Korea; and Formosa. The sisters are planning missions in South America. In the United States, they teach, conduct retreat houses, care for orphans, and give catechetical instructions to migrant workers.

Spiritual Life: The religious exercises include Holy Mass, the chanting of the Office of the Blessed Virgin in Latin, one-half hour of meditation, adoration, and other community prayers and devotions.

Training Program: The community conducts an aspirancy for high school girls interested in the religious life. The six-month postulancy is followed by a two-year novitiate. The first year of the novitiate is dedicated to the religious development of the novices. During the second year, the novices continue the college courses begun in the postulancy toward the fulfillment of their professional degrees or they take up the various works of the community. Perpetual vows are made after three years in temporary vows.

Qualifications:
* Age: 17 to 30.
* The willingness to adapt oneself to the missionary life.

Habit: The sisters wear a black habit, scapular and veil, and a white collar, coronet, and cord.

Write to: Mother Superior
16535 S. W. Tualatin Valley Highway
Beaverton, Oregon

46

ST. JOSEPH OF CLUNY SISTERS (S.J.C.)

History: Assured that God intended her to found a new congregation to evangelize the colored races, Anne-Marie Javouhey with her own three sisters pronounced religious vows as Sisters of St. Joseph of Cluny on May 12, 1807 at Cluny, France. The foundress, who died in 1851, was beatified in 1950. The congregation, became a pontifical institute in 1899. The first sisters came to U.S. in 1874 where they worked for twenty-five years. They returned in 1947 and now have establishments in California, Pennsylvania, and Rhode Island.

Purpose: The congregation is primarily, though not exclusively, missionary in character. Among outstanding activities are the leprosaria in India, New Caledonia, Malagasy Republic, French Guiana, and a preventorium for leper children under observation. Pasteur Hospital and Training School in Paris, thirty-five hospitals, and ninety-three dispensaries throughout the world are also staffed by these sisters. They conduct schools at all levels from kindergarten through college.

Spiritual Life: The religious exercises include Holy Mass, mental prayer, the rosary, spiritual reading in private, the Little Office chanted in English, and other community prayers and devotions.

Training Program: The postulancy lasts from six to twelve months. The two-year novitiate training comprises the canonical year in which emphasis is placed upon learning the principles of the religious life; in the second year the novice prepares for her future assignment. Simple temporary vows are taken at the end of this period, and are renewed for three more years. Final vows are preceded by a period of intensive spiritual preparation.

Qualifications:
* The maximum age is 30. Exceptions are sometimes made.
* Completion of high school.

Habit: The sisters wear an azure blue dress, a black scapular and veil, a white guimpe, profession ring, crucifix, and a large rosary.

Write to: Mary Immaculate Queen Novitiate
Brenton Road
Newport, Rhode Island

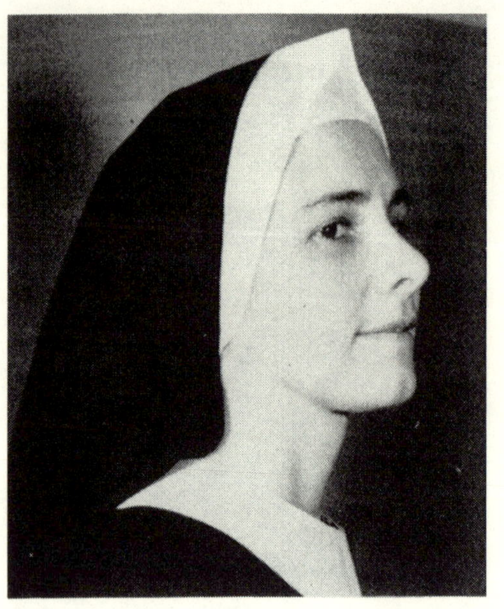

MARIST MISSIONARY SISTERS
(S.M.S.M.)

History: This missionary congregation traces its origin to the valiant members of the Third Order of Mary who set sail in 1845 and 1857 as auxiliaries to the Marist Fathers in the cannibalistic islands of the Southwest Pacific. Fifty years later the community received its first recognition from Rome, at the very time that America was being declared no longer a missionary land. By 1919 America was counting its own daughters among the ranks of Mary's missionaries in the island missions.

Purpose: The apostolate of these missionary sisters embraces catechetical, medical, educational, and social service projects in more than one hundred schools, hospitals, orphanages, dispensaries, medical and maternity centers, and leprosaria in the Polynesian and Melanesian missions of the Southwest Pacific, in Hawaii, Jamaica, Lima, Peru, and Africa.

Spiritual Life: The religious exercises include Holy Mass, meditation, spiritual reading, the rosary, and the chanting of the short breviary form of the Divine Office.

Training Program: The postulancy of six months is followed by a two-year novitiate. Vows are taken annually for three years, then once again for three years. Profession of perpetual vows is then made. During the first part of the six-year period of temporary profession the sisters take courses in their specialized fields as doctors, dentists, anaesthetists, nurses, medical technicians, teachers or artists. Perpetual vows are usually made in the mission field. After twelve to fifteen years following first vows, the sisters are recalled to the United States for a six-month spiritual renewal program which includes a thirty-day retreat.

Qualifications:
* Age: 17 to 30. Exceptions are sometimes made.
* Completion of high school.
* Entrance date: September 8.

Habit: The sisters wear a black tailored habit with scapular, a short circular veil, round collar, profession crucifix, and simple, pointed headpiece with a narrow band.

Write to: Marist Mission Center
62 Newton Street
Waltham 54,
Massachusetts

48

MARYKNOLL SISTERS OF ST. DOMINIC (O.P.)

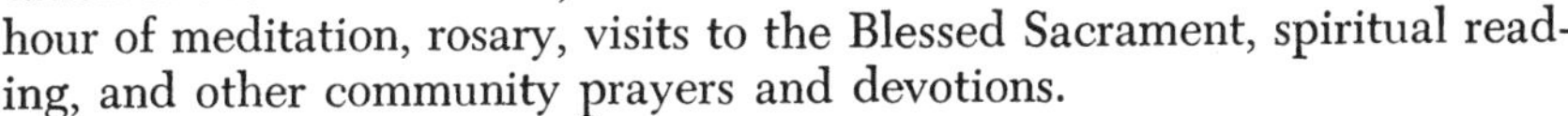

History: Mother Mary Joseph founded this foreign missionary society at Maryknoll, New York, in 1912. The congregation was canonically erected by the Holy See in 1920. Twelve years later, a cloistered branch was instituted. Presently there are approximately sixteen hundred Maryknoll Sisters.

Purpose: The sisters conduct primary and secondary schools and medical clinics in nearly all their missions. They operate three colleges in the Philippines, hospitals in Korea, Hong Kong, Guatemala, Africa, and the United States, social service centers in Peru and Hawaii, refugee centers in Hong Kong, hostels for students in Formosa and Japan, and teach in secular universities in Formosa, Korea, and Chile.

Spiritual Life: The religious exercises include Holy Mass, the recitation of the Divine Office, one-half hour of meditation, rosary, visits to the Blessed Sacrament, spiritual reading, and other community prayers and devotions.

Training Program: The nine-month postulancy is followed by a two-year novitiate. The sisters take temporary vows for six years before they make their perpetual profession. During this time, the sisters continue their spiritual formation while taking courses toward their professional degrees. The congregation has its own teacher-training college. Missionaries return for six months after ten years in the mission fields.

Qualifications:
* The maximum age is 30.
* Applicants are admitted one year after completion of high school.

Habit: The sisters wear a grey tunic, scapular, and cape, a black veil, miraculous medal, and a rosary.

> *Write to:* Mother General
> Maryknoll,
> New York

MEDICAL MISSION SISTERS
(S.C.M.M.)

History: Mother Anna Dengal, M.D., founded this community in Washington, D.C. It was born of the great need for a Catholic response to the vast amount of unrelieved and preventable suffering present in the medically less-developed areas of the world. As a lay doctor in India, Mother Dengal was confronted with these problems daily in her work, especially among women and children. To make this need known, she came to the United States where the society was established in 1925.

Purpose: These sisters were the first group of religious women to dedicate themselves exclusively to the professional care of the sick in the world's less-developed areas. Some are trained as doctors, nurses, and pharmacists; others are engaged in administrative or secretarial work. All contribute equally to the medical mission apostolate. The society conducts hospitals, leprosaria, dispensaries, maternity and child welfare centers in India, Ghana, Pakistan, Venezuela, Vietnam, and Uganda.

Spiritual Life: The religious exercises include Holy Mass, the recitation of the hours of Prime and Compline of the Divine Office in English, one-half hour of mental prayer, the rosary, spiritual reading, and other community prayers and devotions.

Training Program: The ten-month postulancy is followed by a two-year novitiate. Temporary vows are made for three years. These are again renewed for two years, then perpetual vows are pronounced. During the period of temporary profession, the juniorate program of guided work and study is carried on in further preparation for the active apostolate.

Qualifications:
* Age: 17 to 30. Exceptions are sometimes made.
* Completion of high school.

Habit: The sisters wear a grey dress and scapular with a blue veil, silver crucifix, and a rosary.

Write to: Medical Mission Sisters
8400 Pine Road
Philadelphia 11, Pennsylvania

MEDICAL MISSIONARIES OF MARY
(M.M.M.)

History: This community was established in response to the appeal of Pope Pius XI of happy memory for an apostolate designed to meet the changing needs of the missions—missionary sisters trained as doctors and nurses. Mother Mary Martin founded this congregation in Ireland in 1937. The sisters opened their first foundation in the United States at Winchester, Massachusetts, in 1951.

Purpose: The Medical Missionaries have recently established a mission in Formosa and have founded fifteen mission stations in Africa, in Southern Nigeria, Tanganyika, Angola, and Nyasaland. Over twelve thousand lepers are being cared for in one area in Nigeria. Medical work is undertaken in all its branches with special reference for the care of mothers and their children and in everything that helps to provide good medical services, such as, marriage training centers, domestic service schools, and social services.

Spiritual Life: The religious exercises include Holy Mass, Prime, Vespers, and Compline of the Divine Office said in English, and one-half hour each devoted to mental prayer and spiritual reading.

Training Program: After the first profession, the sisters renew their vows annually for five years. Final profession is made at the end of the sixth year. These years may be spent in labors on the missions or, during this time, sisters who have entered without professional training will be given the opportunity to train according to their aptitudes as doctors, nurses, laboratory technicians, or in the allied branches of secretarial, home economics, or social work.

Qualifications:
* Age: 17 to 35.
* High school education is preferred.
* Entrance dates: March and September.

> *Write to:* Directress of Vocations
> 1 Arlington Street
> Winchester, Massachusetts

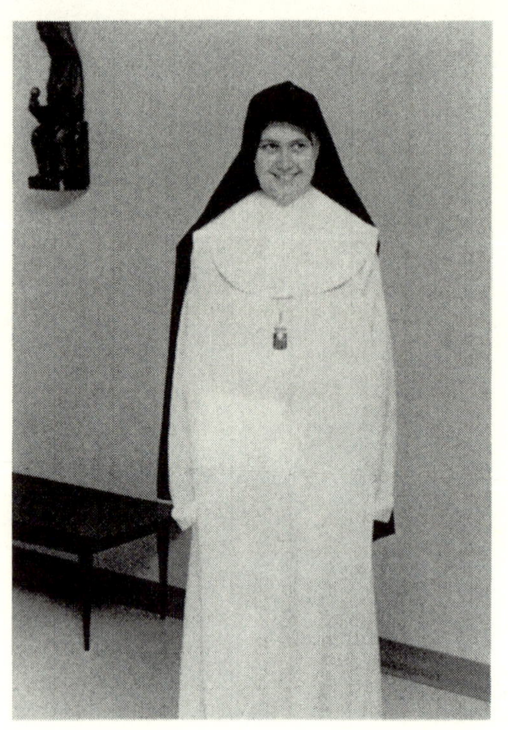

MERCEDARIAN MISSIONARIES OF BERRIZ (M.M.B.)

History: Mother Margarita Maturana founded this congregation in Spain in 1930. In response to the Church's call for active missionaries, she transformed a cloistered convent of nuns of the Order of Mercy into a mssionary institute. Foundations were made in China in 1926, in the Mariana and Caroline Islands in the two following years, and in Japan in 1930. The first three foundations were established while the community was still cloistered. A foundation was opened in the United States in 1946.

Purpose: These missionary sisters strive to bring the faith to non-Christian countries. They teach, maintain dispensaries, visit homes, conduct catechetical classes and other apostolic activities. The main mission fields are located in Formosa, Japan, and the Mariana and Caroline Islands. The vice-province in the United States provides the missionaries for the islands in the South Pacific.

Spiritual Life: The religious exercises include Holy Mass, the recitation of the Divine Office, spiritual reading, the rosary, and other community prayers and devotions.

Training Program: The period of formation from postulancy to final vows is approximately seven and one-half years. The six-month postulancy is followed by a two-year novitiate. After first profession, the future missionary begins her juniorate. During these five years, she continues her spiritual formation and completes the work toward her academic degree. Before final vows all go to the motherhouse in Spain for a tertianship of six months.

Qualifications:
* Choir nuns: high school graduates from 16 to 26. Exceptions are sometimes made.
* Lay sisters: same age requirements but no special education needed.

Habit: The sisters wear a white habit with a black veil. A medallion with coat of arms of the Order of Mercy is also worn.

> *Write to:* Vice-Provincial House
> 918 East Ninth Street
> Kansas City 6, Missouri

MISSIONARY BENEDICTINE SISTERS
(O.S.B.)

History: This community originated in Reichenbach, Germany,
in 1885. The first group of missionaries were sent three years later
to assist the Benedictine Fathers
working in Africa. Four priories
have been established in Africa.
Missions have been founded in
Brazil, the Philippine Islands, and
Korea. The congregation came to
the United States shortly after
World War I.

Purpose: The aim of the congregation is not only the sanctification
of its members but also the spreading of the word of God through its
missionary apostolate. The sisters
teach in elementary and secondary
schools, hospitals, and conduct
teacher training institutions, nursing schools, hospitals, dispensaries
for the poor, and leprosariums in
mission lands.

Spiritual Life: The religious exer-
cises include Holy Mass, the recitation of the Divine Office in Latin,
mental prayer, the rosary, spiritual reading, and other community
prayers and devotions.

Training Program: The community conducts an aspirancy for high
school girls interested in the religious life. After a postulancy of six
months, the postulant receives her Benedictine habit. Following the
year of novitiate, the sister pronounces temporary vows for three years.
Perpetual vows are then pronounced. In each of these stages, appro-
priate instructions relative to the religious life and the apostolate are
given.

Qualifications:
* Applicants are received into the aspirancy after graduation
from elementary school; into the novitiate after high school.
* Entrance dates: arranged with the individual.

Habit: The sisters wear a black habit, belt, scapular, and veil, a linen
wimple, and a gold ring.

> *Write to:* Immaculata Convent
> Box 885
> Norfolk, Nebraska

MISSIONARY SISTERS OF THE IMMACULATE HEART OF MARY (I.C.M.)

History: Mother Marie Louise founded this pontifical congregation in 1897 when she left Belgium to go to the aid of a missionary priest in India. Over thirteen hundred of her spiritual daughters are working in India, the Philippines, the West Indies, the Virgin Islands, the Congo, Ruanda-Urundi, Hong Kong, and Formosa. Home missions aid the Latin Americans in California and Texas.

Purpose: As teachers, catechists, social workers, nurses, midwives, doctors, home economists, the sisters use their womanly capabilities in a joint effort to Christianize the world, to help people help themselves, and to develop Catholic lay-leadership among the women in the foreign missions. They also form and direct communities of native sisters.

Spiritual Life: The religious exercises include Holy Mass, choral recitation of the Little Office of the Blessed Virgin Mary, meditation, stations of the cross, and the rosary, plus other community prayers and devotions.

Training Program: The six-month postulancy is followed by a two-year novitiate. Temporary vows are taken twice for three years, after which profession of perpetual vows is made. During this time, the sisters continue their spiritual formation while taking undergraduate college courses for their professional or nursing degrees.

Qualifications:
* Age: 18 to 30.
* Completion of high school.
* Entrance date: September.

Habit: The Sisters wear a habit with scapular and black veil.

Write to: Mount St. Augustine
Menand Road
Albany 4, New York

MISSIONARY SISTERS OF ST. CHARLES BORROMEO (M.S.S.C.B.)

History: Bishop John Baptist Scalabrini founded this community in 1895 in Piacenza, Italy, to care for the Italian immigrants living in Sao Paulo, Brazil, where the present motherhouse is located. The first foundation in the United States was opened in 1941. Over one thousand sisters are working in more than sixty houses in Europe, South America, and the United States.

Purpose: The sisters devote themselves to teaching in schools and academies, and caring for the aged. They are also engaged in domestic and social work. These institutions are located in Illinois and New York.

Spiritual Life: The religious exercises include Holy Mass, community morning and evening prayers, one-half hour of meditation, the rosary, visits to the Blessed Sacrament, spiritual reading, and the recitation of the Little Office of the Blessed Virgin in Latin.

Training Program: The six-month postulancy is followed by a two-year novitiate. Temporary vows are taken for one year and are renewed every year for five years. Profession of perpetual vows is then made. During this time the sister continues her spiritual formation while engaging in specialized work in preparation for her future apostolate in the missions.

Qualifications:
* Age: 17 to 30. Exceptions are sometimes made.
* Average intelligence.
* Entrance dates: February and August.

Habit: The sisters wear a black skirt, cape, and veil, and a white collar and crucifix.

> *Write to:* Mother Superior
> Bishop Scalabrini Novitiate
> 1414 North 37th Avenue
> Melrose Park, Illinois

MISSIONARY SISTERS OF ST. COLUMBAN (S.S.C.)

History: In 1921, Father John Blowick, co-founder with the late Bishop Edward Galvin of the Society of St. Columban, obtained permission from Rome to found a congregation of sisters who would undertake educational, medical, and social work in the foreign missions. The community was erected in 1922 and became a pontifical institute twenty-five years later.

Purpose: The members of this congregation labor for the salvation of souls in mission countries, especially in China, Korea, the Philippines, Hong Kong, Burma, and South America. More than two thousand out-patients are treated daily in the hospitals and clinics operated by the sisters in Korea and Hong Kong. The sisters conduct two colleges, and secondary and elementary schools in the Philippines and in Burma. Catechetical work forms an important part of their educational program.

Spiritual Life: The religious exercises include Holy Mass, one hour of mental prayer, one-half hour of spiritual reading, the rosary, and other community prayers and devotions.

Training Program: The novitiate continues for two and one-half years. During this time the novices are grounded in the elements of the religious life. In the second year of novitiate, the novices teach catechism to public school children. After they make their temporary vows, the sisters continue their spiritual formation while taking courses toward their professional degrees. The sisters are then given their mission assignments.

Qualifications:
* Age: 17 to 30.
* Completion of high school.
* Entrance date : October 3.

Habit: The sisters wear a black habit, a white collar and cap, a crucifix, rosary, and a ring.

Write to: St. Columban Novitiate
950 Metropolitan Avenue
Hyde Park 36
Massachusetts

MISSIONARY SISTERS OF ST. PETER CLAVER (S.S.P.C.)

History: The congregation originated at a time when the civilized world was gradually becoming aware of the horrors of the traffic in Negro slaves. A young Polish Countess, Mary Theresa Ledochowska, dedicated her life and her pen to the improvement of the spiritual and temporal welfare of the poor peoples of Africa. The community received papal approbation in 1910 from St. Pius X.

Purpose: The primary objectives of this community are the personal sanctification of its members and the spread of Christ's kingdom in Africa, through the Catholic press, catechetical work, and the operation of libraries and study circles. The sisters have the direction of three press centers in Nigeria, Rhodesia, and Uganda, where they also conduct catechetical courses. The society also organizes aid to the missions, and edits and publishes two monthly magazines.

Spiritual Life: The religious exercises consist of Holy Mass, one-half hour of meditation, private spiritual reading, and the recitation of the Little Office of the Immaculate Conception in English.

Training Program: The sixth-month postulancy is followed by a two-year novitiate. During the second year of novitiate, the novices are affiliated to a professed sister in order to gain experience with the different branches of the community. The novices then take their temporary vows and, as professed sisters, they continue their spiritual and professional formation. The sisters are sent to the novitiate in Rome for further spiritual training one year before their final profession.

Qualifications:
* Age: 15 to 35.
* Completion of high school is preferred.
* Entrance dates: Spring and Fall.

Habit: The sisters wear a black habit with a small cape, a black veil, and a red cord with a silver medal.

Write to: Sister Superior   Sister Superior
              3703 West Pine Blvd.   123 West Isabel Street
              St. Louis 8, Missouri   St. Paul 7, Minnesota

MISSIONARY SISTERS OF THE IMMACULATE CONCEPTION (M.I.C.)

History: Mother Marie du Saint Esprit founded this foreign mission society in Montreal, Canada, June 3, 1902. The community, which received pontifical approbation by His Holiness, Pope Pius XI, in 1933, has foundations in twelve countries throughout the world. The congregation opened its first foundation in the United States at Marlboro, Massachusetts, in 1946.

Purpose: The aim of the society is the propagation of the faith among non-Christian nations in a spirit of thanksgiving. Each sister upon taking her vows dedicates her whole life to the extension of the kingdom of Christ and His Immaculate Mother in non-Christian lands and in home missions. The primary apostolic activity in the foreign missions consists in teaching and nursing in dispensaries and hospitals. They also conduct schools and closed retreat centers.

Spiritual Life: The sisters daily recite the rosary which is considered as their "Marian Office." A half hour is dedicated daily to mental prayer to which is added a quarter of an hour for reflective contemplation, and fifteen minutes of spiritual reading.

Training Program: The six-month postulancy is followed by a two-year novitiate. In the post-professional programs, the junior sisters for the three years they are in temporary vows, complete studies toward their academic degrees.

Qualifications:
* Age: maximum is 30.
* Completion of high school.
* Entrance dates: August 8 and February 1.

Habit: The sisters wear a white habit, sky-blue sash, black rosary, silver crucifix, and a plain gold ring with the name of Jesus carved inside.

Write to: Mother Superior
197 Pleasant Street
Marlboro, Massachusetts

MISSIONARY SISTERS OF THE IMMACULATE CONCEPTION OF THE MOTHER OF GOD (S.M.I.C.)

History: Mother Maria Immaculata of Jesus, under the direction of Bishop Amandus Bahlmann, O.F.M., of Santarem, Brazil, founded this missionary branch of the cloistered Conceptionists in 1910 in Brazil. Since that time foundations have been made in the United States, Germany, China, Formosa, and Africa.

Purpose: The special vocation of the members of this congregation is the sacrifice for the missionary works of the Church and the sanctification of priests. The sisters teach in elementary and secondary schools and colleges, nurse in hospitals, and conduct social service work in home and foreign missions.

Spiritual Life: The religious exercises include Holy Mass, the recitation of the Little Office of the Blessed Virgin in Latin, the rosary, way of the cross, fifteen minutes of spiritual reading, and meditation. Exposition of the Blessed Sacrament is held every day in the novitiate houses.

Training Program: During the postulancy, the second year novitiate, and in the juniorate, a basic liberal arts program is given in Tombrock Junior College. At the completion of this program of study, those sisters designated for specialization are sent to resume their professional studies.

Qualifications:

* Age: under 30.
* Completion of high school.
* Entrance date: September.

Habit: The sisters wear a white habit and Franciscan cord, a white seven-decade rosary, a sky-blue scapular, black veil, silver medal of the Immaculate Conception, and a gold crucifix ring.

Write to: Vocation Directress
Box 1858
Paterson 18, New Jersey

MISSIONARY SISTERS OF OUR LADY OF THE ANGELS (M.N.D.A.)

History: This congregation was founded in 1919 specifically for foreign mission work. Mother Mary of the Sacred Heart, the foundress, was in China when she conceived the desire to establish a community which would be especially dedicated to the training of native sisters and catechists. The sisters are now laboring in China, Japan, Oceania, South America, and Africa.

Purpose: The sisters are engaged in all types of missionary work. They maintain hospitals, dispensaries, schools, orphanages, homes for the wayward, and perform social service work. The missions in the jungles of Peru and Africa challenge the most heroic, for practically everything in these mission lands is primitive.

Spiritual Life: The religious exercises include Holy Mass, mental prayer, the rosary, spiritual reading, and other community devotions.

Training Program: The nine-month postulancy is followed by a two-year novitiate. The novices then make their temporary vows. During this period the sisters continue their spiritual formation while preparing themselves to work in the foreign mission lands.

Qualifications:
* The maximum age is 30.
* Completion of high school is preferred.
* Entrance date: September 11.

Habit: The sisters wear a white cotton crape dress, veil, and cord, and a black scapular and rosary.

Write to: Saint Mary's Convent
338 North Main Street
Naugatuck,
Connecticut

MISSIONARY SISTERS OF OUR LADY OF THE HOLY ROSARY (H.R.S.)

History: Known as the Holy Rosary Sisters, this group of sisters was founded in 1924 in Killeshandra, Ireland, by the Most Rev. Joseph Shanahan, C.S.SP., to work for the salvation and sanctification of the women and children of Africa and other missions lands.

Purpose: This community is engaged in various forms of educational, medical, and social work. The sisters work in twelve dioceses in Nigeria, Cameroons, and Sierra Leone, West Africa, in the Transvaal, So. Africa, and in Kenya, East Africa. The works include the instruction of pagan women and children in primitive and remote areas, education on all levels, mobile dispensaries in rural districts, well-equipped general hospitals and maternity homes, training schools for nurses, and leprosaria. Crowning all is the work of formation and direction of African Sisterhoods.

Spiritual Life: The religious life of the sisters is centered in the sacred liturgy, the Holy Sacrifice of the Mass, and the Sacraments. Time is also devoted to mental prayer in the morning and evening. The rosary and Divine Office in choir are said daily.

Training Program: The postulancy lasts six months. This is followed by a two-year novitiate in which the novice is trained in the spiritual and practical formation necessary for a future missionary. After profession, the sisters are introduced to the active work of the congregation while receiving further instruction in catechetics and missiology. They also receive specialized professional training before being assigned to the missions. Perpetual vows are made after three years.

Qualifications:
* Age: 17 to 30. Older candidates will be accepted.
* A desire to give oneself to God.
* Entrance dates: September 24 and February 2.

Habit: The sisters wear a white habit and scapular, a black veil, a silver crucifix, and a rosary of 15 decades.

Write to: Holy Rosary Convent
214 Ashwood Road
Villanova, Pennsylvania

MISSIONARY SISTERS OF THE PRECIOUS BLOOD (C.P.S.)

History: Abbot Francis Pfanner, an Austrian Trappist, founded this congregation on September 8, 1885 at Mariannhill, Natal, South Africa. The rule is based on that of St. Benedict, and the motherhouse is in Holland. The first foundation was made in the United States in 1925 at Princeton, New Jersey.

Purpose: The primary aim of the members of this congregation is to assist priests in the apostolate of the missions. The sisters are engaged in teaching, hospital work, work among the lepers, social work among the aged and orphans, and they help form and instruct independent African communities of religious.

Spiritual Life: The religious exercises include Holy Mass, the recitation of the Little Breviary in English, one-half hour of meditation, the rosary, fifteen minutes of spiritual reading, and the stations of the cross.

Training Program: The one year of postulancy is followed by a year and a half novitiate. The novices then make their temporary profession of vows. Profession of perpetual vows is made after three years in temporary vows.

Qualifications:
* Age: 15 to 30.
* Completion of high school is preferred.
* Entrance date: September 8.

Habit: The sisters wear a black habit, scapular, veil, and rosary, a crucifix suspended from a red cord, and a silver ring.

Write to: Mother Provincial
Precious Blood Convent
Shillington, Pennsylvania

MISSIONARY SISTERS OF VERONA (M.S.V.)

History: Bishop Daniel Comboni established this congregation in Verona, Italy, in 1867. The foundation was the result of continued efforts to bring to Africa volunteer sisters from different communities to aid in the great plan of working among the African Negro. At present over two thousand sisters are working in 186 missions not only in Africa, but also in Asia Minor and in North and South America.

Purpose: The work of this missionary congregation is varied. They teach in elementary and secondary schools, and colleges; nurse in hospitals, leper-colonies, ambulatories, open clinics, and homes, and they are engaged in social work aiding those areas where poverty, famine, misery, and neglect are the greatest hindrances to the appreciation of the goodness of God. In the United States they are located in Virginia, Alabama, Pennsylvania, and Ohio.

Spiritual Life: The religious exercises include Holy Mass, one-half hour of meditation, visits to the Blessed Sacrament, spiritual reading, rosary, and other community devotions.

Training Program: The postulancy of six months is followed by a two-year novitiate. At the end of the novitiate temporary vows are taken for three years. They are then repeated for another three years, at the end of which profession of perpetual vows is made. The junior professed continue their spiritual formation while taking courses toward their academic degrees.

Qualifications:
* Age: under 30.
* Completion of high school.
* A desire to do missionary work in foreign countries.
* Entrance dates: March and October.

Habit: The sisters wear a black serge habit, cape, white collar, and five buttons symbolizing the five wounds of Christ. A silver crucifix is attached to a red cord worn about the neck.

Write to: Reverend Mother Provincial
1307 Lakeside Avenue
Richmond 28, Virginia

MISSIONARY SISTERS SERVANTS OF THE HOLY GHOST (S. Sp.S.)

History: Father Arnold Janssen founded this congregation in Steyl, Holland, in 1889. It grew rapidly. The first group of missionary sisters were sent to South America in 1895. The first foundation in the United States was made at Techny, Illinois, in 1901. Today these missionary sisters number over 4,000 professed members.

Purpose: The sisters teach in all stages of education from kindergarten to the university level, and staff sixty-two hospitals, nurses' training schools, clinics and dispensaries, and homes for the aged. In Africa, India, and New Guinea, they care for 8,000 lepers. Extensive catechetical work is carried on in other mission lands, especially the Philippines, where the sisters instruct 25,000 public school children. In Brazil, Argentina, Japan, and Indonesia, they instruct 15,000 neglected children and adults.

Spiritual Life: The religious exercises include Holy Mass, the recitation of the Divine Office of the Holy Spirit from the Roman breviary—veneration of the Holy Spirit is characteristic of this community—a half hour of mental prayer, the rosary, spiritual reading, and other community prayers and devotions.

Training Program: The community conducts an aspirancy for high school girls interested in the religious life. The nine-month postulancy allows the candidate to attend regular college classes while being introduced to the life of a religious. A two-year novitiate follows. Temporary vows are made for six years. A tertianship of six months' prepares the sister for perpetual vows made at the end of this six-year period. After first vows the sisters complete the college courses necessary for their professional degrees.

Qualifications:
* Age: for the aspirancy—13 to 17.
  for the postulancy—18 to 30.

Habit: The sisters wear a dark blue habit, scapular, and veil, a white collar, cincture, and a crucifix.

Write to: Convent of the Holy Spirit
Techny,
Illinois

PALLOTINE MISSIONARY SISTERS
(C.M.P.)

History: Saint Vincent Pallotti founded his unique society, "The Catholic Apostolate," in Rome, Italy, in 1835 for priests, religious, and lay persons. This group of missionary sisters originated in 1890 when the Pallottine Fathers asked for sister co-workers to assist them in their missionary labors in South Africa. The generalate was transferred to Limburg, Germany. The sisters have foundations in Europe, Central America, Africa, and the United States.

Purpose: The members of this community labor untiringly for souls in the spirit of their founder. Using every kind of apostolic work involved in a missionary society, the sisters are engaged in nursing, filling all the various positions of hospital activities teaching in elementary and secondary schools, and in a school of nursing. They also do catechetical, domestic, and social service work.

Spiritual Life: The religious exercises include Holy Mass, the recitation of the Divine Office, forty minutes of mental prayer, private adoration, and other community prayers and devotions.

Training Program: The postulancy of six to twelve months is followed by a two-year novitiate. The novice makes her temporary vows at the end of the novitiate. Final vows are taken after six years. The sisters continue work for their academic degrees in nursing and teaching at the Catholic University and Dunbarton College in Washington, D.C., and in St. Louis University and Webster College in St. Louis, Missouri.

Qualifications:
* Age: 18 to 30.
* Completion of high school.
* Entrance dates: Fall and early Spring

Habit: The sisters wear a dress and scapular of black serge, a black wool cincture, rosary, a black veil with white lining, and a white guimpe, browband, and headdress.

Write to: St. Mary's Convent
Huntington 2,
West Virginia

WHITE SISTERS

History: This missionary congregation was founded in Algiers, Africa, in 1869 by Cardinal Lavigerie to work in conjunction with the White Fathers. The congregation, which now numbers over two thousand sisters, is primarily engaged in missionary work in Africa.

Purpose: The apostolic activities of the members of this community are to glorify God by their personal sanctification and by embracing every form of educational, medical, and social activity that can help the spiritual and physical welfare of African women. The White Sisters have been instrumental in establishing seventeen congregations of African sisters.

Spiritual Life: Prime and Compline from the Divine Office, recited in English, constitute the sisters' morning and evening prayers. In place of the entire Divine Office, the sisters say the fifteen decades of the rosary at different intervals every day. The other religious exercises include meditation, spiritual reading, and visits to the Blessed Sacrament.

Training Program: The nine-month postulancy is a time during which the postulant is progressively introduced to the life and customs of the congregation. She also studies the land of Africa, its peoples, customs, and languages. This is followed by an eleven-month novitiate. During this time the novice makes a serious study of the evangelical vows, receives instruction in ascetical theology, and continues her studies on Africa.

Qualifications:
* The maximum age is 35.
* It is desirable that candidates further their education for at least two years after graduation from high school by continuing their studies or by seeking employment.
* Entrance date: the latter part of September.

Habit: The sisters wear a white habit, wimple and veil, a silver crucifix attached to a red silk cord, a rosary of black and bone beads, and a silver ring.

Write to: White Sisters
319 Middlesex Avenue
Metuchen, New Jersey

XAVIER MISSION SISTERS (S.F.X.)

History: The late Edward Cardinal Mooney founded this congregation in the Archdiocese of Detroit to work in the rural areas and small villages of India and Japan. It was canonically erected on December 3, 1946. In 1955 the first sisters were sent to the missions and established a mission center in Kochi on the Island of Shikoku, Japan.

Purpose: It is exclusively a foreign missionary society. The sisters give religious, social, medical, and educational assistance to the people of the lands evangelized by St. Francis Xavier. In addition to teaching catechism, the sisters devote themselves to those works which will bring them into personal contact with non-Christians, such as visiting homes and hospitals, teaching English, and working with children.

Spiritual Life: The religious exercises include Holy Mass, one hour of mental prayer, the rosary, spiritual reading, and other community prayers and devotions.

Training Program: The six-month postulancy, the time during which the candidate is introduced to the religious life, is followed by a two-year novitiate. Simple temporary profession is made at the end of the novitiate. During the juniorate period of about five years, the sisters complete their professional training as teachers, nurses, or social service workers, and begin the work of the apostolate.

Qualifications:
* The maximum age is 30.
* Completion of high school.

Habit: The sisters wear a cream white tunic and scapular, a woven cincture, a silver shield of St. Francis Xavier, a rosary, and a black veil.

> *Write to:* Convent of St. Francis Xavier
> 35750 Moravian Drive
> Fraser, Michigan

IV

HOME MISSIONS

CORPUS CHRISTI
CARMELITE SISTERS (O. Carm.)

History: Marie Ellerker founded this congregation in Leicester, England, in 1908. The members who made up this original group worked for some time as Dominican Tertiaries under the direction of Father Vincent McNabb, O.P. They established their first foundation in the United States in 1920. Eight years later they became part of the Carmelite Order, and were given papal approbation in 1958.

Purpose: The sisters cooperate in the priestly ministry by teaching catechism and visiting the sick. Catechetical and parish work is carried on in all houses of the congregation even when the sisters are engaged in administering institutions such as homes for the aged and children and detention homes. They conduct elementary and secondary schools, homes for retarded children, aged, nurseries, and catechetical centers in the West Indies.

Spiritual Life: The religious exercises include Holy Mass, choral recitation of the Divine Office in Latin, and one-half hour of mental prayer. The rosary is said privately.

Training Program: The six to twelve-month postulancy is followed by a two-year novitiate. The novices then make their profession of temporary vows. Profession of perpetual vows is made after five years in temporary vows. During this time the sisters continue their spiritual formation while taking courses toward their academic degrees. The sisters return to the novitiate three months before they make their perpetual vows.

Qualifications:
* Age: 16 to 30.
* Completion of high school preferred.
* Entrance dates: January 10 and July 16.

Habit: The sisters wear a brown tunic, belt, scapular, black veil, and a rosary.

Write to: Mother Vicaress
130 Highland Avenue
Middletown, New York

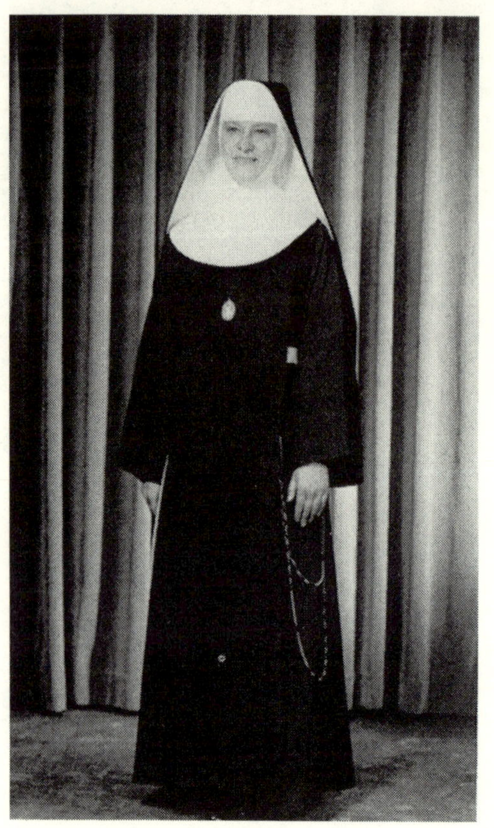

DAUGHTERS OF MARY OF THE IMMACULATE CONCEPTION (C.F.M.)

History: Founded in New Britain, Connecticut, in 1904 by Father Lucian Bojnowski, this pontifical congregation sprang from his desire to honor Our Lady in a special manner and from his deep concern for orphans. His appeal to the Children of Mary Society of his parish was answered by eight Sodalist volunteers who became the nucleus of the new community.

Purpose: Home missions in the New England and Middle Atlantic states are the apostolic activities of the congregation. Its members instruct youth on various levels of education, teach religion on released-time programs in rural and city catechetical centers, and supervise a summer camp for boys and girls. They operate a hospital and nursing home, a home for orphaned and dependent children, a home for the aged, and hospices for working girls, students, and travelers.

Spiritual Life: The religious exercises include Holy Mass, the recitation of the Office of the Blessed Virgin in Latin, one-half hour of mental prayer, the rosary, spiritual reading, and other community prayers and devotions.

Training Program: The six to twelve-month postulancy is followed by a two-year novitiate. Temporary vows are made for five years after which perpetual vows are pronounced. After first vows the sisters are sent to various Catholic centers of learning to obtain the cultural and professional training necessary for their apostolate.

Qualifications:
* Age: 15 to 30.
* Completion of high school is preferred.
* Entrance dates: September 8 and February 2.

Habit: The sisters wear a royal blue habit, a black veil and rosary, and a white sash.

Write to: Motherhouse of the Immaculate Conception
Convent Heights
New Britain, Connecticut

DOMINICAN RURAL MISSIONARIES (O.P.)

History: This congregation was founded in France in 1932 to help in parish work in rural areas lacking sufficient priests. The initial group of ten sisters has grown to a community of five hundred members in seventy convents throughout Europe, North America, and Africa. The sisters came to the United States in 1951 at the request of the Bishop of Lafayette, Louisiana, to help teach religion in his predominantly rural diocese.

Purpose: The main objective of the community is to help rural priests develop a sound Christian life in their parishes.

Spiritual Life: The religious exercises include Holy Mass, the chanting of the Divine Office, mental prayer, the rosary, spiritual reading, and other community prayers and devotions.

Training Program: The six to twelve-month postulancy is followed by a two-year novitiate. Temporary vows are made for two years and then for three years. At the end of five years in temporary vows the sisters pronounce perpetual vows. The sisters continue their spiritual formation and at the same time complete the college studies required for their professional degrees.

Qualifications:
* 18 to 30.
* Completion of high school.

Habit: The sisters wear the traditional white Dominican habit simplified to satisfy the needs of the modern missionary apostolate.

> *Write to:* Dominican Rural Missionaries
> 1318 S. Henry
> Abbeville, Louisiana

EUCHARISTIC MISSIONARIES OF ST. DOMINIC (O.P.)

History: This Dominican congregation originated in 1927 in Louisiana. The founders were two young women who realized the need for catechists to instruct public school children and visit the homes of the sick and poor. In one generation they increased from two catechists to a congregation working in five dioceses in the United States.

Purpose: The works of the community are catechetical and social. Religious instruction is given to children and adults in year-round missions and in religious vacation schools. Instructions are also given to deaf-mutes and to the mentally retarded. Social, religious, and relief work is carried out among the poor. Sisters live in small mission houses, usually in groups of two or three, driving to various places to carry on their apostolate. This work is carried on primarily in the South and Southwest.

Spiritual Life: The religious exercises include Holy Mass, the recitation of the Divine Office in English, half-hour of meditation, the rosary, spiritual reading made privately, and other community prayers and devotions.

Training Program: A two-year novitiate follows the eleven-month postulancy. In the first novitiate year emphasis is placed upon the spiritual development of the novice. During the second year, the novices spend from two to six weeks on active mission duty under the supervision of a professed sister. There is a five-year period of temporary vows. The first two years in temporary vows constitute the juniorate during which studies toward academic degrees are continued.

Qualifications:
* Age: under 30.
* A high school education.
* Entrance date: first Sunday in October.

Habit: The habit is white with a black veil. White is worn in the missions when the climate demands it.

Write to: Eucharistic Missionaries
3453 Magazine Street
New Orleans 15, Louisiana

FRANCISCAN MISSIONARY SISTERS OF THE DIVINE CHILD (F.M.D.C.)

History: The congregation was established in the Diocese of Buffalo, New York, by the late Most Reverend William Turner, August 15, 1927. Institutions have been founded in Texas, Pennsylvania, Louisiana, Florida, and New York.

Purpose: The main objective is teaching religion to public school children and home visitation. The sisters drive from town to town where they teach religion and visit homes of negligent Catholics from the several mission convents which they have established in the rural areas. This community has organized a lay-apostolate known as the Daughters of St. Francis, who help the sisters in their work. The members dedicate a year or more to this apostolate. Provision is made for anyone desiring to devote her life as a Franciscan Missionary Sister.

Spiritual Life: The religious exercises include Holy Mass, the recitation of the Divine Office in English, two periods of mental prayer, the rosary, spiritual reading, and other community prayers and devotions.

Training Program: The six to twelve-month postulancy is followed by a two-year novitiate. Temporary vows are made for five years after which perpetual vows are pronounced. The sisters continue their spiritual formation while taking college courses toward their professional degrees.

Qualifications:
* Age: under 30.
* Completion of high school.
* A desire to serve God's needy on the home missions.

Habit: The sisters wear a dark blue habit and scapular, a white cord, crucifix, and a silver ring.

> *Write to:* Motherhouse
> Regina Coeli Acres
> 6380 Main Street
> Williamsville, New York

FRANCISCAN SISTERS OF THE ATONEMENT (S.A.)

History: Mother Lurana Mary Francis founded this congregation on December 15, 1898 at Graymoor, Garrison, New York, while she was an Episcopalian nun. This Episcopalian community was accepted corporately into the Catholic Church on October 30, 1909. Since that date the congregation has made remarkable progress. Final approbation from Rome was received in 1946.

Purpose: The sisters teach Christian doctrine classes for public school children through high school, train lay catechists, give convert instructions, conduct lay retreats, and operate settlement houses, children's homes, summer camps, kindergartens, and nurseries.

Spiritual Life: The religious exercises include Holy Mass, the chanting of the Divine Office in Latin, the recitation of the Franciscan Crown rosary, spiritual reading, and other community prayers and devotions. Two sisters spend an hour of nocturnal adoration before the Blessed Sacrament each midnight.

Training Program: The eight-month postulancy is followed by a one-year novitiate. These divisions fill a unique role in the sister formation for the Atonement apostolate. During the postulancy the candidate observes the religious life and participates in many of the exercises. In the novitiate the novice lives the life of a religious and studies the obligations which she must freely accept on the day of her profession. After making her first vows, the professed sister continues her spiritual formation while taking courses leading toward her academic degree. A tertianship of one month precedes profession of perpetual vows.

Qualifications:
* Age: 17 to 30. Exceptions are sometimes made.
* Completion of high school.
* Entrance dates: February 2 and September 8.

Habit: The sisters wear a grey-brown habit and scapular, a black veil, a white wimple and cord, a crucifix, rosary, and a silver ring.

Write to: St. Francis Convent
Graymoor, Garrison
New York

GLENMARY HOME MISSION SISTERS

History: Father W. Howard Bishop founded this community in Glendale, Ohio, in 1941, to carry on home missionary work in the United States. In 1946 a Dominican Sister from Adrian, Michigan, was engaged to instruct the sisters in the fundamentals of the religious life. The congregation was canonically erected in 1952.

Purpose: The apostolic activities of these sisters include religious instruction, social work, home nursing, and other works of charity. These works are being carried on especially in the rural sections of the South. Mission centers have been established in Ohio, Kentucky, Virginia, North Carolina, and Georgia.

Spiritual Life: The religious exercises include Holy Mass, mental prayer, the short breviary in English, the rosary, and spiritual reading. The schedule is adjusted according to the demands of the mission work.

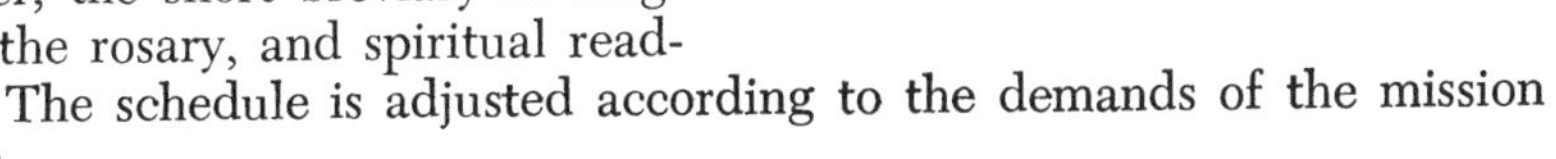

Training Program: The one-year postulancy is followed by a one-year novitiate. Temporary vows are made for five years. Perpetual vows are then pronounced. The professed continue their spiritual formation while taking college courses toward their academic degrees.

Qualifications:
* The maximum age is 30.
* Completion of high school.

Habit: The sisters wear a grey, ankle-length tunic and a grey cape that extends below the waist, a black cincture and veil, white collar and cuffs, and a silver crucifix.

> *Write to:* Motherhouse
> 4580 Colerain Avenue
> Cincinnati 23, Ohio

THE HANDMAIDS OF MARY IMMACULATE (A.M.I.)

History: Bishop Joseph M. Gilmore of Helena, Montana, authorized Mother Mary Stanislaus to found this diocesan congregation on October 13, 1952.

Purpose: The primary objective is the personal holiness overflowing into the apostolate of education and spiritual works of mercy in the spirit of Our Lady of Fatima. The sisters give catechetical instructions, visit the homes of the Blackfeet Indians on their reservation, take censuses, and conduct parish summer vacation schools.

Spiritual Life: The religious exercises include Holy Mass, mental prayer, the complete rosary, spiritual reading, and other community devotions and prayers.

Training Program: The six-month postulancy is followed by a two-year novitiate. The novice is then permitted to make her temporary profession of vows. These vows are renewed annually for five years. At the expiration of this time, the sisters pronounce their profession of perpetual vows. After first profession, the sisters continue their spiritual formation while taking courses toward their professional degrees.

Qualifications:
* The maximum age is 35.
* Completion of high school.

Habit: The sisters wear a blue dress, brown scapular, white headdress, collar, cuffs, and cincture, and a rosary.

> *Write to:* The Convent
> Carroll College
> Helena, Montana

HELPERS OF THE HOLY SOULS (H.H.S.)

History: Blessed Mary of Providence founded this pontifical institute in France in 1856. It soon spread to the Orient and various parts of Europe. Today thirteen hundred Helpers are located in eighteen countries on four continents. The first foundation in the United States was made in New York City in 1892.

Purpose: The sisters are primarily engaged in Confraternity of Christian Doctrine work, teaching catechetics, training lay-catechists, caring for the sick in their homes, and performing other social services. They operate schools, dispensaries, and hospitals in their foreign missions.

Spiritual Life: The religious exercises include Holy Mass, forty-five minutes of mental prayer, the recitation of the office in Latin, the rosary, spiritual reading, and other community prayers and devotions.

Training Program: By the time of profession of perpetual vows, a Helper will have completed six months of postulancy, two years of novitiate, and six years of temporary vows, of which the last ten months are spent in tertianship. In the postulancy and novitiate the rule and spirit of a Helper-vocation are learned along with studies made of the ascetical life. During the time of the juniorate the sister continues her spiritual formation while completing the courses required for her academic degree.

Qualifications:
* Age: 18 to 25. Exceptions are sometimes made.
* Average intelligence.

Habit: The sisters wear a black dress, cape, and veil, and a silver chain and crucifix bearing the motto: "Pray, suffer, work for the souls in purgatory."

Write to: Helpers of the Holy Souls
303 W. Barry Avenue
Chicago 14, Illinois

LITTLE SISTERS OF THE ASSUMPTION
(L.S.A.)

History: Father Stephen Pernet, A.A., founded this pontifical congregation in 1865 in France, in response to one of the greatest problems of the times: families in distress. Growing rapidly, it spread to England, Ireland, and to the United States in 1891. It maintains one hundred and eighty-eight houses in twenty-seven countries.

Purpose: Religious and apostle, nurse and social worker, the Little Sister enters the family circle when sickness strikes. She replaces the mother, assumes the maternal duties regarding the children, remains as long as she is needed, and accepts nothing for her services. Dedicating her life to "Restoring the Family in Christ," the Little Sister's only field of action is the home. She may volunteer for the missions.

Spiritual Life: The religious exercises include Holy Mass, the chanting of the Day Hours of the Divine Office in choir, two periods of meditation, the rosary, spiritual reading, and other community prayers and devotions.

Training Program: The seven-month postulancy is followed by a two-year novitiate. The novice begins her apostolate during the second year, at the end of which temporary vows are made. During the six years of temporary vows, the sisters continue their spiritual formation while training for their nursing or social service degrees in various hospitals and colleges. Perpetual vows are made at the end of this six-year period.

Qualifications:
* Maximum age is 30.
* Completion of high school.
* Entrance dates: March 24 and September 24.

Habit: The sisters wear a black habit and veil, a white headdress, the cincture of St. Augustine, a large crucifix, rosary, and ring.

Write to: Mother Provincial
100 Gladstone Avenue
Walden, New York

SISTERS, HOME VISITORS OF MARY
(H.V.M.)

History: The community was established November 21, 1949, by His Eminence Edward Cardinal Mooney, Archbishop of Detroit, at the request of the Right Reverend John C. Ryan.

Purpose: Convert-making, particularly among the American Negro, is the primary apostolate of the members of this congregation. The sisters are modern saleswomen who go from door-to-door bringing Christ and His Church to families in the friendly atmosphere of their own homes. They strive to encourage faithful Catholics, win back the negligent, and invite non-Catholics to attend information classes. They also teach religion to public school children, conduct recreation programs, instruct girls and women in home nursing and Christian family living, and promote days of recollection for young girls.

Spiritual Life: Daily Mass, mental prayer, the rosary, spiritual reading, and a short form of the Divine Office in English in common give spiritual vigor to the sisters in their apostolic program.

Training Program: The postulancy initiates candidates into convent life and spiritual exercises and gives them an opportunity to test their vocation. The canonical year of the novitiate emphasizes formation toward sanctity, especially through the vows and virtues of religious life. The second year novice either begins or continues her academic studies.

Qualifications:
* Age: 16 to 30.
* At least a high school education.

Habit: The sisters wear a simple navy blue habit, hat, and coat in the style of the day.

> *Write to:* Home Visitors of Mary
> 356 Arden Park
> Detroit 2, Michigan

MARIAN SOCIETY OF DOMINICAN CATECHISTS (M.S.C.)

History: This community was canonically erected on September 8, 1954, by the Most Rev. Charles P. Greco, Bishop of Alexandria, Louisiana, with the cooperation of two lay teachers from Washington, D.C.

Purpose: The teaching of religion according to the program of the Confraternity of Christian Doctrine is the primary objective of this congregation. This involves not only teaching but also the organization and supervision of school-year religion courses and religious vacation schools established in parishes for those children not attending Catholic schools. Training courses are given to the laity, special censuses are taken, and visitations are made among the white and colored in the home missions of the southern part of the United States.

Spiritual Life: The religious exercises include Holy Mass, the recitation of the office of the Blessed Virgin in English, mental prayer, the rosary, spiritual reading, and other community prayers and devotions.

Training Program: The community conducts an aspirancy for high school girls interested in the religious life. The six to twelve-month postulancy is followed by a one-year novitiate. Temporary vows are made for three years after which perpetual vows are pronounced. Interested girls may participate in the work of the community by volunteer summer service involving teaching in religious vacation schools and home visiting.

Qualifications:

* Age: 16 to 30. Exceptions are sometimes made.
* Average intelligence.

Habit: The sisters wear a modernized version of the Dominican habit with a black mantilla, special emblem, and a ring.

Write to: Sister Superior
P.O. Box 176
Boyce, Louisiana

MISSION HELPERS OF
THE SACRED HEART (M.H.S.H.)

History: This community originated in Baltimore, Maryland, in 1890. Mother Mary Demetrias, its foundress, began a great work of organizing religious instruction for the spiritually neglected colored children. The work grew and prospered. Gradually this small congregation extended its apostolate to all ages and races in spiritually depressed areas. Receiving the approbation of James Cardinal Gibbons it became a pontifical institute in 1949.

Purpose: The sisters are primarily engaged in Christian Doctrine Work. They teach religious classes for those not attending Catholic schools, convert classes, and classes for the handicapped, the deaf, blind, and retarded, and give instructions in reformatories. The Mission Helpers publish religious educational literature, and instruct the laity in effective methods of teaching religion and prepare them for their active apostolic work in other divisions of the Confraternity of Christian Doctrine.

Spiritual Life: The religious exercises include Holy Mass, mental prayer, a part of the divine office in English, the rosary, spiritual reading, and other community prayers and devotions.

Training Program: The postulancy and novitiate embrace three years of study in religious formation. The juniorate, or the period of temporary vows, includes college courses leading to their bachelor's or master's degrees and experience in the active mission apostolate. Young women may become familiar with this mission apostolate by working with the sisters for one year as volunteer lay missioners in the organization known as Mary Missioners.

Qualifications:
* Age: 16 to 30.
* Completion of high school.
* Entrance date: September.

Habit: The sisters wear a black habit, scapular, and veil, a white collar, silver crucifix, and a gold ring.

> *Write to:* Vocation Directress
> 1001 West Joppa Road
> Baltimore 4, Maryland

MISSION SISTERS OF THE HOLY GHOST (M.S.)

History: This diocesan community was founded in 1932 by the late Archbishop Joseph Schrembs in Cleveland, Ohio, to carry out the needs of the home mission apostolate. In 1954 the motherhouse was transferred to Saginaw, Michigan. Since that time the sisters have centered their apostolic activities in the Saginaw diocese.

Purpose: These home missionaries have dedicated themselves to the bringing of souls to Christ through catechetical, parish, clinical, and social service work. The sisters help the pastors of the diocese by making religious surveys of each parish. Through their efforts the spiritually weak, lax, and ignorant Catholics of individual parishes are brought to the attention of the pastors.

Spiritual Life: The sisters follow the rule of St. Benedict. They say the short breviary in English. Their daily exercises include a half-hour of mental prayer, and a half-hour of spiritual reading, which is made privately, the rosary, and visits to the Blessed Sacrament.

Training Program: The basic training of all the sisters takes place at Missiondell, the community's headquarters. This consists in the postulancy which lasts from six months to one year. The postulant is introduced to the religious life during this time; following that is the novitiate of one complete year. Here the novice is given a thorough training in the fundamentals of the religious life. After the novitiate is completed, temporary vows are taken for six years. Perpetual vows are made at the end of this period.

Qualifications:
* Age: 18 to 30. Exceptions are sometimes made up to 40.
* Completion of high school.
* Entrance date: September 8. Candidates will be accepted at other times.

Habit: The habit is a trim, dark blue street dress with becoming hat and coat.

Write to: Missiondell
1030 No. River Road
Saginaw, Michigan

MISSIONARY CATECHISTS OF DIVINE PROVIDENCE (M.C.D.P.)

History: Beginning in Houston, Texas, as a small group of zealous young girls organized for the purpose of imparting needed religious instruction to Spanish-speaking children, the Catechists were officially made an adjunct branch of the Sisters of Divine Providence of San Antonio, Texas. This step was taken when the Mother General of the Divine Providence Sisters became convinced of the urgent need in the Southwest of organized catechetical work conducted according to their founder, Blessed Father Moye.

Purpose: Imparting religious instruction and practical Christian training to the poor and neglected are the apostolic activities of these sisters. They are also engaged in clinical work and in parish home visiting programs. The Catechists at present serve eighteen catechetical centers in Texas and New Mexico.

Spiritual Life: Due to the demands of her active apostolic work, the missionary catechist is not required to recite the Little Office of the Blessed Virgin on weekdays. The daily religious exercises include Holy Mass, recitation of the rosary, a half-hour each of mental prayer and spiritual reading, and other community prayers and devotions.

Training Program: St. Andrew's Convent Aspirancy offers a standard secondary school course for young girls of high school age who desire to become Catechist Sisters. The religious formation consists of a candidacy of one to two years depending on religious and educational background, a postulancy of six months, a one-year novitiate, ending with the one year of juniorate. After four years in temporary vows, while engaged in active missionary work, the young sister receives the gold ring, symbol of her final espousal to Christ.

Qualifications:
* The maximum age is 30. Exceptions are sometimes made.
* Completion of high school.

Habit: The sisters wear a black pleated skirt, blouse, and veil, a circular cape, a white collar and head band, crucifix, and a rosary.

Write to: St. Andrew's Convent
2318 Castroville Road
San Antonio 37, Texas

MISSIONARY SERVANTS OF THE MOST BLESSED TRINITY (M.S.B.T.)

History: Founded to meet the present missionary needs of the Church, this American community developed from a lay apostolate movement begun in 1909 by Father Thomas A. Judge, C.M. By 1912 some of the Associates were living a community life with private vows. From this group grew the religious congregation which was canonically erected by Rome in 1932, and raised to a pontifical status in 1958.

Purpose: The sisters have continued the development of the lay apostolate movement by which they endeavor to increase their own missionary effectiveness and also prepare lay people to assume their unique place in the ranks of the Church's missionaries. From two hundred mission centers in twenty-three dioceses in the United States and also Latin America, over five hundred sisters extend their services to the needy and abandoned. The sisters and lay-associates work out from these centers, visting the homes in the areas of each in an effort to strengthen Christian family life through missionary case-work. They provide religious instruction to shut-ins, retarded, deaf, blind, and conduct mission schools, clinics, a hospital, and other social services.

Spiritual Life: The religious exercises include Holy Mass, one-half hour of meditation, periods of adoration, spiritual reading, and other community prayers and devotions.

Training Program: The one-year postulancy is followed by the canonical novitiate year, and the two-year Sister-Formation program, in which a basic liberal arts college curriculum is taken. This is supplemented by initial courses in specific missionary principles and techniques.

Qualifications:
* Age: 16 to 30.
* Completion of high school.
* Entrance date: August 5.

Habit: The sisters wear a black tailored dress and a white collar with a pin bearing the community emblem.

Write to: Missionary Cenacle
3501 Solly Street
Philadelphia 36, Pennsylvania

OUR LADY OF PROVIDENCE
(O.L.P.)

History: The Most Reverend Russell J. McVinney, Bishop of Providence, founded this religious congregation. After four and one-half years, these sisters received papal approbation on January 14, 1960. The community has five houses in the State of Rhode Island.

Purpose: The sisters were founded to work directly under the guidance of the bishop in any field of the apostolate where needs might arise. The sisters are engaged in home visits and social work among the Negroes. They operate two day nurseries and a home for working girls. They teach catechism in several catechetical centers and work with unwed mothers and with children who must be placed for adoption or in foster homes. They also work with delinquent girls.

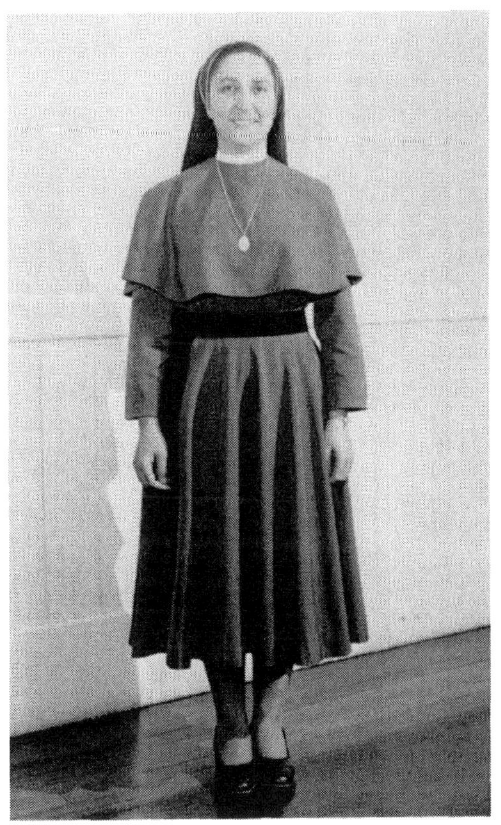

Spiritual Life: The religious exercises include Holy Mass, the recitation of the shortened Divine Office in English, the rosary, spiritual reading, and other community prayers and devotions.

Training Program: During the two and one-half years of the novitiate the sisters receive intensive training in the ideals of the religious life. Here they are also prepared to accept the work of their apostolate. At the novitiate, daily exposition of the Blessed Sacrament brings the novice closer to Christ, her Model. After first vows, the sisters continue their spiritual formation while taking courses toward their professional degrees.

Qualifications:
* Age: 17 to 35.
* At least a high school education.

Habit: The sisters wear a modern habit made of grey material, a grey cape, black veil, and a Medal of Our Lady of Providence.

Write to: Mother of Hope Novitiate
West Main Road
Portsmouth, Rhode Island

OUR LADY OF VICTORY MISSIONARY SISTERS (O.L.V.M.)

History: Father John J. Sigstein founded this congregation in Chicago, Illinois, in 1922. Archbishop John F. Noll, former bishop of the Diocese of Fort Wayne-South Bend and founder of the national Catholic weekly, *Our Sunday Visitor*, built the motherhouse for the sisters at Huntington, Indiana. It is called Victory Noll in commemoration of its great benefactor.

Purpose: This pontifical institute is devoted to religious education and social work. The sisters conduct schools of religion on the elementary and secondary level for Catholic children who attend public schools; catechetical centers are located in every section of the United States. The congregation has no institutions of any kind but is engaged strictly in missionary work. They also conduct parish visitations. In this way they find many who have fallen away from the Church and others who wish to enter the Church. These sisters also staff several clinics for low income groups, and they edit and print their own monthly, *The Missionary Catechist.*

Spiritual Life: The religious exercises include Holy Mass, the recitation of the rosary and the short breviary in English, one-half hour devoted to mental prayer, and spiritual reading.

Training Program: The sisters receive their training at Victory Noll. Postulants enroll in college courses as soon as they enter. Even those with degrees take many of these classes because they must become specialists in religious education. A two-year novitiate follows the year of postulancy. At the end of three years the sisters make their temporary vows. Final profession is made after five years.

Qualifications:
* Age: 18 to 30.
* Completion of high school.
* Entrance date: September 8.

Habit: The sisters wear a dark blue habit and veil, white collar and cuffs, and a medal and chain of Our Lady of Victory.

Write to: Victory Noll
Huntington,
Indiana

PARISH VISITORS OF
MARY IMMACULATE (P.V.M.I.)

History: Mother Mary Teresa Tallon founded this congregation in New York City, August 15, 1920. During the first quarter of the twentieth century, Mother Teresa saw the beginning of a steady and rapid decline in the Christian family life. With unceasing work, she endeavored to restore the spirit of the Holy Family in every home through parish visiting.

Purpose: The specific apostolate of the members of this congregation is the personal visitation of families and Christian Doctrine instruction. The sisters help establish Confraternity of Christian Doctrine in parishes, prepare lay catechists and teachers, and instruct public school children. They reach the families and individuals through a spiritual survey made in urban and rural parishes at the

request of pastors. Convents are located in New York, Illinois, Wisconsin, Connecticut, New Jersey, and Pennsylvania.

Spiritual Life: The religious exercises include Holy Mass, the recitation of the Little Office of the Blessed Virgin in Latin, one-half hour of mental prayer, the rosary, spiritual reading, and other community prayers and devotions.

Training Program: The six-month postulancy is followed by a two-year novitiate. Temporary vows are taken annually for three years. Profession of perpetual vows is then made. During the juniorate years, the sisters continue their spiritual formation while taking courses toward their academic degrees.

Qualifications:
* Age: 15 to 30.
* Completion of high school is preferred.
* Entrance date: December 1.

Habit: The sisters wear a black habit and veil, a white collar and head-piece, an emblem of the Immaculate Conception, and a rosary.

Write to: Mother Superior
Marycrest
Box 535
Monroe, New York

SOCIETY OF CHRIST OUR KING
(Soc. C.R.)

History: This community was founded in 1931 in North Carolina. Its foundress, Mother Teresa, was a cloistered Carmelite nun until she received the permission to enter the field of the missionary apostolate and undertake the guidance of a missionary institute of sisters. The foundation of the society took place in the home of two ladies who gave their property for the foundation and entered as its first novices.

Purpose: The ideal of the society is that its members cooperate in teams to aid persons through medical aid, social services, in retreat and library work, as counselors and guidance directors in recreation, and in manual skills; and in these and other approved areas find opportunity for the orientation of those whom they help toward a knowledge and love of Christ.

Spiritual Life: The religious exercises include Holy Mass, the recitation of the Divine Office, meditation, spiritual reading, and other community prayers and devotions.

Training Program: This is geared to fit the purpose of the society, namely, to bring the other sheep into the fold of Christ. The personality of Christ, His Church, and the social program of the Holy See are the bases of preparation for an active apostolate. This objective is carried through the postulancy and novitiate. The sisters and associates share this preparation. After first vows, the sisters continue their spiritual formation while taking courses toward their professional degrees.

Qualifications:
* Age: at least 17 with a high school education.
* The lay sisters should have some training or experience.
* Entrance dates: September 8 and February 2.

Habit: The sisters wear a modern dress and hat, and in season a coat. A crucifix worn on a neck chain identifies the members as disciples of Christ.

> *Write to:* Mother Superior
> Society of Christ Our King
> Danville, Virginia

SISTERS OF THE SOCIETY DEVOTED TO THE SACRED HEART (S.D.S.H.)

History: The community, originally founded behind the Iron Curtain in Hungary, 1941, opened its first foundation in the United States in 1956 at Los Angeles, California. This diocesan religious community of women is one of the few groups of sisters who do not wear the customary religious habit. They go about their apostolic work mostly in California and Nevada wearing simple street clothes, in order to be more accessible to everyone they meet in their wide field of apostolate.

Purpose: The work of these "plain clothes" sisters, like their dress, is attuned to the modern world and its needs. Their special aim is to contact those who are hard to reach because of their indifference, ignorance, or prejudice. Besides teaching religion to public school students on the elementary

and high school level, they moderate clubs and sodalities, give convert classes to young and old, and develop Catholic leaders through catechetical teacher training and leadership courses.

Spiritual Life: Great emphasis is laid on the life of prayer and character formation, which is the source of a spirit of unity and joyfulness by which the community is noted. Religious exercises include Holy Mass, mental prayer, rosary, spiritual reading and other community prayers.

Training Program: The six-month postulancy is followed by a one-year novitiate. Perpetual vows are pronounced after six years of temporary profession. Each sister receives a thorough spiritual training and practical knowledge right from the beginning in order to start her apostolate with professional skill and confidence.

Qualifications:
* Age: 17 to 30.
* Completion of high school.

Habit: The sisters wear dresses of current fashion which are similar only in color. All wear a silver Sacred Heart badge.

Write to: Vocation Directress
728 South Hudson Avenue
Los Angeles 5, California

V

NURSING

CARMELITE SISTERS OF THE THIRD ORDER (O.C.D.T.)

History: Mother Luisa Josefa of the Blessed Sacrament founded this community in Mexico in 1904. Sixteen years later the congregation was affiliated with the Discalced Carmelites and later became a pontifical institute. In 1927 during the religious persecution raging in Mexico, Mother Luisa Josefa brought the community to the United States.

Purpose: The primary aim of the congregation is the personal sanctification of its members. Their apostolic activities include nursing, teaching, retreat work, and the care of orphan children and those from broken homes.

Spiritual Life: The religious exercises include Holy Mass, one hour of mental prayer, the recitation of the Office of the Blessed Virgin in Latin and English, visits to the Blessed Sacrament, the rosary, and spiritual reading.

Training Program: The sisters conduct an aspirancy for junior and senior high school girls interested in the religious life. The six-month postulancy is followed by a two-year novitiate. This time is spent preparing the novice to make her temporary vows of religion. These vows are renewed annually for five years. At the conclusion of this period, the sister prepares to consecrate herself to God forever by making a six-month tertianship.

Qualifications:
* Age: 17 to 30.
* Average intelligence.

Habit: The sisters wear a brown tunic and scapular. The white mantle is worn for Mass and other religious solemnities.

Write to: Province of the Most Sacred Heart
920 East Alhambra Road
Alhambra, California

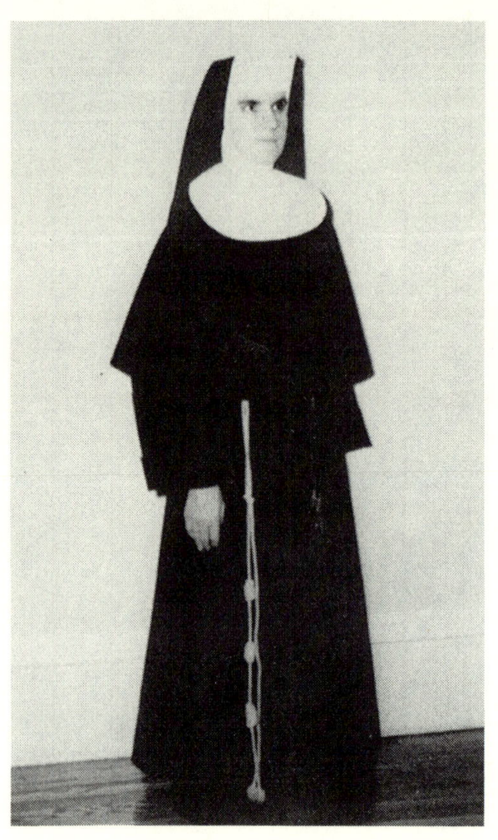

DAUGHTERS OF ST. FRANCIS OF ASSISI (D.S.F.)

History: Mother M. Bruenner founded this congregation in 1890 in Austria-Hungary. The community is active in Hungary, Czechoslovakia, Romania, and the United States. The American Province originated in 1946 when fifteen sisters came from Slovakia and settled in Peru, Illinois, and began their apostolic labors at St. Bede's College. In 1948 the motherhouse was transferred to Lacon, Illinois.

Purpose: The members of this pontifical institute are actively engaged in nursing in hospitals and conducting homes for the aged. Their institutions are located in Illinois, Ohio, and Missouri.

Spiritual Life: The religious exercises include Holy Mass, the Office of the Blessed Virgin in Latin, one-half hour of mental prayer, spiritual reading, and other community prayers and devotions.

Training Program: The community conducts an aspirancy for teen-age girls who are interested in becoming religious. The six-month postulancy is followed by a two-year novitiate. After the novitiate is completed the novice pronounces temporary vows for three years. Perpetual vows are then made. During the period of the temporary profession, the sisters continue their spiritual formation while completing the courses required for their professional and nursing degrees.

Qualifications:
* Age: 15 to 30. Late vocations are sometimes accepted.
* Average intelligence.
* Entrance dates: February 15 and August 15.

Habit: The sisters wear a black habit, veil, and cape, a white head dress and cord, and a Franciscan rosary.

> *Write to:* Mother Superior
> St. Joseph's Convent
> Lacon, Illinois

DAUGHTERS OF SAINT MARY OF THE PRESENTATION (F.S.M.)

History: Father Joachim Fleury and Mother St. Louis founded this congregation in France in 1828. When the religious persecution broke out in 1902 and the French government confiscated community property and closed its schools, the sisters, seeking new fields of labor, established foundations in Belgium, Holland, England, Canada, and the United States. Missions were opened in Africa in 1956.

Purpose: The sisters conduct one hospital, a grade school and catechetical centers in the state of Illinois, and operate three hospitals, a school of nursing, elementary and secondary schools, and catechetical centers in the state of North Dakota.

Spiritual Life: The religious exercises include Holy Mass, the recitation of the Office of the Blessed Virgin in English, one-half hour of mental prayer, the rosary, spiritual reading, and other community prayers and devotions.

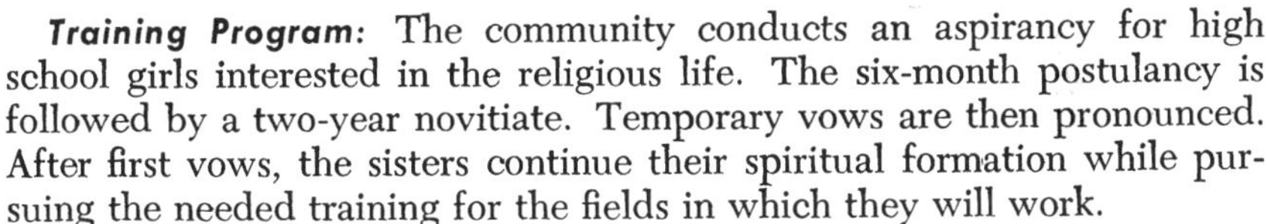

Training Program: The community conducts an aspirancy for high school girls interested in the religious life. The six-month postulancy is followed by a two-year novitiate. Temporary vows are then pronounced. After first vows, the sisters continue their spiritual formation while pursuing the needed training for the fields in which they will work.

Qualifications:

* Age: 16 to 30.
* Completion of high school is desired.
* Entrance dates: September 5 and January 9.

Habit: The sisters wear a black habit and veil, a white head band and collar, a rosary, crucifix, and a silver band ring.

Write to: St. Margaret's Convent   St. Catherine's Convent
Spring Valley,   Valley City,
Illinois   North Dakota

DAUGHTERS OF ST. MARY OF PROVIDENCE (D.S.M.P.)

History: Father Aloysius Guanella, a co-worker of Don Bosco, established this congregation in Italy, in 1881. The sisters opened a foundation in the United States in Chicago, Illinois, in 1913. More than one hundred houses are operating in Europe, and North and South America.

Purpose: The aim of this pontifical institute is to glorify God and do His work by nursing the sick and the aged, and—its special vocation—caring for mentally handicapped children. The foundations of this congregation are located in Illinois, Pennsylvania, Michigan, South Dakota, and Minnesota.

Spiritual Life: The day begins with a half-hour of meditation, community prayers, stations of the cross, and Holy Mass. A visit to the Blessed Sacrament and spiritual reading are made in the afternoon. In the evening, the sisters and those under their care who are able to attend recite the rosary and attend daily Benediction, granted them by special privilege. The spiritual day closes with community evening prayers.

Training Program: The six-month postulancy is followed by a two-year novitiate. Temporary vows are made annually for five years. At the end of this time perpetual vows are pronounced. Professional training is given after the canonical novitiate year is completed and consists of both formal and in-service training. The works of charity call for professionally prepared personnel in nursing, special education, and social work.

Qualifications:
* Age: under 30. Exceptions will be made.
* Average intelligence.
* Entrance dates: February 2 and July 2.

Habit: The sisters dress simply in a black habit with a short cape, a white collar, and crucifix (suspended on a cord) containing their motto: "Pray and Suffer."

Write to: St. Mary of Providence Convent
4200 North Austin Avenue
Chicago 34, Illinois

DAUGHTERS OF ST. RITA (D.S.R.)

History: Father Hugolinas Dach founded this community in Würzburg, Bavaria, in 1911. Established directly from the Bavarian motherhouse, the American foundation has been independent since September, 1954. This autonomy was sought at the request of the Most Reverend William T. Mulloy, the late bishop of Covington, Kentucky.

Purpose: The Daughters of St. Rita are engaged in nursing the convalescent and chronically ill.

Spiritual Life: The community devotions include Holy Mass, meditation, visits to the Blessed Sacrament, the chanting of the Divine Office in English, and other community prayers and devotions.

Training Program: The six-month postulancy is followed by a year novitiate. After receiving her vows, the newly professed is educated according to her talents and the needs of the community.

Qualifications:
* The maximum age is 30.
* Completion of high school.

Habit: The sisters wear a black habit with a black leather cincture, a five decade rosary, and a pectoral cross.

> *Write to:* St. Rita's Convent
> Versailles,
> Kentucky

DAUGHTERS OF THE MOST HOLY REDEEMER (D.M.H.R.)

History: This congregation, which now numbers around three thousand sisters, is a branch of the foundation established in Alsace, North France, by Maria Alphonsa Eppinger in 1866. Twelve sisters came to the United States from the general motherhouse in Würzburg, Bavaria, and opened their first convent in Baltimore, Maryland, on the Feast of St. Joseph, 1924. Twelve houses have been founded in the eastern part of the United States.

Purpose: Following in the footsteps of the Most Holy Redeemer, these sisters devote their lives to nursing the sick, conducting homes for the aged, and nursing the sick in their own homes in the state of Pennsylvania. They also conduct a home for working girls in New York City and maintain household departments in several eastern diocesan seminaries.

Spiritual Life: The religious exercises include Holy Mass, the office of the congregation, the daily recitation of the fifteen decades of the rosary, one-half hour of mental prayer, adoration, and spiritual reading.

Training Program: The three-month candidacy and six-month postulancy gradually initiates the beginner into the secrets of the religious life. An eight-day retreat prepares the postulant for reception of the holy habit. The first year of the novitiate is entirely given over to the spiritual formation of the novice. In the second year, the novice prepares for her life's apostolate in the field assigned. Temporal vows are taken at the end of the novitiate for three years. They are renewed for three more years. Profession of perpetual vows is then made.

Qualifications:
* Age: 16 to 30.
* Completion of high school is preferred.
* Entrance date: August 1.

Habit: The sisters wear a black serge habit held at the waist by a black cincture, a black rosary, short cape, and a small crucifix.

Write to: Most Holy Redeemer Convent
Meadowbrook,
Pennsylvania

DAUGHTERS OF WISDOM (D.W.)

History: St. Louis Marie de Montfort founded this pontifical congregation on February 2, 1703 in Poitiers, France. At the beginning of the twentieth century, when religious orders were expelled from France, the community spread to North and South America as well as to mission fields.

Purpose: The sisters nurse in hospitals as well as in child clinics for orthopedics and those afflicted with cerebral palsy, conduct elementary and secondary schools, and staff a school for mentally retarded children and an infant home. These institutions are located in New York, Virginia, Maine, and Connecticut. In the Belgian Congo, Nyassaland, Madagascar, Haiti, Colombia, and Indonesia, the sisters conduct schools, a teacher-training college, and an institute for the deaf and blind. They also maintain hospitals, nurses' training schools and leper colonies in these missions.

Spiritual Life: The religious exercises include Holy Mass, the recitation of the Little Office of the Blessed Virgin in Latin, meditation, the rosary, spiritual reading, and other community prayers and devotions.

Training Program: The six-month postulancy is followed by a one-year novitiate. A one-year juniorate follows first vows. Temporary vows are made for five years after which a two-month spiritual preparation takes place before profession of perpetual vows at the motherhouse in France. During this time, the sisters continue their spiritual formation while taking undergraduate courses toward their professional and nursing degrees.

Qualifications:
* Age: under 30. Exceptions will sometimes be made.
* Completion of high school is preferred.
* Entrance dates: February 2 and August 2.

Habit: The sisters wear a grey habit with a white linen coif and neckerchief, a black mantle and rosary, and a large crucifix. White is worn in the missions and by the hospital sisters.

Write to: Provincial House
101-19 103 Street
Ozone Park 16, New York

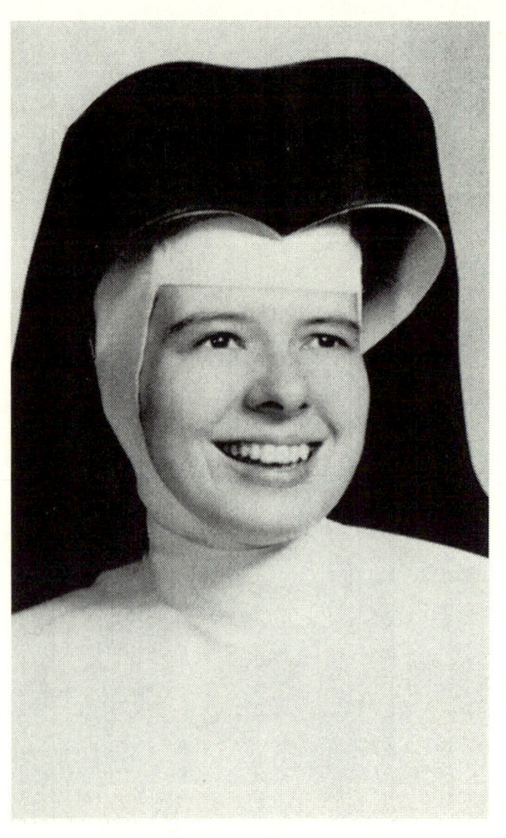

DOMINICAN SISTERS OF
THE SICK POOR (O.P.)

History: This congregation of Dominicans was founded in New York City by Mother Mary Walsh, O.P., with co-founders the Most Reverend John T. McNicholas, O.P., Archbishop of Cincinnati, and Father Peter O'Callaghan, C.S.P. In 1879 she and a few companions began their apostolate of caring for the sick poor in their own homes. After receiving diocesan approbation they were affiliated with the Dominican Order in 1910.

Purpose: The sisters strive to preserve family life in the homes of the needy sick through bedside nursing, allied case work services, and spiritual counsel. Professionally skilled, they care for young and old afflicted with chronic or acute illness. Their service is personalized. Each family's problem is evaluated to give the members every possible assistance. The sisters administer to indigent cancer patients in New York and do home nursing in Colorado, Massachusetts, Minnesota, and Ohio.

Spiritual Life: The religious exercises include Holy Mass, the chanting of the Little Office of the Blessed Virgin, the rosary, an hour of mental prayer, and other community prayers and devotions.

Training Program: The postulancy of one year is followed by another year of novitiate, after which the novice makes temporary vows for six years. During the two-year juniorate program, the sisters continue their spiritual formation while taking an active participation in the works of the community. After having acquired sufficient professional training, the sisters are sent to colleges and hospitals to obtain their professional and nursing degrees.

Qualifications:
* Age: 16 to 30.
* Average intelligence.

Habit: The sisters wear the traditional white Dominican habit.

Write to: Mother General
Mariandale,
Ossining,
New York

FRANCISCAN SISTERS OF THE BLESSED VIRGIN MARY OF THE ANGELS (B.M.V.A.)

History: Mother Mary Rosa Flesch founded this community in Germany in 1863. The first convent which she built in Waldreitbach, Germany, became the motherhouse of around one hundred daughter-houses in Europe, the United States, and South America. The sisters established their first foundation in the United States in 1923.

Purpose: The primary objective of the members of this community is to help spread the kingdom of God on earth by doing works of charity. The sisters are engaged in nursing the sick in hospitals and in caring for the aged. Social work of different kinds, and business and domestic work wherever it is necessary to help support their nursing or educational apostolate, are also included in the sisters' charitable activities.

Spiritual Life: The religious exercises include Holy Mass, the recitation of the Divine Office in Latin, one-half hour of mental prayer, spiritual reading, and other community prayers.

Training Program: The postulancy of eight months is followed by a two-year novitiate. Profession of temporary vows is then made. The sisters are then permitted to make their profession of perpetual vows after five years of temporary vows. During this time, the sisters continue their spiritual formation while taking courses toward their professional degrees.

Qualifications:
* Age: 16 to 30. Exceptions are sometimes made to 35.
* Completion of elementary school.
* Entrance dates: January 6 and September 8.

Habit: The sisters wear a brown habit, a white guimpe and cincture with three knots, a black veil, and rosary of the seven joys.

> *Write to:* Mother Superior
> St. Mary's Home
> 1925 Norfolk Avenue
> Saint Paul 16, Minnesota

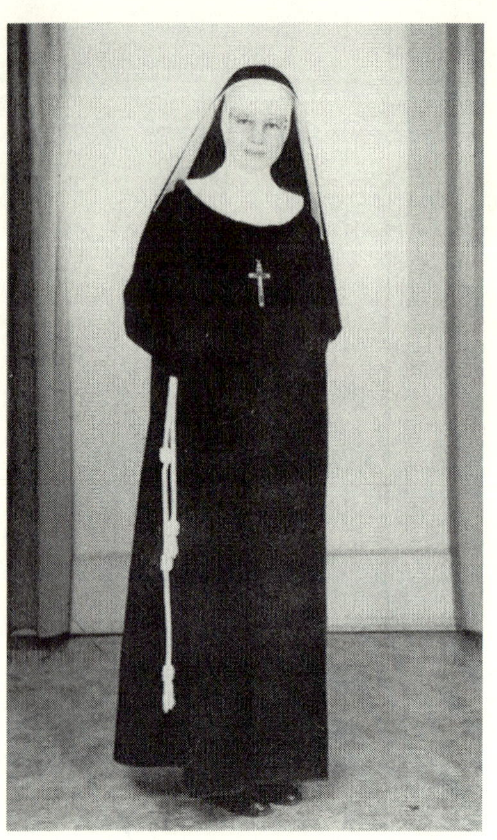

FRANCISCAN SISTERS OF THE IMMACULATE CONCEPTION (O.S.F.)

History: Faustin M. Mennel, a pious parish priest, founded this community in 1856 at Bonlanden, Germany. Hardship and privations marked its early history but the community prospered under the guidance of its beloved founder. The sisters came to the United States in 1928, and after a number of years the provincial motherhouse was founded in Buffalo, New York. This pontifical institute has provinces in Europe, Brazil, Argentina, Paraguay, and Uruguay, South America.

Purpose: In the American Province these sisters are engaged in nursing, child care, catechetics, retreats, and domestic service. In the provinces in South America, teaching, nursing, social service, catechetics are the main apostolic activities.

Spiritual Life: The religious exercises include Holy Mass, Little Office of the Blessed Virgin recited in Latin, meditation, rosary, morning and evening prayers, spiritual reading, and other devotional prayers.

Training Program: The postulancy of six months is preceded by a pre-postulancy period of between six to twelve months. This is followed by a one-year novitiate. The postulancy and novitiate are devoted to religious formation and training. The sisters take their temporary vows for three years before making their profession of perpetual vows. At the completion of the novitiate training the sisters pursue courses leading toward their academic degrees.

Qualifications:
* Age: 17 to 30. Exceptions will be made.
* Completion of high school is preferred.
* Entrance dates: February 2 and September 8.

Habit: The professed sisters wear a black habit, veil and scapular, a white wimple and cord, a Franciscan Crown rosary, crucifix, and a gold ring.

Write to: Nazareth Convent
291 W. North Street
Buffalo 1, New York

FRANCISCAN SISTERS OF THE IMMACULATE CONCEPTION (O.S.F.)

History: Upon the invitation of Bishop John Lancaster Spalding of Peoria, Illinois, this congregation of Franciscan Sisters left Little Falls, Minnesota, in 1893 and came to Rock Island, Illinois, to establish a hospital. In 1901 the congregation became an independent diocesan community. Later, other hospitals were opened as well as schools of nursing education. In 1947 the sisters assumed charge of the Schlarman Children's Home for under-privileged children. The community also conducts homes for the aged and a cathechetical center in the Diocese of Tucson, Arizona.

Purpose: The general purpose of the members of this congregation is the sanctification of its members through the evangelical virtues and vows and in following the rules of St. Francis of Assisi. The special purpose is the care of the sick in hospitals and private homes, the care of the aged, catechetical, and social work.

Spiritual Life: The religious exercises include Holy Mass, the recitation of the Little Office of the Blessed Virgin in English, besides several hours devoted each day to mental and vocal prayer.

Training Program: The six-month postulancy is followed by a two-year novitiate. After a period of five years in temporary vows, the members then make their profession of perpetual vows. The first three years of temporary vows are spent in the juniorate in the motherhouse where the sisters prepare for the active apostolate.

Qualifications:
* Age: 16 to 30. Exceptions are sometimes made.
* Completion of high school is preferred.
* Entrance dates: March and September.

Habit: The sisters wear a brown habit and scapular, a white cord with three knots, a seven decade Franciscan rosary, a white coif, bandeau, guimpe, a black veil, and a plain silver band ring.

Write to: Mother General
1000 Thirtieth Street
Rock Island, Illinois

FRANCISCAN SISTERS OF THE IMMACULATE CONCEPTION (O.S.F.)

History: Mother Mary Ignatius Hayes founded this first Franciscan convent at Belle Prairie, Minnesota, in the fall of 1872. In 1889, while Mother Hayes was in Italy, the mission was destroyed by fire. All efforts to communicate with the foundress proved futile for she had succumbed to a serious illness. Under the direction of the ordinary of the newly established Diocese of St. Cloud, the little band of stranded sisters were placed under diocesan protection and began their new foundation at Little Falls, Minnesota.

Purpose: The sisters operate eleven hospitals, a school of x-ray technology, two schools of nursing, one school of medical record technology, and three homes for the aged. They also teach in elementary and secondary schools and one college, and care for dependent children and teen-agers at the diocesan Children's Home, where they conduct classes for the mentally retarded. A mission has also been established in Peru.

Spiritual Life: The religious exercises include Holy Mass, the chanting of the Franciscan short breviary in English, one-half hour of meditation, private recitation of the rosary, spiritual reading, and other community prayers and devotions.

Training Program: The eleven-month postulancy is followed by a two-year novitiate. The novice then makes her temporary profession of vows. During the juniorate the sisters continue their spiritual formation while taking courses toward their professional and nursing degrees. After three years perpetual vows are pronounced.

Qualifications:
* The maximum age is 30.
* Completion of high school.
* Entrance dates: August 22 and September 8.

Habit: The sisters wear a brown habit and scapular, a white cord, black veil, the Franciscan Crown rosary, crucifix, and a silver ring.

> *Write to:* Franciscan Sisters
> Little Falls,
> Minnesota

FRANCISCAN SISTERS OF THE POOR
(S.F.P.)

History: Mother Francis Schervier founded this community in 1845 in Germany. Thirteen years later five sisters were sent to establish a foundation in Cincinnati, Ohio. Rapid growth in that area and in the East necessitated founding two provinces, one in Cincinnati, and another in Warwick, New York.

Purpose: The sisters nurse in hospitals, conduct schools of nursing, homes for the aged, clinics, kindergartens, orphanages, and social service centers, give catechetical instructions, and sponsor lay retreats. A mission in Brazil was opened in 1960.

Spiritual Life: The religious exercises consist in Holy Mass, the recitation of the Little Office of the Blessed Virgin in Latin, one-half hour of mental prayer, visits, and other community prayers.

Training Program: The Cincinnati Province conducts an aspirancy for interested high school girls. The postulancy of about nine months is followed by a two-year novitiate. Temporary vows are then taken. These are renewed annually for five years. Profession of perpetual vows is then made. The sisters continue another year in this program of spiritual formation while taking courses toward their academic degrees.

Qualifications:

* Age: 15 to 30.
* Completion of high school is preferred.
* Entrance dates: Spring and Fall.

Habit: The sisters wear a brown habit, red cord, wooden rosary, black veil, and a plain gold ring. A red cross and the instruments of the passion are embroidered on the scapular.

Write to: Saint Claire Convent 60 Compton Road Cincinnati 15, Ohio	Mount Alverno Convent 20 Grand Street Warwick, New York

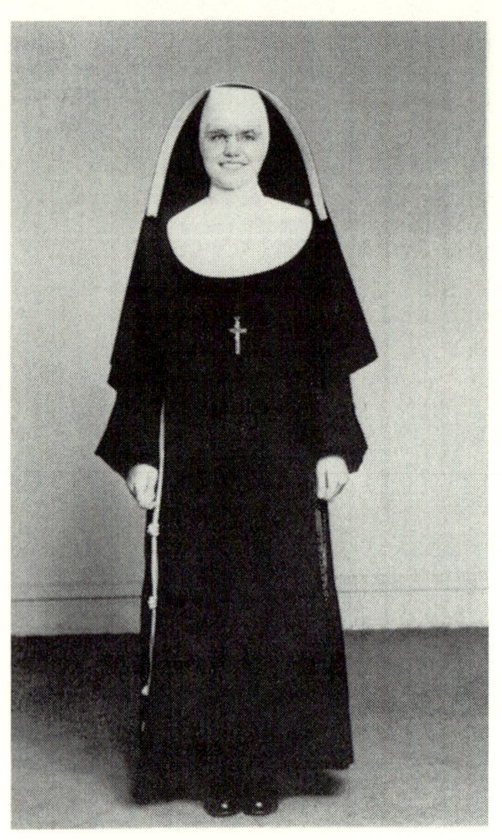

FRANCISCAN SISTERS OF
THE SACRED HEART (O.S.F.)

History: This community, which was founded by Father William Berger in Seelbach, Germany, in 1866 to care for the sick of the village, were ordered to disband or go into exile at the height of the Kulturkampf in 1876. Three of the exiles, Mother Anastasia Bischler, Sister Zita, and Sister Coletta, sailed for America where they established their motherhouse at Avilla, Indiana. In 1833 the motherhouse was transferred to Joliet, Illinois. Permanent approval was granted by the Holy See in 1898.

Purpose: The sisters operate eleven hospitals, six schools of nursing, two schools of practical nursing, teach in elementary and secondary schools, and conduct homes for the orphaned and the aged. These institutions are located in Illinois, Indiana, and California.

Spiritual Life: The religious exercises include Holy Mass, the chanting of the abbreviated divine office in English, a half-hour of meditation, the rosary, spiritual reading, and other community prayers and devotions.

Training Program: The community conducts an aspirancy for high school girls interested in the religious life. The six-month postulancy is followed by a two-year novitiate. Temporary vows are made for three years. Perpetual vows are then pronounced. After first vows, the junior professed sister resides in the novitiate where she continues her preparation for the professional work of teaching or nursing.

Qualifications:
* Age: 16 to 30.
* Average intelligence.

Habit: The sisters wear a black habit and veil, a white collar and cord, a rosary, and a crucifix.

Write to: Franciscan Sisters of the Sacred Heart
372 North Broadway
Joliet, Illinois

SPRINGFIELD FRANCISCANS (O.S.F.)

History: Christopher Behrens-
meyer, O.F.M., founded this community at the Shrine of Our Lady of
Telgte in Europe. The sisters came
to this country in 1875 and established their motherhouse in Springfield, Illinois. They became active
in the hospital and nursing field in
several states and founded missions
in China and Japan.

Purpose: The majority of the
sisters are active in their thirteen
general hospitals in Illinois, Wisconsin, and Missouri. They staff a
tuberculosis sanitorium, two homes
for unwed mothers, three homes for
the aged, and nursing centers.
Their home missionary apostolate
includes catechetical work near
Springfield, in the Ozarks, and the
Indian missions in Arizona where
they carry on home nursing and
dispensary work. Two general hospitals, a novitiate, and a house of
studies have been established in
Japan.

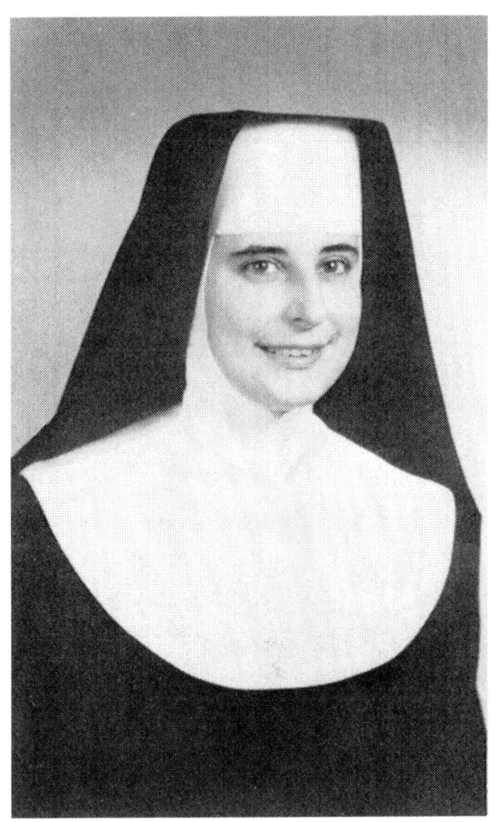

Spiritual Life: Saint Clare of Assisi Chapel of Perpetual Adoration is
the motherhouse of the congregation. There the sisters pray their community prayers, chant the Office of the Blessed Virgin in Latin, and keep
adoration day and night.

Training Program: The congregation conducts an aspirancy for teen-
age girls interested in the religious life. The one-year postulancy is
followed by a two-year novitiate. Temporary vows are then made.
During the juniorate, the sisters continue their spiritual formation while
taking courses toward their professional and nursing degrees. Prior
to final vows the professed make a thirty-day retreat.

Qualifications:
* Age: 17 to 30. Exceptions are sometimes made.
* Completion of high school.
* Entrance date: first week of September.

Habit: The sisters wear a black habit, scapular, and veil, the Franciscan white cord, and a brown rosary. The nursing and medical sisters
wear white.

> *Write to:* Mother Provincial
> P.O. Box 42
> Springfield,
> Illinois

WHEATON FRANCISCAN SISTERS
(O.S.F.)

History: Mother Mary Clara Pfaender founded this congregation in 1859 in Germany. They established the St. Clara Provincial Motherhouse in the U.S., at St. Louis in 1872. This was moved in 1947 to Wheaton, Illinois.

Purpose: These sisters fulfill the spiritual and corporal works of mercy by nursing in hospitals and teaching in elementary and high schools and a college of nursing. They also conduct orphanages and homes for working girls. These institutions are located primarily in the midwestern section of the U.S.

Spiritual Life: The spiritual exercises include Holy Mass, the Little Breviary in English, twenty minutes of vocal prayer, and one-half hour of mental prayer. The rosary and spiritual reading are private devotions.

Training Program: This community operates an aspirancy for girls who have completed the eighth grade. The aspirants are allowed home during the summer and the traditional vacation periods. The postulancy lasts one full year, while the novitiate takes two complete years. The program during these latter periods of formation consists of spiritual training with special emphasis on the vows and Franciscan way of life. Clarean week is offered each June for girls who want to spend a week living and learning about the Franciscan convent life. Invitation sent upon request.

Qualifications:
* Age: the limit is 40 years.
* Education requirements are not fixed.
* Entrance date: August 25.

Habit: The religious habit is brown, the scapular and veil are black, and the head covering and collar are white. Sometimes occupation requires the wearing of an all white habit.

Write to: Wheaton Franciscan Sisters
P.O. Box 166
Wheaton, Illinois

110

LITTLE COMPANY OF MARY
(L.C.M.)

History: Mother Mary Potter founded the community in Nottingham, England, in 1877. During an audience with Pope Leo XIII in 1882, Mother Potter was invited to transfer the motherhouse to Rome, Italy. Foundations were later established in Australia, Ireland, Europe, New Zealand, and the United States.

Purpose: The sisters are consecrated to the maternal heart of Mary at the foot of the cross on Calvary with a special zeal for souls in their last agony. They care for the sick in hospitals, in their own homes, in psychiatric, chronic, and convalescent units, maintain schools of nursing, and foreign missions. Their institutions are located in Illinois, New York, Indiana, California, and Buenos Aires, Argentina.

Spiritual Life: The religious exercises include Holy Mass, recitation of the Office of the Blessed Virgin, one hour of meditation, spiritual reading, fifteen decades of the rosary, the way of the cross, and special community prayers for the dying.

Training Program: The six to twelve-month postulancy consists of an introduction to the spiritual life of the congregation. In the first year of the novitiate emphasis is placed upon religious instruction and the formation of the interior life. During the second year the novices devote themselves with moderation to the works of the institute.

Qualifications:
  * Age: 18 to 24.
  * Completion of high school.

Habit: The sisters wear a black habit and scapular, a red cincture, crucifix, a head piece of white linen, a blue veil, and a silver ring.

> *Write to:* Little Company of Mary
> 9500 So. California Avenue
> Evergreen Park 42,
> Illinois

LITTLE MISSIONARY SISTERS OF CHARITY (P.M.C.)

History: These sisters belong to one of two congregations founded by Don Louis Orione at Tortona, Italy, in 1915. Completely entrusted to God's Divine Providence, the community is dedicated to the spiritual and temporal welfare of the poor. At the invitation of Richard Cardinal Cushing, an American province was founded in the Archdiocese of Boston in 1949. There are presently two thousand sisters in more than three hundred foundations throughout the world.

Purpose: The special objective of the members of this congregation is the apostolate of charity in hospitals, orphanages, homes for abandoned, retarded, and crippled children, the aged, and mentally deficient, schools, and youth organizations. They have foundations in Massachusetts and Indiana.

Spiritual Life: The Divine Office is recited daily in Latin by the blind Sacramentine Sisters, a contemplative branch of the congregation called, "Perpetual Adorers of the Most Blessed Sacrament." The Little Office of the Blessed Virgin is recited at the novitiate on Sundays and Holy Days. One hour is dedicated to mental prayer and two and one-half hours are given to community vocal prayers.

Training Program: The one-year postulancy is followed by a two-year novitiate. The novice spends her second year of novitiate training for the active life in works of charity among the poor. She then makes her temporary vows and receives the crucifix and rosary of a professed sister. Profession of perpetual vows is pronounced after five years of temporary vows.

Qualifications:
* Age: 15 to 35.
* Average intelligence.

Habit: The sisters wear a dark grey habit, black veil, a white linen guimpe, coif and headband, a crucifix, and a rosary.

Write to: Immaculate Conception Convent
120 Orient Avenue
East Boston 28, Massachusetts

NURSING SISTERS OF
THE SICK POOR (C.I.J.)

History: Sister Marie Antoinette, one of the Sisters of the Infant Jesus in France whose work was impeded through religious persecution, looked to the United States as a fertile field in which to spread the Gospel of Christ. When she and two companions arrived in Brooklyn, New York, in 1905, Bishop Charles E. McDonnell offered them the apostolate of nursing the sick in their own homes. Papal approbation was granted in 1907.

Purpose: The community's motto which is: "A strong Christian charity towards the less fortunate of God's creatures and a burning zeal for their spiritual and bodily welfare," expresses itself in the apostolate for nursing the sick in their own homes, hospital nursing, social work, and religious instruction to normal and exceptional children outside of school. Convents have been established in New York and the Bahama Islands. From these convents as centers, the sisters travel, usually alone, to do their assigned work.

Spiritual Life: The religious exercises include Holy Mass, the recitation of the Little Office of the Blessed Virgin in Latin, one-half hour of mental prayer, the rosary, and spiritual reading.

Training Program: The novitiate formation covers a two-year period. The first year is spent as a postulant and the second year as a canonical novice. Temporary vows are then made. These are renewed annually for three years after which perpetual vows are taken. During the juniorate, the sisters begin their professional education. These studies are selected on an individual basis to prepare the sister for her future assignment in the specific works of the congregation.

Qualifications:
* Age: 18 to 30.
* Completion of high school.
* Entrance date: September.

Habit: The sisters wear a black habit, cape and veil, a white metal cross, rosary, and a silver ring.

Write to: Motherhouse
439 Henry Street
Brooklyn 31, New York

SERVANTS OF RELIEF FOR INCURABLE CANCER (O.P.)

History: Rose Hawthorne Lathrop, convert daughter of novelist Nathaniel Hawthorne, appalled by the plight of the poor afflicted with cancer, left the gay social and literary circles of New York City and took a three-month practical nursing course in New York's Cancer Hospital. In 1896 she moved into three small rooms in the Lower East Side, where she nursed destitute victims of cancer. Later, she was joined by Alice Huber. In 1900, encouraged by Father Clement Theunte, O.P., they received the habit of the Third Order of St. Dominic, pronounced their vows, and placed their future entirely upon the support of Divine Providence.

Purpose: These sisters have dedicated themselves to the spiritual and physical welfare of poor incurable cancer patients. There are seven homes which are presently caring for these unfortunate victims. These are located in New York, Pennsylvania, Massachusetts, Georgia, Minnesota, and Ohio.

Spiritual Life: The religious exercises include Holy Mass, the Little Office of the Blessed Virgin recited in English, mental and vocal prayer, and other exercises of piety.

Training Program: The program includes a postulancy of six months and a novitiate of one year. In addition to the customary spiritual exercises of religious formation, classes are conducted by a registered nurse in the highly specialized care of incurable cancer patients.

Qualifications:
* Age: 18 to 35.
* Nursing experience is helpful but not necessary.
* Average intelligence.

Habit: The sisters wear the traditional white Dominican habit.

Write to: Motherhouse
Rosary Hill Home
Hawthorne, New York

SISTERS OF ST. FRANCIS OF THE MARTYR ST. GEORGE (O.S.F.)

History: Mother Anselma Bopp founded this congregation in 1869 in Thuine, Germany. The foundress, facing the dangers of an epidemic of typhoid fever then raging, resolved, with three other women companions, to take the three religious vows of the Franciscan Rule and to travel from home to home nursing the sick and caring for orphans. Numbering at present over 2,000 members, the sisters have foundations in Germany, Holland, Japan, Sumatra, and Africa. The activity of the vice-province in the United States began in 1923.

Purpose: This papal community which became a member of the Franciscan Order in 1906 is engaged in nursing, teaching, and social work. They operate a hospital in Alton, Illinois, and conduct a home for the aged and chronically ill in St. Louis, Missouri.

Spiritual Life: The religious exercises include Holy Mass, the recitation of the Office of the Blessed Virgin, meditation, and other community prayers. The stations of the cross and visits to the Blessed Sacrament are among their private spiritual devotions.

Training Program: The postulancy of eight months is followed by two years of novitiate. At the end of the novitiate, the sister pronounces temporary vows for one year. These vows are renewed annually for the next three years. Profession of perpetual vows is then made.

Qualifications:

    * Age: 16 to 30. Exceptions are sometimes made.
    * Completion of high school is preferred.

Habit: The sisters wear a black habit with scapular, a white collar, veil, and cord, the rosary of the Seven Joys, and a simple crucifix.

> *Write to:* St. Anthony's Convent
> 2120 Central Avenue
> Alton, Illinois

SISTERS OF ST. FRANCIS OF RICE LAKE (O.S.F.)

History: The congregation was founded in Chicago, Illinois, in 1907. In 1916 the sisters were requested to take over a hospital in Rice Lake, Wisconsin. Here they established themselves in 1926 when they were placed under the spiritual direction of the Franciscan Fathers of the Sacred Heart Province in St. Louis.

Purpose: The sisters care for the sick and aged in hospitals, conduct homes for the aged, teach children attending public schools, bake altar breads for parish churches, and are engaged in housekeeping for religious communities of priests.

Spiritual Life: The religious exercises include Holy Mass, the chanting of the Office of the Blessed Virgin, two half-hour periods of mental prayer, the rosary, spiritual reading, and other community prayers and devotions.

Training Program: The community conducts an aspirancy for high school girls interested in the religious life. In the canonical year of the novitiate an intensive study is made of the evangelical counsels and the fundamentals of the spiritual life. During the second novitiate year, the sisters are assigned to in-service training in one or another active works of the community. After first vows, the sisters complete the college courses necessary for their professional degree.

Qualifications:
* The maximum age is 35.
* Completion of high school is preferred.
* Entrance dates: before March 8 and September 25.

Habit: The sisters wear a brown habit, black veil, crucifix, and a white cincture from which is suspended the Franciscan Crown rosary.

Write to: St. Francis Convent
1107 E. Orchard Beach Lane, Route 4
Rice Lake, Wisconsin

SISTERS OF ST. JOSEPH OF ST. MARK (S.S.J.S.M.)

History: Father Peter Blanc and Mother Mary Xavier founded this congregation in 1845 in Alsace-Lorraine, near Strassburg, France, where the motherhouse for the provinces of France, Germany, and America are located. The American province originated in 1937 when Pope Pius XI granted permission to establish a foundation in the Diocese of Cleveland, Ohio. This was brought about by the Most Reverend Joseph Schembs who invited the sisters from the German province to settle in Cleveland in 1926.

Purpose: The sisters are engaged in nursing the sick and aged in their own convalescent home at Mount St. Joseph, as well as being responsible for the registrar office and domestic department of the Cleveland diocesan retreat house and major seminary. In the Youngstown diocese they serve as administrators and nurses at the St. Joseph Hospice for Geriatrics.

Spiritual Life: The religious exercises include Holy Mass, the recitation of the breviary in English, one-half hour of mental prayer, the rosary, spiritual reading, and other community prayers and devotions.

Training Program: The six-month postulancy is followed by a one-year novitiate. Temporary vows are made for six years, after which perpetual vows are pronounced. The sisters during these years continue their spiritual formation while pursuing courses toward their professional degrees.

Qualifications:
* Age: 16 to 30. Exceptions are sometimes made.
* Completion of high school.
* Entrance dates: February 15 and August 15.

Habit: The sisters wear a black habit and veil, a white head piece, a crucifix, rosary, and a silver ring when they receive perpetual vows.

Write to: Mount St. Joseph Convent
21750 Chardon Road
Cleveland 17, Ohio

SISTERS OF SAINT MARY (S.S.M.)

History: Prevented from establishing a religious congregation in her own native Germany because of the Kulturkampf, Mother Mary Odilia with five companions migrated to St. Louis, Missouri. She founded this congregation there in 1872.

Purpose: Following the Rule of the Third Order Regular of St. Francis, the members of this community are engaged in an exclusive program of nursing the sick in hospitals, teaching in schools of nursing, maintaining homes for the aged, and in missionary work. They operate thirteen hospitals in the United States, located in Missouri, Illinois, Wisconsin, and South Carolina, and three schools of professional and two of practical nursing. South America is the site of their foreign mission apostolate.

Spiritual Life: The charity of Christ is kept burning through their religious exercises which include Holy Mass, an hour of mental prayer, the recitation of the Little Office of the Blessed Virgin in English, and other community prayers.

Training Program: The spiritual formation of the sisters is carried on through a six to twelve-month postulancy, a two-year novitiate, and a juniorate for the temporarily professed sisters. Temporary vows are taken annually for two years and then for a period of three years. Profession of perpetual vows is then made.

Qualifications:
* Age: 15 to 35.
* High school education is preferred.
* Entrance date: early September.

Habit: The sisters wear a black or white habit, crucifix, rosary of the Seven Joys suspended from a red cincture, and a gold ring.

Write to: Motherhouse
1100 Bellevue Avenue
St. Louis 17, Missouri

118

SISTERS OF ST. THOMAS
OF VILLANOVA (S.T.DeV.)

History: St. Thomas of Villanova, a religious of the Augustinian Order and Archbishop of Valencia, Spain, died in 1556, and was canonized by Pope Alexander VII in 1658. Three years later, in 1661, a religious of the same order, Reverend Pere Le Proust, gave the name of the great apostle of charity to a new order of nuns which he founded in Lamballe, Brittany, France. Although the community was founded primarily to reorganize the poorest and most abandoned hospitals in France, the society has since added the work of the missions and the education of youth to their work for God and souls. The congregation has established houses in Africa, Belgium, France, Italy, Eire, England, and the United States where the first foundation was made in 1948.

Purpose: The members of this community operate hospitals, schools, and nursing academies, conduct convalescent homes for children, adults, and aged persons, and are engaged in Catholic action and missionary work in Africa.

Spiritual Life: The religious exercises include Holy Mass, the recitation of the Divine Office both in English and Latin, mental prayer, the rosary, and other community devotions.

Qualifications:
* Age: maximum is 30. Exceptions will be made to 35.
* Completion of high school is preferred but not obligatory.

Habit: The sisters wear a black habit and veil. White is worn by the nursing nuns and on the missions.

> *Write to:* Mother Superior
> West Rocks Road
> Norwalk, Connecticut

SISTERS OF CHARITY OF THE INCARNATE WORD (C.C.V.I.)

History: "A multitude of sick and infirm seeks relief at your hands," was the irresistible plea of Rt. Rev. C. M. Dubuis, when he went to France to seek volunteers to help him in his missionary labors in Galveston, Texas. Three young women answered his appeal and with these he founded the congregation in 1866. The community, which built the first Catholic hospital in the state, has papal approval and conducts twenty-six institutions in the South and the West.

Purpose: The most important apostolic labor of this congregation is the care of the sick in hospitals and out-patient clinics. They also teach in elementary schools, care for the aged and orphans, instruct retarded children, and supervise nursing students. These institutions are in Texas, Louisiana, Arkansas, California, and Utah.

Spiritual Life: The religious exercises include the Little Office of the Blessed Virgin chanted in Latin, Holy Mass, one hour of mental prayer, rosary, and spiritual reading.

Training Program: While the community does not have an aspirancy, the period of postulancy is arranged so that a high school graduate will have completed one year of college work by the time she receives the habit. The postulancy is followed by two years of novitiate. A period of six months is required as a preparation for profession of perpetual vows.

Qualifications:
* Age: 15 to 30.
* At least a high school education.

Habit: The habit is black, with a scapular, leather cincture, and rosary. The symbol of the Incarnate Word is embroidered in red on the scapular.

Write to: Villa de Matel
6510 Lawndale Avenue
Houston 23, Texas

SISTERS OF CHARITY OF PROVIDENCE (F.C.S.P.)

History: Compassion for the poor inspired Mother Emilie Gamelin and Bishop Ignatius Bourget to found the community in Montreal, Canada, in 1843. Thirteen years later in response to a plea of the bishops of the northwestern section of the United States, the young congregation sent Mother Joseph of the Sacred Heart to establish a foundation in this territory.

Purpose: The apostolic activity of this congregation is threefold: to honor God in the person of the poor and suffering; to give young women an opportunity to lead a holy life and daily to sanctify their souls in God's service; and to win souls to God through loving service, by caring for the aged and sick in their own homes and in hospitals, teaching, visiting the poor, and in catechetical and interracial work. The St. Ignatius Province has houses in eastern Washington, Idaho, and Montana. The houses of the Sacred Heart Province are located in Oregon, Washington, California, and Alaska.

Spiritual Life: The sisters attend Holy Mass, devote one hour to mental prayer, spend one-half hour in spiritual reading, say the rosary and other vocal prayers, and make visits to the Blessed Sacrament every day.

Training Program: The community has embarked upon a new project —a revised educational program established for the purpose, not only of giving to each of the sisters a deeply-rooted spirituality, but of providing a liberal education and professional preparation that will help each sister to become effective in her vocation to work for Christ in the world. This educational program continues throughout the five-year formation period in Providence Heights College of Sister Formation at Seattle University. A one-year postulancy is followed by a two-year novitiate.

Qualifications:
* Age: 16 to 30.
* Entrance date: August 15.

Write to: Mt. St. Joseph
Nine East Ninth Avenue
Spokane 3, Washington

Providence Heights
Pine Lake
Issaquah, Washington

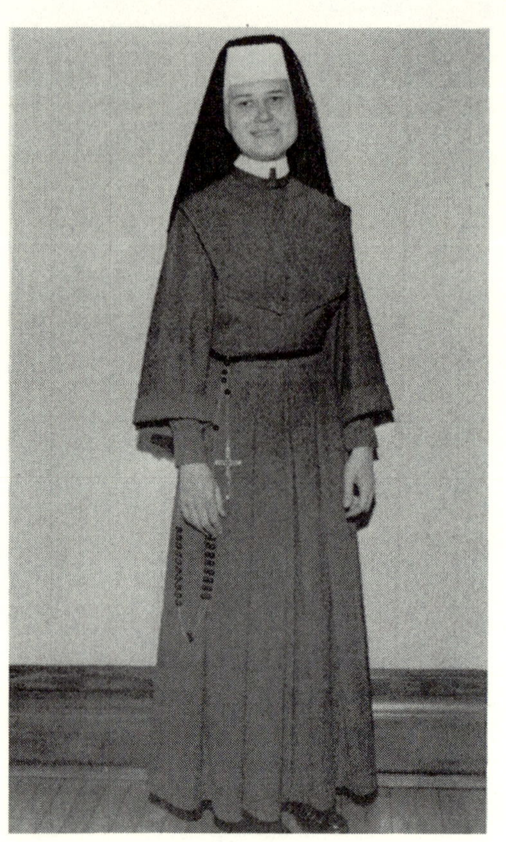

SISTERS OF CHARITY OF SAINT AUGUSTINE (C.S.A.)

History: The congregation originated in 1851 when, in response to the appeal of the first bishop of Cleveland, two Augustinian sisters from St. Louis Hospital, Boulogne-sur-Mer, France, with two postulants, sailed for the United States. Within a year after their arrival they opened Cleveland's first general hospital and in 1898 its first school of nursing.

Purpose: The personal sanctification of its members and the practice of the works of mercy are the primary objectives of this congregation. The sisters conduct seven hospitals, five schools of nursing, a maternity and infant home, and one home for dependent boys and girls. They also teach in secondary and elementary schools and are active in the Confraternity of Christian Doctrine. These institutions are located in Ohio and South Carolina.

Spiritual Life: The religious exercises include Holy Mass, one-half hour of meditation, rosary, spiritual reading, the recitation of the breviary in English, and other community prayers and devotions.

Training Program: The sisters living at the motherhouse attend St. John College, a diocesan institute for teacher-training and education in nursing. Others are assigned to colleges offering various educational programs. The sisters in temporary vows make up the juniorate. Those engaged in teaching and social services avail themselves of in-service training by the attendance of classes and workshops.

Qualifications:
* Age: 15 to 30.
* Average intelligence.
* Entrance dates: January and August.

Habit: The sisters wear a grey serge habit and collar, a white bandeau, coif, and collarband, a black veil, and a large rosary.

> *Write to:* Mother General
> 5232 Broadview Road
> West Richfield, Ohio

SISTERS OF BON SECOURS (C.B.S.)

History: The Most Reverend H. L. de Quelen, Archbishop of Paris, founded this congregation in Paris, France, January 24, 1824. The sisters came to the United States in 1881 at the invitation of James Cardinal Gibbons. As the trend toward institutional care of the sick increased and the value of professional nursing care became better appreciated, the sisters began to exercise their apostolate in hospitals and other institutions.

Purpose: The sisters operate general hospitals in Baltimore, Maryland; Detroit, Michigan; and Methuen, Massachusetts (another is under construction in Richmond), a school of practical nursing in Philadelphia, a house of studies in Washington, D. C., a convalescent home in New Jersey, a home for the aged in Florida, and a three-year nursing school in Baltimore. All these institutions are under the North American Province. They also have provinces in Europe and a mission in Africa.

Spiritual Life: The religious exercises include Holy Mass, the recitation of the office of the Blessed Virgin, two periods of mental prayer, the rosary, spiritual reading, and other community prayers and devotions.

Training Program: The postulancy of six months is followed by a novitiate of two years. Temporary vows are taken for one year. These are renewed every year for five years. Profession of perpetual vows is then made at the motherhouse in Paris when possible. After first profession the sisters are sent to continue or begin their professional training.

Qualifications:
* Age: 18 to 30. Exceptions are sometimes made.
* Completion of high school preferred.
* Entrance date: September.

Habit: The sisters wear a simple dress of black serge with a black veil, a small white cap, collar and cuffs, a silver crucifix and chain, and a rosary of large wooden beads.

Write to: Convent of Bon Secours
2000 W. Baltimore Street
Baltimore 23, Maryland

SISTERS OF PROVIDENCE (S.P.)

History: The Holyoke foundation of Providence sisters was established in 1873 by a small group of religious from Kingston, Ontario, Canada. Nineteen years later, at the suggestion of the Bishop of Springfield, the community was made a diocesan institute, and since then it has functioned as an independent congregation. The community now numbers about five hundred sisters.

Purpose: The sisters are engaged in various phases of charitable ministrations. They conduct hospitals, homes for the aged and orphaned, a home for the chronically ill, an extensive child care center, a residence for business women, day nurseries, and a hospice. These institutions are located in Massachusetts and North Carolina.

Spiritual Life: The religious exercises include Holy Mass, community morning and evening prayers, one hour of mental prayer, spiritual reading, the rosary, and visits to the Blessed Sacrament.

Training Program: The one-year postulancy is followed by a two-year novitiate. The novices then take their temporary vows and become junior professed. There is a five-year juniorate program of weekly conferences for the sisters after their assignment to the active duties of the apostolate. A six-month tertianship at the motherhouse is required before the sisters make their profession of perpetual vows.

Qualifications:
* Age: 18 to 30.
* Completion of high school.
* Entrance dates: July and September.

Habit: The sisters wear a black habit, veil, and cincture, and Chaplet of Our Lady of the Seven Dolors, which has a silver crucifix and a medal of St. Vincent de Paul. A silver cross with the emblem of Our Lady of Seven Dolors is also worn.

Write to: Providence Motherhouse
Sisters of Providence
Holyoke, Massachusetts

History: This congregation was established in Peoria, Illinois, by Bishop John Lancaster Spalding on July 16, 1877. Six pioneer religious with twenty-three companions from Herford, Germany, came to this country in 1875 and settled first in Dubuque, Iowa. Two years later they founded St. Francis Hospital in Peoria, Illinois. Sister M. Frances Krasse became the mother superior.

Purpose: These Franciscans devote their lives to the service of the sick, to teaching in schools, and to community needs. Today the community operates eleven hospitals in Illinois, Iowa, and Michigan.

Spiritual Life: The religious exercises include Holy Mass, the recitation of the Little Office of the Blessed Virgin in Latin, one-half hour of mental prayer, the rosary, spiritual reading, and other community prayers and devotions.

Training Program: The six to twelve-month postulancy is followed by a two-year novitiate. Temporary vows are made for three years and again for another three-year period. At the end of six years, perpetual vows are pronounced. The junior professed sisters attend Quincy College, Quincy, Illinois, where they complete the college work necessary for their professional and nursing degrees. The sisters participate in a six-month in-service program upon completion of their nurses' training.

Qualifications:

* Age: 16 to 35. Exceptions are sometimes made.
* Completion of at least three years of high school.
* Entrance dates: September 8 and February 2.

Habit: The sisters wear a brown habit and scapular, a black veil, a white coif, guimpe, cord and collar, a crucifix, and a Franciscan Crown rosary.

> *Write to:* Mount Alverno Novitiate
> 2327 W. Heading Avenue
> Peoria, Illinois

SISTERS OF THE THIRD ORDER OF SAINT FRANCIS OF THE IMMACULATE VIRGIN MARY MOTHER OF GOD (O.S.F.)

History: This Franciscan community originated in 1865 when, at the request of the Redemptorist Fathers, a group of sisters left the Buffalo foundation and established St. Francis General Hospital in Pittsburgh, Pennsylvania.

Purpose: The sisters operate three hospitals, each with schools of nursing, staff elementary and secondary schools, contribute to the faculty of two diocesan high schools, and are engaged in catechetical instructions in many parishes. These apostolic labors are being carried out in Pennsylvania and Georgia. They also have missions in Puerto Rico.

Spiritual Life: The religious exercises include Holy Mass, two half-hour periods of meditation, Divine Office, the rosary, spiritual reading, and visits to the Blessed Sacrament.

Training Program: The members of this community conduct an aspirancy for high school girls interested in the religious life. The one-year postulancy is followed by a two-year novitiate. Temporary profession of vows is then made. During the juniorate program the sister continues her spiritual formation while taking courses leading toward her academic degree or nursing diploma.

Qualifications:
* Age: maximum is 30. Exceptions are sometimes made.
* Average intelligence.
* Entrance dates: September 8 and February 2.

Habit: The sisters wear a black habit and veil, a seven decade rosary suspended from a white cord, and a white coif, headband, and guimpe.

Write to: Mother Superior
St. Francis Convent
Mount Alvernia
146 Hawthorne Road
Pittsburgh 9, Pennsylvania

SISTERS OF THE THIRD ORDER OF ST. FRANCIS OF MARYVILLE, MISSOURI (O.S.F.)

History: This congregation was founded and organized as a religious body in 1894. Ten years later it became affiliated with the Franciscan Order. In 1931 the constitutions were approved by the Sacred Congregation of Religious and on July 4, 1939 final approbation from the Holy See was given by Pope Pius XII.

Purpose: The sisters are engaged in hospital nursing, teaching, catechetical work, and lay retreats. They own and operate three hospitals in Missouri, a hospital and nursing school in Oklahoma, and one hospital each in Nebraska and North Carolina. Catechetical work is conducted in various sections of Missouri and Oklahoma. Retreats are held at the motherhouse.

Spiritual Life: The religious exercises include Holy Mass, thirty minutes of mental prayer, the Divine Office in English, spiritual reading, and the recitation of the Franciscan Crown rosary.

Training Program: A six-month postulancy followed by a two-year novitiate precedes the reception of temporary vows. Perpetual vows are pronounced three years later. Postulants continue their high school training if this has not been completed. The novices study the principles of the religious life. After first profession, the training varies and the individual is placed in that type of work for which she is best suited.

Qualifications:

* Age: 15 to 30.
* Average intelligence.

Habit: The sisters wear a black habit, a white coif, collar, and cincture, a crucifix, and the Franciscan rosary.

> *Write to:* Sisters of St. Francis
> Mount Alverno Convent
> Maryville, Missouri

SISTERS OF
THE SORROWFUL MOTHER (S.S.M.)

History: Mother Frances Streitel left her native Bavaria and established this community in 1883 in Rome, Italy. Under her guidance the congregation flourished and in 1889 she was able to establish its first foundation and a hospital in the United States. The community which now numbers more than 900 members opened a mission in the West Indies in 1960.

Purpose: The sisters nurse in fifteen hospitals, teach in elementary, secondary, catechetical, and nursing schools, and in their own junior college, conduct homes for the aged, a convalescent and children's home, as well as nursing home units and psychiatric departments in their hospitals. These institutions are located in Wisconsin, New Mexico, Kansas, Oklahoma, New Jersey, Pennsylvania, Iowa, and Minnesota.

Spiritual Life: The religious exercises include Holy Mass, the recitation of the Office of the Blessed Virgin in Latin, the rosary, spiritual reading and other community prayers and devotions.

Training Program: The community conducts an aspirancy for high school girls interested in the religious life. In the postulancy girls are trained in the first steps of the religious life and begin their college studies at the junior college. This is followed by a two-year novitiate. Temporary vows are then made. Perpetual vows are pronounced five years later. Those who are to become nurses enter a three-year period of training in a school of nursing. The future teachers complete studies for their academic degrees.

Qualifications:
* Age: not beyond 35. Exceptions are sometimes made.
* Average intelligence.
* Entrance dates: aspirants, the first Monday in September; postulants anytime—before September preferred.

Habit: The sisters wear a dark grey habit, a black veil, a white wimple and cincture, a rosary, crucifix, and a medal of the Sorrowful Mother.

Write to: Convent of the Sorrowful Mother
6618 Teutonia Avenue
Milwaukee 9, Wisconsin

SISTERS, SERVANTS OF CHRIST THE KING (S.S.C.K.)

History: The community was founded in 1940 at Edgeley, North Dakota, with the approval of the Most Reverend Aloysius Cardinal Muench. Mother Mary Rose and Sister M. Carmelita, under the direction of Father Gerald Walker, O.F.M. Cap., moved the headquarters of the congregation to Mount Calvary, Wisconsin.

Purpose: Nursing, domestic work, and caring for the aged, are the main apostolic activities of this community. The sisters also make altar breads for the surrounding parishes.

Spiritual Life: The religious exercises include Holy Mass, the recitation of the Franciscan short breviary in English, the rosary, stations of the cross, and special devotions to the Sacred Heart. Each sister spends an extra hour a day before the Blessed Sacrament.

Training Program: The postulancy which extends from six months to one year is followed by a two-year novitiate. The novices make temporary vows which are renewed annually. During this time, the sisters continue their spiritual formation while taking courses toward their nursing and professional degrees.

Qualifications:
* Age: 16 to 30. Exceptions are sometimes made.
* Completion of high school is preferred.

Habit: The sisters wear a black habit, veil, and cord, a rosary, and a profession crucifix.

> *Write to:* Mother Superior
> Loretto Convent
> Mount Calvary,
> Wisconsin

VI

RETREAT AND SOCIAL WORK

CONGREGATION OF OUR LADY OF THE RETREAT IN THE CENACLE (R.C.)

History: *"Humble among the humble, she lived humbly."* In the chapel of the first house of the congregation, founded in 1826 in the tiny mountain town of La Louvesc, France, these words are inscribed in marble above the altar of Mother Thérèse Couderc, foundress, declared Blessed in 1951. From the seed of her humility have grown and flourished 70 retreat houses for women, on five continents. At present there are 21 houses in the two North American provinces, oases of prayer, spiritual renewal, and apostolic inspiration for American womanhood.

Purpose: Conducting retreats for women and girls and teaching Christian doctrine constitute the Cenacle's twofold apostolate, which has as its aim the increase of the measure of holiness in the Mystical Body. This work of developing the supernatural life is carried out within the convents by means of

private and preached retreats, catechetical instruction of adults and children, guilds, study clubs, and the training of lay catechists.

Spiritual Life: The religious exercises include perpetual adoration of the Blessed Sacrament, recitation of the Divine Office, an hour of private meditation, and other spiritual exercises which total in all more than five hours daily.

Training Program: The formation of the religious is extended over a period of seven and one-half years which include: six months of postulancy, a two-year novitiate, two years of further study (juniorate) while engaged in the apostolate, and a tertianship. The latter is a six-month period of intensified prayer and recollection, during which the religious are withdrawn from the active apostolate in preparation for perpetual vows.

Qualifications:
* Good cultural background, maturity of character, prudent judgment.
* A desire for the total surrender of self to God.

Habit: Pleated black serge dress, purple cape, fluted white cap and black veil, brown rosary, silver profession cross, a gold ring.

See page 378 for address of nearest Cenacle convent.

CARMELITE SISTERS FOR THE AGED AND INFIRM (O.CARM.)

History: Mother M. Angeline Teresa founded this congregation in New York City, September 3, 1929. With six other sisters, she established the ideals and principles that guide her spiritual daughters in ministering to thousands of aged and infirm souls in many cities throughout the United States.

Purpose: The title identifies the objectives of this community. Every effort is made to minister and brighten the closing days of life for those who seek admission into their houses. The residents of these Carmelite homes are not deprived of their freedom. The spiritual needs are provided for through the resident chaplain. Many of the sisters are trained nurses so that they can give the best possible assistance to the aged and infirm. Homes are located in Iowa, Kentucky, Ohio, Illinois, Florida, and the New England States.

Spiritual Life: The religious exercises include Holy Mass, meditation, spiritual reading, the Little Office of the Blessed Virgin recited in Latin, and other community prayers and devotions.

Training Program: A young girl who enters the congregation spends her first six months in one of the homes for the aged in New York City. Here she is gradually introduced into the spiritual and active life of the sisters. She receives the habit of Carmel at a ceremony at the motherhouse and then enters the novitiate where she is spiritually prepared for her apostolic work.

Qualifications:
* Age: 17 to 30.
* Completion of high school is preferred.

Habit: The sisters wear a brown habit, tunic, and scapular, with a black veil and cincture, a white mantle, and a five decade rosary.

Write to: St. Teresa's Motherhouse
Avila on the Hudson
Germantown, New York

CARMELITE SISTERS OF THE DIVINE HEART OF JESUS (C.D.C.J.)

History: This papal congregation with its motherhouse in Sittard, Holland, was founded in 1891 when Mother Mary Teresa of St. Joseph opened the first of many St. Joseph Homes that she established throughout Europe and America. In 1910, after three journeys to Rome, her inexhaustible efforts were rewarded. She and her companions were allowed to follow the Rule of St. Teresa of Avila. Papal approbation was given in 1930.

Purpose: These Carmelites conduct homes for the aged, orphanages, kindergartens, and day nurseries. They are engaged exclusively in social work—they do not teach school. The two provinces in the United States have twenty homes in Wisconsin, Michigan, Indiana, Missouri, Kentucky, Florida, California, Texas, and Nicaragua, Central America.

Spiritual Life: Although these sisters enjoy all the privileges of the Order of Our Lady of Mount Carmel, they are not cloistered. The religious exercises include Holy Mass, the recitation of the Office of the Sacred Heart of Jesus in Latin, two periods of mental prayer, the rosary, spiritual reading, and other community prayers and devotions.

Training Program: When a girl enters the congregation she is a candidate until she becomes adjusted to convent life. During the six-month postulancy she is initiated into the various works of the community. Upon receiving the habit, the novice spends two years preparing for her temporary vows. Six months before perpetual vows, made after five years, the sister returns to the motherhouse. The sisters preparing to work with the aged are trained as practical nurses at approved hospitals. The other sisters follow collegiate courses leading toward their academic degrees or are trained within the community itself.

Qualifications:
* Age: 17 to 30.
* Average intelligence.
* Entrance dates: July and December.

Habit: The sisters wear a brown habit, scapular, and veil, and a white choir mantle.

See page 378 for address of nearest provincial house.

CONGREGATION OF
THE DIVINE SPIRIT (C.D.S.)

History: The Most Reverend John Mark Gannon, Archbishop-Bishop of Erie, Pennsylvania, in response to the plea of the late Holy Father, Pope Pius XII, for the adaptation and renovation of religious institutes to the needs of the times, founded this community on the Feast of the Sacred Heart 1956.

Purpose: As a congregation which places stress upon work among the laity—and in line with its stated objective of fostering the Propagation of the Faith—the sisters combine prayer with zealous activity of a practical nature. They teach children in parochial schools, nurse in a home for the aged, give catechetical instructions, conduct parish censuses, participate in diocesan religious, educational, and social works, and are engaged in social service work.

Spiritual Life: The religious exercises include Holy Mass, morning and evening prayers, meditation, the rosary, spiritual reading, weekly holy hour, and, after profession of perpetual vows, the Divine Office.

Training Program: Each new member lives with the community from the beginning, joins in all of the spiritual exercises, and accompanies and aids the sisters in the work assigned. The part that each individual plays in the congregation, is, of course, dependent upon her special background, talents, and capabilities. She spends four months as a candidate, eight months as a postulant, two years as a novice, and four years in-service training as part of the Sister Formation Program.

Qualifications:
* Age: 18 to 35. Exceptions are sometimes made.
* Completion of high school.

Habit: The sisters wear an adaptive charcoal grey habit with navy accessories.

Write to: Domus Pacis
409 W. Sixth Street
Erie, Pennsylvania

CONGREGATION OF
THE OBLATES OF BETHANY (C.O.B.)

History: This community was founded by Father Eugene Prevost, a French Canadian. After his ordination he was placed in charge of the "priest adorers." His duties during the thirteen years kept him in close contact with the needs of his fellow-priests and finally led him to the founding of two congregations. In 1901 he received the charter of foundation of the Sacerdotal Fraternity for men and the Oblates of Bethany for women. The first houses were opened in Paris, France, and have spread to other sections of Europe, in Canada, South America, and the United States in 1959.

Purpose: The principal apostolate of the congregation is that of unceasing prayer for the sanctification of all the priests in the world. Each sister is assigned to some special task according to her talents and abilities. Besides making vestments for churches, they engage in the domestic work in priests' rectories.

Spiritual Life: The religious exercises include Holy Mass, one-half hour of meditation, one hour and a half of adoration before the Blessed Sacrament exposed, the rosary, and Solemn Benediction to end each day of adoration.

Training Program: The six-month postulancy is followed by a two-year novitiate. Temporary vows are made for three years. At the expiration of these vows perpetual vows are pronounced. The professed religious continue their spiritual development while pursuing the courses necessary for their professional degrees.

Qualifications:
* Age: 17 to 35.
* Average intelligence.

Habit: The sisters wear a black habit and veil, a white scapular, rosary, and a gold ring.

> *Write to:* Oblates of Bethany
> 4540 Lindell Boulevard
> St. Louis 8, Missouri

DOMINICAN CONGREGATION OF ST. CATHERINE DE' RICCI (O.P.)

History: Lucy Eaton Smith, a young American convert, sailed to Europe late in the nineteenth century to find rest and decide upon her vocation in life. She asked her Dominican spiritual director for permission to enter a European community of sisters. He told her that the United States needed her and that she should return to her homeland and found her own community. This marked the beginning of this Dominican congregation.

Purpose: Personal sanctification and the salvation of souls is the two-fold aim of this community. The members conduct retreats for laywomen, residences for business girls, homes for retired women, and catechetical centers and schools of adult education. These works are carried on in New York, New Jersey, Pennsylvania, Florida, Virginia, Ohio, and New Mexico.

Spiritual Life: The religious exercises include Holy Mass, the chanting of the Little Office of the Blessed Virgin, recitation of the rosary, and private meditation.

Training Program: The postulancy of six months is followed by a two-year novitiate. After making her temporary vows, the sister receives special training and education for the apostolate and gradually assumes her place in the works of the congregation. At the conclusion of her five year period of temporary vows the sister makes her profession of perpetual vows.

Qualifications:
* Age: 15 to 30. Exceptions are sometimes made.
* Completion of high school is preferred.

Habit: The sisters wear the traditionally white Dominican habit and a fifteen decade rosary.

Write to: Mother General
886 Madison Ave.
Albany 8, New York

LITTLE SISTERS OF JESUS

History: This congregation was founded in the Sahara, North Africa, in 1939, following the footsteps of Little Brother Charles of Jesus, Father Charles de Foucauld, in imitation of the hidden life of Jesus at Nazareth. It received diocesan status in 1947 from the Most Reverend Charles de Provencheres, Archbishop of Aix-en-Provence, France. From this original foundation, this community has grown to include over eight hundred and fifty members, of forty-five different nationalities, in over fifty countries.

Purpose: The primary objective of the congregation is to carry the message of the Gospel across the world by the silent testimony of a life of prayer, friendship and love, and through a life of contemplation and manual labor without engaging in any formal apostolic activity. The Little Sisters share the

life of the poor and of the abandoned minorities among whom they live in very small groups, adapting themselves to the particular environment, country, and race. They earn their own living by working in factories, by doing housework, or handicrafts, undertaken in an effort to establish universal unity in the love of God and through a closer understanding between classes, races, and countries.

Qualifications:
* Age: 16 to 30.
* Average intelligence.
* Sound health.

Habit: The sisters wear a white scapular habit with a blue veil for the professed. For work and everyday life, the sisters wear a uniform of blue cotton with a leather belt, sandals, and a wooden rosary.

Write to: The Little Sisters of Jesus
700 Irving Street N.E.
Washington 17, D.C.

LITTLE SISTERS OF THE POOR
(P.S.D.P.)

History: Jeanne Jugan founded this congregation in France in 1839. Divinely inspired to help the abandoned aged, Jeanne received a few elderly ladies into her home. God blessed the work. Foundations have been established on six continents. Around 5,400 sisters care for forty-five thousand aged guests.

Purpose: The main work of the community is caring for the aged. The sisters receive them into their homes, provide for their needs, and nurse them in sickness all the while endeavoring to give them comfort in order to foster their spiritual life and help them get ready to meet their Eternal Master. The sisters have no other income than the liberality of Divine Providence coming to them through their benefactors.

Spiritual Life: The religious exercises include Holy Mass, the recitation of the Office of the Blessed Virgin in Latin, one hour of mental prayer, adoration, the rosary, spiritual reading, and other community prayers and devotions.

Training Program: The sisters conduct an aspirancy for high school girls interested in the religious life. The six-month postulancy is followed by an eighteen-month novitiate. Temporary vows are made for five years, after which perpetual vows are pronounced. After first profession the sisters continue their spiritual formation while taking courses in practical or registered nursing. A tertianship of one year is made about four years after first vows in preparation for final vows. The sisters have organized a new community called Oblates who help the sisters in their work. They make promises, not vows.

Qualifications:
* Age: 18 to 40. Completion of high school.
* Age for the Oblates: 17 to 50. Widows will be accepted.

Habit: The sisters wear a black habit and mantle, and a white bonnet.

See page 378 for address of nearest provincial house.

140

POOR SISTERS OF NAZARETH
(P.S.N.)

History: Mother St. Basil, at the request of Nicholas Cardinal Wiseman, founded this congregation in London, England, in 1851. He wanted her to provide homes for the aged, the orphaned and abandoned children, and for those from broken homes. The community was approved by the Holy See in 1864.

Purpose: The primary objective is to care for the poor of both sexes, young and old alike. Through charity, devotion, and zeal the sisters try to promote in the hearts of their senior citizens a great love for God, and to prepare them for a happy death. They give the under-privileged children motherly care and affection, educate them in their own schools, give them sound moral training, and help them prepare for the difficult battle of life.

Spiritual Life: The religious exercises include Holy Mass, meditation, the recitation of the Little Office of the Blessed Virgin, the rosary, and other community prayers and devotions.

Training Program: The candidate begins her religious life in the postulancy. When she becomes a novice she receives the holy habit and is given her religious name. In the novitiate the novice learns about the principles of the life of a religious and here she receives the foundations for her future life of close union with God. Temporary vows are made annually for three years and then renewed for three more years. At the end of this six year period, the sister pronounces her perpetual vows. During this time, the sisters continue their spiritual formation while taking courses toward their professional degrees.

Qualifications:
* Age: aspirants 14-16; postulants 17-30.
* Average intelligence.

Habit: The sisters wear a black habit, scapular, and veil, a white band, cap and wimple, a leather cincture, a rosary, and a crucifix.

Write to: Provincial House
3333 Manning Avenue
Los Angeles 64, California

History: Father Nikolas Schuler and Mother Josefa Nikolina founded this congregation at Zams, Austria, in 1823. The rule of St. Vincent de Paul was adopted. Foundations were established in other sections of Austria, in Hungary, and in the United States at Kirkwood, Missouri, in 1927. The motherhouse was transferred to Watertown, Wisconsin, in 1946.

Purpose: The greater honor of God through their own sanctification and the practice of the spiritual and corporal works of mercy toward the sick, poor, aged, and the education of youth are the apostolic activities of the members of this community. In the United States they are presently engaged in caring for the aged in two homes in Wisconsin and in taking care of the domestic duties of two major seminaries in Wisconsin and Missouri.

Spiritual Life: The religious exercises include Holy Mass, meditation, spiritual reading, the short breviary in English, and other community prayers and devotions.

Training Program: The postulancy of six months is followed by a two-year novitiate. The sisters take temporary vows for six years, and then vows for life. After first profession, the sisters continue their spiritual formation while taking courses toward their teaching or nursing degrees.

Qualifications:
* Age: 17 to 35.
* Completion of high school.
* Entrance dates: September and February.

Habit: The sisters wear a black habit and veil, a white wimple, and a large rosary.

Write to: Mother Provincial
705 Clyman Street
Watertown, Wisconsin

SISTERS OF THE GOOD SHEPHERD
(R.G.S.)

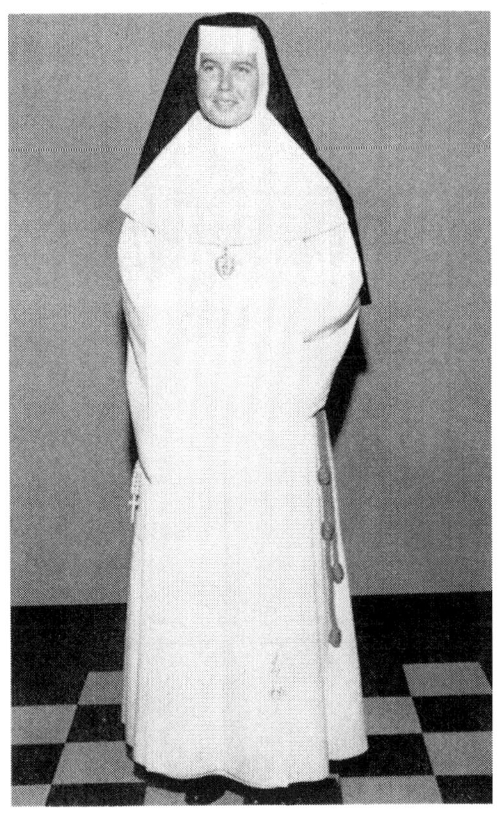

History: These sisters originated in France in 1641 under St. John Eudes, the apostle of devotion to the Sacred Hearts of Jesus and Mary. In 1835, St. Mary Euphrasia, then superior at Angers, France, was given permission by Rome to form a generalate. Her purpose was to facilitate the development of the congregation and infuse into it the vigor which unity alone can insure. There are around ten thousand Good Shepherd Sisters working in over four hundred and sixty foundations throughout the world. There are seven provinces in the United States.

Purpose: The work of the sisters is primarily re-education and formation of character in girls with personality or behavior problems. To the sisters, these girls are not juvenile delinquents but rather children of God. These are girls who cannot cope with their own problems. The Good Shepherd Sisters provide them with needed love, understanding care, and religious guidance.

Spiritual Life: The religious exercises include Holy Mass, the recitation of the Office of the Blessed Virgin in Latin, two periods of meditation, the rosary, spiritual reading, and other community prayers and devotions.

Training Program: The six to nine-month postulancy is followed by a two-year novitiate. Temporary vows are made annually for three years after which perpetual vows are pronounced. During the juniorate years the sisters receive continued intensive intellectual, spiritual, and professional formation. After ten years in vows, the sisters make a spiritual renewal of two months at the provincial house or the motherhouse in Angers, France.

Qualifications:
* Age: 17 to 35.
* Completion of high school.

Habit: The sisters wear a white habit with a blue cincture and a black veil.

See page 379 for address of nearest provincial house.

SISTERS OF THE LAMB OF GOD (A.D.)

History: Father R. M. de la Chevasnerie, S.J., founded this congregation in Brest, France, in 1945. The community has eleven houses in France and one in Owensboro, Kentucky.

Purpose: The sisters care for the sick in their homes, conduct homes for children and for the convalescent, give catechetical instructions, and take parish censuses.

Spiritual Life: The religious exercises include Holy Mass, the recitation of the Office of the Blessed Virgin in English, one-half hour of meditation, spiritual reading, the rosary, and other community prayers and devotions.

Training Program: The ten-month postulancy is followed by a two-year novitiate. Temporary profession of vows is then made. After first profession, the sisters continue their spiritual formation while taking courses toward their professional degrees.

Qualifications:
* There is no age limit.
* Physically handicapped will be accepted.
* Average intelligence.

Habit: The sisters wear a white habit and veil, a red cord, crucifix, leather belt, and a rosary.

Write to: Our Lady of Hope Convent
1516 Parrish Avenue
Owensboro, Kentucky

SISTERS OF MISERICORDE (S.M.)

History: This pontifical institute owes its origin to Mother of the Nativity who founded the congregation in Montreal, Canada, in 1848, upon the request of Bishop Ignace Bourget. In the United States they are represented in New York, Illinois, Wisconsin, and Massachusetts. Recently the congregation has undertaken missionary work in the Cameroons, Africa.

Purpose: Membership in this community provides the means of uniting the active with the contemplative life by performing the work of rehabilitation of unwed mothers and the care of orphans, nursing the sick in general and specialized hospitals, and by conducting retreat houses and missionary work in foreign lands.

Spiritual Life: The religious exercises include Holy Mass, one-half hour of mental prayer, the chanting of the Office of the Blessed Virgin in Latin weekly, the recitation of the rosary, spiritual reading, and other community prayers and devotions.

Training Program: Following a probationary period of six months, the postulant is eligible for acceptance into the eighteen-month novitiate. The canonical year is devoted to an intensive study of the religious life, the formation of religious character, and the development of the spirit which typifies the Misericorde Sister. Five years intervene between the first profession and perpetual vows. During this time the sister acquires competence, skills, and the necessary academic degrees needed for her future apostolate.

Qualifications:

* Age: 17 to 30. Exceptions are sometimes made.
* Entrance dates: January 16 and July 16.

Habit: The professed sisters wear a black habit and veil, a cross, rosary, and a silver ring.

> *Write to:* Misericorde Novitiate
> 288 South Avenue
> Beacon, New York

SISTERS OF
THE MOST HOLY CRUCIFIED (S.S.C.)

History: Father Giovanne Quilici founded this congregation at Livorno, Italy, in 1840. The sisters opened their first foundation in the United States in 1951.

Purpose: The sisters are principally engaged in conducting charitable institutions for the re-education of youth. Most of the apostolate is in Italy. In the United States they conduct a home for the aged in Rhode Island and assist with the domestic work in the seminaries and schools of the Augustinian Fathers.

Spiritual Life: The religious exercises include Holy Mass, the recitation of the Office of the Blessed Virgin, a half-hour of meditation, the rosary, spiritual reading, and other community prayers and devotions.

Training Program: The sisters conduct an aspirancy for high school girls interested in the religious life. The one-year postulancy is followed by a two-year novitiate. Temporary vows are made for five years. Perpetual vows are then pronounced. After first vows, the sisters continue their spiritual formation while taking courses toward their professional degrees.

Qualifications:
* Age: 15 to 35.
* Average intelligence.
* Entrance dates: May and September.

Habit: The sisters wear a black habit and veil, a white wimple, Augustinian cincture, rosary, and a large crucifix.

Write to: Sisters of the Most Holy Crucified
Bishop Scalabrini Home
North Kingston,
Rhode Island

THE SISTERS OF OUR LADY OF CHARITY OF REFUGE (O.L.C.R.)

History: St. John Eudes founded this congregation in Caen, France, in 1642. He organized the community to assist him in the work of reclamation and salvation of girls who had led sinful lives. For over three hundred years the sisters have been practicing the fundamentals of modern sociology according to Christian social principles. In 1855 the first foundation was made in Buffalo, New York.

Purpose: In its apostolate, the congregation acts in a three-fold capacity of home, church, and school. The sisters specialize principally in the rehabilitation of adolescent problem girls who are the victims of modern social evils, bad environment, weakness of character, and broken homes. They are engaged in the scholastic education as well as the moral re-education of these girls.

Spiritual Life: The religious, in addition to the three vows of poverty, chastity, and obedience, make a fourth vow to labor for the salvation of souls entrusted to their care. They observe minor papal enclosure.

Training Program: The six-month postulancy is followed by a two-year novitiate. The novices then make temporary vows for three years. At the expiration of this time, perpetual vows are pronounced. During this five and one-half years of spiritual training, the sister is prepared to do the work for which she is most capable: group supervisor, social worker, teacher, secretary, nurse, or domestic work.

Qualifications:
* Age: 16 to 35. Exceptions are sometimes made.
* A right intention and the ability to bear the burdens of religious life.

Habit: The sisters wear a white habit, scapular, and chaplet, a black veil, and a silver heart bearing an embossed image of Our Lady and the words *"Vive Jesu et Marie."*

See page 379 for a list of monasteries.

SISTERS OF SOCIAL SERVICE OF LOS ANGELES (S.S.S.)

History: This community was originally founded in Budapest, Hungary, for religious social service work. The sisters opened their first foundation in the United States in 1923. They were established as a diocesan institution by the Sacred Congregation in 1955.

Purpose: The special objective of the society is to engage in the works of mercy with specific reference to the social welfare of the Church according to the needs of the diocese.

Spiritual Life: The religious exercises include Holy Mass, the Divine Office in English, (Lauds and Prime are said in the morning, Vespers and Compline are said in the evening), the rosary, meditation, spiritual reading, and other community prayers and devotions.

Training Program: The six-month postulancy is followed by a two-year novitiate. Temporary vows are taken for six years, after which perpetual vows are made. During these years of the juniorate, the sisters continue their spiritual formation while taking courses toward their professional degrees.

Qualifications:
* Age: 18 to 30.
* Completion of high school.
* Entrance dates: February and September.

Habit: The sisters wear a simple grey uniform and the emblem of the society and a silver medal bearing the dove, the symbol of the Holy Spirit.

> *Write to:* Mother General
> 1120 Westchester Place
> Los Angeles 19, California

SISTERS OF SAINT ELIZABETH (S.S.E.)

History: The congregation was founded in Milwaukee, Wisconsin, in 1931 by the Most Rev. Benno Aichinger, O.F.M., with authority received from His Eminence Samuel Cardinal Stritch, then Archbishop of Milwaukee. The sisters follow the rule of the Third Order Regular of St. Francis of Assisi given and approved by His Holiness, Pope Pius XI, on October 5, 1927.

Purpose: In imitation of their divine leader Jesus Christ, the active apostolate of the members of this congregation is the spiritual and corporal welfare of the works of mercy involved in caring for the crippled, blind, and chronically ill women, both young and old. The work fills a crying need in our troublesome times of housing problems, disrupted family life, when chronic invalids of all ages have no place in the homes of their relatives and friends.

Spiritual Life: The religious exercises include Holy Mass, the recitation of the short breviary in English, meditation, the rosary, spiritual reading, and other community prayers and devotions.

Qualifications:
* Age: under 30.
* Older women who qualify will be accepted.
* Average intelligence.

Habit: The sisters wear a light brown habit, a black veil, white cord, and a rosary.

> *Write to:* Mother General
> St. Elizabeth's Convent
> 745 No. Brookfield Road
> Brookfield, Wisconsin

VII

TEACHING AS A MAJOR APOSTOLATE

BETHLEMITA SISTERS (S.C.I.F.)

History: This community, also known as the Daughters of the Sacred Heart of Jesus, was established in 1852 for the education of girls in both grade and high schools and for the care of children in orphanages. The motherhouse is in Bogota, Colombia, South America. The congregation has five provinces located in Italy, South and Central America, and one foundation in Dallas, Texas.

Purpose: The members of this congregation, who take the three simple vows, have dedicated themselves to the salvation of souls through the apostolate of teaching and Catholic Action.

Spiritual Life: The religious exercises of this community include Holy Mass, meditation, spiritual reading, and the rosary. They also say the Office of the Sacred Heart in Latin.

Qualifications:

* Age: 16 to 30.
* Completion of high school.
* The desire to dedicate oneself to the apostolate of teaching.

Habit: The habit is black with a white guimpe and a metal heart representing the Heart of Jesus. The sisters wear white in hot climates.

> *Write to:* Mother Superior
> 331 W. Pembroke
> Dallas 8, Texas

BRIGIDINE CONGREGATION (C.S.B.)

History: The Right Reverend Daniel Delany, Bishop of Kildare and Leighlin, founded this pontifical congregation in Tullow, Ireland, in 1807. The title suggests a link with the ancient order of St. Brigid which was suppressed in the sixteenth century. The roots of the foundation lay in a Confraternity of the Blessed Sacrament. Six of these zealous member-catechists, who were trained to give religious instruction to children and adults in Sunday schools, formed the nucleus of the community.

Purpose: The sisters are engaged in teaching children in primary and secondary, and boarding schools. They have houses in Ireland, Australia, New Zealand, England, Wales, and in Texas.

Spiritual Life: The religious exercises include Holy Mass, the Divine Office, mental prayer, the rosary, spiritual reading, and other community prayers and devotions.

Training Program: The six-month postulancy is followed by a two-year novitiate. Temporary vows are made annually for three or six years. Perpetual vows are then pronounced. After first profession, the sisters continue their spiritual formation while taking courses toward their professional degrees.

Qualifications:

* The age limit is 16.
* Completion of high school is preferred.
* Entrance dates: September 24 and February 1.

Habit: The sisters wear a black habit, scapular, and veil, a white coif, bandeau, and guimpe, a rosary, silver heart, and a ring.

> *Write to:* Brigidine Convent
> 402 John Adams Drive
> San Antonio 28, Texas

History: In 1830, Bishop Edward Dominic Fenwick, O.P., first Bishop of Cincinnati, Ohio, called four sisters from St. Catherine's, Kentucky, the oldest American Dominican foundation, to make a second foundation in Somerset, Ohio. This new establishment was later transferred to Columbus in 1868.

Purpose: This pontifical institute is primarily engaged in teaching. The sisters staff two colleges, four academies, forty-one parochial and thirteen secondary schools, and a hospital. These institutions are located in Ohio, Michigan, Connecticut, New York, New Mexico, Texas, and Pennsylvania.

Spiritual Life: The religious exercises include Holy Mass, mental prayer, the chanting of the Little Office of the Blessed Virgin, the recitation of the rosary, spiritual reading, and other community prayers and devotions.

Training Program: The one-year postulancy is followed by a two-year novitiate. During the postulancy and the second year of the novitiate, the candidates attend college classes. Following first profession of vows, the sisters remain for two years in the House of Studies for further spiritual, intellectual, and professional development.

Qualifications:
* Age: 18 to 30. Exceptions are sometimes made.
* Average intelligence.

Habit: The sisters wear a white habit, black veil and belt, and a fifteen decade rosary.

> *Write to:* Mother General
> St. Mary of the Springs
> Columbus 19, Ohio

DOMINICAN SISTERS, HOUSTON, TEXAS (O.P.)

History: This Dominican community traces its origin in Texas back to 1882. On the Feast of St. Michael, Mother M. Agnes Magevney, O.P., and her community of twenty sisters arrived in Galveston, Texas, having been summoned from Columbus, Ohio, by the Most Reverend Nicholas A. Gallagher, to spread the truths of the Gospel in Texas. The motherhouse was established in Houston in 1926.

Purpose: The Christian education of youth is the chief apostolic activity of this congregation. The sisters conduct a college for women, a dormitory for girls attending the State University in Austin, Texas, academies for girls, a co-educational high school, and teach in parish elementary schools. These institutions are located in Texas, Louisiana, and California.

Spiritual Life: The religious exercises include Holy Mass, the recitation of the Little Office of the Blessed Virgin in Latin, forty-five minutes of mental prayer, the rosary, spiritual reading, and other community prayers and devotions.

Training Program: The nine-month postulancy is followed by a one-year novitiate. Temporary vows are then made. During the years of the juniorate, after first vows, the spiritual, academic, and cultural training of the religious is continued.

Qualifications:
* Age: 16 to 35.
* Average intelligence.

Habit: The sisters wear a white tunic, scapular and cape, a black veil and mantle, and a rosary.

Write to: Sacred Heart Convent
6501 Almeda Road
Houston 21, Texas

DOMINICAN SISTERS OF MISSION SAN JOSE, CALIFORNIA (O.P.)

History: This congregation stems from the Dominican Holy Cross Convent, Brooklyn, New York. In 1876, three sisters were sent from the Brooklyn convent to undertake a foundation in San Francisco. Fourteen years later, the flourishing western community became a separate congregation.

Purpose: The primary apostolic work of the congregation is the Christian education of children with special devotion to the needs of the poor. The community conducts elementary and secondary schools in California and Oregon, and operates a college for the professional training of its sisters at the motherhouse in Mission San Jose. The sisters are also engaged in social work.

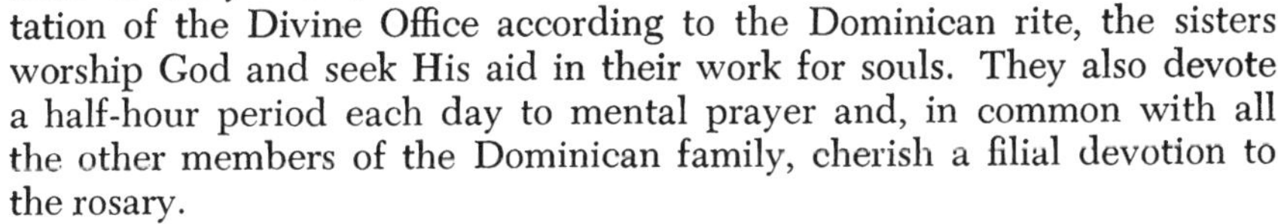

Spiritual Life: Through the attendance of Holy Mass, and the recitation of the Divine Office according to the Dominican rite, the sisters worship God and seek His aid in their work for souls. They also devote a half-hour period each day to mental prayer and, in common with all the other members of the Dominican family, cherish a filial devotion to the rosary.

Training Program: The training program comprises a five year period of integrated spiritual and professional development that includes the following: the postulancy, a nine month period which emphasizes the human and Christian formation; the novitiate, a one year program of ascetical formation, followed by the reception of temporary vows, renewed annually for three years, and finally, the juniorate, a time of spiritual development in which the sister takes courses in preparation for her apostolic work.

Qualifications:
* Age: 17 to 30.
* Completion of high school. Exceptions are made for those who wish to devote themselves to works other than teaching.

Habit: The sisters wear a white tunic, scapular, guimpe, and black veil. A fifteen decade rosary is worn on the side.

> *Write to:* Dominican Convent
> Mission San Jose,
> California

DOMINICAN SISTERS OF NASHVILLE, TENNESSEE (O.P.)

History: In the spring of 1860, shortly before the outbreak of the Civil War, the Most Reverend James Whalen, O.P., Bishop of Nashville, applied to St. Mary's Dominican Convent, Somerset, Ohio, for a number of sisters to conduct a school for girls in his see city. Four sisters were assigned to this new responsibility, and in October of the same year these Dominican pioneers opened St. Cecilia Academy. Soon after the arrival of the sisters, the Civil War broke out. In spite of the prevailing hardships and difficulties, the sisters carried on their work of teaching.

Purpose: Education is the primary apostolic activity of this community. The sisters conduct a junior college, secondary, elementary and religious vacation schools in Tennessee, Virginia, Ohio, and Alabama.

Spiritual Life: The religious exercises include Holy Mass, the recitation of the Office of the Blessed Virgin in Latin, one-half hour of mental prayer, the rosary, spiritual reading, and other community prayers and devotions.

Training Program: The six-month postulancy is followed by a two-year novitiate. Temporary vows are then made. The sisters continue their spiritual formation while completing the requirements for their teaching degrees.

Qualifications:
* Age: 17 to 30. Exceptions are sometimes made.
* Completion of high school for those who desire to teach.

Habit: The sisters wear the traditional white and black habit of the Dominican Sisters.

Write to: Prioress General
St. Cecilia Convent
8th Avenue, N., and Clay Streets
Nashville 8, Tennessee

FRANCISCAN SISTERS OF BALTIMORE (O.S.F.)

History: Mother Mary Francis, formerly a leading member of an Anglican Sisterhood, founded this congregation in England in 1868. The motherhouse was established at Mill Hill, London, England, and the community was approved by the Holy See as a papal institute in 1880. One year later, in response to the invitation of James Cardinal Gibbons, a foundation was made in Baltimore, Maryland. The generalate was established there in 1953.

Purpose: The sisters teach in elementary and secondary schools, and conduct catechetical centers and schools for special education. These institutions are located in Maryland, New York, Virginia, and Pennsylvania. Missions have been opened in Natal, South Africa.

Spiritual Life: The religious exercises include Holy Mass, the recitation of the Franciscan Short Breviary in English, mental prayer, the rosary, spiritual reading, and other community prayers and devotions.

Training Program: The community conducts an aspirancy for teen-age girls interested in the religious life. The six to twelve-month postulancy is followed by a two-year novitiate. Temporary vows are then pronounced. During the postulancy and the second year of novitiate, the candidates take college courses in the community's Teacher Training Institute. After first vows, the sisters complete the courses necessary for their professional degrees.

Qualifications:
* 16 to 30. Exceptions for those under 40 will sometimes be made.
* Completion of high school is desired.
* Entrance dates: September 8 and February 2.

Habit: The sisters wear a grey habit and scapular, a white kerchief, headdress and cord, a black veil, and the Franciscan Crown rosary.

Write to: Convent of Our Lady and St. Francis
2226 Maryland Avenue
Baltimore 18, Maryland

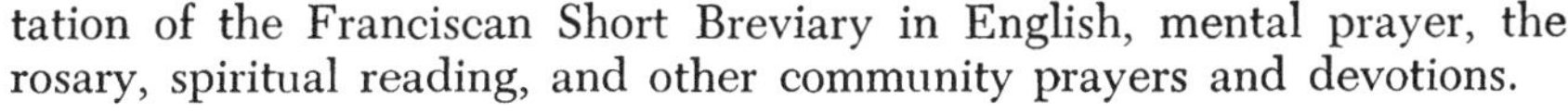
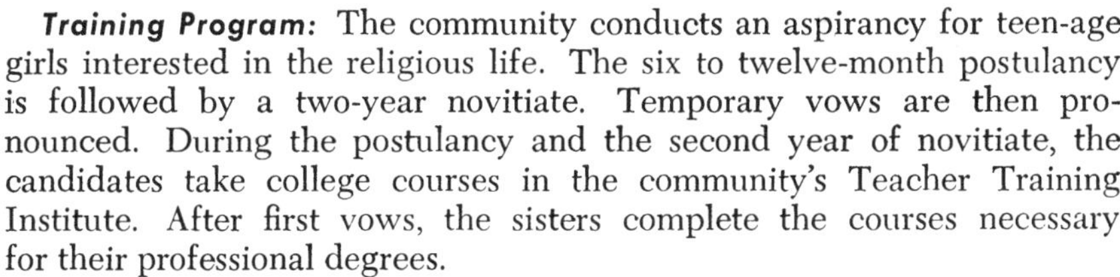

FRANCISCAN SISTERS OF MARY IMMACULATE (O.S.F.)

History: Seven sisters volunteered to leave their cloistered convent of Mary, Help of Christians, at Alstetten, Switzerland, in 1888 to do mission teaching in Ecuador, South America. An impending revolution drove them to Colombia. Their work spread to Panama, Costa Rica, and back again to Ecuador. The first foundation was made in the United States at Amarillo, Texas in 1932 at the invitation of Bishop Rudolph A. Gerken. The more than seven hundred sisters have houses in Texas, New Mexico, and California.

Purpose: Teaching is the principal work of the members of this pontifical institute. The sisters conduct schools in the United States and Latin America, from the kindergarten to the college level.

Spiritual Life: The religious exercises include Holy Mass, the daily recitation of the Little Office of the Blessed Virgin in Latin, the rosary, two half-hour periods of mental prayer, and one hour a week of adoration.

Training Program: The community operates an aspirancy for interested girls of high school age. The postulancy of six months to one year is followed by a two-year novitiate. During the cannonical year the novice studies the basic fundamentals of the religious life. In the second year and after her temporary profession the sister continues taking courses leading to her academic degree. Profession of perpetual vows is made after five years in temporary vows.

Qualifications:
* Girls are admitted any time after completing the eighth grade.
* While the maximum age is 30, exceptions will be made.
* Entrance date: September 1.

Habit: The professed sister wears a brown habit and scapular, with a white guimpe, cord, black veil, and a gold ring.

Write to: St. Francis Convent
4301 N. E. 18th Avenue
P. O. Box 5664
Amarillo, Texas

160

RELIGIOUS OF THE SACRED HEART OF MARY (R.S.H.M.)

History: Father Gailhac founded this congregation in Béziers, southern France, in 1849. The rule was approved by Pope Leo XIII in 1899. Mother St. John is known as the foundress. Before the end of the nineteenth century the sisters had foundations in Ireland, Portugal, England, Spain, and the United States. By 1910 they were in Brazil; by 1930 in Italy; between 1930 and 1960 they were in Canada, Colombia, Portuguese East Africa, Southern Rhodesia, and Mexico.

Purpose: The sisters are dedicated to teaching—in colleges, secondary, and elementary schools. Besides the teaching religious, there are auxiliary sisters who devote themselves to the material needs of the congregation. The institutions of the Eastern Province are located in New York, Virginia, Missouri, Illinois, and Florida with missions in Colombia and Southern Rhodesia. The members of the Western Province are principally found in California and Mexico.

Spiritual Life: The religious exercises include Holy Mass, the Office of the Blessed Virgin in Latin once a week, a half-hour of mental prayer, the rosary, spiritual reading, and other community prayers and devotions.

Training Program: The six-month postulancy is followed by a one-year novitiate. Temporary vows are made for five years. At the expiration of these vows, perpetual vows are pronounced. During the time of temporary profession the sisters continue their spiritual formation while pursuing courses toward their professional degrees. A tertianship of one year, concluded by a thirty-day retreat, is made as a special preparation for perpetual vows.

Qualifications:
* Age: 16 to 25.
* Completion of high school.
* Entrance date: September 8.

Habit: The sisters wear a blue habit, black veil, a headpiece of white linen, and a silver cross and chain.

Write to: Marymount College
Tarrytown,
New York

Marymount College
Palos Verdes Estates,
California

CONGREGATION de NOTRE DAME
(C.N.D.)

History: Marguerite Bourgeoys of Troyes founded this community in Montreal during the middle of the seventeenth century. At the age of thirty-three, she came to New France where her great charity soon earned for her the name of "Mother of the Colony." In 1657 she founded the first uncloistered teaching congregation in North America. Unfailing trust in God enabled Mother Bourgeoys to endure poverty and hardship. Since her death in 1700, her firmly established congregation has spread through Canada, to the United States, and to Japan. Blessed Marguerite Bourgeoys was beatified by Pope Pius XII on November 13, 1950.

Purpose: The nearly four thousand sisters of this congregation are engaged in teaching young girls on the elementary, secondary, and college levels.

Spiritual Life: The religious exercises include Holy Mass, meditation, the rosary, spiritual reading, and other community prayers and devotions.

Training Program: Entrants spend the entire two year probation at the American novitiate in Bourbonnais, Illinois. A juniorate program has been established in Staten Island, New York. Final profession takes place eight years after the candidates' first entrance. After first vows, the sisters continue their spiritual formation while taking college courses toward their professional degrees.

Qualifications:
* Age: at least 18.
* Completion of high school.

Habit: The sisters wear a black habit and veil, a white starched linen coif, a large rosary, and a plain silver cross.

> *Write to:* Provincial House
> 76 Howard Avenue
> Grymes Hill
> Staten Island 1, New York

SISTERS OF NOTRE DAME de NAMUR
(S.N.D. de N.)

History: Blessed Julie Billiart founded this pontifical institute in Amiens, France, in 1803. A foundation was made in the United States in 1840. Today there are over 5,000 religious carrying out the educational ideals of Blessed Mother Julia in eight countries throughout the world.

Purpose: These sisters teach on every level of education from kindergarten through college. They conduct Emmanuel College, Boston, Massachusetts; Trinity College and Kennedy Institute For Retarded Children, Washington, D.C.; Notre Dame College, Belmont, California; Villa Junior College, Stevenson, Maryland; and the Child Guidance Center, Columbus, Ohio.

Spiritual Life: The religious exercises include Holy Mass, two periods of mental prayer, the recitation of Prime and Compline of the Divine Office in English—Vespers are added on Sundays—the rosary, spiritual reading, and other community prayers and devotions.

Training Program: The six to nine-month postulancy is followed by a two-year novitiate. During the first year of novitiate emphasis is placed upon spiritual formation. In the second year, the novice continues her collegiate studies while developing in herself the religious ideals of the Notre Dame spirituality. After first vows, the sisters enter the juniorate for a five-year period of formation in which she completes the college courses required for her degree. A thirty-day renovation period is made before the sister makes her perpetual vows and again for those fifteen years in vows.

Qualifications:
* Age: not over 30. Exceptions are sometimes made up to 40.
* Completion of high school is necessary for those who desire to teach.

Habit: The sisters wear a black habit and veil, a white guimpe, and a rosary.

See page 379 for address of nearest provincial house.

SISTER HANDMAIDS OF THE SACRED HEART OF JESUS FOR REPARATION (A.R.Ss.C.I.)

History: Monsignor Antonio Celona and Mother M. Serafina Fachele founded this congregation in Messina, Sicily, in 1918. Pope Pius XII gave papal approval in 1941. The foundation in the United States was made in Steubenville, Ohio, in 1958, with the approval of Bishop John King Mussio.

Purpose: The apostolic activity consists in a life of reparation to the Sacred Heart of Jesus for all the sins of all mankind according to the teachings of Pope Pius XI. The sisters also teach catechism and conduct kindergartens, schools, and colleges for girls.

Spiritual Life: The religious exercises include Holy Mass, the recitation of the Divine Office, perpetual reparation before the Blessed Sacrament, mental prayer, the rosary, spiritual reading, and other community prayers and devotions.

Training Program: The six-month postulancy is followed by a two-year novitiate. Temporary vows are then made. The sisters continue their spiritual formation while taking college courses toward their professional degrees.

Qualifications:
* Age: 15 to 26.
* Average intelligence.

Habit: The sisters wear a white tunic and scapular, a red cincture, and a medallion of the Sacred Heart.

Write to: Sacred Heart Convent
725 North Fourth Street
Steubenville, Ohio

SISTERS OF CHARITY OF
THE BLESSED VIRGIN MARY (B.V.M.)

History: An American institute of pontifical right, this congregation was founded in Philadelphia, Pennsylvania, in 1833 by Mother Mary Frances Clarke and Father Terence James Donaghoe. Ten years later the foundation was transferred to Dubuque, Iowa, on the invitation of Bishop Matthias Loras. His Holiness, Pope Leo XIII, gave final approval of the community in 1885. Today more than two thousand sisters conduct schools in twenty states including Hawaii.

Purpose: Devoted exclusively to education, the sisters conduct elementary and secondary schools, own and staff Clarke College, Dubuque, and Mundelein College, Chicago, Illinois. Heavily concentrated in the Midwest and the states bordering the Pacific Ocean and with foundations in the South and East, the sisters follow the footsteps of their revered foundress.

Spiritual Life: The religious exercises include Holy Mass, mental prayer, spiritual reading, vocal prayers, the Office of the Blessed Virgin in Latin, the rosary, adoration, and other community prayers and devotions.

Training Program: The orientation program and postulancy of six months is followed by a two-year novitiate. In the scholasticate, which takes about two and one-half years, the sisters prepare themselves for their apostolate of teaching by pursuing courses leading to their academic degrees.

Qualifications:
* Age: 16 to 30.
* Completion of high school.

Habit: The sisters wear a black serge habit, a cape with white collar, a white cap and black veil, and a cincture with rosary and crucifix attached.

> *Write to:* Mount Carmel
> Dubuque, Iowa

SISTERS OF CHARITY OF ST. VINCENT DE PAUL (S.C.H.)

History: These sisters trace their origin through the New York congregation to Blessed Elizabeth Ann Seton, foundress of the American Sisters of Charity at Emmitsburg, Maryland. A group of sisters from New York established a mission in Halifax, Nova Scotia, in 1849. It became independent in 1856 and was approved by the Holy See in 1913. There are two provinces in the United States.

Purpose: The principal work is teaching on all levels of education. The congregation has thirty-three schools in the United States. Five regional high schools for girls are conducted by the Boston province and two large high schools in the New York province. The latter also staffs a private academy in Bermuda.

Spiritual Life: The religious exercises include Holy Mass, a half-hour's meditation, the rosary, a half-hour of adoration, spiritual reading, and other community prayers and devotions.

Training Program: The eleven-month postulancy is made at the motherhouse, Mt. St. Vincent, Halifax, Nova Scotia. It is followed by a two-year novitiate. The first two years after temporary vows are devoted to study and spiritual formation at the juniorate house of studies. The sister enters active service at the conclusion of this training. A tertianship of six weeks precedes the profession of perpetual vows which is made after six years of temporary vows.

Qualifications:
* Age: not over thirty.
* Willingness to give themselves to the works of charity for the love of God.
* Entrance date: September 12.

Habit: The sisters wear a black habit and veil, a pleated cape, a white collar and coif, and a rosary.

Write to: Academy of the Assumption
Wellesley Hills,
Massachusetts

Resurrection-Ascension
Convent
Rego Park 74,
New York

SISTERS OF THE DIVINE PASSION
(R.D.C.)

History: Monsignor Thomas S. Preston and Mother Mary Veronica founded this community in New York City in 1886. It grew out of a charity they had established together in 1870 to educate and aid unfortunate girls. Laywomen supervised the home and school from its foundation until the community was established to carry on its apostolate.

Purpose: Education of youth on all levels and the service of the poor by showing Our Lord's compassion are the principal apostolic activities. The sisters conduct elementary and secondary schools, and a college, all located within the Archdiocese of New York.

Spiritual Life: The religious exercises include Holy Mass, one-half hour of mental prayer, the recitation in choir of the Little Office of the Blessed Virgin, the rosary, spiritual reading which is made privately, and other community prayers and devotions.

Training Program: The nine-month postulancy is followed by a two-year novitiate. After making her temporary profession of vows for one year, the sister enters the juniorate. During the following three years, the sisters continue their spiritual formation while completing the undergraduate courses leading to their academic degrees. After two years of in-service training, profession of perpetual vows is made.

Qualifications:
* Age: ordinarily under 30.
* Completion of high school is preferred.

Habit: The sisters wear a black habit and veil, a white coif, and a fifteen decade rosary.

Write to: Good Counsel Convent
White Plains,
New York

SISTERS OF THE INCARNATE WORD AND THE BLESSED SACRAMENT (S.I.W.)

History: Jeanne Chezard de Matel founded this congregation in Lyons, France, in 1625. The community, originally cloistered, was suppressed during the French Revolution and re-established in 1832. The Lyons Convent sent the first sisters to Brownsville, Texas, in 1852. The cloister was lifted in 1913.

Purpose: To seek the glory of God and the personal sanctification by the three vows according to the rule of St. Augustine are the goals. The sisters are engaged in the education of youth, the conversion of sinners, adoration and imitation of the Incarnate Word, with special homage to the Blessed Sacrament and devotion to the Immaculate Conception. Their institutions are located in Texas and Ohio.

Spiritual Life: The religious exercises include Holy Mass, recitation of the Office of the Blessed Virgin in Latin, rosary, and other community prayers and devotions.

Training Program: The sisters conduct an aspirancy for high school girls who are interested in the religious life. The six to twelve-month postulancy is followed by a two-year novitiate. Temporary profession of vows is then made. During the next two years the sisters continue their spiritual formation while working for their academic degrees.

Qualifications:

* Age: maximum is 35.
* Completion of at least three years of high school for the postulancy.
* Entrance dates: August 15 to September 21 and February 2.

Habit: The sisters wear a white habit, crimson scapular and cincture, a black veil, and rosary.

See page 380 for address of nearest motherhouse.

SISTERS OF LORETTO AT THE FOOT OF THE CROSS (S.L.)

History: Father Charles Nerinckx founded this congregation in Kentucky in 1812. In covered wagon and stage coach the sisters pioneered to bring Christian education to American children. By 1923 they sailed to China and worked in schools there until 1952 when the Communists expelled them. Over one thousand sisters continuing the pioneering spirit that is still the Loretto heritage are presently educating over forty thousand children.

Purpose: The Christian education of youth is their primary apostolic activity. However, nurses, housekeepers, secretaries, accountants, seamstresses, librarians, and dieticians are indispensable to the success of the educational and missionary activities both in La Paz, Bolivia, and other South American missions, as well as the three provinces in the United States. In this country the sisters teach in Kentucky, Missouri, New Mexico, Colorado, Texas, Illinois, Alabama, Arizona, California, Wyoming, and Virginia.

Spiritual Life: The sisters attend Holy Mass, recite a short form of the Divine Office in English, and make a half-hour of meditation. Privately they say the rosary, and spend twenty minutes in spiritual reading and a short time in preparation for the next morning's meditation.

Training Program: The postulancy of eight months is followed by a two-year novitiate. The vows which the novice takes at the end of this time are renewed annually for four years. The sister then makes her final profession. Before entering into the active apostolate the sister completes the courses leading toward her academic degree.

Qualifications:
* Age: 18 to 30.
* Completion of high school.
* Entrance date: September 15.

Habit: The sisters wear a habit and cape of black washable material, and a Seven Dolor rosary suspended from a black cincture.

See page 380 for address of nearest provincial house.

SISTERS OF THE MOST HOLY TRINITY (O.SS.T.)

History: Two French saints, John of Matha and Felix of Valois, founded this congregation in France in 1198. Throughout the centuries these white-robed sisters have shared in the merciful work of the Trinitarian Fathers. In 1920 at the invitation of Dennis Cardinal Dougherty, Mother Theresa opened the first American foundation in Pennsylvania. Later the congregation established a foundation and novitiate in Cleveland, Ohio.

Purpose: The sisters teach in elementary and secondary schools in Ohio, Pennsylvania, and Florida. Non-teaching members are engaged in domestic and office work. They also may be assigned to assist at the Shrine of Our Lady of Lourdes, Euclid, Ohio, where pilgrimages are conducted.

Spiritual Life: The religious exercises include Holy Mass, the recitation of the Office of the Blessed Virgin in Latin, mental prayer, the rosary, spiritual reading, and other community prayers and devotions.

Training Program: The six-month postulancy is followed by a two-year novitiate. Temporary vows are made and renewed annually for three years. Perpetual vows are then pronounced. After first profession, the sisters continue their spiritual formation while taking courses toward their teaching degrees.

Qualifications:
* Age: 15 to 30.
* Average intelligence.
* Entrance dates: August and February.

Habit: The sisters wear a white habit, collar, and bandeau, a black and white veil, a red and blue cross worn on a white scapular, and a five-decade rosary.

> *Write to:* Mother Provincial
> Our Lady of Lourdes Shrine
> 21320 Euclid Avenue
> Euclid 17, Ohio

SISTERS OF OUR LADY OF THE HOLY ROSARY (R.S.R.)

History: Bishop Jean Langevin, while a priest of the Archdiocese of Quebec, and Elizabeth Turgeon founded this congregation in Rimouski, Province of Quebec, Canada, April 3, 1875. The community today numbers over nine hundred professed members.

Purpose: The sisters are engaged in the instruction and education of children especially in parish schools. The congregation is composed of choir and lay sisters. The latter, although leading a life entirely in common with the choir sisters, are in charge of the housework and manual labor.

Spiritual Life: The religious exercises include Holy Mass, thirty minutes of mental prayer, the complete rosary of fifteen decades, spiritual reading, and other community prayers and devotions.

Training Program: The congregation accepts aspirants into the postulancy as soon as they reach sixteen regardless of their high school status. Opportunity of continuing their high school education is provided for at the motherhouse. The six-month postulancy is followed by a two-year novitiate. During the five years in temporary vows, the sisters continue their spiritual formation while completing the studies necessary for their professional degrees. Perpetual vows are then made.

Qualifications:
* Age: not over 30.
* Average intelligence.

Habit: The sisters wear a grey habit, black scapular and veil, a white guimpe and coif, a silver crucifix, and a large rosary.

> *Write to:* St. Martin's Convent
> Maine Avenue
> Millinocket (Penobscot Co.),
> Maine

SISTERS OF PROVIDENCE OF SAINT MARY-OF-THE-WOODS (S.P.)

History: This congregation was founded in the mid-nineteenth century by Mother Theodore Guerin, who came to Indiana with five other sisters from Ruille, France, in 1840. Today more than fifteen hundred of her spiritual daughters staff elementary and secondary schools plus two colleges. The community was the first American congregation to send sisters to China and today it maintains a junior college in Taichung, Taiwan.

Purpose: Teaching is the major apostolic activity of this community. Today more than sixty thousand students are being educated in schools conducted by these sisters.

Spiritual Life: The religious exercises include morning and night prayer in common, community Mass, one hour of spiritual reading and meditation, Lauds, Vespers, and Compline of the Office of the Blessed Virgin chanted in English, and five decades of the rosary recited in common.

Training Program: For eleven months the postulant follows a college course while she is being introduced to the daily life of a sister. As a novice she spends two years in prayer and study before taking temporary vows. The junior sister remains at the motherhouse for further spiritual and intellectual formation. During this time she obtains her degree, renews her temporary vows, and is assigned to active duty in the classroom. At the expiration of these vows, the sister returns to the motherhouse for three months, where as a tertian she makes a thirty-day retreat in preparation for her perpetual vows. A school for aspirants at Saint Mary-of-the-Woods welcomes those girls at the end of grade school who feel that they have a vocation to this community.

Qualifications:
* Completion of high school.
* Ability to be trained for teaching or supplementary duty.

Habit: The sisters wear a black habit and veil, a white headdress and collar. A chaplet is worn at the side and a crucifix is suspended from a black cord.

Write to: Sisters of Providence
Saint Mary-of-the-Woods
Indiana

172

SISTERS OF ST. ANN OF PROVIDENCE (S.S.A.)

History: Marchioness Julia Galletti di Barolo founded this congregation in Turin, Italy, in 1834. Pope Gregory XVI granted it papal approbation in 1846. The community has one mission province in India with twenty-five separate houses. They established their first foundation in the United States in 1952 in the Diocese of Altoona-Johnstown, Pennsylvania.

Purpose: Education of youth is their primary work. The sisters teach in elementary and nursery schools, conduct women's retreats, and are engaged in catechetical work.

Spiritual Life: The religious exercises include Holy Mass, the recitation of the Office of the Blessed Virgin in Latin on Sundays only, the rosary, mental prayer, spiritual reading, and other community prayers and devotions.

Training Program: The six to twelve-month postulancy is followed by a two-year novitiate. Temporary vows are made for three years. These are renewed for another three years. Perpetual vows are pronounced at the end of this six-year period. Those who have the ability begin their college courses during the postulancy. These are resumed in the second year of novitiate. After first profession, the sisters complete the studies necessary for their academic degrees.

Qualifications:
* Age: usually under 30. Exceptions are sometimes made to 35.
* Completion of high school.
* Entrance date: between August and September.

Habit: The sisters wear a black habit and veil, and a white bonnet and collar.

> *Write to:* Mother Superior
> Mount Saint Ann
> Ebensburg, Pennsylvania

SISTERS OF ST. FRANCIS OF THE HOLY CROSS (O.S.F.)

History: The origin of these sisters resulted from the attempt of Father Edward Daems, O.S.C., to provide religious instruction for children in the rural districts of Green Bay, Wisconsin. In 1874 four young women became the nucleus of the congregation. With the help of the Most Reverend Sebastian G. Messmer, Bishop of Green Bay, the community became incorporated as an educational and charitable institution.

Purpose: One of the principal apostolic activities of these sisters is the education of children in parochial schools. They also conduct a home for the aged and staff schools in Madison, Wisconsin, and San Antonio, Texas.

Spiritual Life: The religious exercises include Holy Mass, the daily recitation of the short breviary in English, a half-hour devoted to mental prayer, the rosary, and other community prayers and devotions.

Training Program: Teen-age aspirants to this community may continue their secondary education at the school for aspirants. In the postulancy the candidate begins or continues her college training, usually for one year. This is followed by the two-year novitiate. In the first year emphasis is placed upon spiritual formation. During the second year the spiritual and educational formation is continued. After making temporary vows, the sisters continue their spiritual formation while receiving professional training necessary for the apostolate.

Qualifications:
* The maximum age is 30. Exceptions will sometimes be made.
* Completion of high school.

Habit: The sisters wear a black habit, scapular, and veil, a white cord and collar, a silver crucifix, and a Franciscan rosary.

Write to: St. Francis Convent
Route 1
Green Bay, Wisconsin

SISTER OF ST. FRANCIS, NEVADA, MISSOURI (O.S.F.)

History: Mother John Hau founded this congregation in Switzerland in 1893. To provide a safe place of refuge in the event of confiscation of property due to the civil unrest in Switzerland at that time, Mother John Hau sent five sisters to establish a foundation in the United States. This pioneer band utilized a university building in Missouri as a boarding school for orphans. At the request of the bishop they began teaching in parochial schools, and later became an independent community.

Purpose: The members of this community teach in elementary and secondary schools, conduct religion classes and summer vacation religion schools, and are engaged in domestic work in seminaries.

Spiritual Life: The religious exercises include a half-hour of meditation each morning before Holy Mass, the short breviary in English, the fifteen minutes of spiritual reading, all made in common. They pray the stations of the cross and say the rosary privately.

Training Program: The postulancy of six months is followed by the canonical year of novitiate. At the end of this period the sisters make temporary vows for three years. These are renewed twice for one-year periods. Perpetual vows may then be taken. During the postulancy and the three-year juniorate, the sisters follow a college educational program adjusted to their specific needs, conducted by the community teacher-training institute. Those who are destined to become teachers transfer to major colleges to complete the work necessary for their degrees.

Qualifications:
* Age: 15 to 30.
* Completion of high school is preferred.

Habit: The sisters wear a brown habit and scapular, a white cord with three knots, a white head covering, a black veil, rosary, and a gold ring.

> *Write to:* St. Francis Convent
> Nevada, Missouri

SISTERS OF THE THIRD ORDER OF ST. DOMINIC (O.P.)

History: The community traces its origin to the first Dominican convent for women founded by St. Dominic in 1206. From this convent at Prouille, France, a seed was brought to Bavaria, and Blessed Jordan of Saxony established the Convent of the Holy Cross at Ratisbon, Germany. Arriving in the United States in 1853, Sister Mary Augustine helped to found the first American convent to spring from the cloister at Ratisbon. Mother Mary Augustine opened an academy and convent in the parish of St. Nicholas, Manhattan, New York. This first branch house shortly thereafter became the nucleus of this independent congregation.

Purpose: The sisters teach in every level of education from the nursery school on through to college. Their institutions are located in Connecticut, New York, New Jersey, the District of Columbia, Alabama, North Carolina, Florida, and Puerto Rico.

Spiritual Life: The religious exercises include Holy Mass, the recitation of the Office of the Blessed Virgin in Latin, a half-hour of mental prayer, the rosary, spiritual reading, and other community prayers and devotions.

Training Program: The six-month postulancy is followed by a one-year novitiate. Temporary vows are made for three years at the end of which perpetual vows are pronounced. After first profession, the sisters continue their spiritual formation while resuming their college courses at Mount St. Mary College of Newburgh.

Qualifications:
* Age: 16 to 30. Exceptions are sometimes made.
* Completion of high school.
* Entrance date: August 30.

Habit: The sisters wear a simple white tunic with a full-length scapular, soft guimpe, and a white-lined black veil.

Write to: Mount St. Mary on the Hudson
Newburgh,
New York

SOCIETY OF THE SACRED HEART
(R.S.C.J.)

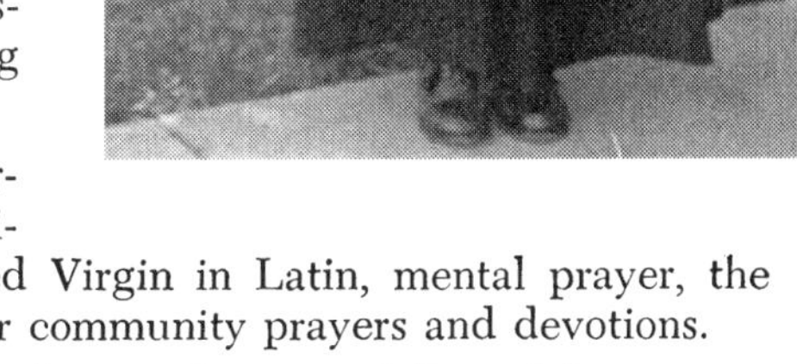

History: Saint Madeleine Sophie Barat founded this congregation in 1800. It was born of an urgent need for a new type of education for girls and the necessity of combating the effects of Jansenism and the terrors of the French Revolution. Under the guidance of Joseph Varin, S.J., Mother Barat governed the society for sixty years. Blessed Philippine Duchesne opened the first convent of the community in the United States in 1818 at St. Charles, Missouri.

Purpose: The primary objective of the congregation is to glorify God and to spread the worship of the Sacred Heart by laboring for the sanctification of its members and the salvation of souls. The sisters are engaged chiefly in teaching on all levels of education.

Spiritual Life: The religious exercises include Holy Mass, the recitation of the Office of the Blessed Virgin in Latin, mental prayer, the rosary, spiritual reading, and other community prayers and devotions.

Training Program: The six-month postulancy is followed by a two-year novitiate, at the end of which simple vows are pronounced. For the choir-religious a year of juniorate follows the first vows. During this time they continue their spiritual formation, to which is added a strong scholastic formation to fit them for their work as educators. Towards the end of the fifth year following first vows, there is a period of spiritual renewal, termed probation, which lasts between five and six months. During this time all teaching and scholastic duties are set aside and the religious devote themselves exclusively to the spiritual life and manual work. This terminates with a retreat and the pronouncing of perpetual vows.

Qualifications:
* The maximum age is 30.
* Completion of high school.
* Entrance dates: September and February.

Habit: The sisters wear a simple black dress with a cape, a long veil over a white cap with fluted border, a rosary, silver cross, and a plain ring.

See page 380 for address of nearest convent.

TERESIAN SISTERS (S.T.J.)

History: Don Enrique de Osso y Cervello founded this community at Tarragona, Spain. His first intention was to form a group of lay teachers who would follow the spirit and maxims of St. Teresa of Jesus. God intervened; he founded a religious congregation instead. The foundation of this society took place June 21, 1876. The community suffered many attacks but the fiercer the persecution, the stronger became Don Enrique's trust in God and the firmer became the roots of the society. Today the Teresians number about 3,000.

Purpose: The principal aim of the society is the personal sanctification of its members. For this they make an hour of mental prayer daily and strive to live a life of union with God. The secondary objective is to procure the greater glory of God through teaching. The American province comprises the United States and Central America. There are at present seven parochial schools and one academy in the United States and one academy in Managua, Nicaragua, and one orphanage in Granada, Nicaragua, Central America.

Spiritual Life: Although the sisters do not recite the Office, they make an hour of meditation daily before Mass, recite one part of the rosary, pray their morning and evening prayers, make their examination of conscience, and spend fifteen minutes in spiritual reading.

Training Program: The six-month postulancy is followed by a two-year novitiate. Temporary vows are pronounced for five years. Perpetual vows are then made. In the juniorate, which follows first vows, the sisters complete their professional preparation for teaching while continuing their spiritual advancement. Four years after taking perpetual vows the sisters return to the novitiate for a five-month tertianship. Here they also make the thirty-day Ignatian retreat.

Qualifications:
* Age: 15 to 30.
* Completion of high school is preferred.

Habit: The sisters wear a dark brown habit and cape, a black fluted cap and veil, white collar and cuffs, and a large crucifix.

Write to: St. Teresa's Academy
4018 S. Presa Street
San Antonio 23, Texas

URSULINE SISTERS OF MT. CALVARY
(O.S.U.)

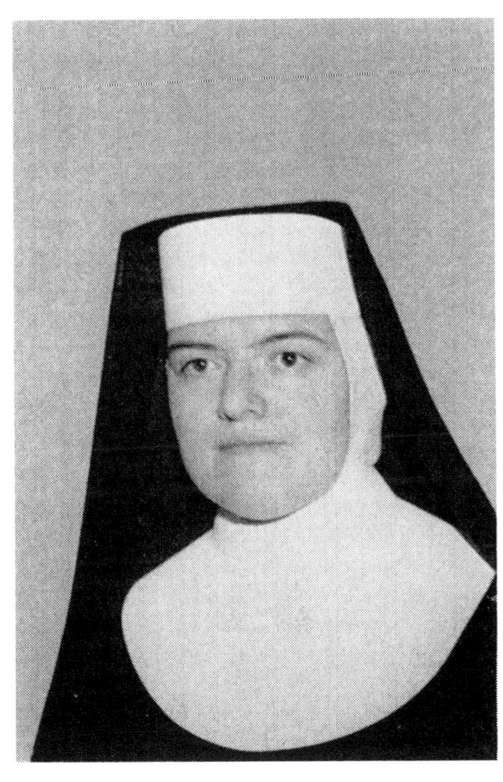

History: This congregation is a branch of the Ursuline Order founded by St. Angela Merici in Italy in 1535 for the education of girls. The motherhouse for the community is at Mt. Calvary, Ahrweiler, Germany. The provincial residence for the American Province was originally established in 1910 in North Dakota. It was later transferred, in 1945, to Belleville, Illinois.

Purpose: The sisters are actively engaged in teaching in elementary and secondary schools. These institutions are located in North Dakota and Illinois.

Spiritual Life: The religious exercises include Holy Mass, the recitation of the Little Office of the Blessed Virgin in English (the Divine Office is said on certain feast days), one-half hour of mental prayer, the rosary, spiritual reading, and other community prayers and devotions.

Training Program: The community conducts an aspirancy for high school girls interested in the religious life. The one-year postulancy is followed by a two-year novitiate. Temporary vows are then made. College studies are either begun or continued during the postulancy and the second year of novitiate. After first profession, the sisters complete the studies for their A.B. degree for teaching on the elementary level or an M.A. for high school teaching. Five years after their perpetual vows all the sisters return to the motherhouse for a period of spiritual renewal.

Qualifications:
* Age: 16 to 33. Exceptions are sometimes made.
* Completion of high school is desired.
* Entrance date: August 15.

Habit: The sisters wear a black habit, veil, and cincture.

Write to: Mother Superior
1026 North Douglas Avenue
Belleville, Illinois

VISITATION SISTERS (S.V.M.)

History: On June 8, 1952, responding to the present needs of the Church and under the direction of the Most Rev. Leo Binz, Archbishop of Dubuque, Iowa, these sisters formed a congregation in which they combine both the active and contemplative life. The community stems from the Order of the Visitation which was originally founded by St. Francis de Sales in cooperation with St. Jane Frances de Chantal in Annecy, France, in 1610. Under their new title and status, the sisters continue the work they began in 1871 when the first Visitation Sisters arrived in Dubuque from St. Louis, Missouri, to open a private academy for girls.

Purpose: The sisters staff their own private academy for girls, a private kindergarten, a parochial grade school, and are engaged in catechetical mission work in the Archdiocese of Dubuque.

Spiritual Life: The religious exercises include Holy Mass, the recitation of the Office of the Blessed Virgin on Sundays, holydays, and special feast days, forty-five minutes of mental prayer, the rosary, spiritual reading, and other community prayers and devotions.

Training Program: The Sister Formation Program which provides a balance of spiritual and professional growth includes one year of postulancy, two years of novitiate, and five years in temporary vows. Candidates receive their college degrees and teacher training certificates before they enter the classroom.

Qualifications:
* Age: 16 to 35.
* Average intelligence.
* Entrance date: September 8.

Habit: The sisters wear a black habit, veil, and head band, a white coif guimpe, and a silver cross.

Write to: Convent of the Visitation
900 Alta Vista Street
Dubuque 3, Iowa

VIII

TEACHING

also Nursing . . .

Social Work . . .

Missions . . .

Retreat Work . . .

Catechetics . . .

Specialized Education . . .

SISTERS OF ST. AGNES (C.S.A.)

History: Father Casper Rehrl, a zealous pioneer from Austria, founded this community at Barton, Wisconsin, in 1858. Mother Mary Agnes Hazotte was the first Superior General. In 1870 she transferred the motherhouse to Fond du Lac, Wisconsin. Father Frances Haas, O.F.M.Cap., spiritual director of the congregation, wrote the rules approved on July 11, 1880, by Pope Leo XIII.

Purpose: The more than eight hundred professed sisters teach on the elementary, secondary, and college levels, maintain four hospitals, and two schools of nursing, and conduct a home for the aged, an orphanage, and a hospice for travelers. These institutions are located in nine states extending from New York through the midwest to Kansas. The sisters also conduct schools in Nicaragua, Central America.

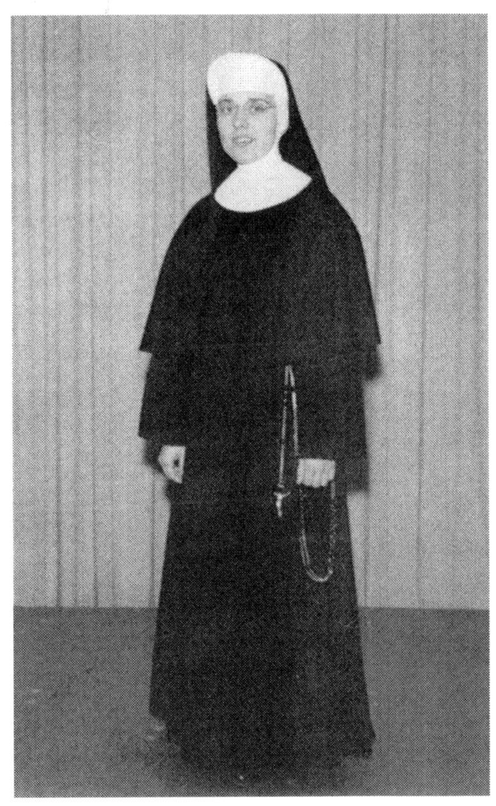

Spiritual Life: The religious exercises include Holy Mass, the recitation of the Office of the Blessed Virgin in Latin, one-half hour of meditation, the rosary, and other community prayers and devotions.

Training Program: The sisters conduct an aspirancy for high school students interested in the religious life. The postulancy is followed by a two-year novitiate. Temporary vows are then made. After first profession, the sisters continue their spiritual formation while taking college courses in preparation for their professional degrees.

Qualifications:
* Age: under 35. Exceptions are sometimes made.
* Completion of high school for the postulancy.
* Entrance date: early September.

Habit: The sisters wear a black habit and veil, and a white wimple and guimpe.

Write to: St. Agnes Convent
390 E. Division Street
Fond du Lac, Wisconsin

SISTERS OF SAINT ANNE (S.S.A.)

History: Mother Marie Anne founded this congregation in Quebec, Canada, in 1850. The motherhouse was later moved to Montreal, Canada. Presently the community has two thousand sisters.

Purpose: The sisters staff elementary, secondary, normal, homemaking, and Indian schools, and three colleges. In the United States the sisters are found principally in the New England States. In British Columbia the community maintains hospitals, homes for the aged, and schools. The sisters also have missions in the Yukon, Alaska, and Haiti.

Spiritual Life: The religious exercises include Holy Mass, one-half hour of mental prayer, the recitation of the Office of the Blessed Virgin on Sundays, the rosary, and other community prayers and devotions.

Training Program: The six-month postulancy is followed by an eighteen month novitiate. The novices pronounce temporary vows for five years. At the expiration of the temporary profession, perpetual vows are made. During the period of temporary vows, the sisters continue their spiritual formation while taking courses toward their professional degrees. After fifteen years, the professed religious withdraws for "100 days" into the seclusion of the tertianship for an inventory of their spiritual life.

Qualifications:
* Age: at least 16.
* Average intelligence.
* Entrance date: August 22.

Habit: The sisters wear a black habit and veil, a white linen coif, brown rosary, and a silver cross and ring.

Write to: Mother Provincial
22 Broad Street
Marlboro, Massachusetts

MISSIONARY SERVANTS OF ST. ANTHONY (M.S.S.A.)

History: Father Peter M. Baqué founded this congregation in 1929 in San Antonio, Texas. It became a diocesan institute in 1956. In his priestly works Father Baqué contacted thousands of spiritually neglected Latin Americans. He realized that the reclamation of these people for God could not be undertaken by one man but required the efforts of many apostolic minded women willing to consecrate themselves to God for this purpose. Mother M. Theresa became the first Mother General.

Purpose: The sisters teach in elementary schools and catechetical centers, conduct day nurseries and health clinics, and operate homes for the infirm and for retired priests. Their work at present is confined to the state of Texas.

Spiritual Life: The religious exercises include Holy Mass, one-half hour of mental prayer, spiritual reading, the perpetual novena to St. Anthony every Sunday and Tuesday, and fifteen decades of the rosary. One set of decades is said in common in the morning and the other in the evening as part of their community prayers. The third part of the rosary is said privately.

Training Program: Elementary school graduates are accepted as aspirants and become postulants in the senior year of high school. During the postulancy of six months the candidates begin their college training. The novices study the fundamentals of the spiritual life in the two years of novitiate which follows. The professed sisters during the juniorate years continue their spiritual formation while taking courses toward their academic degrees.

Qualifications:
* Age: 15 to 30.
* Completion of high school is preferred.
* Entrance date: January 22.

Habit: The sisters wear a black habit and veil, a narrow white collar, cincture, rosary, and a cross medal of St. Anthony.

Write to: Missionary Servants of St. Anthony
100 Peter Baqué Road
San Antonio 9, Texas

SISTERS OF ST. BASIL THE GREAT (O.S.B.M.)

History: St. Basil the Great founded this community in 358 A.D. The saint with his sister, Saint Macrina, founded a monastery on the banks of the River Iris in Asia Minor. The American foundation was made in Uniontown, Pennsylvania, in 1921, by Mother Macrina.

Purpose: The sisters teach in elementary and high schools, give catechetical instructions, care for the aged and orphans, conduct a nursing and retreat home, and an ecclesiastical art department which makes church vestments, sponsor an annual pilgrimage, and edit a magazine.

Spiritual Life: The religious exercises include Holy Mass, the recitation of the Divine Office in Old Slovanik, a half-hour of mental prayer, the rosary, spiritual reading, and other community prayers and devotions.

Training Program: The six-month postulancy is followed by an eighteen-month novitiate. Temporary vows are made for three years. The sisters then make their profession of perpetual vows. During the juniorate the sisters continue their spiritual formation while taking courses toward the fulfillment of their academic degrees.

Qualifications:
* Age: 16 to 30.
* Average intelligence.
* Entrance dates: October 1 and February 1.

Habit: The sisters wear a black habit, scapular, and veil, a white wimple, rosary, and a crucifix.

> *Write to:* Mount Saint Macrina
> West National Pike
> Uniontown, Pennsylvania

SISTERS OF ST. CASIMIR (S.S.C.)

History: Mother Maria, and two co-foundresses, Mother Mary Immaculata and Mother Mary Concepta, founded this congregation in Scranton, Pennsylvania, in 1907. They received their religious formation with the Sisters Servants of the Immaculate Heart of Mary at Mount St. Mary in Scranton. In 1911 they established their motherhouse and novitiate in Chicago, Illinois.

Purpose: Their apostolic activities embrace the field of education from the kindergarten to the college level, nursing in hospitals, caring for the aged, and in social work. These institutions are located in Maryland, Illinois, Nebraska, Pennsylvania, Minnesota, New Mexico, Ohio, Indiana, Michigan, Florida, Rhode Island, Massachusetts, and Argentina, South America.

Spiritual Life: The religious exercises include Holy Mass, mental prayer, the rosary, spiritual reading, and other community prayers and devotions.

Training Program: The congregation conducts an aspirancy for high school girls interested in the religious life. The one-year postulancy is followed by a two-year novitiate. Temporary vows are then made. During the postulancy and the second year of novitiate the sisters take college courses toward their academic degrees. This training is continued after first profession.

Qualifications:
* Age: 15 to 35. Exceptions are sometimes made.
* Completion of high school.

Habit: The sisters wear a black habit, scapular and veil, a large white collar, blue cord, a rosary, a silver crucifix, and a gold ring.

> *Write to:* Mother General
> 2601 West Marquette Road
> Chicago 29, Illinois

SISTERS OF ST. CHRETIENNE (S.S.Ch.)

History: This community was founded in Metz, France, in 1807 by Anne Victoire de Majanes, under the guidance of the Bishop of Metz. Exiled from France by the religious persecution in 1903, fifteen sisters came to the United States, to offer their services to the French-Canadian population of New England. St. Chretienne Academy is the central house of the one hundred and twenty-six sisters of the American foundation.

Purpose: Education is their principal work. These sisters staff schools in the New England states and in Mexico. They have founded three missions at Fox Lake and Trout Lake, Alberta, Canada, and at Djibouti in French Somaliland, Africa.

Spiritual Life: The religious exercises include Holy Mass, one hour of meditation, the rosary, recitation of Lauds and Vespers of the Office of the Blessed Virgin, spiritual reading, and other community prayers and devotions.

Training Program: These sisters conduct an aspirancy for prospective candidates. Close ties are maintained with the other members of the congregation in Canada and France. Each candidate spends three years in the Canadian novitiate during which time the study of French is emphasized. Every professed sister may look forward to a summer in France during which they visit the motherhouse and other community convents. Every six years, a thirty-day retreat is planned for those sisters who have the desire and aptitudes for such spiritual exercises. After the canonical year of novitiate temporary vows for five years are pronounced, after which profession of perpetual vows is made. Upon the reception of first vows, the sisters continue their spiritual formation while taking courses toward their professional degrees.

Qualifications:
* Age: 16 to 30.
* Average intelligence.

Habit: The sisters wear a black habit, guimpe, and veil, a white linen coif, a rosary, silver cross, and a gold ring.

Write to: Central House
262 Loring Avenue
Salem, Massachusetts

SISTERS OF SAINTS CYRIL AND METHODIUS (SS.C.M.)

History: The early 1900's was a critical period for the many immigrants from Slovakia who settled in the United States. Father Matthew Jankola of the Scranton diocese was keenly aware that this adjustment required not only the building of schools but also of securing sisters to staff them. As a result of his efforts, this diocesan congregation was established in 1909 at Scranton, Pennsylvania, under the auspices of Mother M. Cyril, I.H.M.

Purpose: The active apostolate of the members of this congregation is expressed in their motto: "Thy Kingdom Come." The sisters conduct elementary and secondary schools in seven eastern and midwestern states, catechetical classes, reading and speech remedial clinics, an orphanage, and two homes for the aged.

Spiritual Life: The religious exercises include Holy Mass, meditations both morning and evening, community prayer, spiritual reading, and visits to the Blessed Sacrament, all made in common. The stations of the cross and rosary are said privately. The Office of the Blessed Virgin is chanted on Sundays and holydays in Latin.

Training Program: The basic training of the young members follows the Sister Formation Program. The six-month to one-year postulancy is followed by a two-year novitiate. The canonical year is devoted to the spiritual and religious formation of the novices. During the second year they resume the studies for their academic degrees. Upon receiving first vows the junior sisters are transferred to the scholasticate where they spend two more years before entering the apostolate. Perpetual vows are taken after completing five years of temporary vows.

Qualifications:
* Age: 15 to 25. Exceptions are sometimes made.
* Completion of high school.
* Entrance dates: September 8 and February 2.

Habit: The sisters wear a black habit and veil and a white headdress. A rosary, crucifix, and a silver ring are also worn.

> *Write to:* Mother Superior
> Villa Sacred Heart
> Danville, Pennsylvania

CONGREGATION OF THE SISTERS OF ST. DOROTHY (S.S.D.)

History: Paola Frassinetti founded this congregation in Quinto, Italy, in 1834. Convents were soon opened in Rome and elsewhere. In 1866 horizons broadened, mission fields beckoned; Brazil and Portugal welcomed the Dorotheans. They were exiled from Portugal in 1910 when religious congregations were suppressed. Belgium, England, Spain, and Switzerland received them. It was during this persecution that John Cardinal Farley, Archbishop of New York, and Bishop Matthew Harkins of Providence invited the sisters to their dioceses. The congregation is now established on four continents and its 2,300 members work zealously in 84 convents of St. Dorothy.

Purpose: Although the principal object of the community is the moral and religious education of girls in boarding or day schools, or in orphanages, the Dorotheans gladly accept other apostolic works. The sisters conduct retreats for young ladies, and altar societies, give catechetical instructions, visit prisons, organize pious sodalities, and form Catholic Action groups.

Spiritual Life: The religious exercises include Holy Mass, mental prayer, the rosary, spiritual reading, and other community prayers and devotions.

Qualifications:
* Age: 16 to 30.
* Average intelligence.

Habit: The sisters wear a black habit, cape, and veil, a white bonnet, five decade rosary, and a crucifix.

> *Write to:* Mother Provincial
> Villa Fatima Novitiate
> 26 County Street
> Taunton, Massachusetts

SISTERS OF ST. LOUIS, MONAGHAN
(S.S.L.)

History: This congregation, which takes its name from St. Louis, King of France, was founded in Juilly in 1842 by l'Abbe Bautain and La Baronne de Vaux. In 1859, Mother Genevieve Beale established at Louisville, Monaghan, the first Irish foundation from which the work of education has spread to two continents. Convents have been founded in Europe, Africa, and in the United States in 1949.

Purpose: The sisters conduct training colleges, schools of domestic science, elementary and secondary schools, kindergartens, and orphanages, and operate hospitals and maternity centers in Africa. In the United States they teach in grade and high schools located in the Archdiocese of Los Angeles.

Spiritual Life: The religious exercises include Holy Mass, one half-hour of meditation, the Little Office of the Blessed Virgin in Latin, adoration, spiritual reading, the rosary, and other community prayers and devotions.

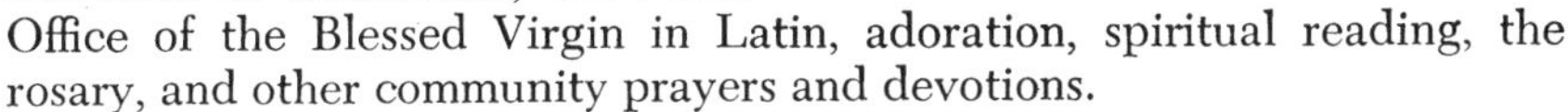
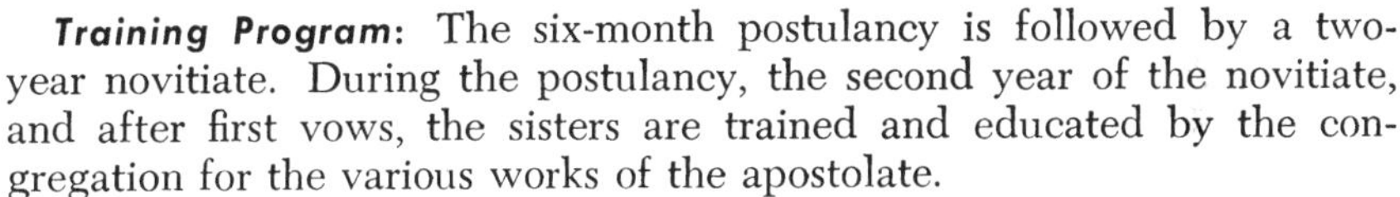

Training Program: The six-month postulancy is followed by a two-year novitiate. During the postulancy, the second year of the novitiate, and after first vows, the sisters are trained and educated by the congregation for the various works of the apostolate.

Qualifications:
* Age: 16 to 30.
* Teachers are needed in California. Doctors, nurses, teachers, and catechists are wanted for Africa. Only those who volunteer are sent to Africa.

Habit: The sisters wear a black habit, cincture and cross, a white coif, band and collar, a rosary, and a gold ring.

> *Write to:* Louisville Convent
> 22300 Mulholland Drive
> Woodland Hills,
> California

SISTERS OF THE ASSUMPTION OF THE BLESSED VIRGIN (A.S.V.)

History: A school, but no teachers, and none to be had from any religious community in spite of numerous requests by Father Jean Harper, pastor of St. Gregoire parish, Province of Quebec, Canada. He decided to act upon his curate's suggestion: "We cannot obtain nuns? Then, let us make some!" And so this congregation came into existence on the Feast of the Nativity, September 8, 1853. Today over two thousand six hundred members are found in four countries.

Purpose: Teaching and its auxiliary services both at home and on the mission fields are the apostolic activities of the members of this pontifical institute. Divided into seven provinces throughout Canada and the New England States, these sisters are engaged in teaching in elementary and secondary schools and in catechetical work. They are planning establishments in Brazil and have a convent and novitiate in Japan.

Spiritual Life: The religious exercises include Holy Mass, the recitation of the breviary, the rosary, visits, thirty minutes of meditation in the morning and fifteen in the evening, the stations of the cross, and spiritual reading.

Training Program: The two-year novitiate is preceded by a six-month postulancy. Temporary vows are pronounced annually for five years; profession of perpetual vows is then made. The sisters spend a month of spiritual recollection at the motherhouse after ten years in perpetual vows.

Qualifications:
* Age: 16 to 35.
* A high school education is preferred.
* Entrance date: September 24.

Habit: The sisters wear a simple black dress with a white collar, and a white headdress with a short black veil.

> *Write to:* Provincial House
> Main Street
> Petersham, Massachusetts

SISTERS AUXILIARIES OF THE APOSTOLATE (A.A.)

History: Father Francis Olszewski founded this congregation in Canada in 1903. In 1910 the first motherhouse was destroyed by fire. Instead of rebuilding in Canada, the sisters established their new home in North Dakota in 1911. Ten years later, at the request of Bishop Patrick Donahue, the entire community moved to the Diocese of Wheeling, West Virginia. The present motherhouse and novitiate are located in Monongah, West Virginia.

Purpose: The sisters devote themselves to the education of youth, especially the children of the poor and destitute, care for altars and sacristies, and are engaged in social and domestic work. The apostolate is carried on in West Virginia, Pennsylvania, and Texas.

Spiritual Life: The religious exercises include Holy Mass, the Office of the Blessed Virgin in English, a half-hour of mental prayer, the rosary, spiritual reading, and other community prayers and devotions.

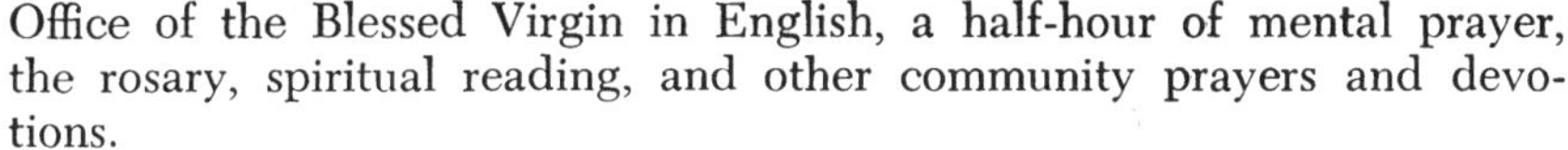

Training Program: The six to twelve-month postulancy is followed by a two-year novitiate. Temporary vows are made for three years. Perpetual vows are pronounced at the end of this period. After first profession the sisters continue their spiritual formation while taking college courses toward the completion of their academic degrees.

Qualifications:
* Age: 16 to 30. Exceptions are sometimes made.
* Completion of high school is preferred.

Habit: The sisters wear a black habit, veil, and cape, a white guimpe, and a silver crucifix.

> *Write to:* SS. Peter and Paul's Convent
> Maple Avenue
> Monongah, West Virginia

BAPTISTINES (C.S.JB.)

History: Canon Alphonsus Maria Fusco, who had become deeply interested in the spiritual and material well-being of the orphaned and abandoned children of his native town, founded this congregation in Italy in 1878. The history of the sisters in the United States is a story of sacrifice, hard work, and a deep faith in the providence of God. Bishop John O'Connor invited them to Newark, New Jersey, in 1906.

Purpose: The sisters are engaged in educational works on the elementary and high school levels, in parochial, diocesan and private schools, and in one college. They are active also in the apostolate among the aged, and conduct a retreat and a guest house, catechetical centers, and orphanages. These institutions are located in the eastern section of the United States.

Spiritual Life: The religious exercises include Holy Mass, one half-hour of mental prayer in the morning and another in the evening, visits to the Blessed Sacrament, the recitation of the Little Office of the Blessed Virgin in Latin on Sundays and holydays, rosary, and spiritual reading.

Training Program: The congregation conducts an aspirancy for high school girls interested in the religious life. The six-month to one-year postulancy is followed by a one-year novitiate. After profession of temporary vows the junior professed remains for a year or more in the House of Studies to pursue further academic courses and for extended religious formation. Profession of perpetual vows is made after five years in temporary vows.

Qualifications:
* Age: 18 to 30. Widows and late vocations sometimes accepted.
* Completion of high school.
* Entrance date: July 16.

Habit: The sisters wear a black tunic, scapular, and veil, and a white wimple, leather belt, rosary, silver crucifix, and a gold ring.

Write to: Mt. St. John's Convent
Anderson Hill Road
White Plains, New York

194

BENEDICTINE SISTERS OF THE CONGREGATION OF ST. BENEDICT (O.S.B.)

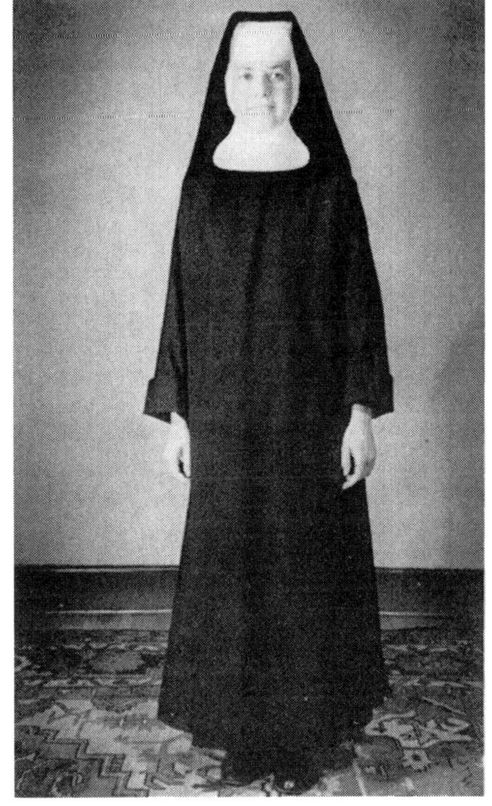

History: The sisters belonging to this congregation trace their American beginnings to St. Mary's Convent, St. Mary's Pennsylvania, where in 1852 two nuns and a lay sister from St. Walburga's Convent, Eichstatt, Bavaria, had introduced the Benedictine life in the United States. In 1947, with the suggestion and approval of the Holy See, the Congregation of St. Benedict was established. This congregation which observes episcopal enclosure now numbers seven priories.

Purpose: These Benedictines teach in elementary and secondary schools, and colleges, nurse the sick in hospitals, conduct orphanages and homes for the aged, and are engaged in catechetical work.

Spiritual Life: The religious exercises include Holy Mass, the chanting of the Divine Office either in Latin or English, one half-hour of mental prayer, spiritual reading, and other community prayers and devotions.

Training Program: Most of the priories have aspirancies for high school girls interested in the religious life. The six to twelve-month postulancy is followed by a one-year novitiate. Temporary vows are made for three years and may be renewed for three more years. Perpetual vows may be made at the end of three or six-year period. After first vows the sisters continue their spiritual formation while completing the studies toward their professional degrees.

Qualifications:

* Age: 15 to 30. Exceptions are sometimes made.
* Average intelligence.
* Entrance date: early September.

Habit: The sisters wear a black habit, scapular and veil, a white coif and band, and a gold ring.

See page 380 for a list of St. Benedict priories.

BENEDICTINE SISTERS OF THE CONGREGATION OF ST. GERTRUDE THE GREAT (O.S.B.)

History: The Order was founded by St. Scholastica, the sister of St. Benedict, in the sixth century. This congregation, which numbers twelve member priories, was officially organized in 1937. Each priory is independent.

Purpose: The main work of the congregation is teaching. The sisters teach from the kindergarten to the college level. All but one house has two or more hospitals and that one has a nursing home. All are engaged in one or more phases of the Confraternity of Christian Doctrine Program, religious vacation schools, weekly classes for public school children, and training classes for lay teachers.

Spiritual Life: The religious exercises include Holy Mass, the recitation of the Divine Office in English, one half-hour of mental prayer, the rosary, spiritual reading, and other community prayers and devotions.

Training Program: The priories at Ferdinand, Indiana; Crookston, Minnesota; and Minot, North Dakota, conduct aspirancies for teen-age girls interested in the religious life. Each priory has its own novitiate. The general practise is a ten-month postulancy during which the postulant takes a year of college work along with her religious formation. After one year of novitiate the novice makes her temporary vows. The newly professed receives one or two years pre-service training in the juniorate. A five-year juniorate program is planned for the future. According to this plan the sister will complete the requirements for a degree and have experience in the active apostolate before making perpetual vows.

Qualifications:
* Age: completion of fifteenth year.
* Average intelligence.

Habit: The sisters wear a black habit and scapular, a white coif and band, and a gold ring.

For a list of St. Gertrude the Great priories see page 381.

BENEDICTINE SISTERS OF THE CONGREGATION OF ST. SCHOLASTICA (O.S.B.)

History: This congregation of Benedictines, which is under papal jurisdiction, was established in 1922. While each of the priories retains its independence, they have united for the purpose of uniform observance and discipline. The congregation, which now numbers seventeen motherhouses, extends from Mexico to Wisconsin, and from New Jersey to California.

Purpose: The apostolate embraces the education of children from the grades through college, hospital work, care of the aged and orphans, household duties, practical and fine arts, and secretarial work. Summer catechetical work, missions among the Negro, in Mexico, and South America also come within the sphere of the sisters' activities.

Spiritual Life: The liturgical prayer life of the Church—the Mass and the recitation of the Divine Office—form the principal religious exercises of each community. Meditation, spiritual reading, and private devotions provide further opportunity for self-sanctification.

Training Program: Since each community in the congregation independently pursues the family ideal according to its own house customs and organization, there is no strict uniformity in the externals of the training program. In general, those entering the Benedictine family are postulants for six to nine months, novices for one year, and in temporary vows for three years. During these four and one-half or five years, the sisters follow a basic program for intellectual and spiritual development, broadened later for professed sisters to provide for advanced study and the privilege of consecration of virgins.

Qualifications:
* The maximum age is 30. Exceptions are sometimes made.
* A desire to serve God in all things.

Habit: The sisters wear a black habit, scapular, and a soft veil. The professed sisters wear a ring with the initials IHS.

For the address of the nearest St. Scholastica priory see page 381.

REGINA PACIS
BENEDICTINE SISTERS (O.S.B.)

History: Mother Abbess Euphemia Skorulski founded this community in Lithuania over 300 years ago. Originally it was a cloistered congregation. In 1944, due to the difficulties then present in their country, two sisters, Sister M. Raphaela and Sister M. Alphonsa, sought refuge in Italy. Through the encouragement of Pope Pius XII, the two sisters came to the United States in 1957 and established their motherhouse foundation at Bedford, New Hampshire.

Purpose: The community is very young and in need of vocations. The superior hopes to begin teaching in a kindergarten using the Montessori system and then as vocations increase to gradually expand their teaching program. Presently they are engaged in retreat work.

Spiritual Life: The religious exercises include Holy Mass, the Divine Office, mental prayer, the rosary, spiritual reading, and other community prayers and devotions.

Training Program: The six to twelve-month postulancy is followed by a two-year novitiate. Temporary vows are made for three years. Perpetual vows are then pronounced.

Qualifications:
   * The maximum age is 30. Exceptions will sometimes be made.
   * Completion of high school is preferred.
   * Entrance date: early September.

Habit: The sisters wear a black habit and scapular and a white coif and bandeau.

> *Write to:* Regina Pacis
> 75 Wallace Road
> Bedford, New Hampshire

BERNARDINE SISTERS (O.S.F.)

History: The American foundation of this congregation dates back to 1894 when Mother Veronica and four companions left their homeland to establish a foundation in the United States. The small nucleus of five has since increased to eleven hundred sisters working in three provinces. Foundations have also been established in Brazil, South America, and Liberia, Africa.

Purpose: The community is actively engaged in education on all levels, in hospital nursing, social, and foreign missionary work. The members of the two eastern provinces, from Massachusetts to Virginia, conduct a college, secondary and elementary schools, three hospitals, orphanages, and retreat houses. The sisters of the midwestern province operate secondary and elementary schools, two hospitals, and one home for the aged. These institutions are located in California and in the Midwest from Michigan to Texas.

Spiritual Life: The religious exercises consist in Holy Mass, one half-hour of mental prayer, thirty-five minutes of vocal prayer, the rosary, stations, period of adoration, spiritual reading, and the chanting of the Little Office of the Blessed Virgin in Latin.

Training Program: The community conducts an aspirancy for girls of high school age. The six to twelve-month postulancy is followed by a two-year novitiate. Temporary vows are then made. The Sister Formation program which begins with the juniorate is carried on to completion. Each sister makes a spiritual tertianship around ten years after her profession of perpetual vows.

Qualifications:
* The maximum age is 30. Exceptions will sometimes be made.
* Completion of high school.
* Entrance dates: September 2 and December 8.

Habit: The sisters wear a dark brown habit, scapular, and mantle, a black veil, white coif, band, and collar, a white cincture with the Franciscan Crown rosary attached, a crucifix, and a ring.

See page 382 for address of nearest provincial house.

SISTERS OF BETHANY (C.V.D.)

History: Mother Dolores de Maria and Mother Maria de la Cruz founded this congregation in El Salvador, Central America, in 1928. Papal approbation of the community was given by the Holy See in 1937. The first foundation was made in the United States at Los Angeles, California, in 1949.

Purpose: This teaching community is also engaged in social and missionary work. The sisters teach in elementary and secondary schools in North, Central, and South America. The social and missionary apostolate in Central and South America consists in restoring religion and Christian morality in the home by giving catechetical instructions to children, adults, and Catholic couples preparing for marriage.

Spiritual Life: The religious exercises include Holy Mass, the recitation of the Office of the Blessed Virgin is English, mental prayer, the chaplet of the seven dolors, and other community prayers and devotions.

Training Program: The community conducts an aspirancy for high school girls who are interested in the religious life. Temporary vows are made after completing the novitiate. Following first profession, the sisters continue their spiritual formation while taking courses in preparation for their professional degrees.

Qualifications:
* Age: 15 to 30.
* Completion of high school is preferred.

Habit: The sisters wear a navy blue habit, veil, and cord, a white guimpe, rosary, and crucifix.

> *Write to:* Mater Dolorosa Novitiate
> 552 North Normandie Avenue
> Los Angeles 4, California

SISTERS OF THE BLESSED SACRAMENT FOR INDIANS AND COLORED PEOPLE (S.B.S.)

History: Mother Katherine Drexel founded this missionary community in the United States in 1891, to serve Christ in the Indians and Colored People. Through the generosity of Mother Drexel numerous educational and social institutions for Indians and Negroes were built, staffed, and maintained. The community today carries on the spirit of the foundress in her efforts toward unity in the spirit of the Blessed Sacrament.

Purpose: In twenty-one states from New York to California nearly 600 missioners carry on an apostolate which includes education, home visitation, and social work. The home mission work reaches into the rural areas of the deep South and the Indian reservations of New Mexico, Arizona, and South Dakota. In New Orleans they conduct Xavier University of Louisiana.

Spiritual Life: The religious exercises include Holy Mass, the recitation of the Office of the Blessed Virgin in English, mental prayer, the rosary, spiritual reading, and other community prayers and devotions.

Training Program: The eleven-month postulancy is followed by a two-year novitiate. Temporary vows are then made. After first vows the sisters continue their spiritual formation while completing the courses toward their professional degrees at Blessed Sacrament College on the motherhouse grounds.

Qualifications:
* The maximum age is 30.
* Completion of high school.
* Entrance date: September 8.

Habit: The sisters wear a black habit, veil, and scapular which has an ebony crucifix, a white cord, and a large rosary.

> *Write to:* Motherhouse
> 1663 Bristol Pike
> Cornwells Heights, Pennsylvania

History: The foundress, spoken of by Pope Pius XII as "that incomparable woman," was Mother Mary Ward, an Englishwoman of post-reformation times who was obliged to flee her country's persecutions to consecrate herself to God. The foundations flourishing in the United States stem from the motherhouse, Loretto Abbey, Toronto, Ontario, which was founded in 1847 by the Irish branch of the Institute.

Purpose: The apostolic activities of this pontifical congregation are designed to develop true Christian womanhood in girls, that they may be a source of happiness and blessing as lay workers working for God and the Church. The sisters teach in co-educational and co-institutional schools in the elementary, secondary, and university levels, and conduct catechetical classes on released time basis and correspondence as well as vacation schools. These foundations are located in Illinois, Michigan, California, and Arizona. This congregation has had long experience working with the adult deaf and retarded hard-of-hearing children.

Spiritual Life: The rule is Ignatian and the spiritual exercises are made annually. The religious exercises include Holy Mass, the recitation of the Office of the Blessed Virgin, said in English privately at the convenience of each sister, the rosary, spiritual reading, one-half hour of meditation, and other community prayers and devotions.

Training Program: The postulancy of six months to one year is followed by a two-year novitiate. At the end of this time temporary vows are made for six years and the sisters receive their sister-formation training and complete their professional work at either the college connected with the novitiate at Wheaton, Illinois, or at Loretto College, Toronto, Canada. Three months before the expiration of temporary vows, a tertianship provides intensive preparation for perpetual vows.

Qualifications:
* Age: 16 to 30.
* At least two years of high school.

Habit: The sisters wear a black habit and veil, white collar and cuffs, a woven cincture, beads with a brass chain, crucifix with a brass corpus, and a silver ring.

> *Write to:* Loretto Convent
> Box 508
> Wheaton, Illinois

CARMELITE SISTERS OF CHARITY
(C.a. CH.)

History: St. Joaquina de Vedruna founded this congregation in 1826 in Spain, to fill an imminent need in that country for counteracting the irreligious atmosphere resulting from the French Revolution. The community received diocesan approval in 1850. Final approbation later came from the Holy See, granting all the privileges and indulgences of the first and second order of Carmelites. The congregation has foundations in Europe, Central America, India, Japan, Africa, South Africa, and in the United States since 1955.

Purpose: Teaching and nursing are the main apostolic activities of this Carmelite community. The rule of the order combines the austerity and prayerful approach of the Carmelites with the simplicity of the Franciscans. The community operates hospitals, homes for the aged, orphanages, schools, and missions. In the United States schools are staffed in California.

Spiritual Life: The religious exercises include Holy Mass, the Office of the Blessed Virgin in Latin, one hour and a quarter of private mental prayer, the rosary, spiritual reading, and other community prayers and devotions.

Training Program: The congregation conducts an aspirancy for high school girls interested in the religious life. The six-month postulancy is followed by a two-year novitiate. Temporary vows are then made. These are renewed annually for five years at which time perpetual vows are pronounced. After first vows the sisters continue their spiritual formation while taking courses toward their professional degrees.

Qualifications:
* Age: 15 to 25. Exceptions are sometimes made.
* Normal intelligence.

Habit: The sisters wear a black habit, scapular, veil, and leather belt of Our Lady, a five-decade rosary, a white linen wimple, crucifix, and a gold ring.

> *Write to:* Carmelite Sisters of Charity
> 19950 Anita Avenue
> Castro Valley, California

CARMELITE SISTERS OF ST. THERESE OF THE INFANT JESUS (C.S.T.)

History: Father Edward Soler, O.C.D., founded this congregation among the Indians of Bentley, Oklahoma, in 1917. Papal approbation was received in 1928. Among those of the early group to respond to the missionary call was Mother Agnes Cavanaugh, who guided and led the community until her death in 1951.

Purpose: The Carmelite sisters follow the teaching of Little Therese, especially that of complete abandonment to the loving will of God. The sisters teach in elementary and high schools, nurse in hospitals, operate day nurseries, and care for the mentally retarded. Their institutions are located in Oklahoma, Texas, and California. Guatemala is their foreign mission field.

Spiritual Life: The religious exercises include Holy Mass, the recitation of the Little Office of the Blessed Virgin in English, one half-hour of mental prayer, and other community prayers and devotions.

Training Program: The congregation has a novitiate program of spiritual formation and teacher-preparation at the present time. At the conclusion of the novitiate, the novices made their temporary profession of vows. The spiritual formation is continued as the sisters complete the courses leading toward their professional and nursing degrees.

Qualifications:

* Age: 17 to 35.
* Completion of high school.
* Entrance dates: August 22 and February 2.

Habit: The professed sisters wear a dark brown habit, black leather cincture and veil, a white choir mantle, large rosary, and a crucifix.

Write to: Mother General
Villa Teresa
1300 Classen Drive
Oklahoma City 3, Oklahoma

SISTERS OF THE
CATHOLIC APOSTOLATE (C.S.A.C.)

History: On January 22, 1950, Pope Pius XII, for the first time in the Jubilee Year, performed the solemn rite of Beatification which raised the Blessed Vincent Pallotte, "Pioneer of Catholic Action," to the dignity of the altar, just one hundred years after his death. He instituted this congregation at Rome, in 1843, for the purpose of caring for girls made homeless by the plague. The sisters formed a part of Blessed Vincent's three-branched society of the Catholic Apostolate, priests, sisters, and lay apostles all working together in the labors of Catholic Action. They established institutions in the United States before the end of the century. In 1933 they opened a mission in Brazil and another in Argentina in 1948.

Purpose: The sanctification of their own souls and of others in the various activities of the Catholic Apostolate is their primary objective. They teach in nursery, elementary, and high schools, do census work, and conduct orphanages, summer camps, and give catechetical instructions.

Spiritual Life: The religious exercises include Holy Mass, the private recitation of the Divine Office in English, one half-hour devoted to mental prayer, the rosary, and other community prayers and devotions.

Training Program: A teacher-training program functions in the community's Queen of the Apostles College, which was established primarily for the purpose of preparing its younger members for the teaching field.

Qualifications:
* Age: 16 to 30. Exceptions are sometimes made.
* Completion of high school.
* Entrance date: September 8.

Habit: The sisters wear a black habit, veil and belt, a white band and coif, a seven-decade rosary, a crucifix, and a gold ring.

Write to: Mother Superior
St. Patrick's Villa
Harriman, New York

DAUGHTERS OF CHARITY OF THE SACRED HEART OF JESUS (F.C.S.C.J.)

History: Rose Giet and Father J. M. Catroux founded this congregation during the post-revolutionary days in France. Father Catroux, unable to find sisters to help him rebuild his parish, discovered in Rose Giet, one of his parishioners, the instrument whom God had prepared for him. A foundation was opened in the United States in 1905. The United States province was formed in 1949 with headquarters in Colebrook, New Hampshire.

Purpose: The sisters devote their lives to the education of children in kindergartens, elementary, and secondary schools, nurse the sick in hospitals, and conduct homes for the aged. These institutions are located in New Hampshire, Maine, and New York. A mission was opened in Africa in 1935.

Spiritual Life: The religious exercises include Holy Mass, the recitation of the Office of the Blessed Virgin, mental prayer, the rosary, spiritual reading, and other community prayers and devotions.

Training Program: The candidates begin with a ten-month postulancy. During this time a full scholastic year is completed by the postulants who prepare for teaching or nursing. This is followed by a two-year novitiate. Temporary vows are made for five years after which perpetual vows are pronounced. During the juniorate the sisters continue their spiritual formation while completing the requirements for their professional degrees.

Qualifications
* Age: 16 to 30. Exceptions are sometimes made.
* Completion of high school is preferred.

Habit: The sisters wear a simple black dress, a white collar, band, and veil, a rosary, and a silver cross.

Write to: Mother Provincial
166 Main Street
Colebrook, New Hampshire

DAUGHTERS OF CHARITY OF ST. VINCENT DE PAUL (D.C.)

History: St. Vincent de Paul and St. Louise de Marillac founded this congregation in France in 1633. Social conditions of the seventeenth century called for dedicated women who, not restricted to a cloister, would consecrate their lives to the service of the poor. The first Daughters of Charity were village girls who visited the poor and sick in their homes, instructed children, and served in hospitals. In 1809 Blessed Elizabeth Ann Seton established the Sisters of Charity at Emmitsburg, Maryland.

Purpose: The needs of the poor determine the works of the Daughters of Charity. Included among these works are child-caring institutions, social centers, visiting the sick in their homes, hospitals, teaching in two colleges and in elementary and secondary schools, one leprosarium, and missions in Latin America and Japan.

Spiritual Life: The religious exercises include Holy Mass, two meditations, examination of conscience, spiritual reading, and the recitation of the rosary. The sisters do not recite the Divine Office.

Training Program: The nine-month postulancy is followed by a one-year novitiate. The sisters make annual vows after five years of probation. The vows are not public in the canonical sense, but are private and privileged, recognized by the Church and renewed each year. During the juniorate years the sisters continue their spiritual formation while pursuing college courses toward their academic degrees.

Qualifications:
* Age: 18 to 35.
* Average intelligence.

Habit: The sisters wear a blue-grey habit, a white cornette, and a chaplet at the side.

Write to: Marillac Seminary
Normandy,
Missouri

St. Joseph Central House
Emmitsburg,
Maryland

THE SISTERS OF CHARITY
(R.S.C.)

History: Mother Mary Aikenhead, founded this congregation in Ireland in 1815. Ireland, at this time, was suffering from the ravages of cholera and from religious persecution. Discrimination was practiced against Catholics and every effort was made to ostracize them from society. The benefits of education were denied to the mass of the population, as only wealthy Catholics could afford to send their children to the continent to be educated. Mother Aikenhead saw in the slums of her native Ireland the appalling plight of the poor and realized it was her vocation to help them spiritually and physically. Today her nuns conduct schools, hospitals, and social services on four continents. The first foundation was made in the United States in 1953.

Purpose: The sisters teach in elementary and secondary schools, give catechetical instructions to public school children, conduct a convalescent home and a Mexican mission where they visit the Mexican people in their homes. The houses of the community are located in the Archdiocese of Los Angeles.

Spiritual Life: The religious exercises include Holy Mass, mental prayer, the rosary, spiritual reading, and special community prayers and devotions. The sisters make the spiritual exercises of St. Ignatius each year.

Training Program: The six-month postulancy is followed by a two-year novitiate. Temporary vows are then made. The second-year novices are given a period of trial in the active works of the congregation to test further their suitability. After first profession the sisters take courses to fit them for their particular field in the apostolate. Perpetual vows are made after three years of temporary vows.

Qualifications:
* Age: 16 to 40.
* Average intelligence.

Habit: The sisters wear a black habit, veil, and cincture, a white linen cap and collar, a rosary, crucifix, and a gold ring.

Write to: St. Cornelius Convent
3350 Bellflower Boulevard
Long Beach 8, California

SISTERS OF CHARITY OF CINCINNATI
(S.C.)

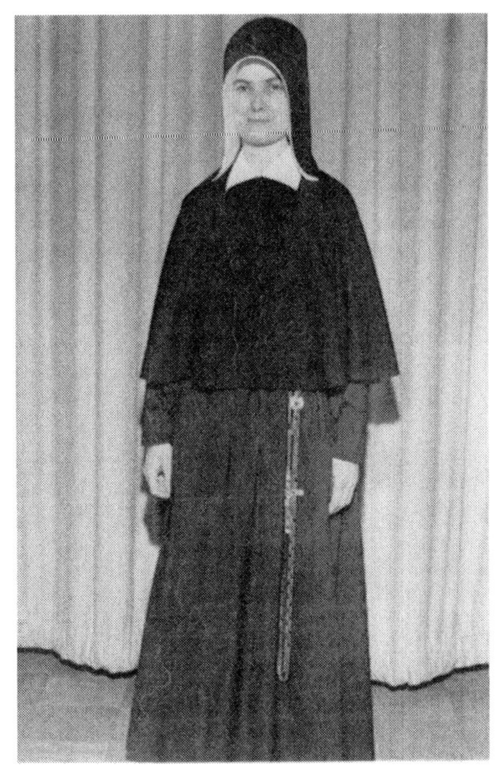

History: From Emmitsburg, Maryland, where Blessed Elizabeth Seton had founded the American Sisters of Charity in 1809, four sisters were sent to Ohio to open a free school and an orphanage. To meet the needs of the Church in the Midwest, this mission became an independent motherhouse in 1852, under Mother Margaret Cecilia George, a friend and co-worker of Mother Seton. The 1,600 members of this congregation are found in Italy, South America, and the United States.

Purpose: The apostolate of the sisters is education, hospital service, and social work. They operate a college for women, an academy for girls, secondary and elementary schools, training schools for nurses, and catechetical religion schools during the summer vacation. They also conduct nine general hospitals, orphanages, day nurseries, a school for the deaf, an institute for children with educational problems, a social center, and a retreat house for women. In Peru, South America, they teach Indian children at Huancane and Chinese refugees at Lima.

Spiritual Life: The observance of the three evangelical vows forms a spiritual bond of union among the sisters. Besides a half-hour of private devotion, the sisters assemble as a community for meditation, examen, spiritual reading, and vocal prayers.

Training Program: The spiritual and professional training of the sister of this congregation is conducted at the motherhouse through a five-year program in the postulancy, novitiate, and juniorate. A spiritual renovation program is offered about eight years after final profession.

Qualifications:
* Age: 16 to 28.
* The applicant should have an earnest desire to achieve holiness by the dedication of her life to the glory of God and salvation of souls.
* Entrance date: September 8.

Habit: The sisters wear a black habit with a circular cape and white collar. A black veil covers a simple white cap.

> *Write to:* Mother General
> Mount St. Joseph,
> Ohio

SISTERS OF CHARITY OF THE INCARNATE WORD (C.C.V.I.)

History: The Most Reverend Claude M. Dubuis founded this congregation at Galveston, Texas, in 1866. The first sisters received their religious training at the Monastery of the Incarnate Word and Blessed Sacrament, Lyons, France. The foundation made at San Antonio, Texas, in 1869, became an independent congregation in 1870. The community which received papal approbation in 1910 has a house of studies in Ireland and a province in Mexico.

Purpose: The sisters teach in elementary and secondary schools and colleges, nurse the sick in hospitals, train and educate nurses as well as other hospital personnel, and conduct orphanages, clinics, and community centers. These institutions are located in Texas, Louisiana, Missouri, Oklahoma, and Illinois.

Spiritual Life: The religious exercises include Holy Mass, the recitation of the Office of the Blessed Virgin in Latin, one hour of mental prayer, the rosary, spiritual reading, and other community prayers and devotions.

Training Program: The congregation conducts an aspirancy for those girls who have not attained senior standing in high school. The nine-month postulancy is followed by a two-year novitiate. The canonical year is devoted primarily to intense concentration on spirituality. In the second year the novice continues her spiritual formation while spending some time on her college studies. The juniorate, which follows the novitiate, ends when the sister completes her formal education.

Qualifications:
* Age: 15 to 30. Exceptions are sometimes made to 35.
* At least a senior in high school.
* Entrance date: September 7.

Habit: The sisters wear a black habit, veil, and scapular, a red cincture, rosary, guimpe, and a bandeau of white linen.

Write to: Motherhouse   Incarnate Word Convent
4515 Broadway   2800 Normandy Drive
San Antonio 9, Texas   St. Louis 21, Missouri

SISTERS OF CHARITY OF LEAVENWORTH (S.C.L.)

History: This pontifical institute came to Leavenworth, Kansas, in 1858 under the leadership of Mother Xavier Ross. The motherhouse was later transferred to Xavier, Kansas.

Purpose: Over nine hundred professed sisters teach in elementary and secondary parochial schools, a senior college, and schools of nursing, conduct hospitals, homes for the aged and children, and are engaged in catechetical teaching for public school children and summer religious vacation schools. The institutions are located in Kansas, California, Colorado, Illinois, Missouri, Montana, Nebraska, New Mexico, Oklahoma, and Wyoming.

Spiritual Life: The religious exercises include Holy Mass, morning and night prayers said in common, one hour of meditation, spiritual reading, periods of adoration, and the rosary.

Training Program: The six-month postulancy is followed by a two-year novitiate. The novices then make their profession of temporary vows. The junior professed continue their religious formation while taking courses leading toward their academic degrees. After six years in temporary vows, the sisters undergo an intensive spiritual training of six weeks in preparation for their profession of perpetual vows.

Qualifications:
* Age: under 30.
* Completion of high school.
* Entrance date: latter part of August.

Habit: The sisters wear a black habit with circular cape and veil.

> *Write to:* Mother General
> Motherhouse
> Xavier, Kansas

SISTERS OF CHARITY OF NAZARETH
(S.C.N.)

History: Father John B. David, who later became auxiliary bishop of Bardstown, and Mother Catherine Spalding founded this congregation in December, 1812 near Bardstown, Kentucky.

Purpose: The sisters teach in one hundred and forty-five schools from the elementary to the college level in ten states in the southern, eastern, and central sections of the United States. They staff eleven hospitals and care for orphans, the aged, the insane, abandoned infants, and unwed mothers. They staff a general hospital, a leper clinic, nurses' training school and an academy in the Patna district of India.

Spiritual Life: The religious exercises consist of Holy Mass, a half-hour of mental prayer, and a half-hour of adoration, community prayers, the rosary and private spiritual reading. Some of the community prayers will soon be replaced by the Divine Office.

Training Program: The postulancy of ten months is followed by a two-year novitiate. During the first year of novitiate the program is directed almost exclusively to spiritual formation. In the second year, the novice continues working toward her academic degree while fulfilling the spiritual requirements. The young professed sister then enters the juniorate where a program of studies based upon the recommendations of the Sister Formation Conference is conducted.

Qualifications:
* Age: 16 to 30. Late vocations are sometimes accepted.
* Good will, good judgement, good health.
* Entrance date: September 8.

Habit: The sisters wear a black habit, circular cape, apron, and a white cap. White is worn in hospitals and on the missions.

Write to: Motherhouse
Sisters of Charity of Nazareth
Nazareth, Kentucky

SISTERS OF CHARITY OF OUR LADY OF MERCY (O.L.M.)

History: This congregation originated in 1829 when John England, first Bishop of Charleston, South Carolina, sought assistance in caring for the orphans and slave children of his diocese. Three young women, originally from Ireland, came from Baltimore, Maryland, to help Bishop England in the work of his vast missionary diocese which then comprised three states.

Purpose: These sisters teach in parochial, elementary and high schools, operate hospitals and a school of nursing, and conduct social and catechetical centers, and an orphanage. These institutions are located in South Carolina and New Jersey.

Spiritual Life: The religious exercises include the recitation in English of Lauds and Prime from the Short Breviary, Holy Mass, thirty minutes of mental prayer, visits to the Blessed Sacrament, common recitation of the rosary, spiritual reading, and evening prayers consisting of Vespers and Compline.

Training Program: The six to twelve-month postulancy is followed by a two-year novitiate. The novices make temporary vows at the conclusion of the novitiate. As junior professed the sisters are guided by a Mistress on the missions where they continue their spiritual formation and when it is possible they pursue courses toward their professional degrees.

Qualifications:
* Age: 16 to 30.
* Average intelligence.

Habit: The sisters wear a black habit, cape, and apron, and a white bonnet and close fitting white cap.

> *Write to:* Mother Superior
> Fort Johnson Road
> P.O. Box 3345, St. Andrew's Branch
> Charleston, South Carolina

SISTERS OF CHARITY OF SETON HILL (S.C.)

History: The establishment of the Sisters of Charity of Seton Hill was the response of the Sisters of Charity of Cincinnati, Ohio, to the appeal of Bishop Michael Domenec, C.M., the second Bishop of Pittsburgh, for an independent foundation of Mother Seton's sisters in his diocese. Four sisters were welcomed in 1870 by Father John Tuigg, later the third Bishop of Pittsburgh. Mother Regina Mattingly came from Cincinnati in November of the same year to install the first superior. Sister Aloysia Lowe and Sister Regina Ennis were the first two mother superiors elected by the community which now numbers 850 members.

Purpose: The sisters teach in elementary and secondary schools, Seton Hill College, and De Paul Institute for the deaf, nurse in hospitals, and conduct a home for the aged, a foundling home, and a social service center. These institutions are located in Maryland, California, District of Columbia, Louisiana, Pennsylvania, and Arizona. They have a mission in Korea.

Spiritual Life: The religious exercises include Holy Mass, a half-hour of adoration, mental prayer, the rosary, spiritual reading, and other community prayers and devotions.

Training Program: The period of religious formation embraces the postulancy, the novitiate of two years, and five years in temporary vows, after which perpetual vows are pronounced. After first vows the sisters receive the professional education and training necessary for the works of the congregation. At the end of ten years in perpetual vows, a thirty-day retreat is devoted to renovation of fervor.

Qualifications:
* Age: under 31.
* Completion of high school.
* Entrance dates: September 8 and January 1.

Habit: The sisters wear a black habit and cap of Mother Seton, a white inner cap, collar, and sleeves, and a separate cape and apron.

Write to: Mother General, Seton Hill
Greensburg, Pennsylvania

SISTERS OF CHARITY OF SAINT ELIZABETH (S.C.)

History: The rule and spirit of St. Vincent de Paul were the foundation stones on which Elizabeth Ann Seton founded the first American Sisters of Charity in the early nineteenth century. James Roosevelt Bayley, first bishop of Newark, sought assistance from Mother Seton's daughters in New York to promote the works of education and charity in his diocese. Among these New York sisters was Sister Mary Xavier Mehegan who became the first Mother of the Sisters of Charity in New Jersey, September 29, 1859.

Purpose: The more than 1,700 sisters teach in elementary and secondary schools, nursing schools, and a college, conduct a catechetical center, nurse the sick in seven hospitals, care for the motherless in orphanages and a foundling home, and operate homes for the aged and business women.

Spiritual Life: The religious exercises include Holy Mass, one half-hour of mental prayer, the rosary, spiritual reading, and other community prayers and devotions.

Training Program: The one-year postulancy in which the candidate becomes acquainted with the religious life is followed by a year of novitiate. This latter year is devoted to the spiritual formation of the novice according to the spirit of the congregation. Perpetual vows are pronounced after five years in temporary vows. Undergraduate studies are completed at Mother Xavier Juniorate. Guidance and formation are continued during this period and during the early days of the apostolic works in schools, hospitals, or other houses until the sister makes her final vows.

Qualifications:
* The maximum age is 30.
* Completion of high school.
* Entrance date: September 6.

Habit: The sisters wear a black habit and veil, with a separate cape and apron, and a rosary.

Write to: Convent of St. Elizabeth
Convent,
New Jersey

SISTERS OF CHARITY OF ST. JOAN ANTIDA (S.C.J.A.)

History: Saint Joan Antida Thouret, who was declared a saint by the Holy See in 1934, founded this pontifical institute in France in 1799. Emerging from the ruins of the French Revolution, the foundress became one of the first social workers to contribute to the moral and social reconstruction of France leading back souls to Christ through a vast program of Christian charity. The 10,000 members are serving Christ in Italy, France, Switzerland, England, Malta, the Middle East, Laos, Africa, and in the United States since 1932.

Purpose: The sisters nurse in hospitals, sanitoriums, and homes for the aged, teach in colleges, kindergartens, and in secondary and elementary schools, and conduct asylums, nurseries, and social centers. Their apostolate is centered in the state of Wisconsin.

Spiritual Life: The religious exercises include Holy Mass, two periods of mental prayer, the recitation of the Penitential Psalms on Wednesdays and Fridays, the rosary, spiritual reading, and other community prayers and devotions.

Training Program: The community conducts an aspirancy for high school girls interested in the religious life. The six-month postulancy is followed by a one-year novitiate. At the expiration of the novitiate year, the sisters may be assigned either to the House of Studies or sent to one of the missions to prepare herself for those activities for which she is suited or talented. Temporary vows are then made. These are renewed annually for six years after which perpetual vows are pronounced.

Qualifications:
* Age: 16 to 28. Exceptions are sometimes made.
* Average intelligence.

Habit: The sisters wear a grey habit, a black veil and apron, a white coif and guimpe, a five-decade rosary, and a crucifix.

Write to: St. Joan Antida Convent
6640 West Beloit Road
West Allis 14, Wisconsin

SISTERS OF CHARITY OF
SAINT LOUIS (S.C.S.L.)

History: Madame Louise Elizabeth Mole founded this congregation in 1802 in France. The community was the first of its kind to devote itself to the welfare of the victims of war. In 1803, Madame Mole came to Vannes, France, and secured a convent which became the motherhouse of the congregation. She took the name of Mother St. Louis as first superior general. There are four separate provinces located in France, England, Western, and Eastern Canada. The United States foundation is part of the Canadian Province.

Purpose: The members of this pontifical institute take, besides the three evangelical vows, the vow of educating children. The sisters teach in elementary, secondary, normal, and specialized commercial schools, pray for the conversion of sinners, conduct retreat houses, and care for the sick in clinics, hospitals, and nursing homes.

Spiritual Life: The religious exercises include Holy Mass, two periods of meditation of one half-hour each, the rosary, spiritual reading, the chanting of the Divine Office either in English or French, and other community prayers and devotions.

Training Program: The six to twelve-month postulancy is followed by a two-year novitiate. Temporary vows are made at this time. These are renewed annually for five years. The sisters then pronounce their perpetual vows. After professing temporary vows, the sisters continue their spiritual formation while completing the studies necessary for their professional degrees.

Qualifications:
* Age: 16 to 30. Exceptions are sometimes made.
* Completion of high school is preferred.
* Entrance dates: August 21 and February 21.

Habit: The sisters wear a black dress and veil, a white headdress, guimpe, a crucifix, Seven Dolor chaplet, and a silver ring.

Write to: Mother Superior
405 Maple Avenue
Cheshire, Connecticut

SISTERS OF CHARITY OF ST. VINCENT DE PAUL (S.C.)

History: Blessed Elizabeth Seton founded this congregation in 1809 in Emmittsburg, Maryland. The first mission was established in New York City in 1817 when Mother Seton sent a group of sisters to care for the needy dependent children of that city. In 1847 the New York community became an independent congregation.

Purpose: The purpose of the community is "To honor Jesus Christ, the source and model of all charity, by rendering Him every possible corporal and spiritual service, in the person of the young whom they educate, and of the poor of every type who may require their assistance." The apostolic activities include teaching, nursing, social service, and missionary work. Working in the archiocese of New York and in the dioceses of Brooklyn, Rockville Center, and Harrisburg, the congregation conducts colleges, academies, secondary and elementary schools, hospitals, a foundling home, and homes for dependent children.

Spiritual Life: The sisters spend nearly four hours each day in spiritual exercises which include the Holy Sacrifice of the Mass, a half-hour of adoration of the Blessed Sacrament, vocal prayers in English, mental prayer, spiritual reading, and private acts of devotions.

Training Program: The postulancy of six months is followed by the two years of novitiate. At the conclusion of the novitiate, the novice takes temporary vows for five years and then pronounces her perpetual vows. Monthly spiritual conferences, days of recollection, and a period of tertianship strengthen the dedicated zeal of the sisters while her professional education is continued by post-graduate studies and in-service training.

Qualifications:
* Age: 17 to 30.
* An earnest desire to serve God faithfully in the religious life.
* Entrance date: September 8.

Habit: The distinctive marks of the New York Sisters of Charity are the black cap and cape as they were worn by Mother Seton.

Write to: Mount St. Vincent-on-the-Hudson
New York 71,
New York

SISTERS OF CHRISTIAN CHARITY
(S.C.C.)

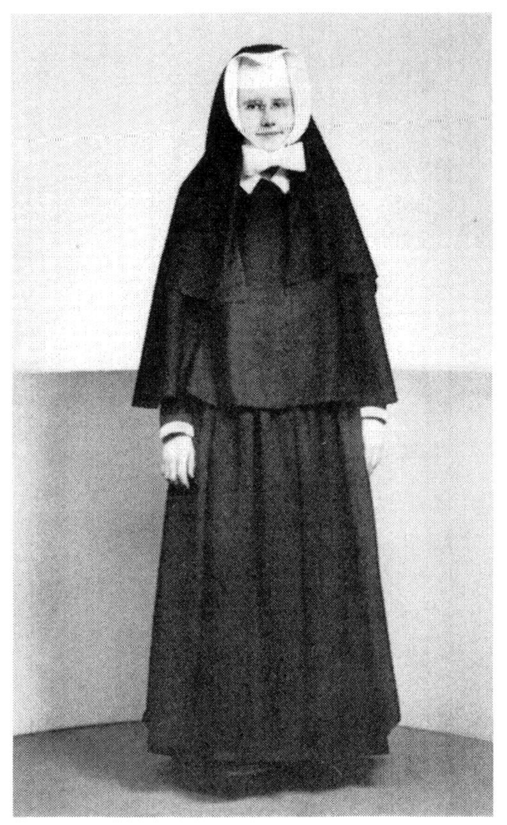

History: Before the tall, gracious woman stood Dr. Herman Schmidt. "May I entrust them to your love?" he questioned. And he put the hands of the little blind girl into hers, knowing that they clasped those of a perfect friend, Pauline von Mallinckrodt. Unable to find a sisterhood that would take charge of her blind, Pauline, on the advice of the Auxiliary Bishop of Cologne, founded this community in Germany in 1849. The first sisters came to America in 1873.

Purpose: Here in the United States and in South America the sisters teach and conduct hospitals, dispensaries, orphanages, homes for delinquents and working girls, catechetical centers, mission schools, homes for the aged, retreat houses, centers for the deaf, blind and mentally retarded.

Spiritual Life: The religious exercises include Holy Mass, the recitation of the Little Office of the Blessed Virgin, a half-hour of mental prayer, and other community prayers and devotions.

Training Program: The sisters conduct an aspirancy for high school girls interested in the religious life. The six to twelve-month postulancy is followed by a two-year novitiate. Temporary profession of vows is made for six years. During these years the sisters continue their spiritual formation while taking courses toward their professional degrees. A tertianship of three months is spent in preparation for the making of perpetual vows.

Qualification:

* Age: 15 to 30. Exceptions are sometimes made.
* Average intelligence.

Habit: The sisters wear a black habit, cape, and veil, white collar and cuffs, and a coif.

Write to: Maria Immaculata Convent   Mallinckrodt Convent
Wilmette,   Mendham,
Illinois   New Jersey

THE COMPANY OF MARY (O.D.N.)

History: St. Jeanne de Lestonnac founded this congregation in Bordeaux, France, in 1606. She died February 2, 1640 after having established thirty schools in her native country. Foundations were made in other parts of Europe, Mexico, the Congo, Japan, and the United States.

Purpose: The sisters teach on all levels of education from kindergarten to college, conduct catechetical centers, and are engaged in social service work. The apostolate in the United States is carried out in California, New Mexico, and Arizona.

Spiritual Life: The religious exercises include Holy Mass, the Office of the Blessed Virgin—the Divine Office is chanted during Holy Week and Christmas—mental prayer, the rosary, spiritual reading, and other community prayers and devotions.

Training Program: The six-month postulancy is followed by a two-year novitiate. Temporary vows are made for five years. During this time the sisters pursue the courses required for their academic degrees and make a tertianship of six months, in which is included a whole month of retreat according to the spiritual exercises of St. Ignatius. The sister then makes her perpetual vows.

Qualifications:
* Age: 15 to 30.
* Completion of high school is preferred.
* Entrance date: arranged with the Mother Superior.

Habit: The sisters wear a black cassock-like habit, hood, and veil, a white wimple, crucifix, and a large rosary.

Write to: Mother Provincial
16791 East Main Street
Santa Ana, California

CORDI-MARIAN MISSIONARY SISTERS (M.C-M.)

History: Father Julian Collell, C.M.F., and Mother Carmen Serrano, M.C-M., founded this congregation in Mexico City, Mexico, March 19, 1921. Due to the religious persecution in Mexico, the sisters came to the United States where they began their first establishment at Martindale, Texas, September 24, 1926. Today the community has foundations in Illinois, Texas, and Mexico.

Purpose: The sisters are engaged in the education of youth and in social work. They teach in elementary and secondary schools, and in colleges, conduct one settlement house, work with the blind and the deaf, and teach catechism after school hours and during the summer months.

Spiritual Life: The religious exercises include Holy Mass, the recitation in Latin of the Office of the Blessed Virgin, one hour of mental prayer, and other community prayers and devotions.

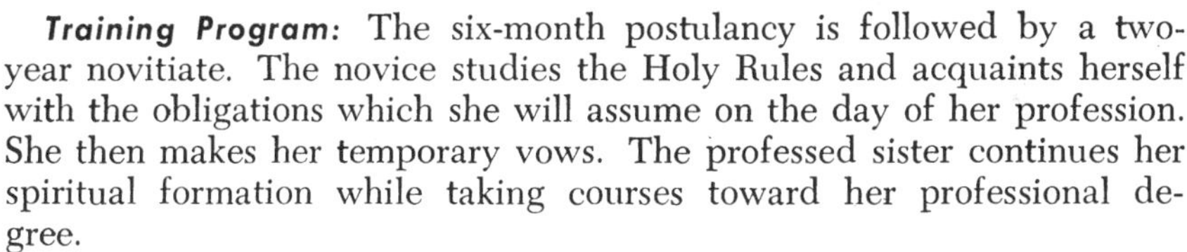

Training Program: The six-month postulancy is followed by a two-year novitiate. The novice studies the Holy Rules and acquaints herself with the obligations which she will assume on the day of her profession. She then makes her temporary vows. The professed sister continues her spiritual formation while taking courses toward her professional degree.

Qualifications:
* Age: 15 to 30.
* Average intelligence.

Habit: The sisters wear a black cassock, sash, scapular, and veil, and a large pendant having on it the symbols of the Immaculate Heart of Mary and of the congregation.

> *Write to:* Mother General
> 2910 Morales Street
> San Antonio 7, Texas

DAUGHTERS OF THE CROSS (D.C.)

History: Marie L'Huillierde Villeneuve founded at Paris, in 1640, one of the very first uncloistered communities of women dedicated to the education of youth and the works of mercy. Using as a basis for her Constitutions the Rule given her by St. Francis de Sales, her spiritual director, Madame de Villeneuve formulated for her daughters a way of life breathing the charity and gentleness of this holy Doctor. Early trials bravely withstood won for the new congregation the admiration of all and the glorius title "Daughters of the Cross." The friend and champion of these struggling beginnings was St. Vincent de Paul. Since 1855, the Daughters of the Cross have been carrying on their apostolic work in the state of Louisiana.

Purpose: The sisters teach in academies and parochial schools and conduct catechetical classes.

Spiritual Life: The religious exercises include Holy Mass, the recitation of the Short Breviary in English—morning prayers are taken from Lauds of the Office and evening prayers from Compline—one half-hour of meditation, the rosary, spiritual reading, and other community prayers and devotions.

Training Program: The six-month postulancy is followed by a two-year novitiate. Temporary vows are pronounced for five years after which perpetual vows are made. After first profession the sisters continue their spiritual formation while taking courses toward their professional degrees.

Qualifications:
* The maximum age is 35.
* Completion of high school.
* Entrance dates: July 19 and January 29.

Habit: The sisters wear a black habit, veil, and guimpe, a white headdress and collar, a rosary, and a silver cross.

Write to: Saint Vincent's Academy
St. Vincent and Southern Avenues
Shreveport 49, Louisiana

DAUGHTERS OF DIVINE CHARITY
(F.D.C.)

History: Mother Franciska Lechner founded this pontifical congregation in 1868 in Vienna, Austria. The first foundation was made in the United States in 1913 at Saint Mary's Residence, the first home for business women in midtown Manhattan, New York.

Purpose: The sisters teach in parish elementary schools and private academies, conduct catechetical centers, and maintain residences for business women and homes for the aged. These institutions are located in New York, Pennsylvania, New Jersey, Michigan, Illinois, Connecticut, Indiana, Ohio, and California.

Spiritual Life: The religious exercises include Holy Mass, the Little Office of Our Lady, meditation on the mysteries of our Faith, regular visits to the Blessed Sacrament, morning and evening prayers, and other community prayers and devotions.

Training Program: The sisters conduct an aspirancy for high school girls who are interested in the religious life. The six-month postulancy is followed by a two-year novitiate. Religious profession follows the novitiate. The sister pronounces her temporary vows and takes the veil. Perpetual vows are made after five years. During this time the sister continues her spiritual formation while taking undergraduate college courses toward her professional degree.

Qualifications:
* Age: under 30.
* Completion of high school is preferred.
* Entrance dates: September 1 and February 1.

Habit: The sisters wear a black habit, cape, and veil, and a white bonnet, a modified form of the headdress worn in the Austrian Province where the community was founded.

> *Write to:* Provincial House
> 850 Hylan Boulevard
> Staten Island 5,
> New York

SISTERS OF DIVINE PROVIDENCE (C.D.P.)

History: Blessed John Martin Moye founded these sisters in Lorraine, France in 1762. After the French Revolution, two sisters, answering the appeal of Bishop Claude M. Dubuis, came to Castroville, Texas, in 1866. The motherhouse was transferred to its present site in 1895. Pope St. Pius X approved the congregation in 1912.

Purpose: The members of this congregation have dedicated themselves to the sanctification of themselves and of others by various apostolic works. While teaching is their main work, they are also engaged in catechetical instruction, nursing, social service, caring for retarded children and the aged, and in foreign missions. The nearly eight hundred members are found in Texas, Oklahoma, Louisiana, Arkansas, New Mexico, and Mexico.

Spiritual Life: The daily prayer schedule includes Holy Mass, the Office of the Blessed Virgin in English, community morning and evening prayers, the rosary, visits, examens, and a half-hour each of mental prayer and spiritual reading.

Training Program: The community has an aspirancy for graduates of elementary school who desire to become religious. The religious formation consists of a candidacy of one year and six months, a postulancy of six months and a novitiate of one year, followed by a juniorate of one full year. Perpetual vows are taken only after four more years are spent in apostolic labors. A full degree program is required of each sister before she begins her apostolic work.

Qualifications:
* The maximum age is 30. Exceptions will be made.
* Average intelligence.
* Entrance date: first week in September.

Habit: The sisters wear a black pleated skirt, blouse, and veil, a circular cape, white collar and band, a crucifix, Franciscan Crown of Mary rosary, and a gold ring.

> *Write to:* Vocation Directress
> Moye High School
> Castroville, Texas

SISTERS OF DIVINE PROVIDENCE (C.D.P.)

History: William Emmanuel von Ketteler, Bishop of Mainz, founded this community in Mainz, Germany, in 1851. The first group of sisters were sent to the United States in 1876 to establish a permanent settlement in Pittsburgh, Pennsylvania. Today there are eight hundred professed sisters in three provinces in the United States.

Purpose: The chief works of the community are teaching and nursing. The area assigned to St. Peter's Province comprises the territory of the middle, central, and southern states east of the Mississippi River and includes Puerto Rico. The St. Louis Province includes all the states west of the Mississippi River. Our Lady of Divine Providence Province embraces all the New England states.

Spiritual Life: The religious exercises include Holy Mass, the Office of the Blessed Virgin recited in English, a half-hour of mental prayer, the rosary, spiritual reading, and other community prayers and devotions.

Training Program: The sisters conduct an aspirancy for high school girls interested in the religious life. The six to nine-month postulancy is followed by a two-year novitiate. The novices then make their temporary vows. If the candidate has completed high school, she begins her college work during the postulancy. During the second year of the novitiate and also in her juniorate years, the sister continues her spiritual formation and professional training toward her teaching or nursing degree.

Qualifications:
* The maximum age is 30. Exceptions for those under 40 are sometimes made.
* Average intelligence.
* Entrance date: early September.

Habit: The sisters wear a black habit, cape, veil, and cincture, a white linen headdress, a rosary, and a small crucifix.

See page 382 for address of nearest provincial house.

DAUGHTERS OF THE DIVINE REDEEMER (D.D.R.)

History: Mother Alphonse Eppinger founded this congregation in 1849 in Alsace-Lorraine. The sisters have foundations in Europe and Africa. The foundation in the United States was established in 1912.

Purpose: The sisters are engaged in teaching in elementary and secondary schools, nursing in hospitals, and caring for the aged and convalescent. Their institutions are located in Pennsylvania, Ohio, New York, and Minnesota.

Spiritual Life: The religious exercises include Holy Mass, the recitation of the Little Office of the Blessed Virgin in English, a half-hour of meditation each morning, spiritual reading, and evening recitation of the rosary.

Training Program: The congregation conducts an aspirancy for high school girls interested in the religious life. The six-month postulancy is followed by a two-year novitiate. The novices then make their temporary profession of vows. The five years of temporary profession following first vows are designated as the period of the juniorate. During the first two years, the junior sisters continue their spiritual and professional training at the motherhouse. The junior sisters take part in the active work of the community during the last three years.

Qualifications:

* The maximum age is 30. Exceptions are sometimes made.
* Students may enter after graduating from elementary school; postulants after three and one half years of high school, or after completing high school.
* Entrance dates: September 15 and February 15.

Habit: The sisters wear a black habit, cape, and veil, a white guimpe, headdress, large black rosary, and a crucifix.

> *Write to:* Divine Redeemer Motherhouse
> R.D. 1, Box 356
> Elizabeth, Pennsylvania

DAUGHTERS OF THE HEART OF MARY
(D.H.M.)

History: Adelaide de Cice and Father De Clorivière, S.J., founded this community in 1790 during the persecution of the French Revolution. It is a religious congregation that combines community life with life in the world. The members of this pontifical institute take the three evangelical vows but they do not have a habit or a cloister. It was first approved by Pius VII in 1801 and received full papal approbation in 1890. The congregation has foundations in Europe, North and South America, Africa, and Asia. They arrived in the United States in 1851 and opened an orphanage in Cleveland, Ohio, schools in Chicago and New York, and Nardin Academy in Buffalo, New York.

Purpose: Through its two-fold apostolate in the community and in the world, the congregation aims to penetrate a de-Christianized society with the spirit of Christ. The works of this congregation includes schools, retreat work, catechetical centers, social service centers, homes, and foreign missions. The sisters who are retained in the world by family obligations or apostolic commitments live a no less consecrated life while engaged in their chosen professions and fulfilling their ordinary occupations. All the sisters take the same vows and observe the same rule.

Spiritual Life: Ample opportunities toward achieving a deep interior life of union with God are provided by the daily program of one-hour of mental prayer, Holy Mass, examens, spiritual reading, visits, and the rosary.

Training Program: During the postulancy and the two years of novitiate the candidates are given the basic fundamentals of the religious life. The two-year juniorate is one of intensive growth in the spiritual life and of professional training for the apostolate.

Qualifications:
* Age: 17 to 37.
* Ability to love, to laugh, and to work.
* A sincere desire for the consecrated life.

> *Write to:* Provincial House
> 103 East 20th Street
> New York 3, New York

DAUGHTERS OF THE MOST HOLY SAVIOR

History: Mother Mary Alphonsa founded this congregation in France in 1849. In 1941 the Holy Father gave the sisters permission to establish an independent foundation in Slovakia, with the motherhouse in Bratislava. Papal approbation was obtained in 1942. There are provinces in Czechoslovakia, Hungary, and in Germany. Due to communistic pressure only the latter remains free. The American province was founded in Oakland, California in 1951.

Purpose: The active apostolate of this congregation includes teaching in both kindergarten and elementary schools, caring for the sick and aged, and domestic work.

Spiritual Life: The religious exercises include Holy Mass, a thirty minute meditation, the recitation of the short breviary in English, spiritual reading, the rosary, and other community prayers and devotions.

Training Program: The postulancy extends from six months to one year. The novitiate, which is a period of training in the principles of the religious life, lasts for one full year. Perpetual vows are made at the end of the three years of temporary vows.

Qualifications:
* Age: the maximum is 30. Exceptions are sometimes made.
* Completion of high school. Exceptions will be made for those desiring domestic work.

Habit: The sisters wear a black habit, cincture, veil, and cape, and a five decade rosary.

Write to: House of Nazareth Convent
Box 5007 Eastmont Station
Oakland 5, California

DAUGHTERS OF THE IMMACULATE HEART OF MARY (C.M.F.)

History: The Right Reverend Joachim Masmitja founded this pontifical congregation in Olot, Spain, on July 2, 1848. Saint Pius X sanctioned its official constitution in 1907. Today the sisters have twenty-six convents in Spain, twelve in the United States, and mission foundations in France, Italy, and South America. The American motherhouse was established in Tucson, Arizona in 1917.

Purpose: The sisters teach in elementary and high schools, give catechetical instructions, visit homes, and are engaged in social work. Their apostolic labors are carried out in Arizona, California, New Mexico, Texas, and Illinois.

Spiritual Life: The religious exercises include Holy Mass, two periods of meditation, spiritual reading, the recitation of the Little Office of the Blessed Virgin, and other community prayers and devotions.

Training Program: The sisters conduct an aspirancy for high school girls interested in the religious life. The six-month postulancy is followed by a two-year novitiate. At the end of this time the sister pronounces her temporary vows. The junior professed then begins a three-year period of temporary vows during which she engages in the active works of the community. She then makes her profession of perpetual vows.

Qualifications:
* The maximum age is 30.
* Completion of high school for the postulancy.
* Entrance dates: August 22 and February 2.

Habit: The sisters wear a navy blue habit, a black scapular, veil, and cincture, and a white coif.

> *Write to:* Immaculate Heart Academy
> 35 East Fifteenth Street
> Tucson, Arizona

DAUGHTERS OF JESUS (F.J.)

History: Mother Saint Angela and Father Coeffic founded this congregation in Brittany, France, in 1834. As a result of the religious persecution in France in the early twentieth century, several hundred sisters were forced to abandon their schools and other institutions and seek refuge in other countries. The first American foundations, a grade school and hospital, were opened in Lewistown, Montana, in 1903. The sisters also have a school in California. The three thousand sisters are actively working in Europe, Canada, United States, Africa, and Central America.

Purpose: Education, the care of the sick and elderly, and foreign missions are the apostolic activities of the members of this community. The congregation seeks to help the poor and middle classes. The sisters take a special pride and joy in being able to help the clergy in every way possible.

Spiritual Life: The religious exercises include Holy Mass, the chanting of the Office of the Blessed Virgin in Latin, one hour of mental prayer divided into two periods of a half-hour each, the rosary, and other community prayers and devotions.

Training Program: The nine-month postulancy is followed by a two-year novitiate. Temporary vows are then made and are renewed annually for five years. Following first vows, the sister begins a program of preparation for the work she will be assigned to do. One month every summer is spent in spiritual renewal. The two months of preparation for perpetual dedication to God are made at the motherhouse in France.

Qualifications:
* Age: 16 to 30. Exceptions are sometimes made.
* Average intelligence.
* Entrance date: second week in September.

Habit: The professed sisters wear a black habit with a waist length veil, a rosary, crucifix, and a silver ring.

Write to: Mother Superior
P.O. Box 580
Lewistown, Montana

DAUGHTERS OF MARY HELP OF CHRISTIANS (F.M.A.)

History: Saint John Bosco founded this congregation in 1872. Also known as the Salesian Sisters, they now number more than seventeen thousand and are established in fifty-two countries throughout the world. The community came to the United States in 1908. The co-foundress, Saint Mary Mazzarello, was canonized in 1951.

Purpose: The Salesian Sister aims to achieve the all-important goal of personal sanctification by way of an apostolate among youth. The field of labor includes teaching at the elementary, secondary, and college levels, conducting orphanages, hospices for young working girls, recreation centers, young girls' retreats, and in foreign missions. They have been in South America since 1877.

Spiritual Life: Because of the active quality of the sister's life, simplicity and brevity characterize the daily religious practices. The religious exercises include Holy Mass, a half-hour of meditation, examens, visits, the rosary, spiritual reading, and other community prayers and devotions. Matins, Lauds, and Vespers of the Office of the Blessed Virgin are recited in Latin on Sundays and holydays.

Training Program: At least one entire year must be spent at the juniorate before the candidate is eligible for the six months of postulancy, which immediately precedes the two-year novitiate. Temporary vows are made at the completion of the novitiate. Profession of perpetual vows is made six years later. The professed sister is given an additional year of preparation during which she deepens and strengthens her own spiritual life and continues by specific instructions her training for the active apostolate.

Qualifications:
* Age: 14 to 25.
* Average intelligence.
* Entrance date: September 8.

Habit: The sisters wear a black habit, veil, and cape, and a white bonnet headband, guimpe, and crucifix.

Write to: Provincial House
41 Ward Street
Paterson 1, New Jersey

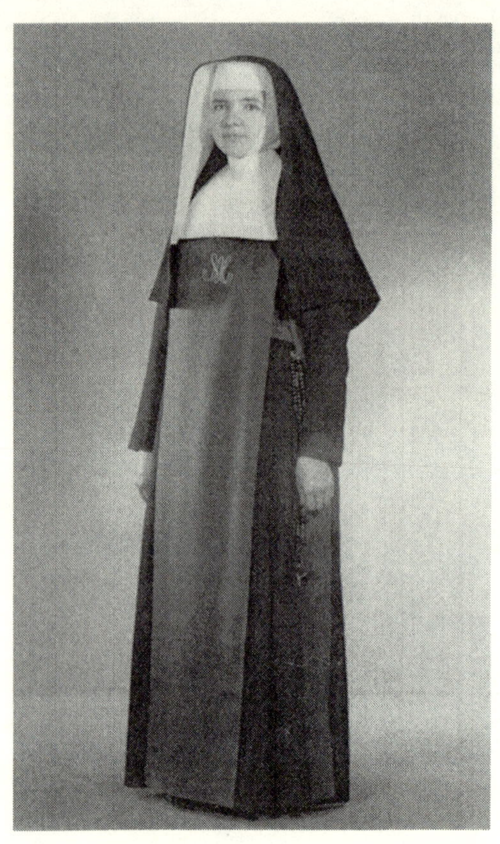

DAUGHTERS OF MARY AND JOSEPH
(D.M.J.)

History: Canon Constant G. Van Crombrugghe founded this congregation in Belgium in 1817. Having established numerous educational institutions in Belgium, the sisters made foundations in England and the United States. At the invitation of Archbishop John J. Cantwell, the sisters settled in California in 1926.

Purpose: In the state of California the sisters teach in parochial elementary and high schools and conduct one retreat center. They also serve as nurses and social workers in the Congo and British West Africa.

Spiritual Life: The religious exercises include Holy Mass, the abridged Divine Office in English, a half-hour of mental prayer, visits to the Blessed Sacrament, rosary, and other community prayers and devotions.

Training Program: The ten-month postulancy is followed by a two-year novitiate. The novices then make their profession of temporary vows. During the juniorate the sisters continue their spiritual formation while taking courses toward their academic degrees.

Qualifications:

* The maximum age is 30.
* Completion of high school.

Habit: The sisters wear a black habit and veil, a blue scapular, and a white headdress and guimpe.

Write to: Daughters of Mary and Joseph
12935 San Vicente Boulevard
Los Angeles 49, California

DAUGHTERS OF
OUR LADY OF MERCY (D.M.)

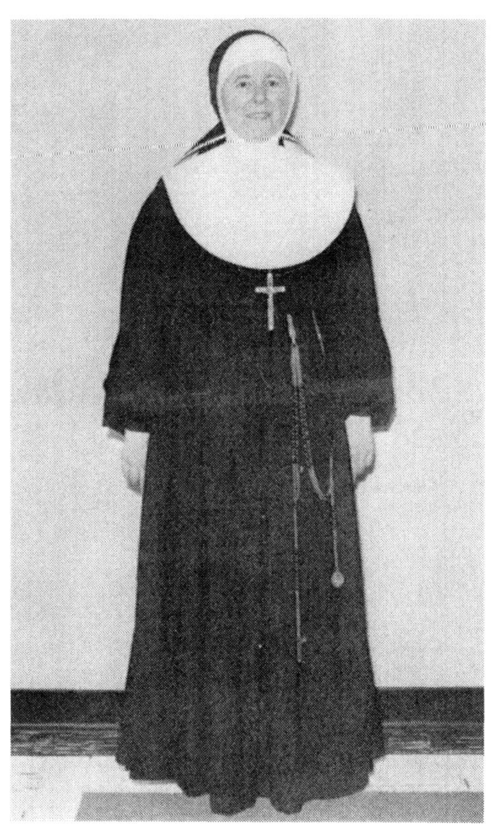

History: Saint Mary Joseph Rossello founded this congregation in northern Italy, August 10, 1837. Bishop De Mari of Savona, Italy, requested the foundress to organize a community of sisters to educate and care for the neglected and abandoned youth of his diocese. The foundress was canonized June 12, 1949. During the lifetime of the saint, the congregation spread throughout northern Italy and missions were opened in South America.

Purpose: The Christian education of youth, especially the poor and the abandoned, is the primary apostolic concern of this community. The sisters teach in elementary and secondary schools and conduct a convalescent hospital and a day nursery. These institutions are located in Massachusetts, upper New York, Pennsylvania, and New Jersey.

Spiritual Life: The religious exercises include Holy Mass, the recitation of the Office of the Blessed Virgin on Sundays and holydays, an hour of mental prayer, the rosary, spiritual reading, and other community prayers and devotions.

Training Program: The congregation conducts an aspirancy for high school girls interested in the religious life. The eight-month postulancy is followed by a two-year novitiate. Temporary vows are made. These are renewed annually for five years after which perpetual vows are pronounced. During the second year of novitiate, the novices continue their education in preparation for the active works of the community.

Qualifications:
* Age: 15 to 30.
* Average intelligence.

Habit: The sisters wear a tailored habit of black serge, a black veil, white guimpe, and a Franciscan rosary.

> *Write to:* Villa Rossello
> Newfield,
> New Jersey

DOMINICAN SISTERS OF ADRIAN, MICHIGAN (O.P.)

History: First established in Prouille, France, in 1206, the Dominican sisters have shared in the glorious apostolate of the Dominican Order for seven centuries. The first four sisters came to New York from the Ratisbon Convent in Bavaria, in 1853. Twenty-five years later, they founded a school in Traverse City and in 1892 established a provincial house at Adrian, Michigan. In 1923 the Adrian community became an independent congregation. It now numbers more than twenty-four hundred members divided into five provinces in the United States.

Purpose: The sisters teach in schools on all levels from kindergarten to university. They also conduct hospitals, catechetical schools, missions, and social service centers throughout the United States and in Latin America.

Spiritual Life: The religious exercises include Holy Mass, the choral rendition of the Office of the Blessed Virgin, the rosary, mental prayer, spiritual reading, and other community prayers and devotions.

Training Program: After spending between eighteen months and two years in the postulancy and simple novitiate, the sisters receive their professional training at their own colleges, Siena Heights in Adrian, and Barry College in Miami, Florida. After graduating they attend various universities in the United States, Latin America, and Europe in order to perfect themselves in their special fields of study. Many of the sisters have achieved national and international recognition for their excellence in many areas of scholarship, especially science and the fine arts.

Qualifications:
* Age: 18 to 30.
* A sincere desire to serve God and save souls.
* Entrance dates: June, September, and February.

Habit: The sisters wear a white tunic, scapular, and cape, and a black veil. A black cloak is worn for travel.

Write to: Mother General
Dominican Motherhouse
Adrian, Michigan

SISTERS OF ST. DOMINIC OF THE IMMACULATE HEART OF MARY (O.P.)

History: This congregation came from Caldwell, New Jersey, in 1887 to found a mission in Ravenna and in 1893 to establish another mission in Akron, Ohio. The members of this community trace their descent to the original convent at Prouille, France, founded by St. Dominic in 1206. The community became a separate independent diocesan congregation with a canonically established novitiate in 1929.

Purpose: The members of this Dominican congregation teach in schools from the pre-school to the college level. They also specialize in music, art, and nursing, and do a great deal of catechetical work on the home missions, work at summer camps, care for the aged, and teach deaf children.

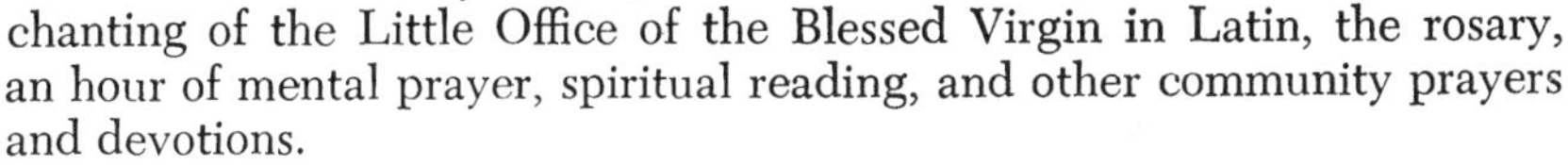

Spiritual Life: The religious exercises include Holy Mass, the chanting of the Little Office of the Blessed Virgin in Latin, the rosary, an hour of mental prayer, spiritual reading, and other community prayers and devotions.

Training Program: The congregation conducts an aspirancy for interested high school girls. The one-year postulancy is followed by a two-year novitiate. The novices then pronounce their temporary vows. During these years of the juniorate, the sisters continue their spiritual formation while taking courses toward the fulfillment of their teaching certificates.

Qualifications:
* Age: 16 to 30.
* Average intelligence.
* Entrance date: August 15.

Habit: The sisters wear the white Dominican habit, collar, and scapular, black veil and belt, and a fifteen decade rosary.

Write to: Our Lady of the Elms Convent
1230 West Market Street
Akron 13, Ohio

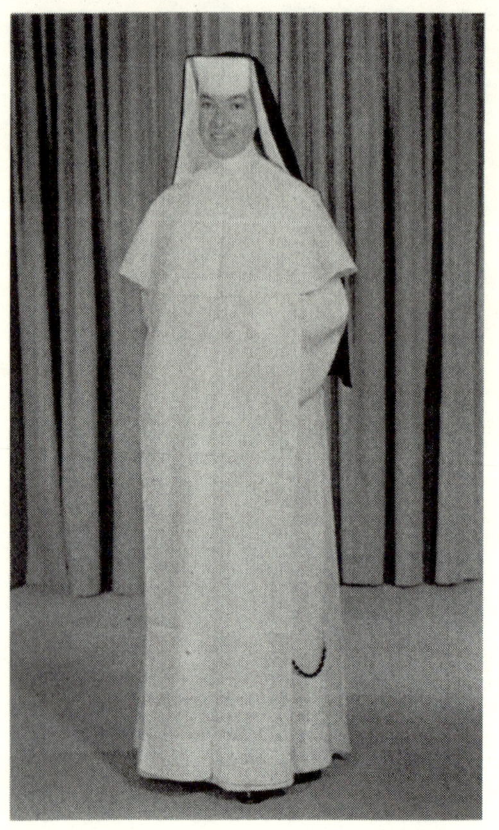

DOMINICAN SISTERS, AMITYVILLE, NEW YORK (O.P.)

History: The first foundation of Dominican sisters was made in Prouille, France, in 1206. Holy Cross Convent, Ratisbon, Germany, was established in 1237. From here four sisters, led by Mother Josepha, came to Most Holy Trinity parish, Brooklyn, New York in 1853. The apostolate, now staffed by sixteen hundred sisters, radiates throughout Long Island, New York, and Puerto Rico.

Purpose: The apostolic works of this congregation include teaching on elementary, secondary, and college levels, nursing in two hospitals in the diocese of Brooklyn, a home for the aged, a dispensary in Puerto Rico, instructing in the nurses' training schools attached to these hospitals, and service in two seminaries, and summer camps.

Spiritual Life: The religious exercises include Holy Mass, forty-five minutes of meditation, a half-hour in the morning and fifteen minutes in the evening, and the chanting in Latin of the Office of the Blessed Virgin in choir. The Blessed Sacrament is exposed daily in the motherhouse.

Training Program: The one-year postulancy is followed by the canonical year of novitiate. First profession of temporary vows brings the novitiate year to a close. The junior professed sister continues her spiritual formation while taking courses toward her academic degree. After three years the sister makes her profession of perpetual vows.

Qualifications:
* Age: 18 to 25. Exceptions are sometimes made.
* Average intelligence.

Habit: The professed sister wears a white habit, a blessed scapular, a black mantle, and a soft black veil lined with white.

Write to: Queen of the Rosary Convent
Amityville, New York

DOMINICAN SISTERS, BLAUVELT, NEW YORK (O.P.)

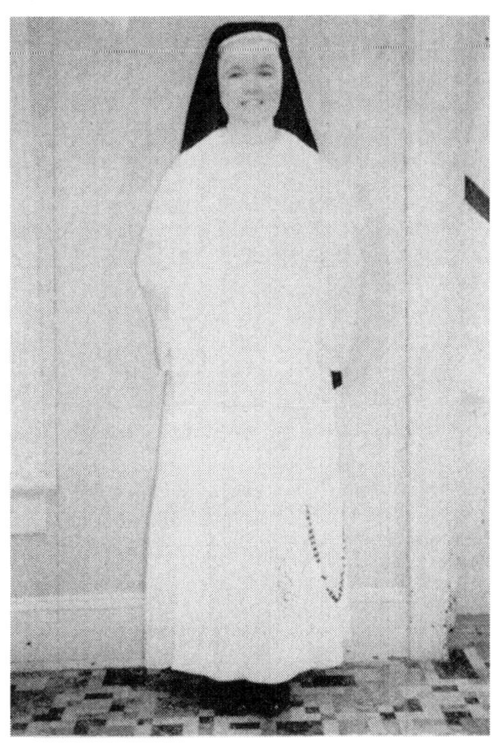

History: The Dominican nuns who were first established in the Convent of the Holy Cross, Ratisbon, Germany, in 1237, founded many branches of the congregation in the United States. Among them was the Convent of St. Dominic, which was founded in 1853 in Blauvelt, New York. Here an orphanage was erected by Mother Mary Ann Sammon.

Purpose: The sisters teach in elementary and secondary schools and care for blind and dependent children. These apostolic works are being carried out in New York, Rhode Island, and Florida. The sisters also conduct a hospital and mission school in Jamaica, West Indies.

Spiritual Life: The religious exercises include Holy Mass, the chanting of the Little Office of the Blessed Virgin in Latin, the rosary, spiritual reading, and other community prayers and devotions.

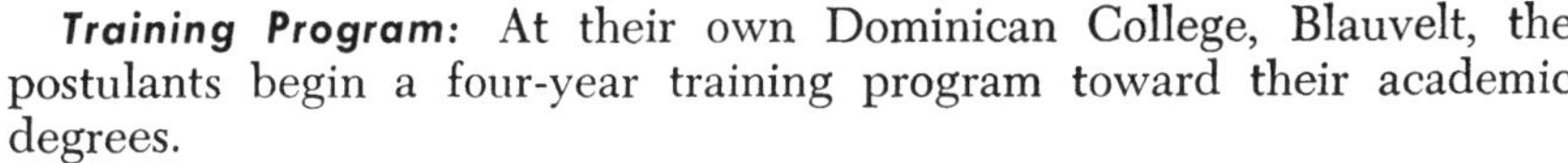

Training Program: At their own Dominican College, Blauvelt, the postulants begin a four-year training program toward their academic degrees.

Qualifications:

* The maximum age is 28.
* Completion of high school.

Habit: The sisters wear a white habit, scapular, a black veil, and a fifteen decade rosary.

> *Write to:* Mother General
> St. Dominic's Convent
> Blauvelt, New York

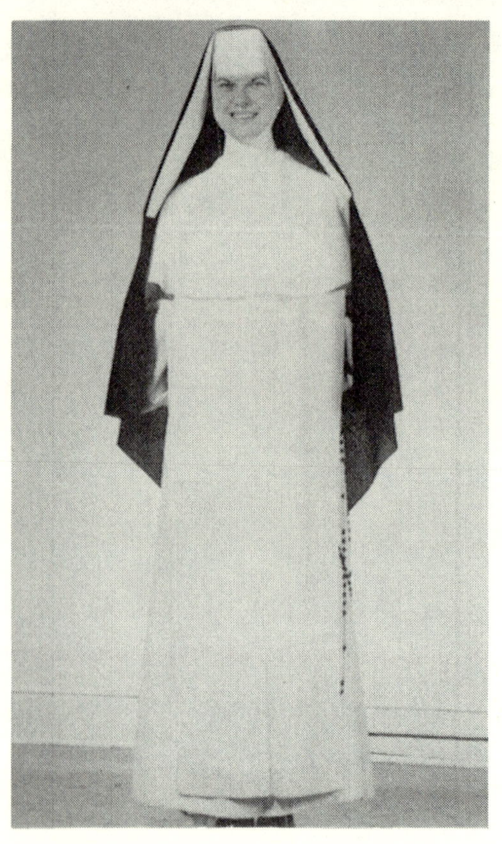

CONGREGATION OF THE SACRED HEART OF JESUS (O.P.)

History: This community traces its origin in the United States from the first American Dominican foundation made in New York City in 1853. In 1872 a pioneer group of sisters was sent to Jersey City, New Jersey, from the New York convent. The immediate beginnings of the present congregation occurred in 1881 when the sisters from Jersey City purchased the motherhouse and novitiate property in Caldwell, New Jersey.

Purpose: Through the Dominican motto, "To contemplate and to give to others the fruit of contemplation," the sisters attain personal sanctification in their work which embraces every level of education from pre-primary classes through college. They are also engaged in nursing and administrative and auxiliary offices, both business and domestic.

Spiritual Life: The religious exercises include Holy Mass, mental prayer, the rosary, spiritual reading, and other community prayers and devotions.

Training Program: The six to twelve-month postulancy is followed by a one-year novitiate. Temporary vows are then made. During the period of the juniorate the sisters continue their spiritual formation while taking courses toward their teaching or nursing degrees.

Qualifications:
* Age: 16 to 30.
* Completion of high school is preferred.

Habit: The sisters wear the traditional white Dominican habit and black veil.

Write to: Mount Saint Dominic
Caldwell,
New Jersey

DOMINICAN SISTERS, EDMONDS, WASHINGTON (O.P.)

History: This congregation traces its origin to a convent established in 1237 at Ratisbon, Germany, by Blessed Jordan. The first American foundation was made in Brooklyn, New York in 1853 and a second in New York City in 1859. At the request of Bishop Egidius Junger of Nisqually in 1890, seven sisters left this convent and established a mission in Aberdeen, Washington. The community, which has papal approbation, became independent in 1923.

Purpose: The sisters staff thirteen schools, conduct numerous catechetical schools, and operate two general hospitals and one nursing home. These institutions are located in Washington, California, and Montana.

Spiritual Life: The religious exercises include Holy Mass, the Office of the Blessed Virgin, a half-hour of meditation, the rosary, spiritual reading, and other community prayers and devotions.

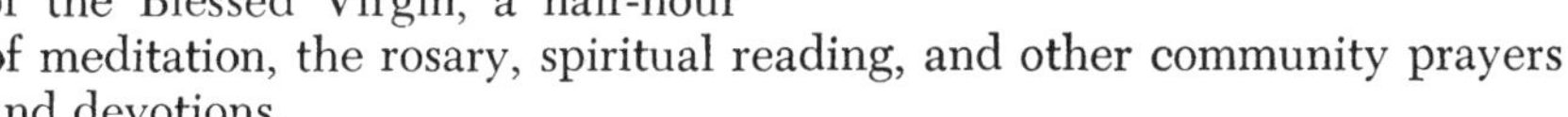
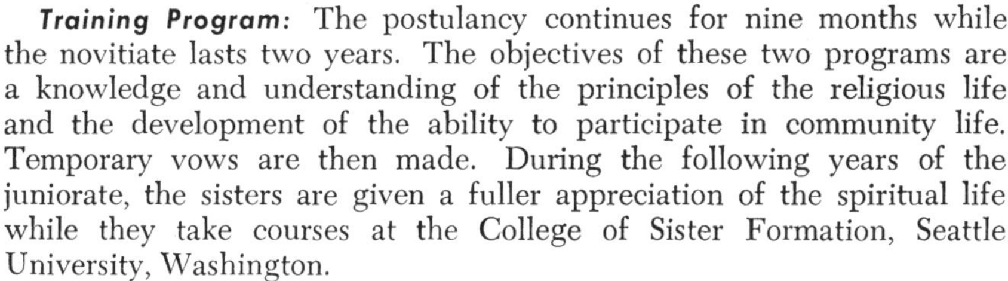

Training Program: The postulancy continues for nine months while the novitiate lasts two years. The objectives of these two programs are a knowledge and understanding of the principles of the religious life and the development of the ability to participate in community life. Temporary vows are then made. During the following years of the juniorate, the sisters are given a fuller appreciation of the spiritual life while they take courses at the College of Sister Formation, Seattle University, Washington.

Qualifications:
* Age: usually under 30. Exceptions are sometimes made.
* Completion of high school.
* Entrance date: August 27.

Habit: The sisters wear a white habit and a black mantle and veil.

Write to: Sisters of St. Dominic
Rosary Heights
P.O. Box 280
Edmonds, Washington

DOMINICAN SISTERS, FALL RIVER, MASSACHUSETTS (O.P.)

History: Mother M. Bertrand Sheridan and two companions founded this community at Fall River, September 4, 1891. By 1922 the congregation had increased sufficiently to be erected as community.

Purpose: The sisters conduct parochial schools and private academies, teach religion through released time programs for pupils in public schools, and take care of nurseries in Massachusetts, New York, and Connecticut.

Spiritual Life: The religious exercises include Holy Mass, the recitation of the Office of the Blessed Virgin in Latin, forty-five minutes of mental prayer, private spiritual reading, the rosary, and other community prayers and devotions.

Training Program: The postulancy ranges from six months to one year. The postulants reside at the novitiate and continue their studies. At the end of this time they receive the habit and begin their novitiate training. The first canonical year is entirely devoted to religious formation. In the second year the novices continue the spiritual training in the Dominican way of life while applying themselves to advanced study. Temporary vows are made for one year. These vows are renewed for two consecutive years, after which time perpetual vows are pronounced.

Qualifications:
* Age: at least 15.
* The completion of high school for a teaching sister or practical aptitudes for manual work as a domestic sister.
* Entrance dates: September 1 and February 2.

Habit: The sisters wear the traditional white Dominican habit, scapular guimpe, black veil, and rosary.

Write to: St. Catherine of Sienna Convent
Park Street
Fall River, Massachusetts

DOMINICAN SISTERS, GREAT BEND, KANSAS (O.P.)

History: This congregation traces its origin to the first community of Dominican Sisters founded by St. Dominic in 1206 at Prouille, France. Thirty-one years later, Blessed Jordan established a foundation at Ratisbon, Germany. Four sisters left this foundation and came to America where they established a foundation in Brooklyn, New York, in 1853. In 1902 upon the invitation of Bishop John J. Hennessy, Wichita, Mother Antonina and six companions established an independent foundation in Great Bend.

Purpose: The members of this pontifical institute teach in elementary schools, staff a high school, a college, a school of nursing, and a field center in logopedics, operate three hospitals, and conduct homes for the aged. These institutions are located in Kansas, Oklahoma, Colorado, and Nebraska. Two missions have been founded in Nigeria, Africa.

Spiritual Life: The religious exercises include Holy Mass, the Office of the Blessed Virgin recited daily in Latin for all Hours except Compline (which is said in English), mental prayer, and the rosary. Vespers and Compline of the Divine Office are sung in Latin on Sundays and holydays.

Training Program: This community conducts an aspirancy for high school girls interested in the religious life. The nine-month postulancy is followed by a two-year novitiate. Temporary vows are then taken for a period of six years. The junior sisters continue their spiritual formation while taking courses toward their academic degrees.

Qualifications:
* Age: 15 to 30. Exceptions are sometimes made.
* At least two years of high school.
* Entrance date: August 30.

Habit: The sisters wear a white tunic, scapular, cape, a black veil, and a fifteen decade rosary.

Write to: Immaculate Conception Convent
3600 Broadway
Great Bend, Kansas

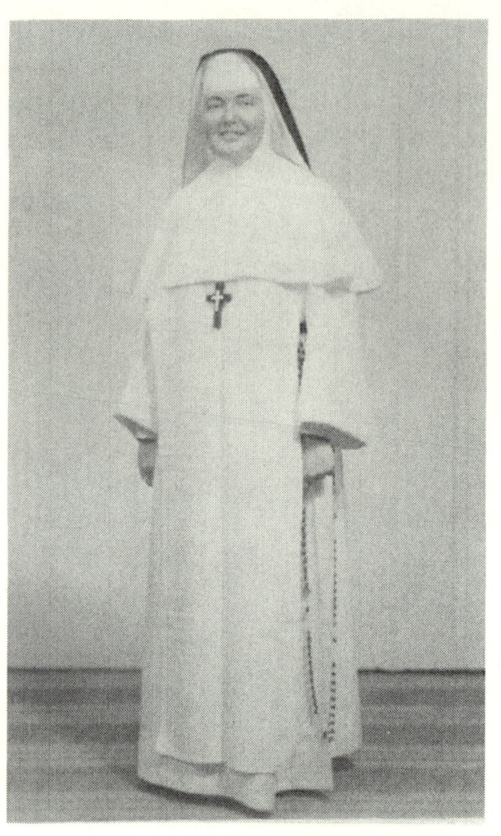

DOMINICAN SISTERS OF ST. CATHERINE OF SIENNA, KENOSHA, WISCONSIN (O.P.)

History: Lady Theresa Catherine Saldanha founded this pontifical institution in 1886 at Lisbon, Portugal. Her first spiritual daughters were trained under the cloistered contemplative nuns of the Dominican Convent of Sienna, Drogheda, Ireland. Although the Irish heritage still remains, the European ties were severed when the American foundation became a distinct congregation in 1952.

Purpose: The two-fold apostolic activities consist in the sanctification of its members and the salvation of souls. The sisters teach in schools, nurse in hospitals, care for the aged, and give catechetical instructions. These institutions and activities are being carried on in the middle and western sections of the United States.

Spiritual Life: The religious exercises include Holy Mass, the recitation of the Divine Office, mental prayer, the rosary, spiritual reading, and other community prayers and devotions.

Training Program: In the six-month postulancy the postulant is introduced to the Dominican way of life. The one-year novitiate follows. After first vows the sister enters the juniorate. Here the religious continues her spiritual formation while pursuing the necessary academic courses for her professional degree. A thorough professional training is strongly encouraged so that the sisters may bring into the apostolate maturity, spirituality, and professional competence.

Qualifications:
* Age: 15 to 30.
* Completion of high school is necessary for those who want to teach or nurse.
* Entrance dates: September 1 and February 1.

Habit: The sisters wear a white habit, scapular, and a black veil. A black and white cross symbolizes the missionary characteristic of their work.

Write to: St. Catherine's Motherhouse
3556 Seventh Avenue
Kenosha, Wisconsin

242

KENTUCKY DOMINICANS (O.P.)

History: This community originated in 1822 when nine girls under the direction of Father Samuel Thomas Wilson, O.P., established the first American foundation of Dominican Sisters in the United States, near Springfield, Kentucky. Mother Angela Sansbury became the first superior. At present, over eight hundred members devote their lives and talents to the ideals of their thirteenth-century founder, St. Dominic.

Purpose: The primary objective of the congregation is the sanctification of its own members and the salvation of souls through the apostolate of teaching, and since 1921, through nursing the sick in hospitals. In thirteen states of the south, the east, the midwest, and in Puerto Rico, the sisters minister to thousands of souls in their many schools ranging from kindergarten to the university level and to countless others in the five hospitals under their supervision.

Spiritual Life: The religious exercises include Holy Mass, the chanting of the Little Office of the Blessed Virgin, the rosary, mental prayer, and other community prayers and devotions.

Training Program: During the eleven-month postulancy, the candidates study the subjects leading to their academic degrees. The canonical year of the novitiate is devoted exclusively to their religious development. After taking first vows, the sisters enter the juniorate where they continue their spiritual formation while resuming their college courses. Profession of perpetual vows is made after five years in temporary vows.

Qualifications:
* The maximum age is 30. Those under 40 are sometimes accepted.
* Completion of high school is preferred.
* Entrance date: September 6.

Habit: The sisters wear a white habit, a black and white veil, a black mantle, and a fifteen decade rosary.

> *Write to:* Motherhouse
> St. Catharine P.O.,
> Kentucky

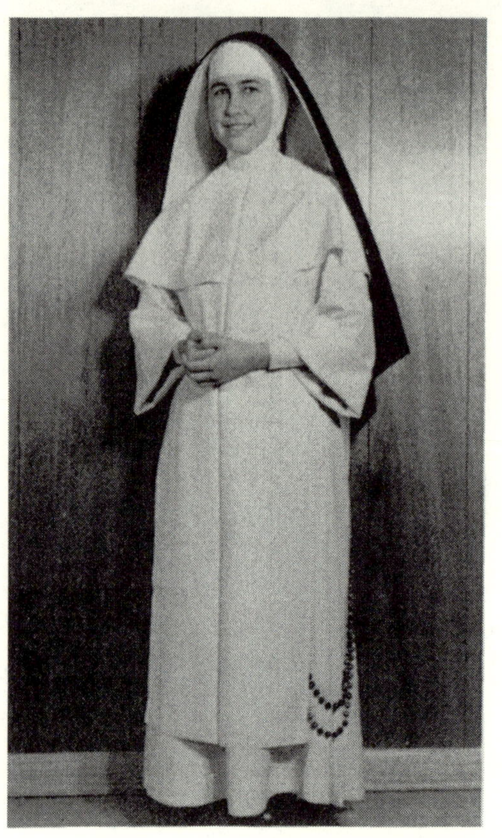

KETTLE FALLS DOMINICANS (O.P.)

History: A pioneer group of twelve Dominican sisters left Speyer, Germany, and came to Carroll College in Montana in 1925. Later, they established the American Province of the Immaculate Heart of Mary with headquarters in Kettle Falls, Washington. The congregation has over one hundred and twenty-five sisters in America, one thousand in Germany, and several missionaries in the Gold Coast African province.

Purpose: The sisters are engaged in education, nursing, and retreat work. They operate grade and high schools and conduct five hospitals in the states of Montana and Washington. They also staff the diocesan retreat house in Spokane, Washington, and the Bishop's residence in Helena, Montana.

Spiritual Life: The religious exercises include Holy Mass, the Little Office of the Blessed Virgin in English, forty-five minutes of mental prayer, the rosary, and spiritual reading.

Training Program: The community conducts an aspirancy for those girls of high school age who are interested in the religious life. The one-year postulancy is followed by a one-year novitiate. Plans are being made to lengthen the novitiate to two years. At the conclusion of this time the novices make their temporary vows. The sisters then continue their religious formation while taking college courses toward their professional degrees.

Qualifications:
* The maximum age is 30. Exceptions are sometimes made.
* Average intelligence.
* Entrance date: August 28.

Habit: The sisters wear the white Dominican habit, black veil, and a fifteen decade rosary.

> *Write to:* Mother Provincial
> Our Lady of the Valley Convent
> Kettle Falls, Washington

DOMINICAN SISTERS
OF MARYWOOD (O.P.)

History: This congregation of Dominicans traces its origin to the historic convent of the Holy Cross in Ratisbon, Germany. In 1853 four sisters answered a missionary call from the United States and established Holy Cross Convent in Brooklyn, New York. A few years later they made a foundation in New York City, from which in 1871, Mother Mary Aquinata Fiegler was chosen to establish the Michigan foundation.

Purpose: The sisters teach from the kindergarten to the college level, nurse in hospitals and a sanitorium, and conduct an orphanage. These institutions are located in Michigan, New Mexico, Texas, and California.

Spiritual Life: The religious exercises include Holy Mass, the chanting of the Office of the Blessed Virgin in Latin, half-hour of mental prayer, the rosary, spiritual reading, and other community prayers and devotions.

Training Program: The community conducts an aspirancy for high school girls interested in the religious life. The six to nine-month postulancy is followed by a one-year novitiate. Temporary vows are made for three years, and renewed for another two years. After five years perpetual vows are pronounced. After first profession the sisters complete the college courses necessary for their professional degrees.

Qualifications:
* Aspirants: a "B" average.
* Postulants: age 16 to 30. Completion of high school.
* Entrance dates: September 8 and January 30.

Habit: The sisters wear a white habit and a black veil and rosary.

Write to: Mother General
2025 East Fulton Street
Grand Rapids 3, Michigan

DOMINICAN SISTERS, OXFORD, MICHIGAN (O.P.)

History: Sister Mary de Sales founded this congregation. In 1923 she gave the holy habit to three young ladies who formed the little pioneer group. In 1927 under the guidance of the Very Reverend Joseph Zaliber of Detroit, Michigan, the first motherhouse was built in Warren, Michigan. It was later moved to Pontiac, Michigan. In 1948 the motherhouse was transferred to Oxford, Michigan.

Purpose: This group of sisters who follow the rule of St. Augustine teach in elementary and secondary schools, conduct their own community college, operate a convalescent home and a hospital, and maintain a retreat house for married and single women. These institutions are located in Pennsylvania, Wisconsin, and Michigan.

Spiritual Life: The religious exercises include Holy Mass, the recitation of the Little Office of the Blessed Virgin in English, a half-hour of mental prayer, the rosary, spiritual reading, and other community prayers and devotions.

Training Program: The sisters conduct an aspirancy for high school girls interested in the religious life. The six to twelve-month postulancy is followed by the novitiate. Temporary vows are then made for either three or five years. Perpetual vows are pronounced at the expiration of this time. During the period of the juniorate the sister completes her college education, which she began in the postulancy year, and enters into the apostolate.

Qualifications:
* The maximum age is 30.
* Average intelligence.
* Entrance dates: August 30 and February 15.

Habit: The sisters wear the traditional cream-colored Dominican habit and black veil.

Write to: St. Joseph Convent
775 West Drahner Road
Oxford, Michigan

246

History: Mother Maria Benedicta Bauer, responding to the missionary spirit of the times, left the mother convent in Ratisbon, Bavaria, and founded the present community at Racine, Wisconsin, in 1862. The congregation carries on its apostolate in twelve dioceses in the midwest and in New Mexico.

Purpose: The sisters teach on the elementary, secondary, and collegiate levels; care for the elderly in homes for the aged, and nurse the sick in a hospital.

Spiritual Life: The religious exercises include Holy Mass, the recitation of the Little Office of the Blessed Virgin in Latin, forty-five minutes of mental prayer, visits to the Blessed Sacrament, rosary, and other community prayers and devotions.

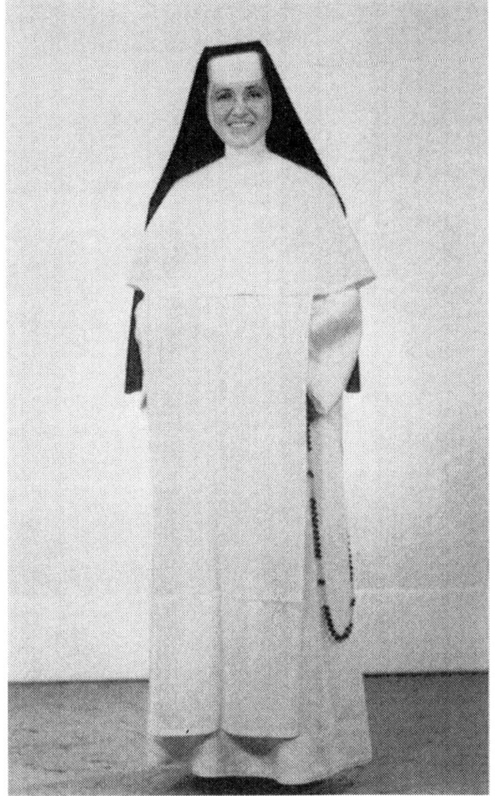

Training Program: The sisters conduct an aspirancy for high school girls interested in the religious life. The one-year postulancy in which the postulants begin or continue their college program is followed by a two-year novitiate. Temporary vows are then made. During the time of temporary profession the sisters continue their spiritual formation while taking courses toward the fulfillment of their professional or nursing degrees. A two-month spiritual rejuvenation is made in preparation for perpetual vows.

Qualifications:

* Age: 16 to 30. Exceptions are sometimes made.
* Completion of high school is required for the postulancy. Non-graduates are accepted into the aspirancy.
* Entrance dates: before the Fall school term.

Habit: The sisters wear a white habit and scapular, a black veil, and a rosary.

Write to: Convent of Saint Catherine
1209 Park Avenue
Racine, Wisconsin

DOMINICAN SISTERS
SAN RAFAEL, CALIFORNIA (O.P.)

History: Mother Mary Goemare, the foundress of this group of Dominicans, came to Monterey, California, in 1850 from the Convent of the Cross in Paris, France, in answer to an appeal by the Most Rev. Joseph S. Alemany, O.P., the first bishop of California. In 1889 the motherhouse was moved to San Rafael where in 1918 their own Dominican College was opened.

Purpose: The work of the sisters is teaching on the elementary, secondary, and college levels and nursing in the two large hospitals maintained by the congregation. All of the foundations are located in California and Nevada. For those not interested in teaching or nursing, there are opportunities for administration, office, library, and other work.

Spiritual Life: Community Mass, the Divine Office said in Latin according to the Dominican Rite, with sung Compline, the rosary said in common (there are no other vocal prayers), forty-five minutes of mental prayer and at least fifteen minutes of spiritual reading constitute the spiritual exercises.

Training Program: The six-month postulancy is followed by a one-year novitiate. Temporary vows are then made. During the juniorate years, the professed sister continues to work for her degree while attending special classes in theology and religion.

Qualifications:
* Age: usually under 30. Exceptions are sometimes made.
* Completion of high school.
* Entrance dates: late July or January.

Habit: The habit consists of a white tunic, scapular and cape, a black mantle and veil, and a white bandeau and wimple.

Write to: Mother General
Dominican Convent
San Rafael, California

DOMINICAN SISTERS
SINSINAWA, WISCONSIN (O.P.)

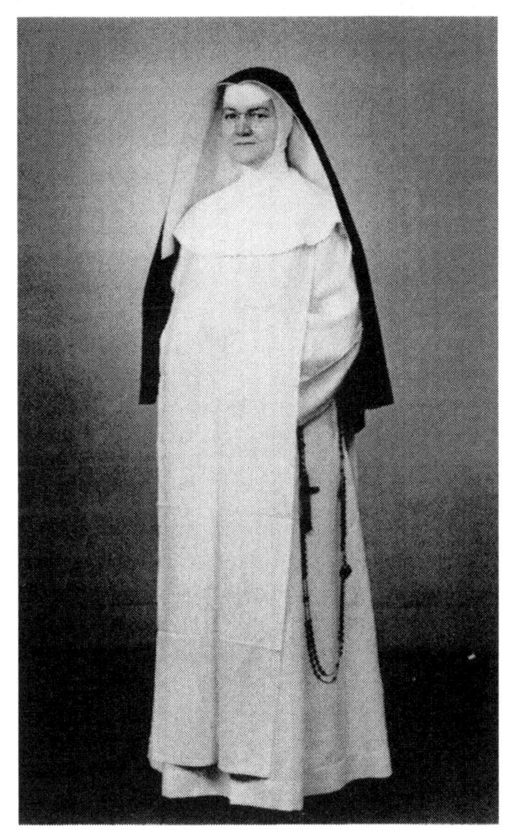

History: The American congregation of the Most Holy Rosary was
founded by the Very Reverend
Samuel C. Mazzuchelli, O.P., at
Sinsinawa, Wisconsin, on August
15, 1849, when four American girls
made their first profession. Since
then it has continued to expand in
numbers and to widen the scope of
its apostolic activities. This congregation which now numbers
nearly two thousand members became a pontifical institute in 1888.

Purpose: This Dominican community is primarily engaged in
teaching. It conducts Rosary College, River Forest, Illinois, with a
European branch in Fribourg,
Switzerland, Edgewood College of
the Sacred Heart, Madison, Wisconsin, and a Graduate School of
Fine Arts in Florence, Italy. It has
foreign missions in Santa Cruz, and
Cochabamba, Bolivia.

Spiritual Life: The religious ex-
ercises include Holy Mass, the choral Office of the Blessed Virgin in
Latin, two periods of mental prayer, the rosary, and other community
prayers and devotions.

Training Program: The one-year postulancy is followed by a one-year
novitiate. Temporary vows are made for three years and are then renewed for second three year period, after which perpetual vows are
made. Studies on the undergraduate, graduate, and post-graduate levels
are undertaken to qualify for the educational apostolate. Sisters preparing for perpetual vows, and those professed ten years undergo a
period of spiritual preparation at the motherhouse.

Qualifications:
    * Age: 16 to 30. Exceptions will sometimes be made.
    * Average intelligence.
    * Entrance date: September 8.

Habit: The sisters wear a white tunic and scapular, a black veil and
mantle, and a fifteen decade rosary.

> *Write to:* Mother General
> Dominican Motherhouse
> Sinsinawa, Wisconsin

SPRINGFIELD DOMINICANS (O.P.)

History: The Springfield Dominicans came to Illinois in 1873 from St. Catherine's, Kentucky. Six sisters of the original group staffed a school in Jacksonville, Illinois, where two years later a novitiate was established. After twenty years the community moved its motherhouse and novitiate to Springfield, Illinois. The congregation which now numbers almost six hundred members became a pontifical institute in 1929.

Purpose: The sisters teach in elementary and secondary schools and colleges, conduct hospitals and homes for the aged, care for dependent children, and are engaged in catechetical work. The works of the community are carried out in Illinois, Colorado, Michigan, Texas, California, Arkansas, Mississippi, and Minnesota.

Spiritual Life: The religious exercises include Holy Mass, the chanting of the Little Office of the Blessed Virgin, a half-hour of mental prayer, the rosary, spiritual reading, and other community prayers and devotions.

Training Program: After a candidacy of three months, the aspirant is admitted into the one-year postulancy. This is followed by a one-year novitiate. Temporary vows are made for three years after which perpetual vows are pronounced. After first profession of vows the sisters complete the courses toward their professional degrees which they began during their year of postulancy.

Qualifications:
* Age: 16 to 30. Exceptions are sometimes made.
* Completion of high school.
* Entrance date: last Sunday in August.

Habit: The sisters wear the white and black of St. Dominic, symbolic of innocence and penance.

Write to: Sacred Heart Convent
1237 West Monroe Street
Springfield, Illinois

DOMINICAN SISTERS, TACOMA, WASHINGTON (O.P.)

History: The convent of the Holy Cross, Ratisbon, Bavaria, was founded in 1237. Four sisters left this convent for the United States where they founded a convent in 1853 in Brooklyn, New York. The Tacoma Dominican convent was established from the Brooklyn foundation in Pomeroy, Washington in 1888 by three Dominican sisters. The motherhouse was transferred to its present site in 1921.

Purpose: The sisters conduct a boys' military academy in Tacoma and teach in parochial elementary and secondary schools, in Confraternity of Christian Doctrine classes throughout the year, and in religious vacation schools during the summer. These apostolic activities are carried on in the states of Washington and California.

Spiritual Life: The religious exercises include Holy Mass, the chanting in Latin of the Little Office of the Blessed Virgin, mental prayer, recitation of the rosary, spiritual reading, and other commuunity prayers and devotions.

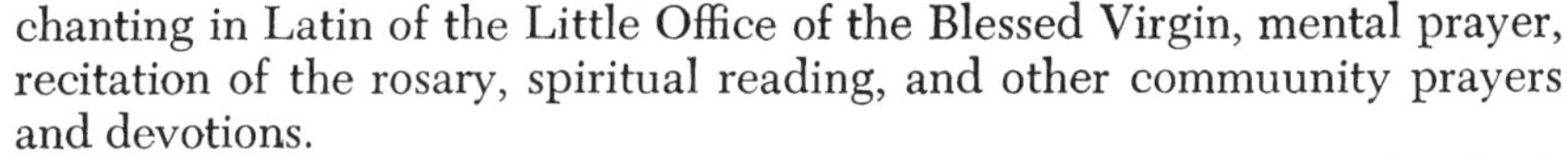

Training Program: The community operates an aspirancy for high school girls interested in becoming Dominican sisters. During the ten-month postulancy, the candidates begin or continue their college training after which they take the habit and enter the canonical year of novitiate. In the second year the novices resume their college studies and take temporary vows at the end of this year. The junior sisters continue their spiritual and intellectual training at the College of Sister Formation, Providence Heights, a special college within Seattle University. After two years of active participation in the apostolate of teaching, the junior sisters pronounce their perpetual vows.

Qualifications:
* The maximum age is 30.
* Completion of high school.
* Entrance date: September 8.

Habit: The sisters wear a white tunic and scapular, a black veil, mantle, and leather belt from which is suspended a fifteen-decade rosary.

Write to: Prioress General
423 East 152nd Street
Tacoma 44, Washington

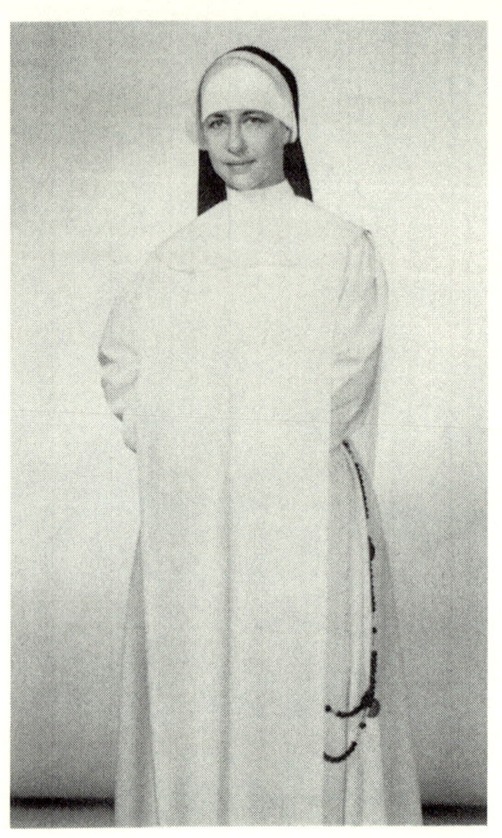

DOMINICAN SISTERS OF CHARITY OF THE PRESENTATION OF TOURS (O.P.)

History: Marie Poussepin founded this congregation in Sainville, France, in 1696. She was an outstanding figure of the French seventeenth century, a pioneer in social improvement, and an apostle burning with zeal for the glory of God. More than five thousand sisters serve the Church in nine provinces located in Europe, Iraq, and North and South America.

Purpose: The members of this congregation are engaged in teaching, nursing, parish, and social work. They also have missions in South America, Iraq, and Africa.

Spiritual Life: The religious spirit of the members of this community is centered around charity. The sisters are taught a life of prayer and the practice of the evangelical virtues through the observance of their vows and rule. The religious exercises include devotions to Mary, mental prayer, recollections, and spiritual reading, fostering a family-like community.

Qualifications:
* Age: 16 to 35.
* Completion of high school is preferred.
* Entrance date: October 2.

Habit: The sisters wear the traditional white Dominican habit.

> *Write to:* Presentation Novitiate
> 3012 Elm Street
> Dighton, Massachusetts

FELICIAN SISTERS (C.S.S.F.)

History: Mother Mary Angela Truszkowska founded this congregation in Warsaw, Poland, in 1855. The sisters follow the rule of the Third Order Regular of St. Francis under the patronage of St. Felix of Cantalice. These sisters came to the United States at the request of Father Joseph Dabrowski, a pastor in Polonia, Wisconsin, in 1874. Over 4,800 sisters are found in Europe, Canada, South America, and the United States.

Purpose: In the United States the Felicians teach on all levels from kindergarten to college, including retarded children and the deaf, nurse in hospitals and in homes for the aged, care for children in institutions, and perform other social work. The institutions of the seven provinces in this country are located in the northwest, midwest, and southwest. They also have missions in Brazil.

Spiritual Life: The religious exercises include Holy Mass, exposition of the Blessed Sacrament in the provincial houses with visits and half-hour adorations, a minimum of forty-five minutes of mental prayer, the rosary, spiritual reading, the Little Office of the Blessed Virgin in Latin, and other community prayers and devotions.

Training Program: Each province conducts an aspirancy for girls of high school age. The twelve-month postulancy is followed by a one-year novitiate. Temporary vows are made for six years, after which final vows are pronounced. A six-week tertianship after the completion of fourteen years of religious life deepens the spirit of the community and enkindles spiritual fervor. Each province has its own college where the postulants and newly-professed attend teacher training courses.

Qualifications:
* Age: 15 to 30.
* Completion of high school preferred.

Habit: The sisters wear a brown habit, scapular, and mantle, the Franciscan Chaplet suspended from a white cord, a black veil, a small wooden crucifix suspended from the neck, and a profession ring.

See page 382 for address of nearest provincial house.

ALLEGHANY FRANCISCANS (O.S.F.)

History: Father Pamphilo da Magliano, O.F.M., founded this congregation in 1859 for the purpose of teaching the children of his mission area in western New York State.

Purpose: Today in the United States this Franciscan congregation conducts elementary and secondary schools, three colleges, six schools of nursing, thirteen hospitals, six homes for the aged, and one home for working girls. These institutions are located in Massachusetts, Connecticut, New York, New Jersey, Florida, Alabama, Mississippi, Indiana, Pennsylvania, Rhode Island, North Carolina, Virginia, Georgia, and Minnesota. They have missions in the West Indies and Brazil.

Spiritual Life: The religious exercises which are said in common include the Little Office of the Blessed Virgin and the Crown of the Seven Joys of Our Lady. Three-quarters of an hour daily is devoted to mental prayer, and twenty minutes is devoted to spiritual reading, except Fridays when the stations of the cross are made.

Training Program: The postulancy of ten months is followed by one year of novitiate. The junior professed remain at the motherhouse an additional year for further spiritual formation and apostolic training. The sisters make simple, temporary vows annually for six years. Perpetual vows are then made.

Qualifications:

* Age: the maximum age is 30. Exceptions are sometimes made.
* Completion of high school.
* Entrance dates: September 8.

Habit: The sisters wear a brown habit, a black veil, a white cord, headband, and guimpe, and a seven decade rosary. The hospital sisters and those working in the missions wear white.

Write to: St. Elizabeth Motherhouse
Alleghany,
New York

SISTERS OF THE THIRD ORDER OF ST. FRANCIS OF THE IMMACULATE CONCEPTION OF THE BVM (O.S.F.)

History: A community without a foundress! Five volunteers in 1866 answered the prayer of Gethsemani's Dom Benedict Burger for sisters to teach in the Kentucky Abbey School for Girls. After a Franciscan novitiate under Mother Antonia at Oldenburg, Indiana, the sisters began an independent community in the newly built Mt. Olivet motherhouse adjacent to the abbey grounds. In 1873 their odyssey began: Mt. Olivet to Shelbyville, Kentucky; Shelbyville, to Dubuque, Iowa; Dubuque to Anamosa to Clinton, Iowa.

Purpose: The chief works of the apostolate are teaching, nursing, caring for the aged, and foreign missions. The teaching level ranges from kindergarten through college. A clinic in Clinton provides training for children with speech and hearing handicaps. Schools are located in California, Kentucky, Illinois, Iowa, Missouri, Nebraska, and Grand Bahama, British West Indies.

Spiritual Life: The religious exercises include Holy Mass, the recitation of the Divine Office in English, half-hour of mental prayer, the rosary, spiritual reading, and other community prayers and devotions.

Training Program: The ten-month postulancy is followed by the two-year novitiate. Temporary profession is then made. Following the sister-formation program, the sisters complete the requirements for their degrees before being assigned to the active apostolate.

Qualifications:
* Age: 16 to 30. Exceptions are sometimes made for those under 35.
* Completion of high school.
* Entrance date: September 8.

Habit: The sisters wear a black habit, white coif, brow band and coronet, a rosary which hangs from a white cincture, and a silver crucifix.

> *Write to:* Mount Clare Convent
> North Bluff Boulevard and Springdale Drive
> Clinton, Iowa

FRANCISCAN CAPUCHIN SISTERS OF THE INFANT JESUS (O. Cap.)

History: The Capuchin Sisters of the Infant Jesus are affiliated with the Order Friars Minor Capuchin in Rome. In 1922 they opened their first day nursery in Holy Rosary Parish in Jersey City, New Jersey, followed by another in 1925 in Our Lady of Pompeii Parish, Paterson, New Jersey. The sisters began their first endeavor in social work in 1926 in Passaic, New Jersey. In 1930 St. Francis Convent and mother-house were founded on a hundred and thirty acre plot of land in the beautiful Ramapo Hills of New Jersey. Situated here also is a boarding elementary school, a high school, and a summer camp for girls. Since 1930 the sisters have opened numerous schools and centers of catechetical and social work in the states of New Jersey and New York.

Purpose: In fulfilling the primary aim of personal sanctification of the individual members, the sisters devote their energies to the promotion of the spiritual and temporal welfare of mankind by teaching in parish and private elementary and high schools, and by visiting the poor and the sick in their homes.

Qualifications:
* Age: 15 to 30.
* Completion of high school is preferred.

Habit: The sisters wear a brown habit with a scapular completely covering the front and back. For street wear, a full black mantle open in the front with a white collar is worn over the habit and scapular.

Write to: Mt. Saint Francis
R.F.D. 1
Wanaque, New Jersey

FRANCISCAN SISTERS OF BLESSED KUNEGUNDA (O.S.F.K.)

History: Mother Mary Theresa Dudsik and Mother Mary Anna Wisinski founded this congregation in 1894 in Chicago, Illinois. Numbering four hundred members this community has institutions in Illinois, Nebraska, Ohio, Pennsylvania, and South Dakota. It received papal approbation in 1939.

Purpose: This community conducts elementary schools, a girls' high school, a school of nursing, three hospitals, a day nursery, catechetical centers, homes of the aged, and homes for working girls. They also take care of the bookkeeping and domestic departments at Father Flanagan's Boys' home.

Spiritual Life: The religious exercises consist of Holy Mass, thirty minutes of mental prayer, recitation of the Office of the Blessed Virgin in Latin, visits to the Blessed Sacrament, stations of the cross, rosary, and other community prayers.

Training Program: The congregation conducts an aspirancy for high school girls interested in the religious life. The six to twelve-month postulancy is followed by a two-year novitiate. Temporary vows are made for one year. These vows are renewed for five consecutive years after which perpetual vows are professed. During these years, the sisters continue their spiritual formation while taking courses toward the fulfillment of their professional and nursing degrees.

Qualifications:
* Age: 14 to 30. Exceptions are sometimes made.
* Average intelligence.
* Entrance dates: February 2 and the last Sunday in August.

Habit: The professed sisters wear a brown habit, white guimpe, black veil, a white cincture, crucifix, and a rosary.

> *Write to:* Mother General
> 2649 North Hamlin Avenue
> Chicago 47, Illinois

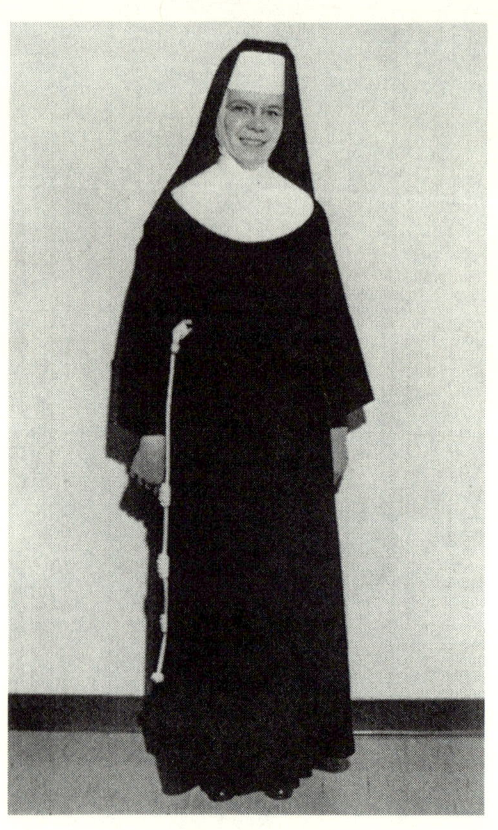

FRANCISCAN SISTERS OF CHRISTIAN CHARITY (O.S.F.)

History: The community had its beginning in 1866 when Teresa Gramlich and three other young women began to teach religion at Clarks Mills, Wisconsin, in the parish of Father Joseph Fessler. By mutual consent they spent the next year in religious training at the novitiate of the School Sisters of Notre Dame, Milwaukee, Wisconsin. On November 9, 1869, they formally established a new religious congregation at Manitowoc, Wisconsin. This pontifical congregation now numbers over one thousand members.

Purpose: The sisters carry on active apostolate in classrooms, hospitals, training schools for nurses and musicians, and in homes for the aged. To meet the growing needs of the Church, the community has extended its activities beyond Wisconsin to Michigan, Ohio, Illinois, West Virginia, District of Columbia, Arizona, Iowa, California, Nebraska, and Hawaii.

Spiritual Life: The religious exercises include Holy Mass, the Little Office of the Blessed Virgin in Latin, two periods of mental prayer, the rosary, and other community prayers and devotions.

Training Program: The community conducts an aspirancy for teen-age girls interested in the religious life. As postulants they devote one year to spiritual and scholastic training at Holy Family College while preparing themselves for the novitiate. The sisters make simple vows annually for five years and then vows for life. During this time their professional training is continued.

Qualifications:
* Age: not over **30**.
* Completion of high school.
* Entrance dates: late August and early September.

Habit: The sisters wear a black habit, scapular, and veil, a white collar, coif, and wimple, a Franciscan rosary, and a cincture.

> *Write to:* Holy Family Convent
> Route 1
> Manitowoc, Wisconsin

FRANCISCAN SISTERS OF ST. ELIZABETH (F.S.S.E.)

History: Venerable Father Louis of Casoria, O.F.M., founded this pontifical institute in Naples, Italy, in 1862 to aid him in his work of mercy and charity. Father Louis was declared Venerable in 1907. With the aid of Margaret Salatino, he established the congregation and placed it under the protection of St. Elizabeth of Hungary. In 1919 a small group of sisters arrived in the United States and settled in Holy Rosary Parish, Newark, New Jersey, where they opened an orphanage.

Purpose: The sisters promote the works of charity among women and girls by conducting schools, orphanages, day nurseries, homes for the poor, the aged, and the physically handicapped, besides imparting catechetical instructions on various levels. The community is represented in New Jersey, New York, Pennsylvania, Indiana, and the Republic of Panama.

Spiritual Life: The religious exercises include Holy Mass, the recitation of the Office of the Dead in Latin, mental prayer, the rosary, spiritual reading, and other community prayers and devotions.

Training Program: The six-month postulancy is followed by a two-year novitiate. Temporary vows are made. These are renewed annually for five years after which perpetual vows are pronounced. After first profession, the sisters continue their spiritual formation while resuming academic training for the active apostolate.

Qualifications:
* Age: 16 to 30. Exceptions are sometimes made.
* Average intelligence.

Habit: The sisters wear a simple ash-colored habit, a black veil, a white wimple, head band, and cord, and a Franciscan Crown rosary.

> *Write to:* Mother Superior
> 185 Parkhurst Street
> Newark 14, New Jersey
>
> St. Francis of Assisi Novitiate
> R.R. 4 Box 156
> Logansport, Indiana

FRANCISCAN SISTERS OF THE IMMACULATE CONCEPTION AND ST. JOSEPH FOR THE DYING (O.S.F.)

History: Father Hugolinus Joseph Storff, O.F.M., founded this congregation in Monterey, California, in 1919. He desired to establish a community whose members would dedicate their whole life and activities for the salvation of poor dying sinners.

Purpose: In imitation of the Divine Master, the sisters combine prayer and the active life in the classroom with the care of children, the convalescent and the aged, give catechetical instructions, and are engaged in domestic occupations.

Spiritual Life: The religious exercises include conventual Mass, two half-hour periods of meditation, the recitation in English of the Little Hours from the Franciscan Short Breviary, the rosary, prayers to St. Joseph for the dying, spiritual reading, and other community prayers and devotions.

Training Program: The six-month postulancy is followed by a one-year novitiate. Profession of perpetual vows is made after three years as junior professed. During this time the religious pursue courses toward their academic degrees.

Qualifications:
* Age: 17 to 30. Exceptions are sometimes made.
* Completion of high school is preferred.
* Entrance date: before January 1.

Habit: The professed sisters wear a brown habit and cape, a white cincture, coif, frontpiece and guimpe, a black veil and mantle, crucifix, and a silver ring.

> *Write to:* St. Joseph Convent
> Monterey,
> California

FRANCISCAN SISTERS OF ST. JOSEPH
(F.S.S.J.)

History: Mother M. Colette Hilbert and Father Hyacinth Fudzinski, O.F.M., founded this community in Trenton, New Jersey, in 1897. The first motherhouse, which was opened in 1898 in Buffalo, was later moved to Hamburg, New York. The sisters are working in four archdioceses and twelve dioceses from Massachusetts to Michigan and from Wisconsin to Alabama.

Purpose: The sisters teach in elementary, secondary, and professional schools, nurse the sick in hospitals and in convalescent homes, care for the aged, work among the colored in home missions, and are engaged in giving catechetical instructions.

Spiritual Life: The religious exercises include Holy Mass, the recitation of the Office of the Blessed Virgin in Latin, spiritual reading, the rosary, and other community prayers and devotions.

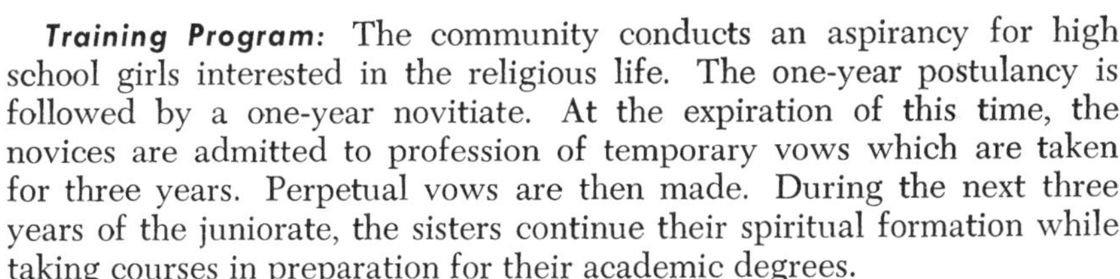

Training Program: The community conducts an aspirancy for high school girls interested in the religious life. The one-year postulancy is followed by a one-year novitiate. At the expiration of this time, the novices are admitted to profession of temporary vows which are taken for three years. Perpetual vows are then made. During the next three years of the juniorate, the sisters continue their spiritual formation while taking courses in preparation for their academic degrees.

Qualifications:
* Age: 16 to 30.
* Completion of high school is necessary for entrance into the postulancy.
* Entrance dates: August 22 and January 6.

Habit: The sisters wear a black habit and veil, a white cincture, coif, band, and round collar, Franciscan rosary, and a crucifix.

> *Write to:* Mother General
> Immaculate Conception Convent
> 5286 South Park Avenue
> Hamburg, New York

FRANCISCAN SISTERS OF OUR LADY OF PERPETUAL HELP (O.S.F.)

History: Mother M. Solanda Leczna, Mother M. Ernestine Matz, and Mother M. Hilaria Matz, members of the Joliet Francisans founded this congregation in St. Louis, Missouri, in 1901. Directed by the Archbishop of St. Louis, John J. Kain, and Father Urban Stanowski the sisters answered the needs of immigrants settling the Mississippi Valley at the turn of the century.

Purpose: Teaching in elementary and high schools, caring for the aged, and sick, giving special education and catechetical classes in mission schools among the Negro and Navajo, domestic work, and caring for altars are among the apostolic activities of the members of this community.

Spiritual Life: The religious exercises include the recitation of the Divine Office in English, a half-hour of meditation, and short community prayers. The Franciscan Crown rosary and the Way of the Cross are private devotions.

Training Program: The congregation maintains a four year high school for aspirants. In the postulancy of six months to one year, the postulant is orientated to the Franciscan way of life. This is followed by a two-year novitiate. In the first year the novice concentrates on her spiritual perfection, the knowledge of the vows, and the practice of virtue. The second-year novice, in addition to continuing her spiritual development, pursues a liberal arts program designed to prepare her for the apostolate. She pronounces her temporary vows at the end of the second year of novitiate.

Qualifications:
* The maximum age is 30. Occasionally candidates up to the age of 40 will be accepted.
* Completion of high school or equivalent.
* Entrance dates: July 6 and February 6.

Habit: The sisters wear a brown habit and scapular, a white cincture from which a Franciscan rosary is suspended, a small white collar, and a black veil.

Write to: Villa St. Joseph
201 Brotherton Lane
St. Louis (Ferguson) 35, Missouri

FRANCISCAN SISTERS OF PERPETUAL ADORATION (F.S.P.A.)

History: This congregation originated in Milwaukee, Wisconsin, in 1849 with a group of Franciscan Tertiaries who had emigrated from Bavaria. Solemn perpetual adoration of the Blessed Sacrament introduced in the motherhouse in 1878 gives the community its title. The more than 1,100 members are located throughout the United States and on the island of Guam.

Purpose: The sisters conduct schools on the elementary, secondary, and college levels, nurse the sick, the infirm, and the aged in hospitals, maintain homes for the aged, care for wayward and emotionally disturbed children, and labor in the home and foreign mission field.

Spiritual Life: The religious exercises include Holy Mass, the recitation of the short breviary in English, a half-hour of adoration before the Blessed Sacrament, the rosary, spiritual reading, and other community prayers and devotions.

Training Program: The community conducts an aspirancy for high school girls interested in the religious life. The six-month postulancy is followed by a two-year novitiate. At the expiration of the novitiate, the novice makes her temporary profession of vows. During the following years of the juniorate, the sister continues her spiritual formation while taking courses toward her academic or nursing degree.

Qualifications:
* Age: 14 to 30. Exceptions are sometimes made.
* Completion of high school is necessary for entrance into the postulancy.
* Entrance date: first week in September.

Habit: The sisters wear a black habit and veil, a white coif, guimpe, and cord, and a gold ring.

Write to: St. Rose Convent
912 Market Street
La Crosse, Wisconsin

SCHOOL SISTERS OF ST. FRANCIS (O.S.F.)

History: Mother Alexia, Mother Alfons, and Sister Clara founded this congregation in 1874 at Campbellsport, Wisconsin. In 1887 the Generalate was transferred to Milwaukee, Wisconsin. This pontifical institute, which is divided into two provinces, now numbers over twenty-six hundred professed sisters.

Purpose: Education is the principal activity. The sisters staff over two hundred educational institutions including a liberal arts college in Milwaukee, St. Clare College in Costa Rica, and secondary and elementary schools. They also own and staff a sanitarium, a hospital for psychiatric patients, and three general hospitals. These institutions are located in Central America, Colorado, Illinois, Indiana, Iowa, Michigan, Minnesota, Mississippi, Missouri, Montana, Nebraska, New York, South Dakota, and Wisconsin.

Spiritual Life: The religious exercises include Holy Mass, the short breviary in English, a half-hour of mental prayer, the rosary, spiritual reading, and other community prayers and devotions.

Training Program: The one-year postulancy is devoted to community orientation and academic studies at Alverno College in Milwaukee. After taking the habit the sisters enter the canonical year of novitiate where they study the Franciscan rule and the basic concepts of the religious life. During the second novitiate year the sisters resume their college work. The time of juniorate is devoted to the completion of the college requirements necessary for their professional degrees and in learning the needs of the apostolate.

Qualifications:
* Age: 17 to 30.
* Completion of high school.
* Entrance dates: August 17 and 18.

Habit: The sisters wear a black habit, veil, scapular and crucifix, a white cincture, headband, coif and collar, and a rosary.

See page 383 for address of nearest provincial house.

SCHOOL SISTERS OF ST. FRANCIS (O.S.F.)

History: In 1723, Mother Mary Hyacintha, the foundress, and a few other women who were living according to the Rule of the Third Order of St. Francis, were organized specifically for the purpose of teaching and educating the girls of the poor salt miners at Hallein, Salzburg, Austria. The first foundation was made in the United States in 1931.

Purpose: The apostolic activities include the teaching and guidance of youth in schools and orphanages and the care of the aged. The institutions are located in the diocese of Amarillo, Texas.

Spiritual Life: The religious exercises include Holy Mass, mental prayer, the rosary, spiritual reading and other community prayers and devotions.

Training Program: The six-month postulancy is followed by a two-year novitiate. Temporary vows are then made for five or six years. Perpetual vows are pronounced at the end of this time.

Qualifications:
* The maximum age is 30.
* Applicants need not have completed high school.

Habit: The sisters wear a black habit, scapular, and veil, a white head band, coif, and cord, and a rosary.

Write to: Sancta Maria Convent
Panhandle,
Texas

SCHOOL SISTERS OF ST. FRANCIS
(O.S.F.)

History: This congregation has been active in the United States since 1922. It was founded by a parish priest, Father Sebastian Schwarz of Voecklabruck, Austria, who, alarmed by the effects of the Industrial Revolution on the home, formed a community of sisters to care for pre-school children exposed to the dangers of the street. Papal approval was granted in 1928.

Purpose: Called School Sisters because their first service was the caring for children in nurseries, kindergartens, and elementary schools, the community soon added other apostolic works. The American province conducts schools in Missouri and Iowa, a hospital in Marceline, and a retirement home in Savannah, Missouri.

Spiritual Life: The religious exercises include daily Mass, the recitation of the Divine Office in English, forty-five minutes devoted to mental prayer, which includes the formal half-hour of meditation, stations of the cross, the rosary, and spiritual reading.

Training Program: The community operates an aspirancy for teen-age girls interested in the religious life. The six to twelve-month postulancy is followed by a twelve to eighteen-month novitiate. This time is devoted almost exclusively to the spiritual training of the novice. After she takes her temporary vows, the sister continues her spiritual formation while taking courses toward her professional degree. Profession of perpetual vows is made about five years after the taking of temporary vows.

Qualifications:
* Age: 17 to 30. Exceptions are sometimes made.
* Average intelligence.
* Entrance date: September.

Habit: The sisters wear the traditional black and white habit with a white Franciscan cord.

Write to: Mother Provincial
School Sisters of St. Francis
La Verna Heights
Savannah, Missouri

SCHOOL SISTERS OF ST. FRANCIS OF CHRIST THE KING (O.S.F.)

History: This congregation originated in 1864 through the efforts of Bishop Anthony Slomsek and Bishop Jacob Stepnichar of Marburg. The first sisters came to the United States in 1909 and established a house in Kansas City, Kansas. The congregation has nine provinces on five continents.

Purpose: The sisters teach in elementary and secondary schools, nurse and do social work in homes for the aged and orphanages. These institutions are located in Illinois, Ohio, Pennsylvania, Wisconsin, and Indiana.

Spiritual Life: The religious exercises include Holy Mass, the recitation in Latin of the Little Office of the Blessed Virgin, a half-hour of mental prayer, rosary, spiritual reading, and other community prayers.

Training Program: The community conducts an aspirancy for teen-age girls who are interested in the religious life. The six-month postulancy is followed by a two-year novitiate. First vows are pronounced and are renewed for five years. Perpetual vows are then made. The sisters continue their spiritual formation while pursuing college courses required for their professional and nursing degrees.

Qualifications:

* Age: 15 to 30.
* Average intelligence.
* Entrance dates: early September and February.

Habit: The sisters wear a black habit, white cord, and a Franciscan rosary of the Seven Joys of Mary.

> *Write to:* Mount Assisi Convent
> 1600 Main Street
> Lemont, Illinois

SCHOOL SISTERS OF THE THIRD ORDER OF ST. FRANCIS (O.S.F.)

History: The Most Reverend Roman Sebastian Zaengerle, Prince-Bishop of Seckau, founded this congregation in Graz, Austria, in 1843. Forty-five years later an independent motherhouse was erected in Bohemia. From this new branch an American foundation was established in Pittsburgh, Pennsylvania, in 1913.

Purpose: The general aim of the community is the promotion of God's glory and the sanctification of its members; the special aim is Christian education of youth. The sisters staff parochial schools and girls' academies, conduct retreat houses, nurse in hospitals, and give catechetical instructions. These institutions are located in the eastern United States and in Texas.

Spiritual Life: The religious exercises include Holy Mass, the recitation of the Little Office of the Blessed Virgin, a half-hour of mental prayer, spiritual reading, the rosary, and other community prayers and devotions.

Training Program: The community conducts an aspirancy for high school girls who are interested in the religious life. The six-month postulancy is followed by a one-year novitiate. Temporary vows are pronounced upon the completion of the novitiate. After five years in temporary vows the sister is admitted to profession of perpetual vows. During this time, the sisters continue their spiritual formation while taking undergraduate courses toward the fulfillment of their professional degrees.

Qualifications:
* The maximum age is 30.
* Average ability to meet the requirements of some form of community service.
* Entrance dates: September and January.

Habit: The sisters wear a black habit, veil, and cincture, and a seven decade Franciscan rosary.

Write to: Mount Assisi Convent
934 Forest Avenue
Pittsburgh 2, Pennsylvania

SISTERS OF ST. FRANCIS (O.S.F.)

History: This congregation originated in 1855 in the city of Philadelphia, Pennsylvania. Faced with highly complex problems of a far-flung diocese, the Redemptorist Bishop John W. Neumann was determined to enlist the services of European sisters. However, Pope Pius IX counseled the Bishop to found an American community from within the ranks of his own flock and to place the religious under the rule of St. Francis.

Purpose: The sisters teach in elementary and secondary schools, nurse the sick in hospitals, care for the aged and children in homes, and instruct adults and children in full-time catechetical centers. The four provinces in the United States have foundations in Pennsylvania, Oregon, Washington, Wyoming, Maryland, North Carolina, Florida, Alabama, Oklahoma, Delaware, Massachusetts, and New Jersey.

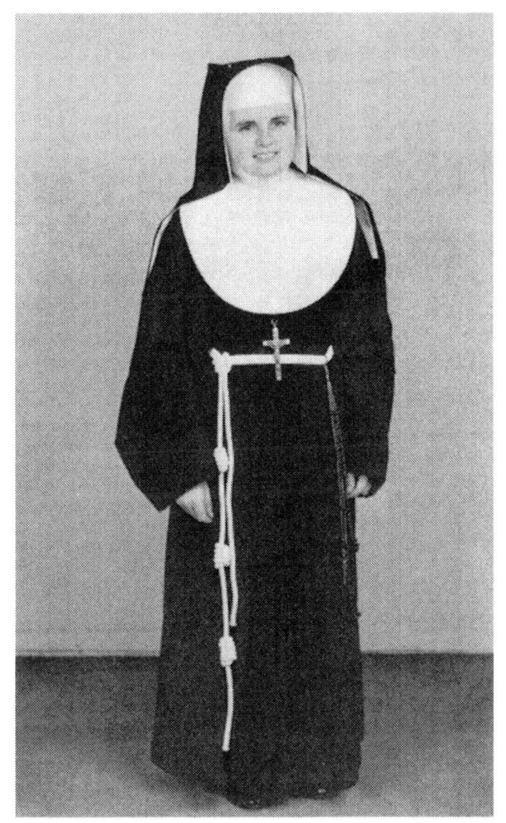

Spiritual Life: The religious exercises include Holy Mass, the recitation of the short breviary in English, mental prayer, the rosary, spiritual reading, and other community prayers and devotions.

Training Program: The nine-month postulancy is followed by a two-year novitiate. Temporary vows are made for six years after which perpetual vows are pronounced. During the postulancy and the second year of novitiate the candidates take college courses. After first profession, the sisters continue their spiritual formation while completing the requirements for their academic degrees.

Qualifications:
* Age: 16 to 30.
* Completion of high school.
* Entrance date: September 8.

Habit: The sisters wear a black habit and veil, white headdress and cord, and a rosary.

See page 383 for address of nearest provincial house.

SISTERS OF ST. FRANCIS (O.S.F.)

History: Father Francis Joseph Rudolph and Mother Theresa Hackelmeier founded this congregation at Oldenburg, Indiana, in 1851. Growth in numbers was paralleled by expansion of the teaching apostolate from one village school to a complete educational system operating chiefly in western and midwestern states.

Purpose: The teaching apostolate extends from kindergarten through college, and it includes religious instruction of children attending non-Catholic schools, special education for the mentally retarded, several schools for Negro and Indian children, two foreign missions, a diocesan orphanage, and a Catholic Charities guidance clinic. These instructions are located in Ohio, Indiana, Missouri, New Mexico, Illinois, Montana, Kansas, and Papau, New Guinea.

Spiritual Life: The religious exercises include Holy Mass, one hour of meditation and spiritual reading, the shortened breviary in English, the rosary, a half-hour of adoration, and other community prayers and devotions.

Training Program: The school for aspirants combines high school studies with opportunities to discover or strengthen a religious vocation. Spiritual and intellectual formation extends from the postulancy of at least six months through the two-year novitiate and a three-year scholasticate. Vows are taken for three years, at the end of which time perpetual vows are professed. Active work begins in the final year of the scholasticate.

Qualifications:
* Age: 16 to 30.
* Completion of high school is preferred.
* Entrance dates: September 8 and February 2.

Habit: A black veil and habit are offset by a white collar, band, and a cord from which is suspended a seven decade rosary.

Write to: Convent of the Immaculate Conception
Oldenburg,
Indiana

SISTERS OF ST. FRANCIS (O.S.F.)

History: Father Joseph L. Bihn, former pastor of St. Joseph's Church, Tiffin, Ohio, founded this Franciscan community to help him care for the many children orphaned as a result of the Civil War. Three of his parishoners, Elizabeth Schaeffer, a widow, and her two daughters, formed the nucleus of this congregation which was established in 1869.

Purpose: The sisters still care for orphaned children at St. Anthony Villa, Toledo, Ohio. They also operate a residence home for the aged in Tiffin, Ohio, and teach in elementary and high schools, and a college extension program, all in the diocese of Toledo, Ohio. These sisters administer two hospitals, one in Linton, South Dakota, and another in Paducah, Kentucky.

Spiritual Life: The community exercises include Holy Mass, a half-hour of mental prayer, and other community prayers and devotions.

Training Program: The community has an aspirancy at the motherhouse where girls of high school age who desire to become religious may continue their secondary school education. When these aspirants reach the senior year they enter the postulancy and are permitted to enter the novitiate one year later. The novices take temporary vows upon the completion of the two years of novitiate. After five years of temporary vows in the juniorate, the sisters are ready for final vows. During the juniorate the sisters attend classes in preparation for teaching and nursing certificates and degrees.

Qualifications:
* Age: 14 to 30. Over-age applicants will sometimes be accepted.
* Entrance dates: last Sunday in August and February 2.

Habit: The sisters wear a brown habit and scapular, a black veil, and a white cord with three knots which symbolizes the three vows of the professed religious.

> *Write to:* St. Francis Convent
> Tiffin,
> Ohio

SISTERS OF ST. FRANCIS (O.S.F.)

History: This community traces its origin to the mother-foundation, founded in Philadelphia in 1855 by the Redemptorist Bishop, Blessed John Neumann. A foundation was made in New York City, through a request made by Father Drumgoole, who asked the sisters to come and establish a home for neglected children. The New York branch became an independent congregation in 1893.

Purpose: These Francisan sisters conduct a day nursery and child care institutions, teach in elementary and secondary schools, and nurse the suffering and afflicted in hospitals and in a convalescent home for physically handicapped children. They also operate two fully accredited schools of nursing.

Spiritual Life: The religious exercises include Holy Mass, two half-hour periods of mental prayer, the recitation of the Little Office of the Blessed Virgin in Latin, the Franciscan Crown rosary, and other community prayers.

Training Program: The six-month postulancy is followed by a two-year novitiate. Here the novice undergoes a spiritual training in preparation for the obligation of the vows. The novice then makes her temporary vows. As a juniorate sister, she continues her spiritual formation and professional training according to the principles of the sister formation movement.

Qualifications:
* Age: under 30.
* Completion of high school.
* Entrance date: September 8.

Habit: The sisters wear a black habit and veil, a white coif, headband, guimpe and cord, a rosary, and a crucifix.

Write to: Immaculate Conception Motherhouse
Hastings-on-the-Hudson 6,
New York

OBLATE SISTERS OF
ST. FRANCIS DE SALES (O.S.F.S.)

History: Mother Frances de Sales Aviat and Father Louis Brisson founded this congregation at Troyes, France, in 1866. From its original work of providing homes for working girls in France, the community soon established other foundations throughout Europe, Africa, South America, and the United States. The American novitiate was established in 1952 at Childs, Maryland. Presently, they number over seven hundred members.

Purpose: The sisters teach in kindergarten, in elementary and secondary schools, conduct a summer camp, and are engaged in retreat work. They also assist the Oblate Fathers in the missions in Africa.

Spiritual Life: The religious exercises include Holy Mass, mental prayer, the rosary, spiritual reading, and other community devotions.

Training Program: The postulancy of six months to one year is followed by a one-year novitiate. The novice then makes her temporary profession of vows. These are renewed annually for five years. At the expiration of this time, the sister makes her profession of perpetual vows. Those who are unable to fulfill the requirements of the convent may be accepted as associate oblates. A special rule based on St. Francis de Sales' spiritual directory has been drawn up for them.

Qualifications:
* Age: 16 to 35.
* Average intelligence.

Habit: The sisters wear a black habit, short scapular, and veil, a white Roman collar, and a silver profession cross.

> *Write to:* Mother Superior
> Villa Aviat
> Childs, Maryland

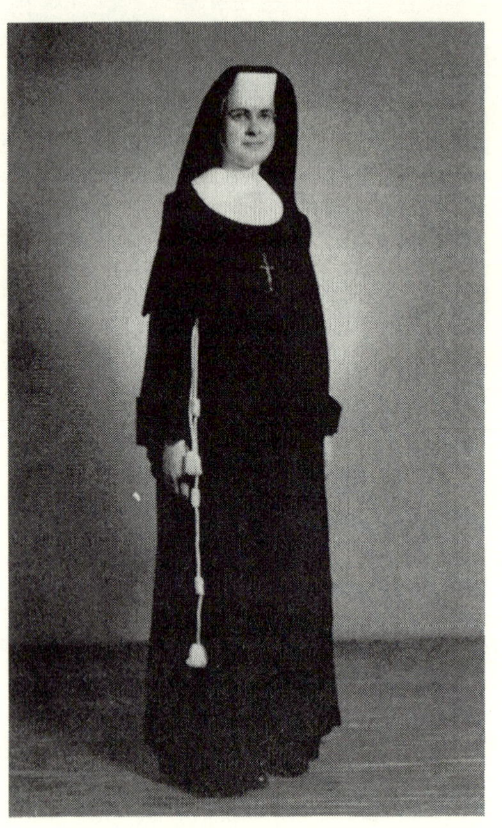

SISTERS OF ST. FRANCIS OF THE HOLY FAMILY (O.S.F.)

History: Mother Mary Xavier Termehr founded the congregation in 1864. Exiled from Germany in 1875, Mother Mary Xavier, twenty-five sisters, and four postulants settled in Iowa City, Iowa. The permanent motherhouse was established in Dubuque, Iowa, in 1878.

Purpose: Primarily, each sister strives for personal sanctity through the regular observance of the rule and constitutions. Collectively, the congregation seeks to give expression to the holiness of the Church. Unrelentingly, the institute proposes to its members the example of the charity and poverty of Christ and of St. Francis and the traditions and the spirituality of the Franciscan Order. Secondarily, the sisters spend themselves for Our Lord in the apostolate by teaching youth in parochial and high schools and by minstering to exceptional children, the sick, and the aged. The community has houses in Iowa, Illinois, Minnesota, California, and Oregon.

Spiritual Life: The religious exercises include Holy Mass, the chanting of the abridged form of the Divine Office in English, mental prayer, spiritual reading, and other community prayers and devotions. The Blessed Sacrament is exposed perpetually at the motherhouse.

Training Program: Three years are devoted to the spiritual and the intellectual formation of the postulant and the novice. Upon the completion of this period, the novices pronounce their temporary vows. These vows are renewed annually for five years. Perpetual vows are then made. After the novitiate, the sisters enter the juniorate where they continue their spiritual and academic formation and progress toward professional competence.

Qualifications:

* The desire to serve God as a Franciscan religious.
* Average intelligence.

Habit: The sisters wear a brown habit and scapular, a black veil, crucifix, a white cincture, the Franciscan Crown rosary, and a ring.

Write to: Mother General
Mount St. Francis
Dubuque, Iowa

SISTERS OF ST. FRANCIS OF THE IMMACULATE CONCEPTION (O.S.F.)

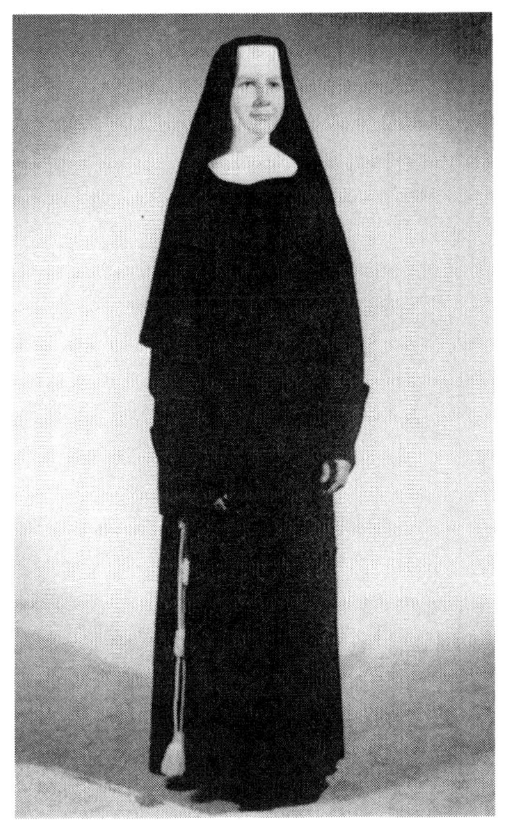

History: Mother Mary Pacifica Forrestal, under the direction of the Franciscan Fathers of the Sacred Heart, founded this congregation in Palmyra, Missouri, in 1888. Two years later, the Most Reverend John Lancaster Spalding invited the sisters to Peoria, Illinois, to direct the diocesan orphanage and to teach. Simultaneously, the sisters established St. Joseph's Home, thus adding the care of the aged to their works of mercy. The constitutions were approved in 1905.

Purpose: The education of youth and the care of orphans and the aged are the principle apostolic works of the congregation. The sisters teach in elementary and secondary schools and give catechetical instructions in those areas without parochial schools. These institutions and apostolic labors are carried on in the state of Illinois.

Spiritual Life: The religious exercises include Holy Mass, a half-hour of meditation the recitation of the short breviary in English, the rosary, private spiritual reading, and other community prayers and devotions.

Training Program: The community conducts an aspirancy for high school girls interested in the religious life. The postulancy and the two-year novitiate provide the new members with a thorough study of the religious life and professional knowledge obtained through the community's junior college. The in-service training begins after temporary profession when the religious are assigned to one of the various works of the congregation. Each summer until perpetual vows, a period of five years, the junior professed return to the motherhouse for a special program of instructions.

Qualifications:
* Age: 17 to 30.
* Average intelligence.
* Entrance date: September 8.

Habit: The sisters wear a black habit, scapular, and veil, a white coif and collar, and a white woolen cord to which is attached the Franciscan Crown rosary.

> *Write to:* Immaculate Conception Convent
> 2408 West Heading Avenue
> Peoria, Illinois

SISTERS OF ST. FRANCIS OF THE IMMACULATE HEART OF MARY (O.S.F.)

History: This pontifical congregation originated in Dilligen, Germany, in 1241, fifteen years after the death of St. Francis, when Count Hartman IV and his son, Bishop Hartman of Dillingen-Augsburg, built a convent for fifteen poor girls. This congregation has more than two thousand members with a motherhouse in Germany, two provinces in Brazil, and an American province of almost two hundred sisters who work primarily in North Dakota.

Purpose: The glory of God through personal sanctification and the salvation of souls is the sister's primary ambition. The sisters teach, nurse, care for the aged, design and prepare vestments, and make and supply altar breads.

Spiritual Life: The religious exercises include Holy Mass, recitation of the short breviary in English, a half-hour of meditation, fifteen minutes of spiritual reading, the rosary, and other community prayers and devotions.

Training Program: The community conducts an aspirancy for high school girls who are interested in following the religious life according to the ideals of St. Francis. The six-month postulancy is followed by a one-year novitiate. Intensified training acquaints the novices with the fundamentals of the Franciscan way of life. During the five-year juniorate the sisters are given further guidance in the application of their religious training and are offered educational opportunities to prepare for their future work.

Qualifications:
* Age: 14 to 30.
* Average intelligence.

Habit: The sisters wear a simple black cross-shaped habit, scapular, and veil, a white cord, rosary, mission crucifix, and a ring upon final profession.

> *Write to:* Mother Provincial
> St. Francis Convent
> Hankinson, North Dakota

SISTERS OF ST. FRANCIS OF MARY IMMACULATE (O.S.F.)

History: As the first religious teachers in Will County and the first Franciscan sisters of Illinois, this congregation was formally established on August 2, 1865. Mother M. Alfred Moss was appointed the first superior. Under the direction of Father Pamfilo da Magliano, the newly founded community was affiliated with the Franciscan Order in 1867. At present, more than one thousand sisters work in nine states in the United States.

Purpose: In accordance with the two-fold purpose of the community, the apostolic work is carried on mainly in the field of teaching. The congregation conducts a liberal arts college, an academy, an aspirancy, an orphanage, and a retirement home. They teach in high schools and grade schools, and are engaged in social and catechetical work.

Spiritual Life: The religious exercises include Holy Mass, chanting the short breviary in English, visits to the Blessed Sacrament, spiritual reading in private, and the recitation of the Franciscan Crown rosary.

Training Program: The community operates an aspirancy for high school girls who are interested in the religious life. The one-year postulancy is followed by a two-year novitiate. The novices take temporary vows upon completion of the novitiate. During the juniorate program, the sisters continue their spiritual formation while pursuing college courses for their academic degrees.

Qualifications:
* Age: 16 to 27.
* Completion of high school.

Habit: The sisters wear a dark brown habit, a black veil, a white cord, and the Franciscan Crown rosary.

> *Write to:* Mother Superior
> St. Francis Convent
> 520 Plainfield Avenue
> Joliet, Illinois

SISTERS OF ST. FRANCIS OF OUR LADY OF LOURDES (O.S.F.)

History: On the Feast of the Immaculate Conception, 1916, in response to the request of the Most Reverend Joseph Schrembs, Mother Mary Adelaide came with twenty-three sisters from the Franciscan Congregation of Our Lady of Lourdes, Rochester, Minnesota, to establish a foundation in the Diocese of Toledo, Ohio. In 1918 the permanent location of the motherhouse was made in Sylvania, Ohio. Twelve years later the foundation became an autonomous Franciscan congregation. The Holy See gave the new community papal approbation in 1957, with Mother M. Adelaide as foundress and Mother M. Justinian as general superior.

Purpose: The sisters teach on all levels of education from kindergarten to the university level and in numerous catechetical centers throughout Ohio, Michigan, Indiana, Minnesota, and Missouri. They staff eleven hospitals in five states from Nebraska to Louisiana.

Spiritual Life: The religious exercises include Holy Mass, a half-hour of mental prayer, the recitation of the Office of the Blessed Virgin, the rosary, spiritual reading, and other community prayers and devotions.

Training Program: The community conducts an aspirancy for high school girls interested in the religious life. In the one-year postulancy the postulants begin their college education. The two-year novitiate follows. During the second year of novitiate, the novices resume their collegiate courses at the community's junior college. Temporary vows are made for three years after which perpetual vows are pronounced. After first profession, the junior sisters continue their spiritual formation while completing the studies leading to their academic or nursing degrees in approved higher institutions in either full time or in-service programs.

Qualifications:
* Age: under thirty-one.
* Completion of the eighth grade.

Habit: The professed sisters wear a dark brown habit, scapular, and cord, a white coif and collar, black veil, silver cross, and a gold ring.

Write to: Vocational Counselor
6832 Convent Boulevard
Sylvania, Ohio

SISTERS OF ST. FRANCIS OF PENANCE AND CHRISTIAN CHARITY (O.S.F.)

History: Catherine Daemen, in religion known as Mother Magdalen, founded this community in Holland in 1835. It soon spread to Germany, Poland, Italy, Indonesia, Brazil, and Tanganyika, East Africa. The motherhouse is in Rome, Italy. In this country the convents and institutions of the three separate provinces extend from New York to California and from North Dakota to South Carolina.

Purpose: The sisters teach in primary, elementary, and high schools, conduct academies, cadet schools, a school of nursing, and a liberal arts college. They also serve in hospitals, orphanages, and in Negro and Indian Missions.

Spiritual Life: Spiritual strength and inspiration for their work are drawn from daily participation in the liturgical life of the Church, in the Holy Sacrifice of the Mass, in chanting the Divine Office in English, in meditation, and in prayer.

Training Program: Ordinarily the training program for the young religious begins with a one-year postulancy, a time of preparation for the habit. In the Denver Province there is an aspirancy for interested young girls of high school age. A two-year novitiate follows the postulancy. During this time the novice is grounded in the principles of the religious life and the Franciscan spirit. The profession of temporary vows is followed by a two-year juniorate, during which the spiritual and educational formation is continued. The religious then begins her apostolate. After five years of temporary vows the sister makes her profession of perpetual vows. There is a tertianship after ten years spent in the apostolate.

Qualifications:
 * Age: 18 to 30.
 * Average intelligence.

Habit: The sisters wear a dark brown habit and scapular embroidered with the instruments of the Passion, a white cord and rosary, and a white head-covering with a black veil.

See page 383 for address of nearest provincial house.

SISTERS OF ST. FRANCIS OF THE PROVIDENCE OF GOD (O.S.F.)

History: This congregation was founded in Pittsburgh, Pennsylvania, in 1922. It traces its descent directly, through the Franciscan communities in Millvale, Pennsylvania, and Buffalo, New York, from the mother foundation in Philadelphia founded in 1855 by the Redemptorist bishop, Blessed John Nepomucene Neumann. Under the leadership of Mother Mary Chrysostom, the community expanded and built the Motherhouse in Pittsburgh, Pennsylvania.

Purpose: The sisters conduct elementary and secondary schools, catechetical centers, and one hospital. These institutions are located in Michigan, Connecticut, Wisconsin, New Jersey, Pennsylvania, Illinois, New York, and Ohio. The missionary work in Sao Paulo, Brazil, includes teaching, nursing, and catechetical work.

Spiritual Life: The religious exercises include Holy Mass, the recitation of the short breviary in English, two periods of mental prayer, the Franciscan rosary, spiritual reading, and other community prayers and devotions.

Training Program: The community conducts an aspirancy for teen-age girls interested in the religious life. The postulants and first year junior professed sisters begin or continue college work in Duquesne University extension courses at the motherhouse. Other phases of study and training are pursued according to individual talents and community needs. After one year in the novitiate, the novices make their temporary vows for three years. These are renewed for two more years before perpetual vows are pronounced.

Qualifications:
* Age: 17 to 30.
* Average intelligence.
* Entrance dates: September 8 and February 2.

Habit: The sisters wear a black habit and veil, a white guimpe and cord with three knots, a Franciscan rosary, and a silver ring.

Write to: St. Francis Convent
Mount Providence
Grove and McRoberts Roads
Pittsburgh 34, Pennsylvania

SISTERS OF ST. FRANCIS SERAPH OF THE PERPETUAL ADORATION (O.S.F.)

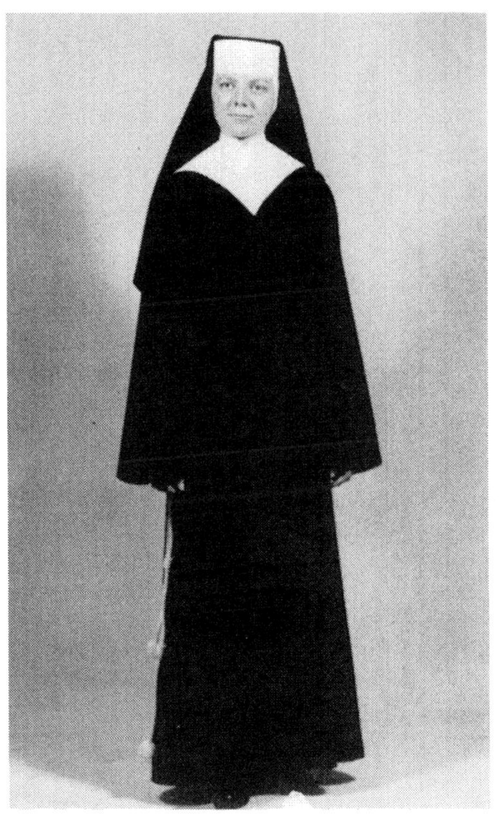

History: Mother M. Theresa Bonzel founded this community in 1860 in Westphalia, Germany. Fifteen years later the members of this congregation established their first foundation in Lafayette, Indiana. Two provinces were erected in 1932. The Western Province covers the states of Colorado, Kansas, Nebraska, and New Mexico. The Eastern Province includes Ohio, Indiana, Illinois, Michigan, Missouri, Kentucky, Tennessee, New York, and Louisiana.

Purpose: The community has a three-fold objective: the perpetual adoration of the Most Blessed Sacrament in its motherhouses, the sanctification of its members, and the active apostolate as expressed in education on all levels, the care of the sick in hospitals, the care of the aged, and orphans. The Western Province conducts Indian missions in New Mexico and the Eastern Province has Negro missions in Louisiana.

Spiritual Life: The religious exercises include Holy Mass, the recitation of the Divine Office in English, a half-hour of mental prayer, and fifteen minutes each of spiritual reading and common vocal prayers. The rosary and the stations of the cross are made privately.

Training Program: The members of this congregation conduct an aspirancy for teen-age girls who are interested in convent life. The one year of postulancy is followed by a two-year novitiate. During the juniorate program the sisters continue their religious formation while taking college courses to complete the requirements for their academic degrees.

Qualifications:
* Age: 17 to 30. Exceptions are sometimes made.
* Average intelligence.

Habit: The sisters wear a dark brown habit and a scapular, a white cincture, collar and cap, a black veil, rosary, and a crucifix.

Write to: Mount St. Francis
P.O. Box 1059
Colorado Springs, Colorado

St. Francis Convent
Mount Alverno
Mishawaka, Indiana

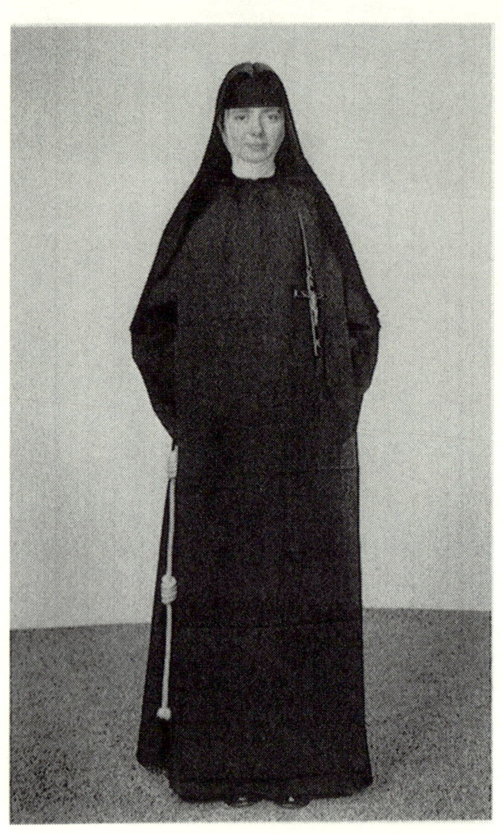

MISSIONARY SISTERS OF THE THIRD ORDER OF ST. FRANCIS (O.S.F.)

History: Erected in Gemona, Italy, in 1861, the congregation was guided in its early years by Father Gregorio Fiorvante dalle Grotte di Castro, O.F.M., and endowed by Laura Leroux. Four years later, at the request of the Franciscan Fathers, the sisters began their work in the United States at West 31st Street in New York City. They have since spread their missionary activities to the Near East, Chile, Bolivia, and Spain.

Purpose: The sisters teach in parochial, secondary, and business schools, and at Ladycliff College, as well as caring for dependent and neglected children at St. Joseph's Home, Peekskill and Lt. Joseph P. Kennedy Jr. Home, Bronx, New York. They also have houses in Pennsylvania and New Jersey. Foreign missionary work in Bolivia includes teaching and social work among the Indians.

Spiritual Life: The religious exercises include Holy Mass, the Office of the Blessed Virgin recited in common, one hour of mental prayer, the rosary, spiritual reading, and other community prayers and devotions.

Training Program: The one-year postulancy is followed by a one-year novitiate. The novitiate is devoted to the study of the rule, the obligations of the vows, and domestic training in preparation for a missionary life. After their first vows, the sisters continue their spiritual formation while taking courses toward their professional degrees.

Qualifications:
* Age: 16 to 30.
* Average intelligence.
* Entrance date: September 8.

Habit: The sisters wear a dark grey habit and scapular, a black veil, a white wimple, wooden rosary, and a large crucifix over the heart.

Write to: Mount St. Francis
250 South Street
Peekskill, New York

SISTERS OF THE THIRD ORDER OF ST. FRANCIS (M.C.)

History: This community was established in Syracuse, New York, in November, 1860, when James F. Wood, Bishop of Philadelphia, introduced a separation of the sisters laboring outside his diocese from the Franciscan community in Philadelphia. Mother Mary Bernardine Dorn was the co-foundress and first mother general.

Purpose: The sisters conduct elementary and high schools, Maria Regina College, catechetical centers, and schools of nursing education. They also operate four general hospitals, a government hospital in Molokai, a home for the aged, a retreat house for laywomen, a house of studies at The Catholic University of America, Washington, D.C., and one in Rome. Their institutions are located in New York, New Jersey, North Carolina, Ohio, Washington, D.C., and Hawaii.

Spiritual Life: The religious exercises include Holy Mass, thirty minutes of mental prayer, the recitation of the Little Office of the Blessed Virgin in Latin, spiritual reading, and other community prayers.

Training Program: The nine months of postulancy is followed by a two-year novitiate. After the completion of the novitiate, the novice makes her profession of temporary vows, which are taken for three years. Profession of perpetual vows is then made. The sisters continue their spiritual formation while taking college courses toward their academic degrees.

Qualifications:
* Age: 16 to 30.
* Average intelligence.
* Entrance date: September 8.

Habit: The professed sisters wear a black habit and veil, a white collar, coronette and band, a white cord, rosary of seven decades, and a pectoral cross.

Write to: St. Anthony Convent
1024 Court Street
Syracuse 8, New York

SISTERS OF ST. FRANCIS OF THE THIRD ORDER REGULAR (O.S.F.)

History: This pontifical congregation is a branch foundation of the mother Franciscan community erected in Philadelphia, Pennsylvania, in 1855 by Bishop Blessed John Neumann. Pius IX asked him to found a Franciscan organization that would work among the indigent. In 1861, Sister Margaret, one of the first three sisters to be clothed in the habit of St. Francis by the bishop, arrived in Buffalo, New York, and opened this daughter foundation. Bishop John Timon, C.M., of Buffalo severed the connection with Philadelphia in 1863.

Purpose: The sisters teach in elementary and secondary diocesan high schools and in Niagara University College of Nursing. They own and operate three hospitals in the Buffalo diocese and three homes for the aged, as well as conducting Confraternity of Christian Doctrine classes and mission schools in Puerto Rico.

Spiritual Life: The religious exercises include Holy Mass, the chanting of the Office of the Blessed Virgin—those in the active apostolate recite it privately—mental prayer, the rosary, spiritual reading, and adoration before the Blessed Sacrament exposed in the motherhouse.

Training Program: During the ten-month postulancy, the postulants carry a full freshman program in the community's own junior college. The first year of the novitiate is devoted to the spiritual formation of the novice. The novices continue their regular college courses in the second year. After receiving temporary vows, the professed sister enters the three-year juniorate program. Profession of perpetual vows is made at the expiration of temporary vows.

Qualifications:
* Age: 16 to 30. Late vocations are sometimes accepted.
* Entrance dates: September 8 and December 27.

Habit: The sisters wear a black habit and veil, a Franciscan rosary attached to a white cord, and a crucifix.

Write to: St. Mary of the Angels Convent
400 Mill Street
Williamsville 21, New York

SISTERS OF THE THIRD ORDER OF ST. FRANCIS OF ASSISI (O.S.F.)

History: This congregation was founded in Milwaukee, Wisconsin, in 1849 by six Franciscan tertiaries from Bavaria. The community, whose motherhouse was one of the first to be founded in Wisconsin, today numbers almost a thousand professed members.

Purpose: The sisters teach on the elementary, secondary, and collegiate levels, conduct two educational clinics, and thirty-five schools of music, maintain three schools for exceptional children, one school for the deaf, and one for pre-delinquent boys, and three orphanages. They also perform domestic services in seminaries, episcopal residences, and in numerous houses of the congregation. The community's apostolate in the United States extends from Massachusetts to California although most of its houses are in the Midwest.

Spiritual Life: The religious exercises include Holy Mass, the chanting of the Franciscan short breviary in English, a half-hour of mental prayer, periods of adoration, and other community prayers and devotions.

Training Program: The sisters conduct an aspirancy for junior and senior girls interested in the religious life. The one-year postulancy is followed by a two-year novitiate. Temporary vows are made for five years. At the end of this time, perpetual vows are pronounced. During the period of temporary profession the sisters continue their spiritual formation while fulfilling the requirements for their advanced degrees.

Qualifications:
* The maximum age is 30.
* Completion of high school is required for the postulancy.
* Juniors and seniors may enroll in the aspirancy.
* Entrance date: September 1.

Habit: In 1963 the sisters adopted a modified habit consisting of a black sleeveless jumper with a jacket, a white collar, and a black cord. Their headdress is a black waist-length veil with a white cap.

Write to: Vocation Directress
3221 South Lake Drive
Milwaukee 7, Wisconsin

SISTERS OF THE THIRD ORDER REGULAR OF ST. FRANCIS OF THE CONGREGATION OF OUR LADY OF LOURDES (O.S.F.)

History: Mother Mary Alfred Moes founded this congregation in Rochester, Minnesota, in 1877. The sisters originally came to establish schools. Due to the devastating results of a tornado which struck Rochester in 1883, a hospital was built. Dedicated in 1889, this hospital has become the world famous St. Mary's Hospital, whose patients are admitted through the Mayo Clinic.

Purpose: Education of youth and nursing are the two-fold apostolic activities of the members of this Franciscan congregation. In urban and rural areas the one thousand sisters serve the sick, the poor, and the aged in two general hospitals, a convalescent hospital, and a home for elderly people; they teach in elementary and secondary schools, and a college.

Spiritual Life: The religious exercises include community Mass, mental prayer, the Little Office of the Blessed Virgin in Latin, and other community prayers and devotions.

Training Program: Postulants are received at the motherhouse where they spend from six to nine months preparing to receive the religious habit. In the two-year novitiate the novice prepares for her profession of triennial vows. On the Assisi Heights Campus, an integral part of the College of St. Teresa, in Winona, Minnesota, a complete program of college studies is available where the sisters may continue their studies toward an academic degree.

Qualifications:
* Age: 16 to 30.
* Freedom to enter the religious state.
* Entrance dates: September and January.

Habit: The sisters wear a brown habit, scapular, and cord, a black veil, a white coif, band, and collar, and a Franciscan Crown rosary.

Write to: Mother Superior
Assisi Heights
Rochester, Minnesota

GREY NUNS OF THE CROSS
(S.G.C.)

History: In 1845, upon the request of Bishop Phelan, of Kingston, Ontario, the Grey Nuns of Montreal, founded in 1783 by Blessed Marguerite d'Youville, sent four sisters under the leadership of Mother Elizabeth Bruyere, to found an autonomous congregation in Ottawa, Ontario, Canada. They received pontifical approbation in 1889. The more than two thousand members are divided into five provinces in Canada, one each in Africa and the United States.

Purpose: The sisters are actively engaged in teaching from the kindergarten to the university levels, nursing in general and chronic hospitals, and operating homes for orphans and the aged. These institutions are located in New York, Massachusetts, and Louisiana. Missions have also been founded in Japan and South America.

Spiritual Life: The religious exercises include Holy Mass, the recitation of the Office of the Blessed Virgin in English, mental prayer, the rosary, spiritual reading, and other community prayers and devotions.

Training Program: The six-month postulancy is followed by an eighteen-month novitiate. Temporary vows are made for three years after which perpetual vows are pronounced. The sisters continue their spiritual formation while taking college courses toward their nursing and professional degrees.

Qualifications:
* Age: at least 16.
* Average intelligence.
* Entrance dates: February 1 and August 1.

Habit: The professed sisters wear a grey dress, black headdress, veil, and cincture, and a silver cross.

> *Write to:* Mother Provincial
> 25 Fairmont Street
> Lowell, Massachusetts

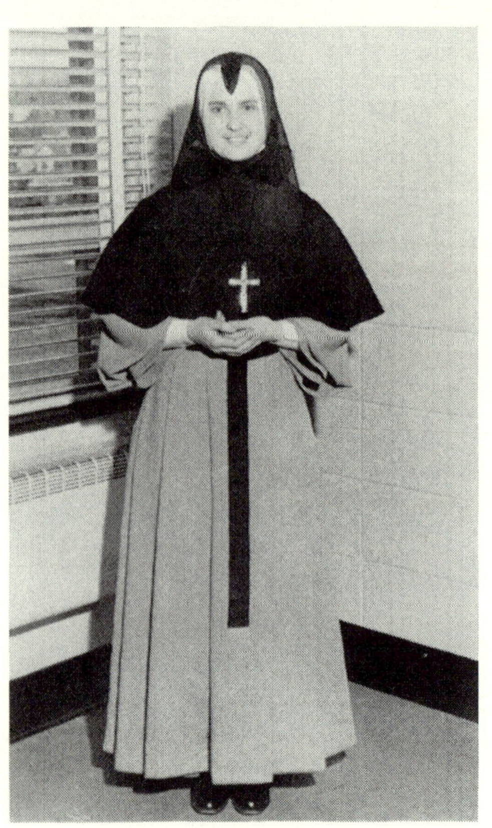

GREY NUNS OF THE SACRED HEART (G.N.S.H.)

History: Blessed Marguerite d'Youville founded this community in Montreal, Canada, in 1738. She wanted to consecrate herself and all the sisters who would follow in her footsteps to the service of all those who were in need. From this small beginning, the Grey Nuns have spread into five autonomous branches. From the foundation in Canada, they established a motherhouse in Philadelphia, Pennsylvania, in 1921 to maintain the works of charity in the United States.

Purpose: The sisters teach on all educational levels from primary schools to college, including schools of nursing. They also maintain hospitals and institutions for the care of the sick and infirm, the aging, orphans, and for the homeless poor. These institutions are located in Pennsylvania, New York, Massachusetts, Georgia, and Alaska.

Spiritual Life: The religious exercises include Holy Mass, a half-hour of mental prayer, recitation of the short breviary in English, the rosary and litanies, spiritual reading and other community prayers.

Training Program: The ten-month postulancy provides an introductory training in the spirit and duties of the congregation. A two-year novitiate follows. During the first year emphasis is placed on a thorough study of the principles of the religious life. The second year supplements this spiritual development while the novice takes courses toward her academic degree.

Qualifications:
* Age: 15 to 30.
* Average intelligence.
* Entrance date: September 8.

Habit: The sisters wear a sand colored habit, with a black gauze coif, cape, veil, and cincture. All the professed wear a silver ring and crucifix.

Write to: Motherhouse
7500 West Avenue
Philadelphia 26, Pennsylvania

SOCIETY OF THE HOLY CHILD JESUS
(S.H.C.J.)

History: This society originated in 1846 in England through the efforts of Cardinal Wiseman who sought help in improving the standard of education of Catholic girls in England. Cornelia Connelly, an American convert, was commissioned to undertake the work. The first foundation in the United States was made in 1862.

Purpose: The chief work of the society is the Catholic instruction and education in colleges, and in parochial and private schools. In Africa the sisters have established a native sisterhood, training colleges, secondary and "bush" schools. The society has foundations in Europe and in the United States from coast to coast.

Spiritual Life: The religious exercises include an hour of meditation before Mass, a half-hour of adoration in the evening, spiritual reading and the community prayers said in common. The Office of the Blessed Virgin is said daily in Latin in the novitiate. In the other houses it is recited on all non-school days. The rosary is said privately.

Training Program: The postulancy of nine months is followed by a two-year novitiate. The novices then profess temporary vows for five years. During these five years, the sisters continue their religious formation and professional training according to the spirit of the society. A tertianship of six months precedes profession of perpetual vows.

Qualifications:
* Age: 17 to 25. Exceptions are sometimes made.
* Average intelligence.
* Entrance date: September 8.

Habit: The professed sisters wear a black habit and veil, a white cap and collar, a gold crucifix, ring, and a silver cross.

Write to: Convent of the Holy Child Jesus
1341 Montgomery Avenue
Rosemont, Pennsylvania
Convent of the Holy Child Jesus
Westchester Avenue
Rye, New York

HOLY CROSS SISTERS (S.C.S.C.)

History: This congregation is a member of the international Franciscan congregation, the Sisters of Mercy of the Holy Cross, founded in 1856 at Ingenbohl, Switzerland, by Father Theodosius Florentini, O.F.M. Cap., and Mother Mary Theresa Scherer. At the request of Bishop Vincent de Paul Wehrle, O.S.B., of Bismarck, North Dakota, the sisters came to the United States in 1912. The present motherhouse was established in 1923 at Merrill, Wisconsin, by Mother Aniceta Regli.

Purpose: Over nine thousand sisters are united in their common dedication to Christ by serving Him through the spiritual and corporal works of mercy. The sisters conduct schools and hospitals in Wisconsin, North Dakota, Illinois, and Ohio. They maintain a year-round catechetical center in northern Wisconsin and carry on a missionary apostolate in southern Louisiana. The sisters are active in CCD work, both in instructing lay catechists and in continuing confraternity programs.

Spiritual Life: The religious exercises include Holy Mass, the recitation of the Divine Office in English, a half-hour of mental prayer, spiritual reading, visits, the rosary, and other community prayers and devotions.

Training Program: High school girls are received into the aspirancy in which they are given a special preparation for the convent life while they continue their secondary school education. The eighteen-month postulancy is followed by a one-year novitiate. During the period following temporary profession the sisters continue working for their academic degrees. Profession of perpetual vows is made after six years in temporary vows.

Qualifications:
* Age: 16 to 32.
* Completion of high school.

Habit: The sisters wear a simple black habit with a small crucifix, both signifying their complete dedication to Christ Crucified.

> *Write to:* Holy Cross Sisters
> Merrill,
> Wisconsin.

CONGREGATION OF THE SISTERS OF THE HOLY CROSS (C.S.C.)

History: The Very Reverend Basil Anthony Moreau founded this pontifical congregation at LeMans, France, in 1841. Two years later, four sisters of the infant community left France for America by appointment of Father Moreau to serve in the first foundation in the United States at Notre Dame, Indiana. Today the sisters have a mother-house at Saint Mary's, Notre Dame, Indiana, and three provinces in the United States.

Purpose: The sisters teach in elementary and secondary schools, administer three liberal arts colleges, operate ten hospitals, schools of nursing, and conduct orphanages. In their apostolic missions abroad, they conduct a college in East Pakistan and another in Sao Paulo, Brazil, teach in elementary and secondary schools, and conduct orphanages. Missions are maintained for the Negroes and neglected Mexicans in the South. The houses and institutions of the Congregation extend through 35 dioceses from Massachusetts to California and from Washington to Texas.

Spiritual Life: The religious exercises include Holy Mass, the recitation of the Little Office of the Blessed Virgin Mary, mental prayer, the rosary, spiritual reading, participation in perpetual adoration, and other community prayers and devotions.

Training Program: The ten-month postulancy is followed by a two-year novitiate. Temporary vows are made for five years after which perpetual vows are pronounced. After first profession, the junior-professed continue their spiritual formation while completing college and university courses to fulfill the requirements for their professional or nursing degrees. Annual summer programs of in-service training are carried out in several centers with an annual tertianship at the motherhouse.

Qualifications:
* The maximum age is 30. Exceptions are sometimes made.
* Completion of high school.
* Entrance date: early September.

Habit: The sisters wear a black habit and veil, a blue cincture in honor of Our Lady, and the Chaplet of Seven Dolors. The fluted cap is characteristic of the French peasants in the province where the sisters were founded.

See page 383 for address of nearest provincial house.

SISTERS OF THE HOLY CROSS AND THE SEVEN DOLORS (C.S.C.)

History: The Very Reverend Basil Antoine Moreau, who, under the auspices of Bishop Bouvier, organized the Fathers of the Holy Cross in 1834, also founded this congregation of sisters at Le Mans, France, in 1841. At the request of the saintly bishop, four sisters embarked for Canada and arrived at Montreal on May 27, 1847. The young community increased and its work prospered. Today, to the zeal and care of its members are entrusted thousands of school children throughout Canada and the United States. The congregation received papal approbation on March 15, 1910.

Purpose: All the members, who form one family, believe that whatever is done in a spirit of faith in the service of God is noble. The special aim of the sisters is to cooperate in the sanctification of souls, by teaching in a college and in elementary and secondary schools, and by the exercise of charity towards the sick.

Spiritual Life: The religious exercises include Holy Mass, the recitation of the Office of the Blessed Virgin in English, mental prayer, the rosary, spiritual reading, and other community prayers and devotions.

Training Program: The six-month postulancy is followed by an eighteen-month novitiate. Temporary vows are made for five years after which perpetual vows are pronounced. After first profession, the sisters continue their spiritual formation while fulfilling the requirements for their academic degrees.

Qualifications:
* Age: 16 to 30.
* Completion of high school is preferred.

Habit: The sisters wear a black habit and veil, a white guimpe and fluted linen headdress, a rosary, and a medal of Our Lady of Sorrows.

Write to: St. George Manor
357 Island Pond Road
Manchester, New Hampshire

SISTERS OF THE HOLY FAMILY
(S.S.F.)

History: Mothers Henriette De Lisle and Juliette Gaudin, under the direction of Father Etienne Rousselon, founded this congregation in New Orleans, Louisiana, on November 21, 1842. Touched by the wretched conditions of the Negro in the United States, these young women dedicated their lives to God for the uplift of their own people. The community apostolate now embraces the continental southern United States and Central America.

Purpose: This pontifical institute conducts a college, secondary and elementary schools, nurseries, kindergartens, orphanages, a home for the aged, and catechetical classes. These works are being carried on in Louisiana, Texas, Mississippi, Oklahoma, Florida, California, and the British Honduras.

Spiritual Life: The religious exercises include Holy Mass, the Office of the Blessed Virgin, mental prayer, the rosary, spiritual reading, and other community prayers and devotions.

Training Program: The six to eleven-month postulancy is followed by a two-year novitiate. The novice then makes temporary vows for three years. These are again renewed for two more years. After five years the sister pronounces her perpetual vows. During the years of the juniorate the sister continues her spiritual formation while taking courses toward the fulfillment of requirements for her academic degree.

Qualifications:
* Age: 16 to 28. Exceptions are sometimes made.
* Completion of high school.
* Entrance date: September 8.

Habit: The sisters wear a black habit cape, and veil, a white band, guimpe and collar, a seven-knotted cincture, a six decade rosary, crucifix, and a gold band ring.

> *Write to:* Holy Family Convent
> 6901 Chef Menteur Highway
> New Orleans 26, Louisiana

SISTERS OF THE HOLY FAMILY OF NAZARETH (C.S.F.N.)

History: Mother Mary Frances Siedliska, a Polish noblewoman, founded this congregation in Rome, Italy, in 1875. International in scope, the community has established foundations in Europe, Australia, and the United States. The more than 1,500 sisters of the four American provinces carry on their apostolate in seventeen states.

Purpose: The sisters teach from kindergarten through college, nurse in the community's eleven hospitals, teach and train hospital personnel in nursing and in medical and X-ray technology, and conduct child care institutions, from New York to Texas.

Spiritual Life: The religious exercises include the conventual Mass, the recitation in Latin of the Little Office of the Blessed Virgin, a half-hour of mental prayer, the rosary, spiritual reading, visits to the Blessed Sacrament, and other community devotions.

Training Program: Each of the four provinces conduct aspirancies for high school girls who are interested in the religious life. The Chicago province has established a sister-formation center at Lourdes College, Des Plaines, Illinois. The sisters in the Atlantic coastal states receive in-service training at Holy Family College, Philadelphia. Undergraduates in the Pittsburgh province and graduate students in all the provinces attend institutions of higher learning both in the United States and Europe.

Qualifications:
* Age: maximum is 30. Exceptions are sometimes made.
* Completion of high school.
* Entrance dates: September 8 and January.

Habit: The sisters wear a black habit, veil, and cincture, and a white coif and collar, and a silver profession cross.

See page 384 for address of nearest provincial house.

SISTERS OF THE HOLY FAMILY OF SAN FRANCISCO (S.H.F.)

History: "I have another work for you to do," Archbishop Joseph S. Alemany, O.P., said to young Elizabeth Armer when she came to consult him about entering a contemplative order. The archbishop unfolded to the future Mother Dolores his plans for an institute to give religious instruction to children who could not attend Catholic schools. In other words, they were to be mothers-by-the-day to children whose own mothers had to work. Mother Dolores and one companion opened the first convent in San Francisco, California, in 1872.

Purpose: The apostolic activities of the members of this congregation include the religious education of public school children, including the handicapped, training of lay catechists, conducting day homes for children of working mothers, and home-visiting of the needy and poor. These works are being carried out in California, Nevada, Utah, Texas, and Hawaii.

Spiritual Life: Holy Mass, morning and evening prayers, meditations, spiritual reading, and the rosary are among the religious exercises which are of daily obligation.

Training Program: The candidates must undergo a nine-month postulancy in which they are introduced to the life of a religious and begin their academic training for two semesters in the community's junior college. The canonical year of the novitiate is a more intensive spiritual formation in the fundamentals of the religious life.

Qualifications:

* Age: 17 to 30.
* Completion of high school.
* Entrance date: September 7.

Habit: The sisters wear a plain black habit, veil, and cape, and a coif.

> *Write to:* Mother Superior
> Mission San Jose,
> California

DAUGHTERS OF THE HOLY GHOST
(F.S.E.)

History: This congregation was founded in Brittany, France, in 1706 by Renée Burel and Marie Balavenne under the direction of Dom Jean Leuduger. A pontifical institute of over 3,500 members, it looks back upon more than a half century of expansion in the U.S.A.

Purpose: The members of this congregation devote themselves to teaching and nursing. They teach on elementary, high school, and college levels in New England, New York, Alabama, California, and Canada. In New England they direct district-nursing centers, conduct a convalescent hospital, a home for the aged, homes for working girls, catechetical centers, and day nurseries. In Alabama and in the North Cameroons they work among the Negroes.

Spiritual Life: The sisters join their active apostolate to a life of prayer and union with God. Each day, they attend Holy Mass, dedicate one hour and a half to mental and vocal prayer, recite the rosary morning and afternoon and devote some time to spiritual reading. The choral recitation of the Office of the Blessed Virgin is prescribed on Sundays and on holy days of obligation.

Training Program: The postulancy is a nine-month period of orientation in the religious life. It is followed by the canonical novitiate, a year spent in serious study of the obligations of a religious. The novices then pronounce simple vows annually for three years. These years are devoted to further spiritual formation and professional training. After this they are assigned to some definite work. The sisters pronounce their perpetual vows five years after the canonical novitiate.

Qualifications:
* Age: not more than 30.
* A high school education is preferred.

Habit: The sisters wear a white habit bound at the waist by a black leather belt from which hangs a rosary. Suspended from the neck on a black cord is a silver dove, the symbol of the Holy Spirit.

Write to: Holy Ghost Novitiate
72 Church Street
Putnam, Connecticut

SISTERS OF THE HOLY GHOST
(C.H.G.)

History: The Most Reverend Francis Regis Canevin, Bishop of Pittsburgh, Pennsylvania, founded this congregation April 25, 1913. He proposed the principles regarding the religious life and marked out the daily routine of the institute.

Purpose: The sisters are engaged in the Christian instruction and education of children, especially those from poor parishes, own and operate a General Hospital in Martinsburg, West Virginia, conduct homes for the aged and summer classes of Christian Doctrine for public school children. Their institutions are located in West Virginia, Ohio, and Pennsylvania.

Spiritual Life: The religious exercises include Holy Mass, the recitation of the Office of the Blessed Virgin in English, a half-hour of mental prayer, the rosary, spiritual reading, and other community prayers and devotions.

Training Program: The community conducts an aspirancy for high school girls interested in the religious life. The one-year postulancy is followed by a two-year novitiate. Temporary vows are made for five years. Perpetual vows are then pronounced. After first vows, the sisters continue their spiritual formation while taking courses toward the completion of their professional degrees.

Qualifications:
* Age: 16 to 40.
* Average intelligence.
* Entrance dates: September 8 and February 2.

Habit: The sisters wear a black habit, scapular, cincture, and veil, a white collar and cap, the rosary, a Holy Ghost medal, and a silver ring.

Write to: Sisters of the Holy Ghost
5346 Clarwin Avenue
Pittsburgh 29, Pennsylvania

History: Mother Mary Josephine Finatowicz founded this community in Palermo, Italy, in 1890. Fifteen years later, Mother Mary Anthony, the co-foundress, and a companion were sent to the United States to solicit funds for the European house. Father Vitold Buhaczkowski, then rector of Orchard Lake Seminary, Detroit, Michigan, asked the sisters to remain in the States and take charge of the domestic department in the seminary. In 1911 the sisters opened their first American foundation at Donora, Pennsylvania. The congregation was erected as an independent diocesan community in 1929.

Purpose: The general aim of the congregation is the glory of God and the sanctification of its members, through the observance of the three simple vows of religion. The special objective is based on the exercise of the works of Christian charity and the education of youth. The sisters are engaged in caring for the aged, sick, and preparing members to enter the educational field.

Spiritual Life: The religious exercises include Holy Mass, a half-hour of meditation, the Office of the Blessed Virgin in Latin, visits to the Blessed Sacrament, spiritual reading, and other community prayers and devotions.

Training Program: The postulancy of six months to one year is followed by a two-year novitiate. At the end of this time the sisters make their profession of temporary vows for three years, after which time perpetual vows are taken.

Qualifications:
* Age: 14 to 30.
* Completion of high school is preferred.

Habit: The sisters wear a black habit and scapular, a red cincture in honor of the Holy Ghost, rosary, crucifix, and, after perpetual vows, a golden ring.

Write to: Mother Superior
10102 Granger Road
Garfield Heights 25, Ohio

SISTER SERVANTS OF THE HOLY GHOST AND MARY IMMACULATE (S.H.G.)

History: In 1893 Mother Margaret Mary Murphy was inspired to initiate a movement for the education of Negro children in San Antonio, Texas. Her dream materialized with the founding of this congregation. She governed as its first superior until her death. Over two hundred and sixty sisters conduct forty schools principally in the South and the Southwest.

Purpose: The sisters work with children of all races on the elementary and high school levels, especially the poor and the colored, and care for the aged.

Spiritual Life: The religious exercises include Holy Mass, the recitation of the Little Office of the Holy Ghost in English, the rosary, two half-hour periods of mental prayer, and other community devotions.

Training Program: The one-year postulancy is followed by a one-year novitiate. The novices are then permitted to make their first profession of temporary vows for three years. During this time, the sisters continue their spiritual formation while taking courses toward their academic degrees. After three years in temporary vows, and if the sisters have passed their twenty-first birthday, they then make their profession of perpetual vows.

Qualifications:
* Age: maximum is 30.
* Completion of high school.
* Entrance date: September 8.

Habit: The sisters wear a black habit and veil, and a white collar, bandeau, and headband, a rosary, and a silver cross.

> *Write to:* Mother Superior
> Convent of the Holy Ghost and Mary Immaculate
> 301 Yucca Street
> San Antonio 3, Texas

SISTERS, SERVANTS OF THE HOLY HEART OF MARY (S.S.C.M.)

History: "The spirit of faith, the spirit of sacrifice, and the spirit of family unity" is the legacy of the saintly Father Francois Delaplace, C.S.Sp., to his spiritual daughters. The congregation was founded in Paris, France, in 1860 to care for the most abandoned children of the famed Ste. Antoine sector of the city. Begun in poverty and humility, tried in the fire of the many religious persecutions in France, the community has maintained its characteristic spirit as expressed in its motto, "One Heart and One Soul." The first American foundation was made in 1889 at St. Viator's College, Bourbonnais, Illinois. The community now exercises its apostolate in Illinois, Minnesota, District of Columbia, and Arkansas.

Purpose: Inspired by the maternal Heart of Mary, the sisters' apostolate extends to the education of youth on all levels of instruction, including nursing programs; the care of the suffering in hospitals; social and catechetical work in Negro missions; and numerous administrative, secretarial and domestic duties of the various institutions entrusted to its care.

Training Program: Pre-service and in-service formation programs are in operation. The novitiate and scholasticate pursue college studies under the direction of the respective superiors. Monthly in-service weekends, including special conferences for the junior professed, foster continued growth in religious ideals and family spirit. Educational and cultural conferences are included in the in-service programs for all religious.

Qualifications:
* Age: 16 to 30. Delayed vocations are given consideration.
* Subjects are prepared for and assigned to duties according to their talents and aptitudes.

Habit: The sisters wear a black habit and cape, a white guimpe, azure-blue cincture, a large rosary, an ebony and silver crucifix, and a ring.

Write to: Holy Heart of Mary Novitiate
717 N. Batavia Avenue
Batavia, Illinois

SISTERS OF THE HOLY NAMES OF JESUS AND MARY (S.N.J.M.)

History: Eulalie Durocher, Mother Mary Rose, founded this congregation more than a century ago in Quebec, Canada. Work of education began on October 28, 1843, with only three members. At present, more than four thousand sisters teach in the United States, Canada, South Africa, and South America.

Purpose: The work of the community embraces all levels of educational development from pre-school through college. The members also conduct graduate schools of music, art studies, mission dispensaries, Catholic Action Centers, and one orphanage. These works are being carried out in New York, Massachusetts, Virginia, Maryland, Florida, California, Oregon, Washington, Minnesota, Illinois, Michigan, and the District of Columbia. Missions have been established in Basutoland, South Africa, and Peru, South America.

Spiritual Life: The daily spiritual preparation includes Holy Mass, meditation for three-quarters of an hour in the morning and a half-hour in the evening, the Little Office of the Blessed Virgin which is said in the motherhouse and the novitiates, and on Sundays and holy days by the sisters actively engaged in the apostolate, and other community prayers and devotions.

Training Program: After a six-month postulancy, the candidate begins her eighteen months of novitiate. Temporary vows are then made for three years. Twice she renews her vows before profession of perpetual vows. During this time, the sisters continue their spiritual formation while taking courses toward their academic degrees.

Qualifications:
* Age: not over 30.
* Completion of high school.

Habit: The sisters wear a simple black habit, cape, veil, and a white linen headdress. A crucifix and a gold ring are worn by the professed members.

See page 384 for address of nearest provincial house.

CONGREGATION OF THE HUMILITY OF MARY (C.H.M.)

History: Abbé John Joseph Begel and Antoinette Potier founded this community in France in 1854. Ten years later the congregation opened a house in the United States. Schools and a motherhouse were established in Missouri in 1870. The Missouri foundation was transferred to Ottumwa, Iowa, seven years later.

Purpose: The primary purpose of the congregation is the salvation of souls through the instruction of children and youth, the care of the sick in hospitals, and social service works. The sisters conduct two colleges for women, a school of nursing, a hospital, co-educational grade and high schools, and children's homes. The congregation has missions in Iowa, Illinois, Minnesota, Montana, and California.

Spiritual Life: The religious exercises include a half-hour of mental prayer followed by Holy Mass and during the course of the day there is the rosary, spiritual reading, and other community prayers and devotions. The office is not prescribed.

Training Program: The six-month to one-year postulancy is followed by a two-year novitiate. The three-year period of temporary vows is climaxed with the taking of perpetual vows. Junior sisters are given special training in religious and secular subjects so as to fit them for the works of the congregation.

Qualifications:

* Age: not over 30. Exceptions are sometimes made.
* Completion of high school.
* Entrance dates: September 8 and January 6.

Habit: The Sisters wear a pleated skirt of light-weight material, with matching sleeves and guimpe, a belt of habit material, a white snap-on-collar, cuffs, and a black veil, a silver ring, and a rosary.

Write to: Convent of the Humility of Mary
Ottumwa Heights
Ottumwa, Iowa

SISTERS OF THE HOLY HUMILITY OF MARY (H.H.M.)

History: The congregation was founded in France in 1854. The educational work of the community was so restricted under Napoleon III, that the sisters decided to emigrate to America at the invitation of Amadeus Rappe, the first Bishop of Cleveland. Ten professed sisters, accompanied by Father Begel, the founder, established their motherhouse at Villa Maria, Pennsylvania. Until 1943, the sisters worked exclusively in the Cleveland diocese, but presently they have houses in the dioceses of Youngstown and Pittsburgh.

Purpose: The apostolate of this pontifical institute consists in works of Christian charity and education. These works include teaching in elementary and secondary schools, nursing in hospitals, performing works of social service, and the conducting of catechetical classes.

Spiritual Life: The religious exercises include Holy Mass, a half-hour of meditation, the recitation of the Office of the Blessed Virgin in English, the rosary, adoration, and spiritual reading.

Training Program: The ten-month postulancy is followed by a two-year novitiate. At the end of this time the candidate makes her triennial temporary vows. She then enters the juniorate for a term of three years, followed by a period of two more years. Profession of perpetual vows is then made. During the juniorate the sister continues her spiritual study and formation, while concentrating on her professional preparation. Throughout her religious life the sister has frequent opportunities to participate in the furthering of her professional background. The community conducts a three-day retreat for prospective candidates each spring.

Qualifications:
* Age: 17 to 30.
* Completion of high school.
* Entrance date: September 12.

Habit: The sisters wear a dark blue habit with matching guimpe, a small white collar, a medal of the Blessed Virgin, and a black veil attached to a white headdress.

> *Write to:* Villa Maria Convent
> Villa Maria,
> Pennsylvania

SISTERS OF THE
MOST HOLY SACRAMENT (M.H.S.)

History: This congregation originated from the Sisters of Perpetual Adoration of the Most Holy Sacrament founded by Father Joseph A. Faller at Bellemagny, France, in 1851. A foundation was established in Louisiana in 1872. Twenty years later the community became independent from the French motherhouse. The community is active in Louisiana, Mississippi, and Alabama.

Purpose: The sisters teach in elementary, secondary, and boarding schools, conduct closed retreats for women every week end, make and distribute altar breads for many parishes, and give catechetical instructions to public school children.

Spiritual Life: The religious exercises include Holy Mass, the recitation of the abbreviated Divine Office in English, the rosary, spiritual reading, and other community prayers and devotions.

Training Program: This congregation conducts an aspirancy for high school girls interested in the religious life. The twelve-month postulancy is followed by a one-year novitiate. At the expiration of the novitiate year, the novice pronounces her temporary vows for a period of three years. Profession of perpetual vows is then made. During this time, the sister continues her spiritual formation while taking courses toward her professional degree.

Qualifications:
* Age: 16 to 30. Exceptions are sometimes made.
* Completion of high school is necessary before entering the postulancy.
* Entrance dates: September, November, February, and June.

Habit: The sisters wear a black habit, scapular, and veil, a white collar, cap, bandeau, and a gold medal.

Write to: Convent of the Most Holy Sacrament
409 W. St. Mary's Boulevard
Lafayette, Louisiana

CALIFORNIA INSTITUTE OF THE SISTERS OF THE MOST HOLY AND IMMACULATE HEART OF THE B.V.M. (I.H.M.)

History: The Institute had its beginnings in Olot, Spain, under the title of "Daughters of the Most Holy and Immaculate Heart of the B. V. M." Its founder was the zealous Dr. Joaquin Masmitja y de Puig, Archpriest of the Cathedral of Gerona. In 1871, at the invitation of Bishop Thaddeus Amat, C.M., ten sisters came to California. In 1924 a new papal institute was established.

Purpose: Its members are bound to honor and serve the Mother of God under her title and to pray especially for the conversion of sinners. They also labor for the salvation of souls through the work of Catholic education in schools and colleges, the care of the sick in hospitals, and the administration of retreat houses.

Spiritual Life: The religious exercises include Holy Mass, the recitation of the Office of the Blessed Virgin Mary in English, two half-hour periods of meditation, the rosary, the Crown of the Seven Dolors, and other community prayers and devotions.

Training Program: After the canonical periods of postulancy and novitiate, the novice is admitted to first vows. The first profession is followed by a scholastic period intended to stabilize the formation begun during the novitiate, and to provide the spiritual, intellectual, and professional education of the sisters as a preparation for their apostolic work. The sisters are admitted to final profession after five years in temporary vows. The sisters are given the opportunity of making their tertianship about ten or more years after their perpetual vows.

Qualifications:
* Age: under 30.
* At least a high school education.
* Entrance date: September 15.

Habit: The habit is blue-violet. The sisters also wear a white coif and guimpe, black scapular, a black veil, and the rosary of the Seven Dolors.

> *Write to:* Immaculate Heart Convent
> 5515 Franklin Avenue
> Los Angeles 28, California

THE LITTLE SERVANT SISTERS OF THE IMMACULATE CONCEPTION
(L.S.I.C.)

History: Mr. Edmund Bojanowski, Mother Leona Jankiewicz, and Father Theophil, Baczynski, S.J., founded this community in Poland in 1850. Its fruitful activity in the education of youth and the care of the sick expanded throughout Poland and later to England, America, and Africa. The first foundation was opened in the United States in 1926.

Purpose: The primary aim of the community is the sanctification and perfection of its members through the observance of the three holy vows and the salvation of others through the apostolate of teaching and caring for the sick and aged. The sisters are located in New Jersey and New York.

Spiritual Life: The religious exercises include Holy Mass, the recitation of the Office of the Blessed Virgin, a half-hour of meditation, the rosary, spiritual reading, and other community prayers and devotions.

Training Program: The six-month postulancy is followed by a two-year novitiate. Temporary vows are made for three years and then are renewed for another two years. Perpetual vows are pronounced at the expiration of this period. After first vows the sisters continue their spiritual formation while taking college courses toward the completion of their professional degrees.

Qualifications:
* The maximum age is 25. Exceptions are sometimes made.
* Completion of high school.
* Entrance dates: December 7 and July 22.

Habit: The sisters wear a blue habit and cincture, a black veil, a roman collar, white coif, and a rosary.

Write to: St. Joseph's Home
184 Amboy Avenue
Woodbridge, New Jersey

MISSIONARY FRANCISCAN SISTERS OF THE IMMACULATE CONCEPTION (O.S.F.)

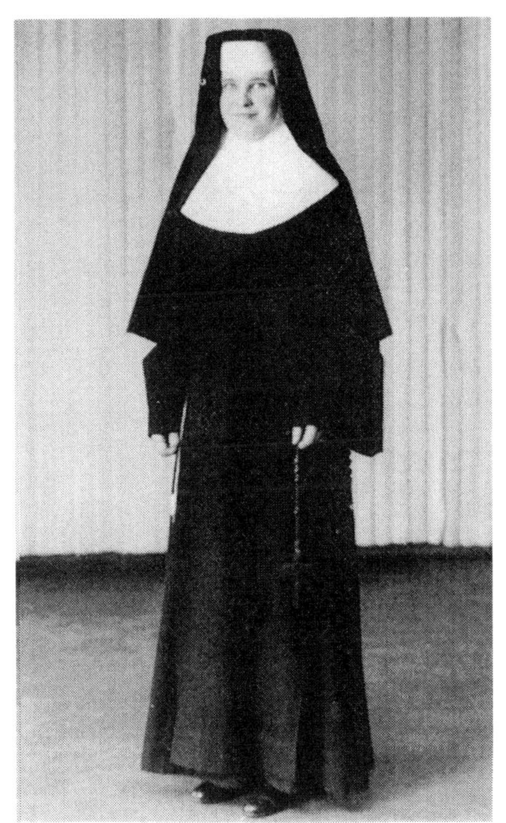

History: Mother Mary Ignatius Hayes founded this institute in Belle Prairie, Minnesota, in 1873. The motherhouse was later transferred to Rome, Italy. The sisters now have establishments in Canada, Australia, Egypt, New Guinea, Peru, South America, and the United States.

Purpose: The sisters teach in elementary and secondary schools, give catechetical instructions, and are engaged in social work. The houses of the community are located in New York, New Jersey, Pennsylvania, Massachusetts, Illinois, Minnesota, and Georgia.

Spiritual Life: The religious exercises include Holy Mass, the chanting of the Office of the Blessed Virgin in English, one hour of mental prayer, the rosary, spiritual reading, and other community prayers and devotions.

Training Program: The period of postulancy is followed by a two-year novitiate. At the expiration of the novitiate, the novice makes her temporary vows. These are made for five years. Perpetual vows are pronounced at the end of this period. After first vows, the sisters continue their spiritual formation while taking courses toward their academic degrees.

Qualifications:
* The maximum age is 30. Exceptions are sometimes made to 35.
* Completion of high school.
* Entrance dates: September and February.

Habit: The sisters wear a brown scapular and tunic, a white cap, guimpe, band, and cord, a Franciscan Crown rosary, and a silver ring.

Write to: Immaculate Conception Convent
20 Manet Road
Chestnut Hill 67, Massachusetts

St. Francis Convent
1601 Central Avenue
Union City, New Jersey

Our Lady of the Angels Convent
Belle Prairie
Little Falls, Minnesota

SISTERS OF THE
IMMACULATE CONCEPTION (C.I.C.)

History: Father Cyprien Venissat, a zealous French priest, founded this congregation in Labadieville, Louisiana, in 1874. Recognizing the imminent need for educating the children of the poor, Father Venissat organized a group of sisters, who with lay-helpers, opened a boarding and day school in his parish. He chose Miss Elvina Vienne as the foundress of the community.

Purpose: The sisters conduct elementary and secondary schools and give catechetical instructions to public school children. These institutions and work are being carried on in the state of Louisiana.

Spiritual Life: The religious exercises include Holy Mass, the recitation of the Little Office of the Blessed Virgin in English, the rosary, a half-hour of mental prayer, spiritual reading, and other community prayers and devotions.

Training Program: The congregation conducts an aspirancy for teen-age girls interested in the religious life. The six-month postulancy is followed by a two-year novitiate. Four years of spiritual formation and professional training follow the novitiate. From five to ten years after final profession, there is a period of tertianship lasting six weeks for the purpose of spiritual renovation.

Qualifications:

* Aspirancy: ninth grade and up.
* Postulancy: not over 35 and completion of high school.

Habit: The sisters wear a black pleated dress, cape and veil, medal of the Immaculate Conception, rosary, and a ring.

Write to: Immaculate Conception Convent
3037 Dauphine Street
New Orleans 17, Louisiana

SISTERS OF THE IMMACULATE CONCEPTION OF THE BLESSED VIRGIN MARY

History: Archbishop George Matulaitis, M.I.C., founded this congregation at Mariampole, Lithuania, in 1918. The sisters arrived in the U.S. in 1936 and established their first foundation at Thompson, Connecticut. This was later moved to Putnam, Connecticut. They are located in the eastern section of the United States and in Canada.

Purpose: The specific purpose of this community is the education of children in day nurseries, summer camps, and schools, care for the sick and aged, and the apostolate of the press.

Spiritual Life: The religious exercises include Mass, a half-hour of meditation, recitation of the rosary, and other community prayers and devotions.

Training Program: Along with their initial spiritual training, the postulants pursue studies in preparation for their future work in the apostolate. The time of novitiate is one year, after which they make their first profession of temporary vows. Perpetual vows are taken after five years of temporary vows.

Qualifications:

* Age: 15 to 30. Exceptions are sometimes made.
* Completion of high school is desirable but not absolutely necessary.

Habit: The sisters wear a full-length, tailored black dress, roman collar and a simple black veil. The crucifix is received at their first profession, a gold ring when they take their final vows.

> *Write to:* Immaculate Conception Convent
> R. F. D. 2
> Putnam, Connecticut

SISTERS SERVANTS OF THE IMMACULATE HEART OF MARY (S.C.I.M.)

History: This community, better known as the Sisters of the Good Shepherd of Quebec, was founded in Quebec City, Canada, by George Manly Muir, Knight of St. Gregory, in 1850. Madame Genevieve Fitzbach became the first religious superior. Three provinces were established in Canada and one in Saco, Maine.

Purpose: The primary apostolic activities include the spiritual rehabilitation and moral preservation of fallen women and education of youth. The sisters operate elementary and secondary schools, an orphanage, a school of religion, homes for the aged, and a maternity hospital for unwed mothers in Massachusetts, Maine, and Tennessee.

Spiritual Life: The religious exercises include Holy Mass, community morning and evening prayers, an hour of meditation, spiritual reading, visits, and the rosary. The Office of the Blessed Virgin is said in Latin on Sundays, on holy days, and on principal feast days of the Blessed Mother.

Training Program: After a year of postulancy and one canonical year of the novitiate, the novice takes her temporary vows. During the five years of her profession of temporary vows, the junior professed sister spends the first two years following a professional educational program in the institute. The other three years are fulfilled in the active apostolate of the community.

Qualifications:
* Age: maximum is 35. Exceptions are sometimes made for those up to 40.
* Completion of high school.
* Entrance date: first Monday in September.

Habit: The sisters wear a black habit, veil, mantle, and rosary, a white headdress, and a silver crucifix.

Write to: Provincial House of the Good Shepherd
Saco,
Maine

SISTERS, SERVANTS OF THE IMMACULATE HEART OF MARY (I.H.M.)

History: Father Louis Florent Gillet, C.Ss.R., founded this congregation in Monroe, Michigan, in 1845 to teach religion in the mission schools for the French settlers in that area. Now nearly 4,000 sisters are divided into three separate motherhouses, working in nineteen dioceses in the United States.

Purpose: The sisters teach from the kindergarten to the college level, nurse in hospitals, and are engaged in social work. This work is being carried on in eight states including Puerto Rico. The community also maintains Pius XII Research Center for the teaching of religion on all levels.

Spiritual Life: The religious exercises include Holy Mass, the Office of the Blessed Virgin recited in Latin on Sundays and on major feast days—the short breviary is said privately at other times—a half-hour of mental prayer, the rosary, spiritual reading, and other community prayers and devotions.

Training Program: The six to nine-month postulancy is followed by a two-year novitiate. The novice makes her temporary vows at the end of the novitiate. Perpetual vows are pronounced after five years in temporary vows. After first profession, the sister continues her spiritual formation while taking courses toward her academic or nursing degree. A tertianship is offered after about fourteen years in religion.

Qualifications:
* The maximum age is 30. Exceptions are sometimes made.
* Completion of high school.
* Entrance date: early September.

Habit: The sisters wear a blue habit in honor of the Immaculate Conception and a black veil.

See page 384 for address of nearest motherhouse.

CONGREGATION OF THE INCARNATE WORD AND BLESSED SACRAMENT (I.W.B.S.)

History: Mother Jeanne de Matel founded this congregation in Roanne, France, in 1625. The first American foundation was made in 1853 in Brownsville, Texas.

Purpose: The members of this community are engaged in teaching in private and parochial schools, and nursing the sick in three hospitals. Most of the works of this community are carried on in South Texas.

Spiritual Life: The religious exercises include Holy Mass, the recitation of the Office of the Blessed Virgin in English, one hour of mental prayer, spiritual reading, and visits to the Blessed Sacrament.

Training Program: This congregation conducts an aspirancy for high school girls who are interested in the religious life. The eleven-month postulancy is followed by a one-year novitiate, after which a five-year scholasticate program begins. The sisters, during this period, renew their temporary vows annually. They continue their spiritual formation while taking courses toward the fulfillment of their academic degrees.

Qualifications:
* Age: 14 to 30.
* Average intelligence.
* Entrance date: usually August.

Habit: The sisters wear a white habit, and a dark red cincture and scapular.

Write to: Mother Superior
105 West Church Street
Victoria, Texas

CONGREGATION OF THE SISTERS OF ST. JOSEPH OF BOURG (C.S.J.)

History: This congregation which was founded in Le Puy, France, by a zealous Jesuit, Jean Pierre Medaille, and his saintly Bishop, Henri de Maupas, disseminated throughout all France during the century and a half preceding the Revolution. It was steeped in the blood of its numerous martyrs in the Reign of Terror. It was revived at Lyons, France, during the Napoleonic regime through the efforts of Cardinal Fesch and the devotedness of Mother St. John Fontbonne. Such is the history of St. Joseph's of Bourg from its inception in 1650 until 1824, the year which marked its separation from the general motherhouse at Lyons, and its erection into a separate congregation. Houses have been established in Europe, the United States, and Canada.

Purpose: The general aim of these sisters is the glory of God through the sanctification of its members by means of the three vows. The special objective is the salvation and service of others through works of charity: elementary and secondary schools, hospitals, social service missions among the Indians and the Negro, prison visitations, and summer camps for youth.

Spiritual Life: The religious exercises include Holy Mass, meditation, the rosary, spiritual reading, and other community prayers and devotions.

Training Program: The formation begins with a nine-month postulancy followed by a two-year novitiate. During the postulancy and the second year of the novitiate an integrated liberal arts college program is simultaneously initiated with a thorough spiritual foundation. After first profession the first level of education is completed before entering into the apostolate.

Qualifications:
* Age: at least 16.
* Average intelligence.

Habit: The sisters wear a black habit with white linen around the face, and a white guimpe.

Write to: Mother Provincial   Mother Provincial
Marywood Road   1200 Mirabeau Avenue
Crookston, Minnesota   New Orleans 22, Louisiana

SISTERS OF ST. JOSEPH (C.S.J.)

History: Bishop Henry Maupas and Father John Peter Medaille, S.J., founded the Sisters of St. Joseph, who now number over 30,000 members, in Le Puy, France, in 1650. Disbanded by the French Revolution, it was reorganized in 1816 in Lyons, France, by Mother St. John Fontbonne, survivor of the Reign of Terror. In 1836 at the request of the Most Reverend Joseph Rosati, first Bishop of St. Louis, six sisters were sent to Carondelet, Missouri. Today around 17,000 Sisters of St. Joseph are serving in the United States from coast to coast.

Purpose: The most extensive work of the congregation is the instruction of youth from kindergarten to college. The constant need for dedicated service has expanded the work to the operation of hospitals with nursing schools, orphanages, care of the deaf and other charitable institutions. Missions have been founded in South America, the Solomon Islands, New Guinea, and Japan.

Spiritual Life: The religious exercises include Holy Mass, the recitation of the Prime and Compline of the Divine Office (the Little Office of the Blessed Virgin is recited on Sundays and holy days by Carondelet and a few of the other communities—some congregations say the short breviary) mental prayer, the rosary, spiritual reading, and other community prayers and devotions.

Training Program: The six to eleven-month postulancy is followed by a two-year novitiate, after which temporary vows are made. These are renewed for three or six years before final vows. During this period, the Sister Formation program is followed, giving the young sister ample time to lay a strong spiritual foundation while at the same time continuing her academic and professional education. The works of the congregation are so varied, both at home and in the missions, that opportunity for the development of special talents and skills is offered, so that any young woman desirous of serving God as a Sister of St. Joseph may use her personal gifts in His Service.

Qualifications:
* Age: 18 to 35.
* Completion of high school is preferred.
* Entrance date: September.

Habit: The sisters wear a black habit and veil, a white band, coronet, and guimpe, profession crucifix, and a rosary.

Write to Mother Superior at the nearest St. Joseph Convent listed below:

SISTERS OF ST. JOSEPH OF CARONDELET

Generalate, 2307 South Lindbergh Boulevard, St. Louis 31, Missouri

*Province of St. Louis—*St. Joseph's Provincial House, 6400 South Minnesota Avenue, St. Louis 11, Missouri

*Province of St. Paul—*St. Joseph's Provincial House, 1890 Randolph Avenue, St. Paul 16, Minnesota

*Province of Albany—*St. Joseph's Provincial House, Watervliet-Shaker Road, Latham, New York

*Province of Los Angeles—*St. Mary's Provincialate, 11999 Chalon Road, Los Angeles 49, California

INDEPENDENT CONVENTS OF THE SISTERS OF ST. JOSEPH

California
Motherhouse of Sisters of St. Joseph, 380 S. Batavia Street, Orange, California

Illinois
Motherhouse of Sisters of St. Joseph, 1515 Ogden Avenue, La Grange, Illinois

Indiana
St. Joseph Convent, Tipton, R.R. 5, Indiana

Kansas
Nazareth Motherhouse, 13th and Washington Streets, Concordia, Kansas

Mt. St. Mary's Convent, 3700 E. Lincoln Street, Wichita 18, Kansas

Massachusetts
Motherhouse of the Sisters of St. Joseph, 444 Centre Street, Milton 86, Massachusetts

Convent of the Sisters of St. Joseph, 62 Elliot Street, Springfield 5, Massachusetts

Michigan
Nazareth College, Nazareth, Michigan

New York
St. Joseph's Convent, Brentwood, New York

Mt. St. Joseph, 2064 Main Street, Buffalo 8, New York

Nazareth Convent, Pittsford, Brighton Station, Rochester 18, New York

Sisters of St. Joseph, 362 Main Street, Watertown, New York

Ohio
Sisters of St. Joseph, 3430 Rocky River Drive, N.W., Cleveland 11, Ohio

Pennsylvania
Mt. Gallitzin Motherhouse, Baden, Pennsylvania

Sisters of St. Joseph, 819 W. 8th Street, Erie, Pennsylvania

Mt. St. Joseph Convent, Chestnut Hill, Philadelphia 18, Pennsylvania

Vermont
Mt. St. Joseph Convent, Rutland, Vermont

West Virginia
Mt. St. Joseph, Pogue Run Road, Wheeling, West Virginia

Wisconsin
Sisters of St. Joseph, 1412 E. 2nd Street, Superior, Wisconsin

SISTERS OF ST. JOSEPH OF CHAMBERY (C.S.S.J.)

History: Bishop de Maupas and Father Medaille founded this congregation in Le Puy, France in 1650. It was later reorganized at Lyons by Mother St. John Fontbonne. Political upheavals forced a separation from Lyons and the foundation at Chambery, France, became the headquarters of the community. It became a diocesan congregation in 1812 and a pontifical institute in 1875. There are eleven provinces located in ten countries in Europe, India, Brazil, Iceland, Pakistan, Madagascar, and the United States.

Purpose: The members of this congregation are engaged in teaching in elementary and secondary schools, nursing in hospitals, and in caring for orphans. Their institutions are found in the states of Massachusetts, Connecticut, and in the District of Columbia.

Spiritual Life: The religious exercises include Holy Mass, two half-hour meditations, vocal community prayers, Lauds from the short breviary chanted every day in English and Compline of the same Office chanted on Sundays, the rosary, and the Litanies of St. Joseph and of Our Lady. On holy days Prime and Vespers are chanted.

Training Program: The six-month postulancy is followed by a two-year novitiate. After the novitiate, temporary vows are renewed annually for five consecutive years. Profession of perpetual vows is then made.

Qualifications:
* Age: 15 to 30.
* Completion of high school is preferred.
* Entrance date: September 1.

Habit: The sisters wear a black habit, cincture, and veil, a white coif, band, guimpe, crucifix, and rosary.

Write to: Provincial House
27 Park Road
West Hartford 7, Connecticut

SISTERS OF ST. JOSEPH OF NEWARK
(C.S.J.)

History: Bishop Bagshawe of Nottingham, England, founded this congregation in 1888. Bishop Michael Wigger of Newark, New Jersey, received the community into his diocese shortly after its establishment. In 1890 the congregation opened a foundation in Tacoma, Washington. At present the community is represented in New Jersey, West Virginia, North Carolina, Washington, Oregon, California, Alaska, and the Philippine Islands.

Purpose: The original purpose of the institute was to conduct homes for working girls and to teach underprivileged children. To these were added the care and education of the blind and orphans, teaching in elementary and high schools, the maintenance of hospitals and nursing schools, catechetical centers, a publishing department, foreign missions, and an institute for the mentally retarded.

Spiritual Life: The religious exercises include Holy Mass, the recitation of the Little Office of the Blessed Virgin, (petition has been made for the right to say the abridged Divine Office), a half-hour of meditation, spiritual reading, and other community prayers and devotions.

Training Program: A ten-month postulancy is followed by a two-year novitiate. Temporary vows are then taken. A two-year advanced program of training is then provided at the juniorate. After the juniorate, one year is spent on an assigned mission before final profession. Ten years after perpetual vows a six-week tertianship is given.

Qualifications:
* Age: 15 to 30.
* Average intelligence.
* Entrance date: September 12.

Habit: The sisters wear a black habit, scapular, veil and leather cincture, a white kerchief and forehead band, a silver crucifix, and a five decade rosary.

> *Write to:* St. Michael's Provincial House
> Englewood, New Jersey
>
> Mt. St. Mary Provincial House
> Bellevue, Washington

SISTERS OF ST. JOSEPH OF THE THIRD ORDER OF ST. FRANCIS (S.S.J.)

History: This pontifical congregation was established at Stevens Point, Wisconsin, with the approval of The Most Reverend Sebastian Messmer, former bishop of the Diocese of Green Bay, Wisconsin. Mother Mary Felicia and Mother Mary Clara with forty-six sisters opened a foundation there in 1901.

Purpose: The members of this community maintain two junior colleges for their own members and conduct elementary and secondary schools, hospitals, and schools of practical nursing. These institutions are located in Illinois, Indiana, Colorado, Connecticut, Michigan, Minnesota, Mississippi, Nebraska, Ohio, and Wisconsin.

Spiritual Life: The religious exercises include Holy Mass, the recitation of the Little Office of the Blessed Virgin in Latin, mental prayer, the rosary, spiritual reading, and other community prayers and devotions.

Training Program: The community conducts aspirancies in all its provinces for teen-age girls interested in the religious life. The six to twelve-month postulancy is followed by a two-year novitiate. Temporary vows are made annually for five years, after which perpetual vows are pronounced. After first profession of vows, the sisters continue taking college courses toward the fulfillment of their professional degrees.

Qualifications:
* Age: 14 to 30.
* Average intelligence.
* Entrance dates: July and August.

Habit: The sisters wear a black habit, scapular and veil, a white collar and cord, a crucifix, and the Franciscan Crown rosary.

See page 384 for address of nearest provincial house.

THE MARIAN SISTERS (M.S.)

History: This community was founded in 1954 when two sisters who escaped the communist regime in Europe were invited by Louis B. Kucera, Bishop of Lincoln, Nebraska, to establish a religious congregation in his doicese. The community is a diocesan institute with its motherhouse in Lincoln.

Purpose: The primary aim is the sanctification of its members through the observance of the evangelical vows of religion. The secondary objective is the sanctification of souls through the various works of teaching, catechetical, and social work.

Spiritual Life: The religious exercises include Holy Mass, the recitation of the short breviary in English, mental prayer, the rosary, spiritual reading, and other community prayers and devotions.

Training Program: The six-month postulancy is followed by a one-year novitiate. Temporary vows are made for five years after which perpetual vows are taken. The sisters continue their spiritual formation while taking college courses toward the fulfillment of their professional degrees.

Qualifications:
* Age: not over 30.
* Completion of high school.
* Entrance date: September.

Habit: The sisters wear a full-length grey tunic, cape and cincture, a white cap, black veil, and a ring.

> *Write to:* The Marian Sisters
> Box 721
> Lincoln, Nebraska

MARIANIST SISTERS (F.M.I.)

History: Father William J. Chaminade and Adele de Trenquelleon founded this community in France in 1816. They are also known as the Daughters of Mary Immaculate. This congregation had its origins in the Sodalities of Our Lady which were established in southern France by Father Chaminade following the French Revolution. The community has foundations in Europe, Japan, Africa, and the United States.

Purpose: The sisters teach in primary and secondary schools, conduct closed retreats and days of recollection, work with youth groups, especially sodalities, operate residences for students and working girls, and are engaged in catechetical work.

Spiritual Life: The religious exercises include Holy Mass, the chanting of the short form of the Divine Office in English, one hour of mental prayer, the rosary, spiritual reading, and other community prayers and devotions.

Training Program: The six to twelve-month postulancy is followed by a two-year novitiate. Temporary vows are made for three years. Perpetual vows are usually pronounced at the end of the three years. After making her first vows, the sisters are assigned either to continue their professional education or to begin working in the active apostolate.

Qualifications:
* Age: at least 16.
* Completion of high school.
* Entrance dates: September and February.

Habit: The sisters wear a simple black habit, a soft linen guimpe, a white sash, and a silver crucifix.

Write to: Our Lady of the Pillar Convent
251 W. Ligustrum Drive
San Antonio 28, Texas

320

MARIANITE SISTERS OF HOLY CROSS (M.S.C.)

History: Father Basil Anthony Moreau and Mother Mary of the Seven Dolors founded this congregation in 1841 in Le Mans, France. In 1843 the first mission was established in the United States. Missions are located also in Canada, East Pakistan, and Haiti.

Purpose: The sisters work for the salvation of souls by conducting schools and hospitals. In the United States, the Louisiana province staffs twenty-four elementary and ten secondary schools, a sisters' college, and a hospital. The New York province staffs four elementary and two secondary schools and a hospital.

Spiritual Life: The religious exercises include daily morning and evening prayers, a half-hour of meditation, Holy Mass, the recitation of the Little Office of the Blessed Virgin, examination of conscience, visits, a half-hour of spiritual reading and the recitation of the rosary of Our Lady of the Seven Dolors.

Training Program: The period of postulancy lasts from six months to one year. The postulant studies the rules of the community, follows the spiritual exercises of the congregation and begins her college studies. Following the reception of the habit, the novice spends two years in the novitiate. At the end of this time, the novice takes her temporary simple vows which are renewed annually for three years. She then continues working toward her academic degree. Upon the completion of the third year of temporary vows, the sister makes her profession of perpetual vows.

Qualifications:
* Age: 16 to 35.
* Normal intelligence.
* Entrance dates: September 8 and February 2.

Habit: The sisters wear a black habit, cape, and veil, a blue cord, the Seven Dolor rosary, a white collar and cap, and a silver heart.

Write to: Our Lady of the Holy Cross Our Lady of Princeton
4123 Woodland Highway Princeton,
New Orleans 14, Louisiana New Jersey

LITTLE FRANCISCANS OF MARY
(P.F.M.)

History: This community was founded in Worcester, Massachusetts, in 1889. It was erected as a diocesan congregation in 1892 and granted papal approbation in 1949. The rule observed is that of the Third Order Regular of St. Francis of Assisi. The congregation now numbers seven hundred sisters.

Purpose: The primary aim of the congregation is the glory of God and the sanctification of its members through the observance of the evangelical counsels. The sisters teach in schools, conduct orphanages and homes for the aged, and operate hospitals. These institutions are located in Massachusetts and Maine.

Spiritual Life: The religious exercises include Holy Mass, meditation, the recitation of the Office of the Blessed Virgin in Latin, spiritual reading, the rosary of the Seven Joys of Mary, and other community devotions.

Training Program: This congregation conducts an aspirancy for girls of high school age interested in the religious life. The six-month postulancy is followed by a two-year novitiate. The novice then pronounces her temporary profession of vows. These are renewed annually for five years. Profession of perpetual vows is then made. During this time, the sisters continue their spiritual formation while taking courses toward their professional degrees.

Qualifications:
 * Age: 15 to 35.
 * Completion of high school is preferred.
 * Entrance dates: February 2 and August 12.

Habit: The sisters wear a brown tunic and scapular, a white hood, wimple, and cord, and a silver crucifix.

Write to: Mother Superior
St. Francis Home
37 Thorne Street
Worcester 4, Massachusetts

SISTERS OF THE PURITY OF MARY
(S.P.V.M.)

History: This congregation was founded in Aguascalientes, Mexico, in 1903. Under the fatherly protection of the Bishop of Aguascalientes, a group of young girls desiring to glorify God, and to console the Most Sacred Heart of Jesus, united to establish a school. They wished to dedicate themselves to the education of youth in solid Christian principles and in the practice of the virtues of purity and sacrifice. Their works has rapidly increased under the protection of the Most Blessed Virgin and has extended to include several states in the Republic of Mexico and in the state of Texas, where three foundations have been established.

Purpose: Its principal purpose is the imitation of the purity of Mary and the consolation of the Sacred Heart of Jesus, and the salvation of souls by prayer and sacrifice. The sisters teach in schools and conduct retreat houses.

Qualifications:
* Age: 15 to 30.
* Average intelligence.

Habit: The sisters wear a black habit, scapular, cincture, and veil, a white collar, rosary, and an embroidered monogram of Mary on the scapular.

> *Write to:* Mother Superior
> P.O. Box 843
> Kingsville, Texas

SISTERS OF ST. MARY OF NAMUR (S.S.M.N.)

History: Father Nicholas Joseph Minsart founded this congregation in Namur, Belgium, in 1819, to help restore Christian family life disrupted by the French Revolution. The first foundation in the United States was opened in the diocese of Buffalo, New York, in 1863, which has since become the eastern province. Within a decade the sisters were in Texas forming the nucleus for the western province.

Purpose: The apostolic activities of the members of this congregation include teaching from the nursery to college level and nursing. They also operate missions among the Mexicans in Texas and the Negroes in South Carolina, and maternity centers and schools in the Congo and Ruanda, Africa.

Spiritual Life: The center of the communal prayer life is daily Holy Mass and the Divine Office. Lauds or Prime in English form each day's morning prayers. Compline closes the day. On Sundays and feast days, all of the day hours are recited. Except for Office and the rosary, the congregation has few vocal prayers. An hour each day is given to mental prayer and adoration.

Training Program: The basic training program extends over the nine years between entrance and perpetual vows. During the postulancy of one year maximum attention is given to an understanding of the religious life. In the canonical year of the novitiate special emphasis is placed on religious formation. During the second year of novitiate and in her juniorate period, the sister continues taking courses toward her academic degree. After ten years in vows the sister spends two months in spiritual renewal.

Qualifications:
* Age: maximum is 30.
* Completion of high school.
* Entrance date: usually August.

Habit: The sisters wear a black dress, scapular, and veil, and a white bandeau, underveil, neckerchief, and a rosary.

Write to: Our Lady of Victory Provincial House   Mount St. Mary
3300 South Hemphill Street   3756 Delaware Avenue
Fort Worth 10, Texas   Kenmore, New York

SISTERS OF SAINT MARY
OF OREGON (S.S.M.O.)

History: The Most Reverend
Archbishop William Gross, C.Ss.R.,
of Oregon City founded this pontifical congregation in Sublimity,
Oregon in 1886. Papal approbation
was granted in 1934. A vastly scat-
tered flock, with less than thirty
priests and only a few religious to
care for them made Archbishop
Gross determined to establish his
own community of sisters. After
testing the sincerity of seven young
women who desired to consecrate
their lives to God and to the service of the Church, the congregation
had its origin.

Purpose: The sisters conduct a
resident and day academy, staff
twenty-five elementary and secondary schools, instruct in colleges,
maintain a convalescent and nursing home, and are engaged in catechetical work. The apostolate is
carried on in Oregon and Washington.

Spiritual Life: The religious exercises include Holy Mass, mental
prayer, the rosary, spiritual reading, and other community prayers and
devotions.

Training Program: The community conducts an aspirancy for high
school girls interested in the religious life. The six to twelve-month
postulancy is followed by a two-year novitiate. Temporary vows are
made for three years. Perpetual vows are pronounced at the end of this
period. College degrees must be earned before commencing the apostolate. This education begins during the postulancy, continues in the
second year of novitiate, and is completed after profession of temporary vows.

Qualifications:
* Age: at least 15.
* Completion of high school is preferred.
* Entrance date: September.

Habit: The sisters wear a black habit, cincture, scapular, and
veil, a white coif, forehead band, and collar, a rosary, crucifix, and a gold
ring.

> *Write to:* St. Mary of the Valley
> 4440 S.W. 148 Avenue
> Beaverton, Oregon

SISTERS OF MERCY (R.S.M.)

History: The Sisters of Mercy were founded by Mary Catherine McAuley in Dublin, Ireland, on December 12, 1831. In the United States since 1834, they number over 14,000 and are found in almost every state of the union. The congregation has spread to South and Central America, British Honduras, Jamaica, the Philippine Islands, Guam, Asia, and Africa. In 1929 many communities amalgamated and are known as the Sisters of Mercy of the Union. Although there are many other independent congregations, there is perfect accord and harmony among them because they are spiritually one.

Purpose: The sisters teach on all levels of education, including work with exceptional children and nursing education, conduct hospitals, visit the sick and imprisoned, and are engaged in social service work in all its aspects with special emphasis on geriatric care, distressed women, and homes for dependent children.

Spiritual Life: The religious exercises include Holy Mass, mental prayer, spiritual reading, the Little Office of the Blessed Virgin, and other community prayers and devotions.

Training Program: The training for the Mercy apostolate consists of three years of postulancy and novitiate, at the end of which profession of temporary vows is made. The next two years are passed in continued formation in the house of studies called the juniorate. This time is followed by three years in the apostolate before perpetual vows. The scholastic and professional development is integrated consistently with the spiritual and apostolic formation. A period of spiritual renewal is planned after ten years in vows and during the silver jubilee year.

Qualifications:
* Age: not over 30. Exceptions are sometimes made.
* Completion of high school.
* Entrance date: usually September.

Habit: The sisters wear a black habit, leather cincture, and veil, a rosary and a silver ring.

Write to the Mother Superior at the nearest Sister of Mercy convent listed below.

SISTERS OF MERCY
(Each of the following communities are independent units of pontifical
right.)

California
Convent of Our Lady of Mercy
  Auburn, California

  Sisters of Mercy
  2300 Adeline Drive
  Burlingame, California

Connecticut
  St. Joseph's Convent
  160 Farmington Avenue
  Hartford 5, Connecticut

Iowa
  Sacred Heart Convent
  Elmhurst Drive
  Cedar Rapids, Iowa

Maine
  St. Joseph's Convent
  605 Stephens Avenue
  Portland 5, Maine

Massachusetts
  St. Gabriel's Convent
  46 High Street
  Worcester 8, Massachusetts

New Hampshire
  Sisters of Mercy
  435 Union Street
  Windham, New Hampshire

New Jersey
  Sisters of Mercy
  U.S. Route 22 at Tirrell Road
  North Plainfield, New Jersey

New York
  Convent of Mercy
  634 New Scotland Avenue
  Albany 8, New York

  St. Francis Convent
  273 Willoughby Avenue
  Brooklyn 5, New York

  Convent of Mt. Mercy
  625 Abbott Road
  Buffalo 20, New York

  Sisters of Mercy
  1437 Blossom Road
  Brighton Station
  Rochester 10, New York

North Carolina
  Sacred Heart Convent
  Belmont, North Carolina

Pennsylvania
  Sisters of Mercy
  Merion, Pennsylvania

  Mt. Mercy College
  3333 Fifth Avenue
  Pittsburgh 13, Pennsylvania

  St. Joseph's Convent
  512 W. Main Street
  Titusville, Pennsylvania

Vermont
  Mt. St. Mary Academy
  Mansfield Avenue
  Burlington, Vermont

SISTERS OF MERCY OF THE UNION IN THE UNITED STATES

General Motherhouse
  Mother General
  1000 Kendale Road
  Bethesda P.O.,
  Washington 14, D.C.

Province of Baltimore
  Holy Family Convent
  Mt. Washington
  Baltimore 9, Maryland
  For further addresses see page 384.

Province of Chicago
  Provincial House
  10024 S. Central Park Avenue
  Chicago 42, Illinois

Province of Cincinnati
  Provincial House
  2301 Grandview Avenue
  Cincinnati 6, Ohio

MINIM DAUGHTERS OF MARY IMMACULATE (C.F.M.M.)

History: Father Pablo de Anda Padilla founded this congregation in Leon, Guanajuato, Mexico, March 25, 1886, where the motherhouse is presently located. The community has foundations in Cuba and in the United States.

Purpose: The members of this congregation are engaged in the education of youth, nursing in hospitals, and care for the aged, orphans, and Indian missions in Mexico. Their institutions in the United States are found in Arizona.

Spiritual Life: The religious exercises include Holy Mass, one hour of mental prayer, the recitation of the Office of the Blessed Virgin, the rosary, spiritual reading, and other community prayers and devotions.

Qualifications:
* Age: 15 to 30.
* Completion of high school is preferred.
* Entrance dates: February-June-December.

Habit: The sisters wear a black habit, veil, and cape, and a white wimple, crucifix, and rosary.

Write to: St. Joseph's Novitiate
Box 636
Nogales, Arizona

SISTERS SERVANTS OF
MARY IMMACULATE (S.S.M.I.)

History: This congregation was founded in the Western Ukraine in 1892. Upon the invitation of the Oblate Fathers the sisters came to Canada in 1902. The community has foundations in Europe, South America, Poland, countries beyond the Iron Curtain, Canada, and the United States.

Purpose: The primary objective of the members of this community is teaching in elementary, secondary schools, and academies. They also conduct day nurseries, orphanages, hospitals, homes for the aged and infirm, homes for girls, culinary departments in ecclesiastical institutions, and give catechetical instructions in rural areas in the summer. Their institutions are located primarily in the eastern section of the United States.

Spiritual Life: The religious exercises include Holy Mass, the recitation of the Office in Old Slavonic, meditation, the rosary, spiritual reading, and other community prayers and devotions.

Training Program: The six-month postulancy is followed by a two-year novitiate. Temporary vows are made at the expiration of the novitiate. After three years of temporary vows, the sister then pronounces her perpetual vows.

Qualifications:
* Age: 15 to 35.
* Average intelligence.
* Entrance dates: June 15 and August 15.

Habit: The sisters wear a navy blue habit, and scapular, a white coif, and head band, and a black veil.

> *Write to:* Mother Provincial
> 209 West Chestnut Hill Avenue
> Philadelphia 18, Pennsylvania

SISTERS OF MARY MOTHER OF GOD
(S.M.M.G.)

History: Mother Francis Xavier founded this community at Long Beach, California, in 1950. The sisters inaugurated their congregation by opening Saint Lucy School. In 1952 the Sacred Congregation for Religious confirmed the establishment of the community. The sisters have been teaching in the Los Angeles Archdiocesan high schools since 1956.

Purpose: Since this is a new community, it is not presently engaged in every area of its specific apostolate. Its apostolic endeavor aspires to meet the needs of body and soul according to the best standards of the times. A variety of sister personnel is needed. This includes teachers on the elementary, secondary, and college levels, nurses, secretaries, dieticians, and administrators.

Spiritual Life: The religious exercises include Holy Mass, the chanting of the Little Office of the Blessed Virgin in Latin, a half-hour of mental prayer, rosary, spiritual reading, and other community prayers and devotions.

Training Program: The six-month postulancy is followed by a two-year novitiate. Temporary profession of vows is then made. During the five years of the juniorate, the sisters continue their spiritual formation while taking college courses in preparation for the particular work to which they will be assigned.

Qualifications:
* Age: under 30.
* Completion of high school.
* Entrance date: September 8.

Habit: The sisters wear a black habit, scapular, and veil, a white headband, coif, and guimpe, a five decade rosary, and a silver crucifix.

> *Write to:* Motherhouse
> 10664 St. James Drive
> Culver City, California

SCHOOL SISTERS de NOTRE DAME
(de N.D.)

History: This congregation traces its origin to the community of religious women established in France by St. Peter Fourier in 1598. Suppressed during the French Revolution, favorable conditions found the congregation re-established in various places throughout Europe. One such place was Bavaria under Caroline Gerhardinger. From these School Sisters, Father Gabriel Schneider founded an entirely separate community in Bohemia in 1853. In 1910 Mother Mary Gualberta led a small group of sisters from their Czechoslovakian motherhouse to the United States.

Purpose: The School Sisters conduct elementary and secondary schools in the Midwestern United States, and perform extensive catechetical work with public school children, especially in rural areas. The sisters staff an Indian Mission in South Dakota and direct facilities for lay retreats.

Spiritual Life: As the source of their apostolate and for their own sanctification, the life of the sisters is devoted to Holy Mass, prayer, and meditation. They chant in English the Little Office of the Blessed Virgin daily and devote an hour to mental prayer. The rosary, spiritual reading, and community vocal prayers are some of the other religious exercises.

Training Program: The sisters conduct an aspirancy for high school girls interested in the religious life. The postulancy of six months is followed by a two-year novitiate. Temporary vows are taken at the end of this time for three years. The professed remain in the juniorate for at least two years during which they take courses toward their professional or academic degrees. There is a one year in-serving juniorate before the profession of perpetual vows.

Qualifications:
* Age: 15 to 27. Exceptions are sometimes made.
* Completion of high school is preferred.

Habit: The sisters wear a simple black habit, belt, and veil, a white linen collar, and a medallion (adopted 1963).

Write to: Convent de Notre Dame
35th and State Streets
Omaha 12, Nebraska

SCHOOL SISTERS OF NOTRE DAME
(S.S.N.D.)

History: This congregation was founded by a dedicated teacher, Caroline Gerhardinger, the future Mother Teresa of Jesus. Directed by Bishop Wittmann of Ratisbon, Bavaria, Mother Teresa opened the first SSND convent in 1833. Just fourteen years later she brought five sisters to the United States. The great need for Catholic schools was recognized by Mother Teresa, and the sisters soon spread throughout the country. Today there are around twelve thousand sisters in eighteen countries. In the United States alone there are more than sixty-five hundred.

Purpose: These sisters are active in the apostolate of Catholic education. Some are teachers, others are housekeepers, typists, nurses, seamstresses, or secretaries, or serve in other occupations. The sisters in the seven American provinces conduct elementary and high schools, colleges, orphanages, schools for deaf mutes, day nurseries, and industrial schools. The overseas missions are located in Guam, Puerto Rico, Honduras, Japan, Bolivia, and Okinawa.

Spiritual Life: The religious exercises include Holy Mass, recitation of the Divine Office in English, a half-hour in the morning and a quarter-hour of meditation in the afternoon, the rosary, spiritual reading, and other community prayers and devotions.

Training Program: Those girls who have not completed high school may enroll in the aspirancy. Entrants with a secondary school education spend one year as candidates and another as novices. After the canonical novitiate year the formation continues in the juniorate, during which the sister is prepared for her active apostolate.

Qualifications:
* Age: high school graduates under 30. Exceptions are sometimes made.
* The scope of the congregation provides for many occupations besides teaching.
* Entrance dates: August and January.

Habit: The sisters wear a black habit, cincture, and veil lined with white, and a white wimple.

See page 385 for address of nearest community.

SISTERS OF NOTRE DAME (S.N.D.)

History: Sister Mary Aloysia and Sister Mary Ignatia founded this pontifical congregation in Coesfeld, Germany, in 1850. The sisters, who observe the rule of Blessed Julie Billiart, are active in ten countries. The first foundation in the United States was made in Cleveland, Ohio, in 1874. Today there are fifteen hundred sisters conducting one hundred and twenty-four institutions in this country.

Purpose: The apostolate is principally teaching from kindergarten to college. The sisters also conduct schools for the mentally retarded, three children's homes, a school for the visually handicapped, homes for women, orphanages, and convalescent homes. The sisters teach in New Guinea and operate a novitiate and conduct schools and a dispensary in India.

Spiritual Life: The religious exercises include Holy Mass, a modified form of the Divine Office in English, mental prayer, the rosary, spiritual reading and other community prayers and devotions.

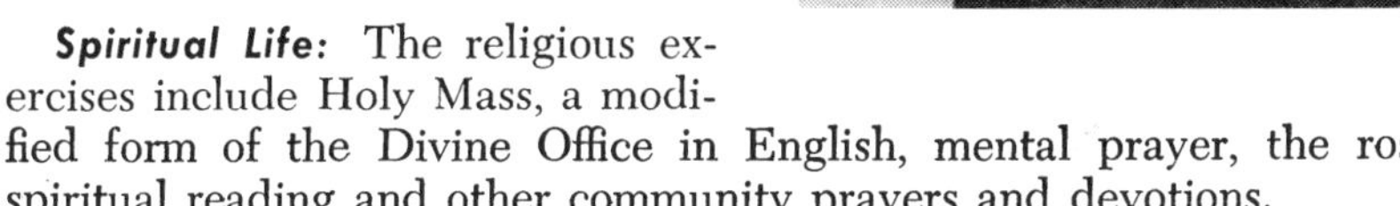

Training Program: Each of the provinces conduct an aspirancy school for teen-age girls interested in the religious life. The program of spiritual formation includes a postulancy of at least six months, a two-year novitiate and a five-year juniorate which terminates with a six-month tertianship. A systematic study is made of the religious life and the educational principles of the Sisters of Notre Dame. Except during the first year of the novitiate, the sisters continue working for their professional degrees.

Qualifications:

* For the aspirancy—completion of elementary school.
* For the postulancy—age: 18 to 30 and average intelligence.
* Entrance dates: February 2 and September 8.

Habit: The sisters wear a black habit, cape and veil, a large rosary, and a silver crucifix.

See page 385 for address of nearest convent.

CONGREGATION OF NOTRE DAME DE SION (N.D.S.)

History: This congregation owes its origin to one of the apparitions of Our Lady. The event took place in Rome, January 20, 1842, where a young Jew, Alphonse Ratisbonne, was instantaneously converted by the Mother of God. The acceptance of Christ by the once skeptical Jew and his reconciliation with his brother, Father Theodore Ratisbonne who had been converted in 1827, were the first of a series of events in which God manifested His will that a congregation be established to work and pray for the chosen people of the Old Testament.

Purpose: The community is made up of three branches. The greater number of the sisters are dedicated to the apostolate of teaching and missionary work. The contemplative sisters aid the active members through their humble life of poverty and labor, and daily and nocturnal adoration before the Blessed Sacrament. The social service sisters live completely dedicated lives in small communities without the exterior form of conventual life. These religious take positions in the business world and bring the Church to those who do not go to her.

Spiritual Life: The religious exercises include Holy Mass, the recitation of the Divine Office, forty-five minutes of mental prayer, spiritual reading, the rosary, and other community prayers and devotions.

Training Program: The six to twelve months of postulancy is followed by an eighteen-month novitiate. Temporary vows are then made. After first profession, the religious and professional training of the professed sisters are continued during the juniorate.

Qualifications:
* Age: 18 to 30.
* Completion of high school.

Habit: The sisters wear a black habit, a rosary, an ebony and silver crucifix, and a chain.

Write to: Provincial House
3823 Locust Street
Kansas City 9, Missouri

SISTERS OBLATES TO DIVINE LOVE
(R.O.D.A.)

History: Mother Margherita Diomira Crispi, assisted by Archbishop Antonio Augusto Intreccialagli, founded this community in Monte Regali, Italy, in 1922. Following the rule of St. Ignatius, this congregation has foundations in Europe, Central America, Puerto Rico, and the United States. The American novitiate was dedicated in 1961.

Purpose: The sisters teach in kindergartens, elementary and secondary schools, and colleges, staff orphanages, and are engaged in sponsoring retreats, and the making of altar linens and vestments.

Spiritual Life: The religious exercises include Holy Mass, the recitation of the Office of the Sacred Heart in Latin, meditation, the rosary and prescribed litanies, and daily exposition of the Blessed Sacrament and regular nocturnal adoration.

Training Program: The community conducts an aspirancy for teen-age girls who are interested in the religious life. The six-month postulancy is followed by a two-year novitiate. The novice then makes her profession of temporary vows. As professed sisters they continue their spiritual formation while taking courses toward their academic degrees.

Qualifications:
* Age: maximum is 30.
* Completion of high school.
* Entrance date: July 30.

Habit: The sisters wear a black habit, veil, and cape, and a cincture, and silver cross.

Write to: St. Clare's Convent
1925 Hone Avenue
Bronx 61, New York

DAUGHTERS OF MARY IMMACULATE FOR THE PROTECTION OF YOUNG GIRLS (F.M.I.)

History: Mother Vincenta Maria Lopez, who was beatified in 1950 by Pius XII, founded this congregation at Madrid, Spain, in 1876. During her lifetime she established six houses in Spain and her work continued to progress rapidly even after her death in 1890. Nine years later the congregation was approved by Pope Leo XIII.

Purpose: The special object of the community is the care and protection of young girls. To achieve this objective, the sisters conduct residences for students and working girls, homes for orphans and neglected children, and provide moral guidance for young girls. The education of young girls is also an important aspect of the community's apostolate. The sisters operate training schools, home economics classes, and night schools for working girls. In India and South America they have dispensaries, schools, and recreation centers.

Spiritual Life: The religious exercises include Holy Mass, the recitation of the Office of the Blessed Virgin in Latin, one hour and a half of mental prayer, the rosary, visits to the Blessed Sacrament, spiritual reading, and daily adoration of the Blessed Sacrament.

Training Program: The candidates begin their religious formation by a six-month postulancy which is followed by a two-year novitiate and a one-year juniorate. After five years of temporary vows, they make perpetual vows which are preceded by one month of spiritual exercises and nine months of tertianship. The sisters receive training for their future work in colleges and universities.

Qualifications:
* Age: 16 to 30.
* Completion of high school is preferred.

Habit: The sisters wear a black wool habit, veil, sash, soft linen guimpe, small cape, rosary, and a silver cross.

Write to: Mother Superior
Villa Maria
719 Augusta Street
San Antonio 2, Texas

OLIVETAN BENEDICTINE SISTERS
(O.S.B.)

History: In answer to an appeal of the Bishop of Little Rock, four Sisters under the leadership of Mother Mary Beatrice arrived in Pocahontas, Arkansas, December 13, 1887 to establish a community. These sisters were from the Maria-Rickenback Convent in Switzerland and had established a foundation in Clyde, Missouri. The first convent was a log house and the first school was partly in a barnlike shanty, and partly in the sacristy of the little frame church. Since 1898 the motherhouse of the community has been located at Jonesboro, a city of about 20,000 inhabitants. Holy Angels Convent, built at that time, accommodated the sisters until 1929, when it became necessary to provide a larger convent home which is a beautiful, fire-proof structure, up-to-date in every detail.

Purpose: The members of this diocesan congregation teach in elementary and secondary schools, operate two hospitals, a nursing home, and maintain a hospice in Hot Springs, Arkansas. The institutions are located in Texas, Missouri, Louisiana, and Arkansas.

Spiritual Life: The religious exercises include Holy Mass, the recitation of the Divine Office in English, mental prayer, the rosary, spiritual reading, and other community prayers and devotions.

Qualifications:
* * Age: 15 to 30.
* * Average intelligence.

Habit: The sisters wear a white habit and scapular and a black veil.

> *Write to:* Holy Angels Convent
> Jonesboro,
> Arkansas

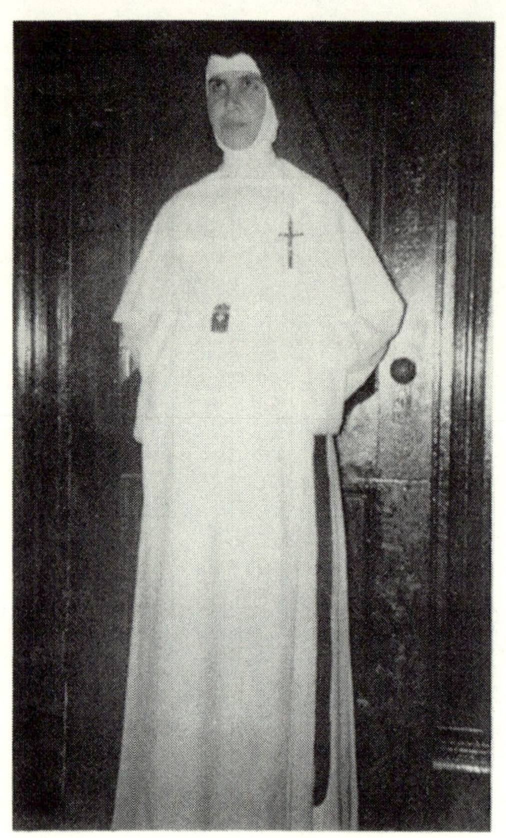

MISSIONARY SISTERS OF OUR LADY OF MERCY (M.M.O.M.)

History: The Most Reverend Inocentio Santamaria founded this community in Piaui, Brazil, in 1938. This diocesan congregation has 18 houses including schools and hospitals in Brazil. The sisters opened their first foundation in the United States at Lackawanna, New York, in 1955.

Purpose: The sisters teach, care for the sick in hospitals, maintain nurseries, and are engaged in catechetical work.

Spiritual Life: The religious exercises include Holy Mass, the recitation of the Office of the Blessed Virgin in Latin, one hour of mental prayer, the rosary, spiritual reading, and other community prayers and devotions.

Training Program: The six-month postulancy is followed by a two-year novitiate. A five-year juniorate in-service program has been inaugurated. After first vows the sisters continue their spiritual formation while taking courses toward their professional degrees.

Qualifications:
* The maximum age is 30.
* Average intelligence.

Habit: The sisters wear a white habit and a black veil, a crucifix, and an emblem of the Mercy Order.

Write to: St. Raymond Nonnatus Convent
Lake Street
Le Roy, New York

SISTERS OF OUR LADY OF MOUNT CARMEL (O. Carm.)

History: Father Charles Boutelou founded this congregation in Tours, France, in 1825. The revolution of 1830, aimed at destroying the Church in France, forced the community to disperse. The founder sought refuge in New Orleans, Louisiana. Upon his arrival there, he told the Bishop of New Orleans of the plight of his sisters. The bishop invited them to his diocese. On September 8, 1833, Mother Theresa Chevral and Mother St. Augustine Clerc left France to establish the community in the United States.

Purpose: The sisters teach in elementary and secondary schools and operate a hospital. Their institutions are located in the state of Louisiana.

Spiritual Life: The religious exercises include Holy Mass, the recitation of the Office of the Blessed

Virgin according to the Carmelite Rite, mental prayer, the rosary, spiritual reading, and other community prayers and devotions.

Training Program: The six-month postulancy is followed by a two-year novitiate. Temporary vows are made for five years after which perpetual vows are pronounced. After first profession, the sisters continue their spiritual formation while taking college courses necessary for their teaching or nursing degrees.

Qualifications:
* Age: 15 to 30.
* Widows under 30 will be accepted.
* Average intelligence.

Habit: The sisters wear a black habit, cape, and veil, a white cap and bandeau, a scapular, and a rosary.

> *Write to:* Mother General
> 420 Robert E. Lee Boulevard
> New Orleans 24, Louisiana

PASSIONIST SISTERS (C.P.)

History: Father Gaudentius Rossi, C.P., founded this community in 1851 in Manchester, England. At the request of the Most Rev. William A. Hickey and Father Felix Ward, C.P., a pioneer group of sisters were sent to Providence, Rhode Island, where they made a foundation in 1924.

Purpose: The primary aim of the congregation was the founding of hostels for young girls employed in the manufacturing districts of large cities. The sisters teach in elementary and secondary schools, conduct retreat houses for women, visit the sick and negligent Catholics in their homes, and maintain missions in Africa and South America.

Spiritual Life: The religious exercises include Holy Mass, meditation, the rosary, spiritual reading, and other community prayers and devotions.

Training Program: The six-month postulancy is followed by a two-year novitiate. Temporary simple vows are made. During the years of the juniorate, the sisters continue their spiritual formation while taking courses toward their professional degrees.

Qualifications:
* The maximum age is 30.
* Completion of high school.

Habit: The sisters wear a black habit and cape with the Passionist Badge and a white fluted cap to which is attached a black veil.

Write to: Mount St. Joseph
Wakefield,
Rhode Island

SISTERS OF THE PIOUS SCHOOLS
(Sch.P.)

History: Paula Montalt, following the Rule of St. Joseph Calasanctius, founded this pontifical congregation in 1829, when she opened schools for girls in her native Spain. The community established houses in South America, Italy, France, Japan, and until June, 1961, they maintained six houses in Cuba. The first sisters arrived in the United States in 1954.

Purpose: The aim of the community is the greater glory of God through the personal sanctification of its members and the Christian education of girls and women. In the countries in which they are working, the sisters are engaged in teaching, give catechetical instructions, and conduct orphanages. In the United States the sisters teach in a parochial school and are in charge of the domestic departments of three seminaries. Their work is centered at present in California.

Spiritual Life: The religious exercises include Holy Mass, the recitation of the Office of the Blessed Virgin, mental prayer, the rosary, spiritual reading, and other community prayers and devotions.

Training Program: The six-month postulancy is followed by a two-year novitiate. Temporary vows are made for three years. During this time, the sisters remain in the House of Studies where they take courses for their teaching assignments and, after three years, pronounce their perpetual vows.

Qualifications:
* Age: 16 to 25. Exceptions are sometimes made.
* Average intelligence.

Habit: The sisters wear a black habit and veil, a white collar, a medallion of Our Lady, and a rosary.

> *Write to:* Mother Superior
> 15101 Mission Boulevard
> P.O. Box 1071
> San Fernando, California

SISTERS OF THE POOR CHILD JESUS
(P.C.J.)

History: Mother Clare Fey founded this pontifical institute in Germany in 1844 to care for poor abandoned children. Born in Aix-la-Chapelle, Germany, Mother Fey was distinguished for her Christian piety and charity. Over 2,000 sisters are working in Europe, North and South America, and in Indonesia. The first American foundation was made in the United States in 1923.

Purpose: The sisters teach in kindergartens, elementary and secondary schools, and are engaged in catechetical and remedial work. Their institutions are located in West Virginia, Illinois, and Ohio.

Spiritual Life: The religious exercises include Holy Mass, the recitation of the Office of the Blessed Virgin in Latin, mental prayer, the rosary, spiritual reading, and other community prayers and devotions.

Training Program: The community conducts an aspirancy for high school girls interested in the religious life. After the postulancy, a two-year novitiate follows. Temporary vows are made for five years. Perpetual vows are then pronounced. The sisters continue their spiritual formation while taking courses toward their academic degrees.

Qualifications:
* Age: 15 to 30. Exceptions are sometimes made up to 40.
* Completion of high school is preferred.
* Entrance dates: August 28, September 8, December 8, February 2.

Habit: The sisters wear a black habit and veil, a white scapular and cord, a medal of the Blessed Sacrament and Holy Family, and a large rosary.

Write to: Our Lady of Bethlehem Convent
4567 Olentangy River Road
Columbus 14, Ohio

History: Catherine Kasper, who with four companions pronounced vows August 15, 1851, founded this congregation in Dernbach, Germany. Upon the invitation of Bishop John Henry Leurs of Fort Wayne and with the help of Father Koenig, the first sisters arrived and made their foundation in the United States in 1868. The community now numbers more than six hundred members.

Purpose: The members of this active congregation work out their apostolic labors through the education of youth, the care of the sick, orphans, and the aged. These activities are centered in college, elementary, and high schools, schools of nursing, hospitals, orphanages, and a home for the aged. These foundations are located in Illinois, Indiana, Minnesota, and Wisconsin.

Spiritual Life: The religious exercises include Holy Mass, meditation, the recitation of the rosary and abbreviated breviary.

Training Program: The aspirancy at Villa Maria provides ample opportunities for high school girls who desire to embrace the religious life. The postulancy program is followed by a two-year novitiate. The canonical novices study intensively the rule and constitutions. The senior novices concentrate on the meaning of the vows. During the juniorate the sisters complete their religious and professional training.

Qualifications:
* Age: under 30.
* Average intelligence.
* Entrance date: latter part of August.

Habit: The sisters wear a black habit of light weight material, with cincture and rosary, a white linen collar, and a black veil attached to a white starched coronet.

Write to: Mother Provincial
Convent Ancilla Domini
Donaldson, Indiana

POOR SERVANTS OF THE MOTHER OF GOD

History: This pontifical institute was founded in 1868 by Mother Magdalen Taylor who was a lady volunteer with Florence Nightingale in the Crimea, Soviet Russia, in 1854.

Purpose: The sisters teach, nurse, give convert instructions, and conduct orphanages, homes for the aged, and hospitals for spastics.

Spiritual Life: The religious exercises include Holy Mass, the Office of the Blessed Virgin in Latin, one hour of mental prayer, and other community prayers.

Training Program: The six-month postulancy is followed by a two-year novitiate. Temporary vows are then made. After five years of temporary profession, the sisters spend a year tertianship in preparation for their profession of perpetual vows. After receiving first vows, the sisters continue their spiritual formation while taking courses toward their professional or nursing degrees.

Qualifications:
* Age: 16 to 25. Exceptions are sometimes made.
* Average intelligence.
* Entrance dates: March 25, July 22, and December 8.

Habit: The sisters wear a black habit, apron, veil, and cincture, and a blue scapular.

Write to: Maryfield Convalescent Home
High Point,
North Carolina

POOR SISTERS OF JESUS CRUCIFIED AND THE SORROWFUL MOTHER
(C.J.C.)

History: Father Alphonsus Maria, C.P., founded this congregation in Elmhurst, Pennsylvania, in 1921. Twenty-four years later the motherhouse and novitiate was transferred to Brockton, Massachusetts.

Purpose: The primary purpose of this congregation is the sanctification of its members through the faithful observance of the evangelical vows of religion. The secondary objective is the active apostolic charity toward their neighbor. This is exercised especially in the instructing and educating of children, the caring for the aged in nursing homes, and in sponsoring retreats. These activities are carried out in Massachusetts, Connecticut, New York, and Pennsylvania.

Spiritual Life: The religious exercises include Holy Mass, the recitation of the Office of the Passion in Latin, mental prayer, the rosary, spiritual reading, and other community prayers and devotions.

Training Program: The two years of novitiate are preceded by a one-year postulancy and followed by five years of post-professional education. Candidates are requested to manifest a diligence and aptitude for acquiring knowledge and a desire for spiritual perfection.

Qualifications:
* Age: 15 to 30.
* Completion of high school is desired. Those who have not yet completed high school will be accepted.
* Entrance dates: September 15 and February 2.

Habit: The sisters wear a black habit, cape, and veil, a white forehead band, a rosary, and a crucifix.

> *Write to:* Our Lady of Sorrows Convent
> 261 Thatcher Street
> Brockton, Massachusetts

SISTERS OF THE PRECIOUS BLOOD (C.PP.S.)

History: Founded by St. Gaspar del Bufalo, this congregation originated at Castle Loewenberg, Canton Grisons, Switzerland, in 1834, under the direction of Maria Anna Brunner and her son, Francis de Sales. In 1844 Father Brunner invited the sisters to follow him to Ohio where they erected several convents of perpetual adoration.

Purpose: The sisters are engaged in teaching on all the stages of education from kindergarten to the university level. Some members direct domestic work in episcopal residences and seminaries. Others follow a nursing profession, while a small contemplative group with minor papal enclosure is devoted to a life of prayer. The sisters conduct three homes for the aged, an orphanage, and a lay retreat house.

Spiritual Life: The religious exercises include Holy Mass, the recitation of the English short breviary, a half-hour of mental prayer, the rosary, spiritual reading, and other community prayers and devotions.

Training Program: The congregation offers a complete educational program beginning with a fully accredited high school course in the aspirancy, continuing through college in the one-year postulancy, two-year novitiate, two-year juniorate, leading to a B.S. in Ed. degree. Those preparing to become teachers, nurses, or dieticians follow the general liberal arts course through the novitiate, and after first vows, as full time students at the University of Dayton. Those who do not aspire for a degree are trained according to the needs of the apostolate.

Qualifications:
* The maximum age is 30.
* Completion of high school is preferred.

Habit: The sisters wear a light grey habit, a black veil attached to a linen head band, and a white linen collar.

Write to: Motherhouse
Regina Heights
4830 Salem Avenue
Dayton 16, Ohio

SISTERS OF THE MOST PRECIOUS BLOOD (C.PP.S.)

History: Founded in 1845 at Steinerberg, Switzerland, by Father Karl Rolfus and Mother Theresa Weber, the community was forced in 1848 to flee France because of religious persecution. After settling in Baden, Germany, it was again the victim of persecution by the German government under Bismark in 1870. Seeking refuge in America, the congregation established its motherhouse in O'Fallon, Missouri, three years later.

Purpose: The sisters teach in elementary and secondary schools, conduct centers for mentally retarded children, and maintain two episcopal residences. They have foreign missions in Helsinki and Tampere, Finland, in Lima, Peru, and La Paz, Bolivia, South America. The motherhouse maintains an ecclesiastical art department, a well known center of the liturgical apostolate.

Spiritual Life: The religious exercises include Holy Mass, the chanting of the Divine Office in Latin, a half-hour of meditation, the rosary, spiritual reading, and other community prayers and devotions.

Training Program: The eleven-month postulancy is followed by a two-year novitiate. The postulants begin their collegiate studies in the community's junior college. The second year novices resume these courses while completing their religious training for the reception of temporary vows. Perpetual vows are pronounced after five years in temporary vows. In the juniorate the sisters continue their spiritual training and complete the studies leading to the bachelor's degree. After ten years in vows the sisters spend a summer in spiritual renewal—the tertianship—at the motherhouse.

Qualifications:
* Age: 16 to 30.
* At least high school juniors.
* Entrance dates: August 26 through January 25.

Habit: The sisters wear a black skirt, blouse, and scapular, a soft white collar, and a silver cross suspended from a red cord.

Write to: Motherhouse
204 North Main Street
O'Fallon, Missouri

SISTERS ADORERS OF THE MOST PRECIOUS BLOOD (Ad.PP.S.)

History: When Blessed Maria De Mattias opened a small school in Aucto, Italy, in 1834, she began also the foundation of the Adorers of the Most Precious Blood. With the general motherhouse in Rome, the community has provinces in Europe, and in North and South America. In the United States, provinces were established at Ruma, Illinois, in 1870; at Columbia, Pennsylvania, in 1906; and at Wichita, Kansas, in 1929.

Purpose: The sisters teach in elementary, secondary schools and in colleges; they conduct hospitals, orphanages, and homes for the aged. Missions have been founded in Brazil and Puerto Rico.

Spiritual Life: The religious exercises include Holy Mass, a half-hour of mental prayer, one hour of adoration in honor of the Precious Blood, and other community prayers and devotions.

Training Program: The three provinces in the United States conduct aspirancy schools for high school girls who are interested in the religious life. The period of postulancy is followed by one-year of novitiate. The novices then make their profession of temporary vows. These are renewed annually for five years. At the expiration of this time, the sisters are permitted to make their profession of perpetual vows. During the juniorate the sisters continue their spiritual formation while taking college courses toward their academic degrees. After six years in perpetual vows, the sisters participate in a spiritual renewal period—several weeks of special study and emphasis on religious life and the spirit of the congregation.

Qualifications:
* Age: maximum is 35.
* Completion of high school is preferred.
* Entrance date: September 1.

Habit: The sisters wear a black habit and veil, a white collar and crown, a gold heart and chain, and a red belt and sash.

See page 385 for address of nearest provincial house.

SISTERS OF THE PRESENTATION OF THE BLESSED VIRGIN MARY (P.B.V.M.)

History: When the penal laws against Catholics were in full force in Ireland in 1775, Nano Nagle founded this congregation to instruct children in their Catholic faith. The community grew and prospered rapidly. Today the sisters are to be found in Europe, America, India, Australia, and Africa. Since their first foundation in the United States in 1884, the congregation, which now numbers twelve independent motherhouses, is in many states from coast to coast. The rule was approved by the Holy See in 1791.

Purpose: The sisters teach in colleges, secondary and elementary schools, are engaged in parish visiting and catechetical summer school teaching, and conduct hospitals, schools of nursing, orphanages, nurseries, and homes for children and the aged.

Spiritual Life: The religious exercises include Holy Mass, the chanting of the Little Office of the Blessed Virgin, mental prayer, the rosary, spiritual reading, and other community prayers and devotions.

Training Program: The six to twelve-month postulancy is followed by a two-year novitiate. Temporary vows are then made. After five years in temporary vows the sisters profess their perpetual vows. Before being assigned to the apostolic work of the congregation, the sisters complete the college work toward their professional degrees.

Qualifications:

* The maximum age is 30.
* Completion of high school.
* Entrance date: September.

Habit: The sisters wear a black habit, cincture, veil and a domino, white bandeau and guimpe, rosary, and a silver ring.

See page 386 for nearest Presentation motherhouse.

History: During the troubled days of the French Revolution, this group of Presentation Sisters was founded by Mother Anne-Marie Rivier in Thueyts, France, in 1796, for the purpose of instructing the sadly neglected youth of her neighborhood. Since the approval of the rules by the Holy See in 1801, the swelling ranks of the community has brought about the present system of organization: one province each in France, Spain, and Portugal; four provinces in Canada, and two in the United States.

Purpose: In the New England States, the members of this congregation who have conducted parochial schools since 1886, are presently engaged in teaching on all levels from kindergarten to college. The Manchester Province supplies missionaries for its missions in the Philippine Islands.

Spiritual Life: The religious exercises include Holy Mass, the recitation of certain "Hours" of the Divine Office on specified days, mental prayer, the rosary, spiritual reading, and other community prayers and devotions.

Training Program: The six-month postulancy is followed by a two-year novitiate. Temporary vows are then made. To further intensify their spiritual development, the sisters are sometimes sent to the general motherhouse for a tertianship or to participate in the Spiritual Exercises of St. Ignatius. The sisters, while continuing their spiritual formation, complete the college courses necessary for their baccalaureate degrees.

Qualifications:
* Age: 16 to 28. Exceptions are sometimes made.
* Completion of high school.
* Entrance dates: February 11 and July 29.

Habit: The sisters wear a simple black dress with broad sleeves, waist-length cape, white coif and black bonnet, a silver cross, and a rosary.

Write to: Presentation of Mary   Presentation of Mary
495 Mammoth Road   207 Lawrence Street
Manchester, New Hampshire   Methuen, Massachusetts

OBLATE SISTERS OF PROVIDENCE
(O.S.P.)

History: Father James Jourbert, a Sulpician priest, founded this congregation in Baltimore, Maryland, in 1829. This was the second foundation for religious women in the United States and the first for Negro girls. Numbering three hundred and fifty members, these sisters are located in fifteen states in the United States.

Purpose: The sanctification of its members through apostolic works and spiritual exercises are the main objectives of the sisters of this congregation. They teach in elementary and secondary schools, and operate an orphanage and one college. Their institutions are found in Alabama, Florida, Illinois, Louisiana, Maryland, North Carolina, South Carolina, Virginia, Mississippi, Missouri, Michigan, Minnesota, Wisconsin and New Jersey.

Spiritual Life: The sisters chant the Divine Office in English and daily devote a half-hour each to mental and vocal prayer.

Training Program: During the five months as a candidate and six as a postulant the future Oblate sister continues her studies at the community's college. The postulant then receives her habit and enters the novitiate. In the novitiate she studies the fundamentals of the religious life, learns to chant the Divine Office and participates fully in the spiritual life of the congregation. After making her temporary vows she enters the two-year juniorate program. Here she continues the studies toward her academic degree. Profession of perpetual vows is made after five years in temporary vows.

Qualifications:
* Age: 16 to 30.
* Completion of high school.

Habit: The sisters wear a pleated skirt, blouse, circular cape, black veil on a white head band, a Miraculous Medal, and a fifteen-decade rosary.

Write to: Our Lady of Mt. Providence Convent
701 Gun Road
Baltimore 27, Maryland

RELIGIOUS OF CHRISTIAN EDUCATION (R.C.E.)

History: This pontifical institute originated in France in 1817 through the efforts of Father Lafosse, who, while looking for catechists to combat the ravages of the French Revolution, founded a community of religious teachers. The congregation was exiled in 1904. The members fled to England, Belgium, and the United States in 1905. The community later prospered in France and established missions in Morocco, and West Africa.

Purpose: The sisters devote themselves to the education of youth by teaching in private and parochial schools on the elementary and secondary levels. They also have missions in North Carolina and Dahomey, West Africa. The sisters work primarily in North Carolina and Massachusetts.

Spiritual Life: The religious exercises include Holy Mass, the recitation of the Office of the Blessed Virgin in English, meditation, spiritual reading, rosary, and visits to the Blessed Sacrament.

Training Program: The ten-month postulancy is followed by a one-year novitiate. After completing the novitiate the novice makes temporary vows for one year. During this period of the juniorate the sister continues her spiritual formation while taking courses toward her professional degree. After five years in temporary vows the professed sister makes her profession of perpetual vows.

Qualifications:
* Age: minimum is 16.
* Completion of high school.
* Entrance date: August 15.

Habit: The sisters wear a black habit, cape, and veil, a white coif framing the face, and a silver crucifix.

Write to: Provincial House
130 Milton Street
Milton 86, Massachusetts

MISSIONARY SISTERS OF THE MOTHER OF GOD (M.S.M.G.)

History: This congregation was founded by the late Archbishop Constantine Bohachevsky and Archbishop Ambrose Senyshyn in Stamford, Connecticut, October 1, 1944. It was founded at a time when the godless powers of Communism were liquidating monasteries and convents in the Ukraine.

Purpose: The members of this congregation work for the greater glory of God among Ukrainian Catholics of the Byzantine-Slavonic Rite. In after school programs, the sisters instill in the Catholic children of this rite, an appreciation and knowledge of the Ukrainian heritage. They are also engaged in cooking, sewing, household duties, embroidering, pysanky designing, and vestment making.

Spiritual Life: The religious exercises include Holy Mass, the recitation of the Divine Office in Old Slavonic, one hour of meditation, spiritual reading, and other community devotions.

Qualifications:
* Age: 16 to 30. Exceptions are sometimes made.
* At least two years of high school.

Habit: The sisters wear a black habit, veil, a white forehead band and collar, and a silver crucifix.

Write to: Mother Superior
111 West North Street
Stamford, Connecticut

RELIGIOUS TEACHERS FILIPPINI
(M.P.F.)

History: Saint Lucy Filippini founded this pontifical institute in Montefiascone, Italy, in 1692. The congregation attracted the attention of Clement XI, who asked St. Lucy to found schools in Rome. In 1910, according to the wishes of Saint Pius X, five sisters established a foundation in the United States at Morristown, New Jersey.

Purpose: The sisters bring the truth of Christ by example and instruction to youngsters in nurseries, to students from the elementary through the college level, and to the handicapped through specialized teaching. They conduct summer camps, retreats for girls and mothers, and are engaged in catechetical and Confraternity of Christian Doctrine work. These institutions are located in Maryland, Connecticut, New Jersey, New York, Pennsylvania, District of Columbia, Ohio, New Hampshire, Rhode Island, Minnesota, and Brazil, South America.

Spiritual Life: The religious exercises include Holy Mass, one hour of mental prayer, the rosary, spiritual reading, and other community prayers and devotions.

Training Program: After one year of postulancy, the candidate receives the habit and remains in the novitiate for three consecutive years. Temporary vows are then pronounced. The sisters continue their spiritual formation while taking college courses to fulfill the requirements for their professional degrees.

Qualifications:
* Age: 15 to 30.
* A desire to dedicate oneself to the education of youth.

Habit: The sisters wear a black habit, veil, bonnet and sash, a white kerchief, and a fifteen-decade rosary.

> *Write to:* Mother Superior
> Villa Walsh
> Morristown, New Jersey

RELIGIOUS VENERINI SISTERS (M.P.V.)

History: Blessed Rosa Venerini, the foundress of this congregation, was born in Viterbo, Italy, on February 1, 1656. With the encouragement of Father Ignazio Martinelli, she opened the first free schools for girls twenty-nine years later. This was followed a few years later by a foundation at Rome which continues today as the motherhouse of the congregation. In the following years, Blessed Rosa formulated a method of teaching which has been carried on by the members of her community to the present day. The first foundation was made in the United States in 1909.

Purpose: The sanctification of its members and the education of youth is the two-fold aim of the congregation. The sisters conduct elementary schools and one high school, catechetical centers, and nursery schools in New York, Massachusetts, and Rhode Island.

Spiritual Life: The religious exercises include Holy Mass, a half-hour of mental prayer, the rosary, and other community prayers and devotions.

Training Program: The six-month postulancy is followed by a two-year novitiate. The novice then makes her temporary vows. During this period of the juniorate the sister continues her spiritual formation and professional training.

Qualifications:
* Age: 16 to 30. Exceptions are sometimes made.
* Average intelligence.
* Entrance dates: September 8 and February 9.

Habit: The sisters wear a black habit, veil, cape, and silk bonnet, a ring, and a fifteen decade rosary on which is a medal bearing the image of St. Ignatius Loyola, the special patron of the community.

Write to: Mother Superior
23 Edward Street
Worcester 5, Massachusetts

CONGREGATION OF THE RELIGIOUS OF JESUS AND MARY (R.J.M.)

History: Claudine Thevenet under the direction of Father Andre Coindre founded this congregation in Lyons, France, October 6, 1818, to aid in the rehabilitation of the working classes after the French Revolution. The congregation soon spread to many other European countries, as well as to India, Canada, the United States, South America, and Africa.

Purpose: The general aims of the members of this congregation are the praise of God and the sanctification of its members through the evangelical virtues. The sisters staff twenty schools and three residences for women in California, Maryland, Massachusetts, New Hampshire, New York, Rhode Island, and Texas. The religious have become known as the "singing sisters" because the Jesus and Mary Choral Group composed of novices and postulants was the first to record for a major recording company.

Spiritual Life: The religious exercises include Holy Mass, the Little Officer of the Blessed Virgin, meditation of one hour which includes Matins, the rosary, spiritual reading, and other community prayers and devotions.

Training Program: The six-month postulancy is followed by a two-year novitiate. Temporary vows are made for five years. Perpetual vows are pronounced at the expiration of this time. During the juniorate years the sisters continue their spiritual formation while taking courses in preparation for their professional degrees. There is a tertianship of eight months.

Qualifications:
* Age: 15 to 30.
* Average intelligence.
* Entrance dates: in the spring.

Habit: The sisters wear a black habit, cape, cap, and veil, a white fluted cap, a silver cross, and a rosary.

Write to: Convent of Jesus and Mary   Mother Provincial
           Route 97   1401 Yandell Boulevard
           Brookeville, Maryland   El Paso, Texas

SISTERS OF THE RESURRECTION
(C.R.)

History: This congregation originated in Rome where the co-foundress, Mother Celine Borzecka and her daughter, Mother Hedwig, first began to lead a community life under the guidance of Father Peter Semenenko, founder of the Resurrection Fathers. After its official establishment in 1891, the new community spread to several European countries. In 1900 four sisters opened the first American foundation in Chicago, Illinois.

Purpose: The sisters teach in elementary and secondary schools, and care for the sick and aged in hospitals and convalescent homes. They also conduct catechetical and boarding schools, day nurseries, orphanages, residences for working girls and students, and retreat centers for girls and women. The institutions for the Western Province are located in Indiana, Wisconsin, Nebraska, North Dakota and Florida. The members of the Eastern Province are principally found in New York and Connecticut.

Spiritual Life: The religious exercises include Holy Mass, a half-hour of mental prayer, the rosary, spiritual reading, and other community prayers and devotions.

Training Program: The congregation conducts an aspirancy for high school girls interested in the religious life. The six-month postulancy is followed by a one-year novitiate. Profession of temporary vows is then made for five years, after which perpetual vows are taken. During this time, the sisters continue their spiritual formation while taking courses toward their professional or nursing degrees. A six-week tertianship is made before final vows.

Qualifications:
* Age: 15 to 35.
* Completion of elementary school for aspirancy.

Habit: The sisters wear a black habit, cincture, and veil, a white cap, wimple, and collar, a rosary, and a silver cross.

Write to: Sisters of the Resurrection   Sisters of the Resurrection
7432 West Talcott Avenue   Mount St. Joseph
Chicago 31, Illinois   Castleton-on-the-Hudson, New York

HANDMAIDS OF THE SACRED HEART OF JESUS (A.C.J.)

History: Dolores and Raphaela Mary Porras founded this congregation in Madrid, Spain, in 1877. Raphaela became the first superior general in 1887, the same year that the community received final approbation from the Holy See. Raphaela was pronounced Blessed by Pope Pius XII in 1952 just twenty-seven years after her death. The congregation has fifty-seven houses in fourteen different countries.

Purpose: The work of the congregation is contemplative as well as active. Characteristic of the first is adoration before the Blessed Sacrament exposed daily. The sisters in their active apostolate teach in elementary, secondary, and parochial schools and conduct retreats. They have opened missions in South America and Japan.

Spiritual Life: The religious exercises include Holy Mass, mental prayer, the rosary, spiritual reading, and other community prayers and devotions.

Training Program: The six to nine-month postulancy is followed by a two-year novitiate. Temporary vows are then made. After first profession, the time of the juniorate, the sisters complete the work toward their academic degrees before they are sent out into the active apostolate. The sisters spend one year of probation in Rome in preparation for the reception of perpetual vows.

Qualifications:
* Age: 16 to 30.
* Completion of high school is preferred.

Habit: The sisters wear a black habit, rosary, and a white linen guimpe over which is pinned a brass heart, emblem of their particular devotion to the Sacred Heart.

Write to: Mistress of Novices
616 Coopertown Road
Haverford, Pennsylvania

358

MISSIONARY SISTERS OF THE SACRED HEART OF JESUS (M.S.C.)

History: Saint Francis Xavier Cabrini (1850-1917) founded this congregation at Codogno, Italy, in 1880. Saint Mother Cabrini established foundations throughout Europe, and at the request of Pope Leo XIII, came to the United States in 1889. She opened foreign missions in Central and South America, and after her death, missions were founded in China, Australia, and Canada.

Purpose: The primary aim of the community is to glorify the Sacred Heart of Jesus and to sanctify its members through the three religious vows. Christian education of youth and hospital work are its main apostolic activities. They teach in kindergartens, elementary and secondary schools, and colleges, and conduct seven hospitals, orphanages, rest homes, retreat houses, and catechetical classes.

These institutions are located in New York, Illinois, Colorado, California, New Jersey, Louisiana, Pennsylvania, and Washington.

Spiritual Life: The religious exercises include Holy Mass, the Office of the Blessed Virgin, mental prayer, the rosary, spiritual reading, and other community prayers and devotions.

Training Program: The six to twelve-month postulancy is followed by a one-year novitiate. Temporary vows are made for one year. These are renewed for seven years after which perpetual vows are pronounced. If they have graduated from high school the postulants begin their college classes. After first profession the sisters continue their spiritual formation, while completing the college courses necessary for their professional degrees.

Qualifications:
* Age: 16 to 30.
* Completion of high school for those who desire to teach or nurse.
* Entrance dates: August 15 and February 2.

Habit: The sisters wear a black habit, veil, cap and bow, a white collar, cincture, silver cross, and a gold ring.

Write to: Sacred Heart Novitiate
West Park, New York

OBLATES OF THE SACRED HEART OF JESUS (O.S.C.)

History: Louise Therese de Montaignac founded this pontifical congregation in 1843. There are fifty-six houses of professed sisters and forty-three schools directed by secular oblates in Europe, Africa, Latin America, and the United States. The first foundation in the United States was made in Washington, D.C., in 1955.

Purpose: All forms of the apostolate are pursued and those of greatest local utility which cannot be undertaken by cloistered congregations are chosen by preference. These include schools, retreats, centers for youth, parish census work, medical centers, and orphanages.

Spiritual Life: The religious life is based on the love of the Sacred Heart carried to the most complete gift of one's self and keeping the spirit of a contemplative while bringing Christ to the world. The spirit of St. Ignatius and St. Teresa of Avila mark the constitutions and the way of life.

Training Program: The six-month postulancy is followed by a two-year novitiate. The sisters then make their temporary vows for five years. At the end of this time they take perpetual vows. The following members are not bound to this program: the secular oblates take vows of chastity and stability only; the teaching secular oblates take these same two vows and that of consecration to Christian education; and the lay members do not take any vows. They consecrate themselves to the Sacred Heart according to their state in life.

Qualifications:
* Maximum age is 25. Exceptions are sometimes made.
* There are no age requirements for the secular oblates.
* Average intelligence.

Habit: The sisters wear a black dress in keeping with the times, a veil, cross, and after perpetual vows, a ring.

Write to: Our Lady of Guadalupe Academy
3233 Ellicott Street, N.W.,
Washington 8, D.C.
Our Lady of Fatima Academy
314 South 4th Street
Camden 3, New Jersey

OBLATE SISTERS OF THE SACRED HEART OF JESUS (O.S.H.J.)

History: Mother Mary Teresa Casini founded this pontifical congregation at Grottaferrata, Italy, in 1894. Through the benevolence of Bishop James A. McFadden of Youngstown, Ohio, the Oblate sisters established their first foundation in the United States in 1949.

Purpose: The life of the Oblates is one of reparation in union with the Sacred Heart of Jesus. They strive for perfection through the practice of the evangelical virtues. They are also dedicated to the sanctification of priests and the success of their apostolate. The sisters serve the person of His priests through teaching in parochial schools, giving catechetical instruction and caring for priests who are in need of assistance.

Spiritual Life: The word "Oblate" expresses the fact that the religious willingly sacrifices herself and all she has to make reparation for the many offenses committed against the Sacred Heart of Jesus. The center of her spiritual life is the Holy Sacrifice. The day also includes adoration before the Most Blessed Sacrament, and the community activities of prayer, meditation, spiritual reading, rosary, and Office.

Training Program: The first six months are spent in the postulancy. This is followed by a two-year novitiate. During this time the novice strives to learn the spirit of the congregation and the principles of the religious life. After five years as a professed religious the sister makes her profession of perpetual vows.

Qualifications:
* Age: 14 to 30.
* Average intelligence.

Habit: The sisters wear a white habit, sash, scapular, and veil.

Write to: Oblate Sisters
50 Warner Road
Hubbard, Ohio

SISTERS OF THE SACRED HEART OF JESUS (S.S.C.J.)

History: A twenty-year old girl who operated an underground movement for hunted priests and Catholics during the French Revolution, founded this community in 1816 at St. Jacut, Brittany, France. This second Joan of Arc, Angelique Le Sourd, had all the zeal of her fiery predecessor. Watching her beloved country crumble under moral and political decay, Angelique decided to organize a congregation of sisters who would battle forces of ignorance and godlessness.

Purpose: The primary objective of the congregation is the personal sanctification of each member and the salvation of the souls under their care. The sisters conduct secondary and elementary schools and are engaged in social work in France, England, Canada, and the United States where they are presently working in Texas and Louisiana.

Spiritual Life: The religious exercises include Holy Mass, meditation, one hour of adoration, community vocal prayers, spiritual reading, and the recitation of the Office of the Blessed Virgin in Latin.

Training Program: The congregation operates an aspirancy for elementary school graduates who desire to enter the convent before completing high school. The postulancy lasts six months. This is followed by a two-year novitiate. During this time the young novice devotes herself to the intense study of the religious life. At the completion of this training the novice becomes a professed religious with temporary vows for five years. Perpetual vows are pronounced at the end of this period. Each sister then continues the necessary college courses required for her academic degree.

Qualifications:
* The maximum age is 30.
* Completion of high school is preferred.

Habit: The sisters wear a black habit and veil, a white bandeau, rosary, and a silver crucifix.

Write to: Sisters of the Sacred Heart of Jesus
606 Mount Sacred Heart Road
San Antonio 1, Texas

MISSIONARY SISTERS OF THE MOST SACRED HEART OF JESUS (M.S.C.)

History: Father Hubert J. Linkkens, M.S.C., founded this congregation at Hiltrup, Germany, in 1899. The American province was established in 1908. Thirty-three foundations in the East and Middle West are directed from the provincial house in Reading, Pennsylvania. Today about nineteen hundred professed sisters are actively working in Europe, South West Africa, Peru, South America, Australia, and the South Pacific Islands.

Purpose: The motto of the community, "May the Sacred Heart of Jesus be loved everywhere," expresses its special objective. The sisters teach in elementary and secondary schools, nurse in hospitals and sanitariums, care for the aged and orphaned, and tend to the domestic needs of missionaries and retreatants.

Spiritual Life: The religious exercises include Holy Mass, a half-hour of mental prayer, the rosary, spiritual reading, and other community prayers and devotions.

Training Program: The community conducts an aspirancy for teen-age girls interested in the religious life. The six to ten-month postulancy is followed by a two-year novitiate. Temporary vows are made for five years after which perpetual vows are pronounced. During the postulancy and the second year of novitiate, the sisters take college courses. Plans are being made for a juniorate to continue the spiritual, intellectual, and professional training of the sisters.

Qualifications:
* Age: 17 to 30.
* Completion of high school is preferred.

Habit: The sisters wear a black habit, scapular, and veil, a silver cross and ring, and a rosary.

> *Write to:* St. Michael's Convent
> Hyde Park
> Reading, Pennsylvania

HOLY UNION OF THE SACRED HEARTS (S.U.S.C.)

History: John Baptist Debrabant founded this pontifical congregation in Douai, France, in 1826 to counteract the ignorance and irreligion of his day through the Christian education of youth. It flourished in northern France and Belgium, and spread to England, Ireland, Argentina, Spain, Africa, and, in 1886, the United States.

Purpose: Completely dedicated to the salvation of souls through the apostolate of teaching, the Holy Union conducts schools from the elementary to the college level in the eastern part of the United States. The two American provinces staff one of the congregation's four African missions at Dschang, Cameroun, where they have established a daughter congregation of native sisters.

Spiritual Life: The religious exercises include Holy Mass, meditation, and the Little Office of the Blessed Virgin which is recited in choir every day.

Training Program: The one-year postulancy is followed by a two-year novitiate and a two-year juniorate during which time the sisters continue their spiritual formation and pursue their professional studies. Temporary vows are taken at the end of their novitiate for six years after which profession of perpetual vows is made.

Qualifications:

* Age: under 30.
* Completion of high school.
* Entrance date: September.

Habit: The sisters wear a black habit and veil, a white coif, and a silver cross.

> *Write to:* Mother Provincial
> 492 Rock Street
> Fall River, Massachusetts
>
> Mother Provincial
> 1 Main Street
> Groton, Massachusetts

SISTERS OF THE SACRED HEARTS (SS.CC.)

History: Countess Henriette Aymer de la Chevalerie, with the help and encouragement of Father Coudrin, her co-founder, founded this congregation in Poitiers, France, in 1797. Imprisoned in 1793, and sentenced to death for having given shelter to a Catholic priest, she was providentially released after a year of seclusion. Upon regaining freedom, Mother Henrietta, promised to give herself whole-heartedly to Our Blessed Lord. The community was approved by the Holy See in 1817.

Purpose: The members, besides their devotion to the Sacred Heart of Jesus, render to the Immaculate Heart of Mary a homage of filial tenderness. The sisters, besides adoration, are engaged in educational, catechetical, and household works in boarding and parochial schools, and guest houses. These sisters have foundations in Europe, Canada, United States, South America, and Hawaii.

Spiritual Life: The religious exercises include the Office of the Blessed Virgin and the Little Offices of the Sacred Heart of Jesus and Mary in English, and thirty minutes each of mental prayer and spiritual reading. Each sister spends one hour in adoration before the Blessed Sacrament every day.

Training Program: The postulancy of six to twelve months is followed by eighteen months of novitiate. After this period of spiritual formation the novice makes her temporary profession of simple vows. The juniorate program lasts five years.

Qualifications:
* Age: 15 to 28. Exceptions are sometimes made.
* Average intelligence.
* Entrance date: July 9.

Habit: The sisters wear a white habit and a scapular which has a medallion of the Sacred Hearts.

Write to: Mother Superior
Sacred Hearts Academy
330 Main Street
Fairhaven, Massachusetts

SALVATORIANS (S.D.S.)

History: Mother Mary of the Apostles, under the direction of Father Francis of the Cross, founded this congregation in Tivoli, Italy, in 1888. The foundress intended to establish an apostolic society which would work in every nation of the world to combat by prayer, word, and action, the evils of the times. Within five years, foundations were established in India and South America. The motherhouse foundation for the United States was made in Milwaukee, Wisconsin, in 1895.

Purpose: The sisters teach in elementary, secondary schools, and colleges, and nurse and care for the aged and orphans both at home and in the foreign missions. More than two thousand members work in the United States, Europe, Africa, South America, Ceylon, Formosa, and the Holy Land.

Spiritual Life: The religious exercises include Holy Mass, the recitation of the Little Office of the Blessed Virgin in Latin, the rosary, one hour of mental prayer, spiritual reading, and other community prayers.

Training Program: The sisters conduct an aspirancy for high school girls interested in the religious life. The postulancy of one year is followed by a two-year novitiate. After the novice makes her profession of temporary vows, she remains at the motherhouse to continue her spiritual formation in the juniorate and complete her college education.

Qualifications:
* The maximum age is 30.
* Average intelligence.
* Entrance date: September.

Habit: The sisters wear a black habit and veil, and a white head band and guimpe.

> *Write to:* Director of Vocations
> Saint Mary's Convent
> 3516 West Center Street
> Milwaukee 10, Wisconsin

SISTERS OF SERVICE (S.O.S.)

History: The community was founded in Toronto, Canada, in 1922 by two Redemptorist Fathers, Rev. Arthur Coughlan and Rev. George T. Daly. There were many thousands of Catholics at this time in the prairie lands of Western Canada who were without churches or Catholic schools. The alarming number of families who had either given up their religion or were in the danger of drifting from the Faith, prompted the foundation of the Sisters of Service. The sisters were first established in the United States at Fargo, North Dakota, in 1939.

Purpose: The sisters are engaged in teaching in rural schools, conducting religious vacation schools, teaching religion to children in isolated districts through the Religious Correspondence Schools, operating small hospitals in rural areas, visiting the sick in their homes, conducting residential clubs for girls in the cities, and meeting and assisting immigrants at ports of entry.

Spiritual Life: The religious exercises include Holy Mass, mental prayer, the rosary, spiritual reading, and other community prayers and devotions.

Training Program: The one-year postulancy is followed by a two-year novitiate. Temporary vows are made for five years. The sisters continue their spiritual formation during this time, while taking college courses in preparation for their professional degrees.

Qualifications:
* Age: 17 to 30. Exceptions are sometimes made for those under 40.
* Completion of high school.
* Entrance date: August 22.

Habit: The sisters wear a grey habit, white collar and cuffs, a head-dress similar to that of a nurse, and a silver cross and ring.

> *Write to:* Sisters of Service
> 608 9th Street
> Fargo, North Dakota

URSULINE NUNS (O.S.U.)

History: Angela Merici founded the Order of St. Ursula in Brescia, Italy, in 1535. The history of the Ursulines is a history of pioneering. Venerable Mary of the Incarnation came to Quebec in 1639 as the first woman missionary. In 1727 a group of French Ursulines landed in New Orleans, Louisiana, to found the first Catholic school for girls in America.

Purpose: The Ursulines have the distinction of being the first group of women dedicated to the teaching of girls. The foundress proposed to prepare thoroughly Catholic women and to reform a paganized and de-Christianized society through the influence of the Catholic wife and mother. The Ursulines have adhered to this objective for four hundred years. They conduct elementary and secondary schools, academies, colleges, and have missions in Africa, Alaska, South America, Mexico, Formosa, Indonesia, and Greece.

Spiritual Life: The religious exercises include Holy Mass, mental prayer, the rosary, spiritual reading, and other community prayers and devotions. Some congregations say the Divine Office while others say the Office of the Blessed Virgin.

Training Program: The postulancy of at least six months is followed by a two-year novitiate. Under the guidance of the mistress of novices, the novice is introduced to the Ursuline spirituality. During the novitiate she also makes her thirty-day retreat. Temporary vows are made for five years, after which perpetual vows are pronounced. During this time, the sister continues the studies toward her academic degrees or is trained in domestic or other duties if she is a co-adjutrix sister. In the Ursulines of the Roman Union, a tertianship of about ten months is made in Rome around the tenth year after first vows. At the end of the tertianship, solemn vows are pronounced.

Qualifications:
* The maximum age is 30. Exceptions are sometimes made.
* Completion of high school.

Habit: The sisters wear a black habit, leather cincture, and veil, a white guimpe and band, crucifix, rosary, and a gold ring.

Write to the Mother Superior at the nearest Ursuline Convent listed below:

URSULINE NUNS OF THE ROMAN UNION

Eastern Province
Provincialate
200th Street and Marion Avenue
New York 58, New York

Central Province
Ursuline Provincialate
399 South Sappington Road
Kirkwood 22, Missouri

Western Province
Ursuline Provincialate
400 Angela Drive
Santa Rosa, California

Northeastern Province
Ursuline Provincialate
65 Lowder Street
Dedham, Massachusetts

URSULINE NUNS OF THE CONGREGATION OF PARIS

Kansas
Ursuline Convent of Our Lady of Lourdes, East Miami Street, Paola, Kansas

Kentucky
Ursuline Motherhouse of the Immaculate Conception, 3115 Lexington Road, Louisville, Kentucky
Mt. St. Joseph Ursuline Motherhouse, Maple Mount, Kentucky

Ohio
St. Ursula Convent, 1339 E. McMillan Street, Cincinnati 6, Ohio

Ursuline Motherhouse, 2600 Lander Road, Cleveland 24, Ohio

Mount St. Ursula, Old Washington, Ohio

Immaculate Heart of Mary Convent, St. Martin, Ohio

Ursuline Convent of the Sacred Heart, 2413 Collingwood Boulevard, Toledo 10, Ohio

Ursuline Convent, 3650 Logan Way, Youngstown 5, Ohio

INDEPENDENT URSULINE MOTHERHOUSE CONVENTS

Michigan
Epiphany Convent, Menominee, Michigan

Convent of Our Lady of Lourdes, Stephenson, Michigan

Ursuline Convent of Our Lady of the Straits, St. Ignace, Michigan

New York
Ursuline Convent, Blue Point, Long Island, New York

SOCIETY OF ST. URSULA OF THE BLESSED VIRGIN (U.T.S.V.)

History: Venerable Anne de Xainctonge founded this society in 1606 at Dole, France. It was founded to offer all girls, rich or poor, the opportunity of a Christian education. The apostolate of education has been carried on in France, Germany, and Switzerland for more than 350 years. The society established its first American foundation in New York on November 9, 1901.

Purpose: In the United States the sisters teach in private and parochial schools, both elementary and secondary, and conduct catechetical work, retreats, and sodalities. The congregation has two missions in the Congo.

Spiritual Life: The daily religious exercises include Holy Mass, an hour of mental prayer, the rosary, and a half-hour of spiritual reading. They also chant the day hours of the Divine Office in Latin. When recited privately it may be in either English or Latin.

Training Program: A three-month postulancy is followed by a novitiate of two years, after which first vows are taken for five years. A tertianship of six months precedes perpetual vows. This is a time of intense spiritual preparation, which the tertians sometimes make in the motherhouse in Tours, France.

Qualifications:
* Age: 17 to 35.
* A sincere desire to devote themselves to the service of God.

Habit: The habit is black with a white guimpe, the simple widow's costume of the Mary Stuart era, when the society was founded.

> *Write to:* Convent of St. Ursula
> Marygrove
> Kingston, New York

VINCENTIAN SISTERS OF CHARITY
(V.S.C.)

History: This Vincentian community dates its origin in the United States to November 14, 1902, when five sisters from the Sathmar Province in central Europe, under the leadership of Mother M. Emerentiana, came to the Diocese of Pittsburgh, Pennsylvania, to work among the poor, sick, and children.

Purpose: The sisters teach in parochial grade and high schools as well as in catechetical centers, nurse the sick in general hospitals, and in homes for the chronically ill, and carry on a missionary apostolate among the colored in Alabama. Their institutions are located in Pennsylvania, Alabama, Missouri, and Ohio.

Spiritual Life: The religious exercises include Holy Mass, the recitation in Latin of the Little Office of the Blessed Virgin, the rosary, a half-hour of meditation, spiritual reading, and other community prayers and devotions.

Training Program: The postulancy of six months to one-year is followed by a two-year novitiate. The novices during the first year are instructed in the matters pertaining to the religious life. In the following year they resume their academic courses while continuing their spiritual formation. Simple vows are then made for three years. Junior professed sisters make a more practical application of the principles of the spiritual life in the daily experiences they meet in community life.

Qualifications:
* Age: 15 to 35. Exceptions are sometimes made.
* Completion of high school preferred.

Habit: The sisters wear a black habit, scapular, and veil, a headdress which consists of a bonnet, coif, and collar, a six-decade rosary, and a silver ring on the left hand.

Write to: Motherhouse
8200 McKnight Road
Pittsburgh 37, Pennsylvania

ZELATRICIAN SISTERS (M.Z.S.H.)

History: Mother Mary Clelia founded this congregation in Tuscany, Italy, in 1894. The first foundation in the United States was made in 1902. The community has four provinces: two in Italy, one in South America, and one in the United States. The congregation is presently working in New York, Connecticut, Rhode Island, Pennsylvania, Florida, Illinois, California, Kansas, and Missouri.

Purpose: The sisters teach on the kindergarten, elementary, and secondary levels. They are active in parish visiting, conduct nurseries, and teach catechism to public school children in many parishes. These sisters are specialists in the field of mentally handicapped children. They operate two nationally famous schools for the mentally retarded, one in Oakmont and the other in Greensburg, Pennsylvania.

Spiritual Life: The religious exercises include Holy Mass, the recitation of the Little Office of the Sacred Heart of Jesus in Latin, two half-hour periods of mental prayer, the rosary, spiritual reading, and other community prayers and devotions.

Training Program: The community conducts an aspirancy for teen-age girls interested in the religious life. The six-month postulancy is followed by a two-year novitiate. Temporary vows are made annually for three or six years. At the end of this time the sisters make their perpetual vows. The sisters continue their spiritual formation while completing the college courses necessary for their professional degrees.

Qualifications:
* Elementary school graduates enter the aspirancy.
* Completion of high school is desirable but not absolutely necessary for the postulancy.

Habit: The sisters wear a black habit, veil and coco bead rosary, and a crucifix.

Write to: Mount Sacred Heart
265 Benham Street
Hamden 14, Connecticut

IX

WRITING AND PUBLICATIONS

DAUGHTERS OF ST. PAUL (D.S.P.)

History: Father James Alberione, S.S.P., founded this congregation in 1915 in Italy. As apostles in twenty-four countries and coast to coast in the United States, the sisters of this community enjoy a common family spirit through the directives of their co-foundress and present Mother General Thecla Merlo.

Purpose: The members of this congregation are engaged in a unique positive use of mass media of communications, by which they endeavor to replace indecent literature, obscene motion pictures, misleading radio programs, and objectionable television programs in order to bring men to a better knowledge and love of God. The sisters write, design, print, and distribute books, pamphlets, and magazines. They also direct, produce, film, and record movies and film strips, and operate book and film centers.

Spiritual Life: The religious exercises include Holy Mass, meditation, spiritual reading, examens, the rosary, and other community prayers and devotions.

Training Program: The community conducts an aspirancy for high school girls. A one-year novitiate precedes the making of first simple vows. Another similar year, called the novitiate of perfection, completes the five years of temporary vows, in which the sister prepares herself for profession of perpetual vows.

Qualifications:
* Age: 14 to 23.
* A desire to help others know and love God better through the press, radio, movies, and television.

Habit: The sisters wear a simple black, floor-length habit, veil, leather cincture, rosary, and a small white collar.

> *Write to:* Mother Superior
> 50 St. Paul's Avenue
> Boston 30, Massachusetts

DOMINICAN NUNS OF THE SECOND ORDER OF PERPETUAL ADORATION (Page 9)

California

Monastery of the Angels
1977 Carmen Place
Los Angeles 28,
California

Corpus Christi Monastery
Oak Grove Avenue
Menlo Park, California

Connecticut

Monastery of Our Lady of Grace
North Guilford, Connecticut

Massachusetts

Monastery of the Mother of God
1430 Riverdale Street
West Springfield, Massachusetts

Michigan

Monastery of the Blessed Sacrament
9704 Oakland Avenue
Detroit 11, Michigan

New Jersey

Monastery of St. Dominic
13th Ave., and S. 10th Street
Newark 3, New Jersey

Monastery of Our Lady of the Rosary
Morris and Springfield Avenues,
Summit, New Jersey

New York

Monastery of the Immaculate Conception
714 New Scotland Avenue
Albany, New York

Corpus Christi Monastery
Lafayette Avenue and Barretto Street
Hunt's Point,
Bronx, New York

Monastery of Our Lady of the Rosary
335 Doat Street
Buffalo, New York

Monastery of Mary the Queen
1310 West Church Street
Elmira, New York

Ohio

Monastery of the Holy Name
3020 Erie Avenue
Cincinnati 8, Ohio

Texas

Monastery of the Infant Jesus
1501 Loftus Lane
Lufkin, Texas

DOMINICAN SISTERS OF THE PERPETUAL ROSARY (Page 11)

Alabama

Dominican Monastery
Marbury, Alabama

Maryland

Dominican Nuns
720 Maiden Choice Lane
Catonsville 28, Maryland

New Jersey

Monastery of Perpetual Rosary
Haddon and Euclid Avenues
Camden 3, New Jersey

Monastery of Dominican Sisters
14th and West Streets
Union City, New Jersey

New York

Monastery of Perpetual Rosary
802 Court Street
Syracuse 8, New York

Pennsylvania

Dominican Monastery
1834 Lititz Pike
P.O. Box 1125
Lancaster, Pennsylvania

Wisconsin

Dominican Sisters
217 N. 68th Street
Milwaukee 13, Wisconsin
St. Dominic's Monastery
3000 South Avenue
La Crosse, Wisconsin

PASSIONIST NUNS (Page 18)

Kentucky
Convent of the Sacred Passions
751 Donaldson Highway
Erlanger, Kentucky

St. Joseph's Monastery
1420 Benita Avenue
Owensboro, Kentucky

Missouri
Immaculate Conception Convent
P. O. Box 145
Ellisville, Missouri

Pennsylvania
St. Gabriel's Monastery
1560 Monroe Avenue
Dunmore 9, Pennsylvania

Our Lady of Sorrows Convent
2715 Churchview Avenue
Pittsburgh 27, Pennsylvania

SISTERS ADORERS OF THE PRECIOUS BLOOD (Page 26)

Indiana
Precious Blood Monastery
1106 State Street
Lafayette, Indiana

Maine
Precious Blood Monastery
166 State Street
Portland, Maine

New Hampshire
Precious Blood Monastery
700 Bridge Street
Manchester, New Hampshire

New York
Precious Blood Monastery
54th St. and Hamilton Parkway
Brooklyn, New York

Ohio
Precious Blood Monastery
R.D. 2, Marywood
Bellevue, Ohio

Oregon
Precious Blood Monastery
1208 S.E. 76th Avenue
Portland 15, Oregon

CONGREGATION OF OUR LADY OF THE RETREAT IN THE CENACLE (Page 133)

Eastern Province
Convent of Our Lady of the Retreat
in the Cenacle
Mt. Kisco, New York

Midwestern Province
Convent of Our Lady of the Cenacle
3288 North Lake Drive
Milwaukee 11, Wisconsin

CARMELITE SISTERS OF THE DIVINE HEART OF JESUS (Page 135)

California
Mother Provincial
8585 La Mesa Boulevard
La Mesa, California

Wisconsin
Mother Provincial
1214 Kavanaugh Place
Milwaukee 13, Wisconsin

LITTLE SISTERS OF THE POOR (Page 140)

Province of Brooklyn
Mother Provincial
Bushwick and De Kalb Avenues
Brooklyn 21, New York

Province of Baltimore
Mother Provincial
4291 Richmond Road
Cleveland 22, Ohio

Province of Chicago
Mother Provincial
2358 Sheffield Avenue
Chicago 14, Illinois

SISTERS OF THE GOOD SHEPHERD (Page 143)

Province of Baltimore
Convent of the Good Shepherd
Mount and Hollins Streets
Baltimore 23, Maryland

Province of Carthage
Convent of the Good Shepherd
North Bend Road
Cincinnati 16, Ohio

Province of New York
Mount St. Florence
Peekskill, New York

Province of Philadelphia
Convent of the Good Shepherd
8550 Verree Road
Philadelphia 11, Pennsylvania

Province of St. Louis
Convent of the Good Shepherd
3801 Gravois Avenue
St. Louis 16, Missouri

Province of St. Paul
Convent of the Good Shepherd
931 Blair Avenue
St. Paul 4, Minnesota

Novitiate House for Home and Foreign Missions
Convent of the Good Shepherd
1500 S. Arlington Avenue
Los Angeles 19, California

THE SISTERS OF OUR LADY OF CHARITY OF REFUGE (Page 147)

Arkansas
Monastery of Our Lady of Charity of Refuge
1125 Malvern Avenue
Hot Springs, Arkansas

New York
Monastery of Our Lady of Charity
485 Best Street
Buffalo 8, New York

Monastery of Our Lady of Charity
1326 Winton Road
Rochester 9, New York

Pennsylvania
Monastery of Our Lady of Charity
Flaugherty Run Road
Coraopolis, Pennsylvania

Sisters of Our Lady of Charity
4635 East Lake Road
Erie, Pennsylvania

Monastery of Our Lady of Charity
1625 Lincoln Avenue
Pittsburgh, Pennsylvania

Texas
Monastery of Our Lady of Charity
415 N. Glenwood Drive
El Paso, Texas

Monastery of Our Lady of Charity
4500 W. Davis Street
Dallas, Texas

Monastery of Our Lady of Charity
1900 Montana Street
San Antonio 3, Texas

West Virginia
Monastery of Our Lady of Charity
Edgington Lane
Wheeling, West Virginia

Wisconsin
Monastery of Our Lady of Charity
918 Porlier Street
Green Bay, Wisconsin

SISTERS OF NOTRE DAME de NAMUR (Page 163)

Massachusetts Province
Notre Dame Novitiate
Jeffrey's Neck Road
Ipswich, Massachusetts

Connecticut Province
Provincial House
1561 North Benson Road
Fairfield, Connecticut

Baltimore Province
Provincial House
Ilchester, Maryland

Cincinnati Province
Convent of Notre Dame
Reading
Cincinnati 15, Ohio

Province of California
Provincial House
Bohlman Road
Saratoga, California

SISTERS OF THE INCARNATE WORD AND BLESSED SACRAMENT (Page 168)

Ohio
  Mother Superior
6618 Pearl Road
Parma Heights (U.S. Rt. 42)
Cleveland 30, Ohio

Texas
  Mother Superior
4600 Richmond Road
Bellaire, Texas

  Mother Superior
2930 South Alameda Street
Corpus Christi, Texas

SISTERS OF LORETTO AT THE FOOT OF THE CROSS (Page 169)

Generalate
  Mother General
Loretto, Nerinx P. O.
Kentucky

Province of Our Lady of Sorrows
  Mother Provincial
470 East Lockwood Avenue
Webster Groves 19, Missouri

Province of St. Joseph
  Mother Provincial
1101 West 39th Street
Kansas City 11, Missouri

Province of the Sacred Heart
  Mother Provincial
3001 South Federal Boulevard
Loretto, Colorado

SOCIETY OF THE SACRED HEART (Page 177)

Vicariate of Albany
  Manhattanville College of the Sacred
  Heart
Purchase, New York

Vicariate of Chicago
  Convent of the Sacred Heart
6250 Sheridan Road
Chicago 26, Illinois

Vicariate of St. Louis
  Convent of the Sacred Heart
Villa Duchesne
334 North Taylor Avenue
St. Louis 8, Missouri

Vicariate of San Francisco
  San Francisco College for Women
Lone Mountain
San Francisco 18, California

Vicariate of Washington
  Convent of the Sacred Heart
9101 Rockville Pike
Washington 14, D.C.

BENEDICTINE SISTERS OF THE CONGREGATION OF ST. BENEDICT (Page 195)

Illinois
  St. Mary Priory
Nauvoo, Illinois

Indiana
  Our Lady of Grace Convent
Beech Grove, Indiana

Minnesota
  St. Scholastica Priory
Kenwood Avenue
Duluth 11, Minnesota
  St. Benedict's Priory
St. Joseph, Minnesota
  St. Paul's Priory
301 Summit Avenue
St. Paul 2, Minnesota

North Dakota
  Annunciation Priory
R. R. 2, Box 119
Bismarck, North Dakota

Washington
  St. Placid Priory
4600 Martin Way
Olympia, Washington

Wisconsin
  St. Bede's Priory
1329 Wilson Street
Eau Claire, Wisconsin

BENEDICTINE SISTERS OF THE CONGREGATION OF ST. GERTRUDE THE GREAT (Page 196)

Idaho
St. Gertrude's Convent
Cottonwood, Idaho

Indiana
Immaculate Conception Convent
Ferdinand, Indiana

Minnesota
Mt. St. Benedict's Convent
Crookston, Minnesota

North Dakota
Our Lady of Peace Convent
Belcourt, North Dakota
Sacred Heart Convent
Minot, North Dakota

Oregon
Convent Queen of Angels
Mt. Angel, Oregon

South Dakota
Sacred Heart Convent
Yankton, South Dakota
Mother of God Priory
Pierre, South Dakota

St. Martin's Priory
Rapid City
South Dakota

Wisconsin
St. Benedict's Convent
Route 1
Waunakee, Wisconsin

BENEDICTINE SISTERS OF DIOCESAN JURISDICTION

Arkansas

St. Scholastica's Motherhouse
Albert Pike and Rogers Street
Fort Smith, Arkansas

Florida

Holy Name Priory
San Antonio, Florida

INDEPENDENT BENEDICTINE CONGREGATIONS

Colorado
Convent of St. Walburga
Boulder, Colorado
Convent of St. Therese
Canon City, Colorado

Louisiana
St. Gertrude's Monastery
(St. Gertrude Rural Station, Covington)
Ramsay, Louisiana

Pennsylvania
St. Emma's Retreat House
Five Point Road
R.F.D. 4, Box 281
Greensburg, Pennsylvania

BENEDICTINE SISTERS OF THE CONGREGATION OF ST. SCHOLASTICA (Page 197)

Alabama
Sacred Heart Convent
Cullman, Alabama

California
St. Lucy's Priory
19045 E. Sierra Madre
Glendora, California

Illinois
Sacred Heart Convent
Lisle, Illinois

St. Scholastica Convent
7430 Ridge Avenue
Chicago 45, Illinois

Our Lady of Sorrows Convent
Tinley Park, Illinois

Kansas
Mount St. Scholastica Convent
Atchison, Kansas

Kentucky
St. Walburg Convent
2500 Amsterdam Road
Covington, Kentucky

Louisiana
St. Scholastica Convent
Covington, Louisiana

Maryland
St. Gertrude Convent
Ridgely, Maryland

New Jersey
St. Walburg Convent
851 N. Broad Street
Elizabeth, New Jersey

Oklahoma
St. Joseph's Convent
2220 South Lewis
Tulsa, Oklahoma

Pennsylvania
Mt. St. Mary Convent
4530 Perrysville Avenue
Pittsburgh 29, Pennsylvania

St. Benedict's Convent
345 E. Ninth Street
Erie, Pennsylvania

St. Joseph Convent
303 Church Street
St. Mary's, Elk Co., Pennsylvania

Texas
St. Scholastica Convent
P. O. Box 905
Boerne, Texas

Virginia
St. Benedict Convent
Bristow, Virginia

BERNADINE SISTERS (Page 199)

Generalate
Mother General
Maryview
647 Spring Mill Road
Villanova, Pennsylvania

Sacred Heart Province
Mother Provincial
Mount Alvernia
Reading, Pennsylvania

Heart of Mary Province
Mother Provincial
159 Sky Meadow Drive
North Stamford, Connecticut

Our Lady of the Rosary Province
Mother Provincial
27405 West 10 Mile Road
Farmington, Michigan

SISTERS OF DIVINE PROVIDENCE (Page 225)

St. Peter's Province
Mother Provincial
Providence Heights
Allison Park, Pennsylvania

St. Louis Province
Mother Provincial
8351 Florissant Road
Normandy 21, Missouri

Our Lady of Divine Providence Province
Mother Provincial
Box 2, Route 80
Kingston, Massachusetts

FELICIAN SISTERS (Page 253)

Presentation of B.V.M. Province
Mother Provincial
36800 Schoolcraft Road
Livonia, Michigan

Immaculate Heart of Mary Province
Mother Provincial
600 Doat Street
Buffalo 11, New York

Mother of Good Counsel Province
Mother Provincial
3800 Peterson Avenue
Chicago 45, Illinois

Immaculate Conception Province
Mother Provincial
South Main Street
Lodi, New Jersey

Our Lady of the Sacred Heart Province
Mother Provincial
1500 Woodcrest Avenue
Coraopolis, Pennsylvania

Our Lady of the Angels Province
Mother Provincial
1333 Enfield Street
Enfield, Connecticut

Assumption of the B.V.M. Province
Mother Provincial
Assumption Villa
Monument Road
Ponca City, Oklahoma

SCHOOL SISTERS OF ST. FRANCIS (Page 264)

General Motherhouse
St. Joseph Convent
1501 South Layton Boulevard
Milwaukee 15, Wisconsin

Mount St. Francis Province
Mother Provincial
839 North Main Street
Rockford, Illinois

Our Lady of the Angels Province
Mother Provincial
625 North 90th Street
Omaha 14, Nebraska

SISTERS OF ST. FRANCIS (Page 269)

Generalate
Convent of Our Lady of the Angels
Glen Riddle P. O.
Pennsylvania

Immaculate Conception Province
St. Agnes Annex
1400 Mifflin Street
Philadelphia 45, Pennsylvania

Sacred Heart Province
Convent of Our Lady of the Angels
0858 S.W. Palatine Hill Road
Portland 19, Oregon

St. Joseph's Province
St. Joseph's Hospital
1400 N. Caroline Street
Baltimore 13, Maryland

St. Anthony's Province
St. Francis Hospital
Trenton 9, New Jersey

SISTERS OF ST. FRANCIS OF PENANCE AND CHRISTIAN CHARITY (Page 279)

Holy Name Province
Seminary of Our Lady of the Sacred
Heart
4421 Lower River Road
Stella Niagara, New York

Sacred Heart Province
Marycrest
2851 W. 52nd Avenue
Denver 21, Colorado

St. Francis Province
Mount Alverno
3910 Bret Harte Drive
Redwood City, California

CONGREGATION OF THE SISTERS OF THE HOLY CROSS (Page 291)

Motherhouse
St. Mary's Convent
Notre Dame, Indiana

Province of the Midwest
Mother Provincial
3720 Miami
South Bend 14, Indiana

Province of the East
Provincial House
10701 Rockville Pike
Rockville, Maryland

Province of the West
St. Mary-of-the-Wasatch
Salt Lake City 8, Utah

SISTERS OF THE HOLY FAMILY OF NAZARETH (Page 294)

Sacred Heart Province
Mother Provincial
353 N. River Road
Des Plaines, Illinois

Immaculate Conception Province
Mother Provincial
Grant and Frankford Avenues, Torresdale
Philadelphia 14, Pennsylvania

St. Joseph's Province
Mother Provincial
285 Bellevue Road
Pittsburgh 29, Pennsylvania

Immaculate Heart of Mary Province
Mother Provincial
Villa Immaculata
Sound Avenue, Riverhead
Long Island, New York

SISTERS OF THE HOLY NAMES OF JESUS AND MARY (Page 301)

Province of Oregon
Convent of the Holy Names
Marylhurst, Oregon

Province of California
Convent of the Holy Names
P. O. Box 907
Los Gatos, California

Province of New York
Provincialate of the Sisters of the Holy Names
1061 New Scotland Road
Albany 8, New York

Province of Washington
Convent of the Holy Names
1114 N. Superior Street
Spokane 2, Washington

SISTERS, SERVANTS OF THE IMMACULATE HEART OF MARY (Page 311)

Michigan
Mother General
610 West Elm Avenue
Monroe, Michigan

Pennsylvania
Mother General
Immaculate Heart of Mary Convent
Scranton 9, Pennsylvania

Mother General
Villa Maria
West Chester, Pennsylvania

SISTERS OF ST. JOSEPH OF THE THIRD ORDER OF ST. FRANCIS (Page 318)

Generalate
St. Joseph Motherhouse
107 South Greenlawn Avenue
South Bend, Indiana

Province of St. Joseph
St. Joseph's Convent
Maria Drive
Stevens Point, Wisconsin

Province of Our Lady of Czestochowa
Marymount Convent
12215 Granger Road
Garfield Heights 25, Ohio

Province of Immaculate Conception
Immaculata Convent
Box 414
Bartlett, Illinois

SISTERS OF MERCY OF THE UNION IN THE UNITED STATES (Page 327)

Province of Detroit
Provincial House
8200 West Outer Drive
Detroit 19, Michigan

Province of New York
Provincial House
Mt. Mercy-on-the-Hudson
Dobbs Ferry, New York

Province of Omaha

Provincial House
1901 S. 72nd Street
Omaha 14, Nebraska

Province of Providence

Provincial House
R. D. #3
Cumberland, Rhode Island

Province of St. Louis

Provincial House
2039 N. Geyer Road
St. Louis 31, Missouri

Province of Scranton

Provincial House
Villa St. Teresa
Dallas, Pennsylvania

SCHOOL SISTERS OF NOTRE DAME (Page 332)

Western Province

Notre Dame of the Lake
Mequon, Wisconsin

Eastern Province

Mother Provincial
6401 North Charles Street
Baltimore 12, Maryland

Northeastern Province

Mother Provincial
345 Belden Hill Road
Wilton, Connecticut

Southern Province

Sancta Maria in Ripa
320 East Ripa Avenue
St. Louis 25, Missouri

Northwestern Province

Convent of Our Lady of Good Counsel
Mankato, Minnesota

South-Central Province

Mother Provincial
2110 Cooper Drive
Irving, Texas

SISTERS OF NOTRE DAME (Page 333)

Cleveland Province

Notre Dame Educational Center
Auburn Road
Chardon, Ohio

Covington Province

Provincial House
1601 Dixie Highway
Covington, Kentucky

Province of Toledo

Notre Dame Provincialate
3837 Secor Road
Toledo 6, Ohio

Canton Province

Maryhill Convent
5228 Everhard Road
Canton 8, Ohio

California

Sisters of Notre Dame
Rancho La Pilarica
Rt. 1, Box 60
Thousand Oaks, California

SISTERS ADORERS OF THE MOST PRECIOUS BLOOD (Page 348)

Province of Ruma

Mother Provincial
Ruma, (P. O. Red Bud, R.R. 1)
Illinois

Province of Wichita

Mother Provincial
1165 Southwest Boulevard
Wichita 13, Kansas

Province of Columbia

Mother Provincial
St. Joseph Convent
Gethsemane,
Columbia, Pennsylvania

SISTERS OF THE PRESENTATION OF THE BLESSED VIRGIN MARY (Page 349)

Arizona

Presentation Convent
1300 E. Cedar Street
Globe, Arizona

California

Presentation Convent
281 Masonic Avenue
San Francisco 18, California

Georgia

Presentation Convent
150 So. Davis Drive
Warner Robins, Georgia

Illinois

Presentation Convent
Oregon, Illinois

Iowa

Mt. Loretto Convent
1229 Mt. Loretto Avenue
Dubuque, Iowa

Massachusetts

Holy Family Convent
366 South Street
Fitchburg, Massachusetts

New York

Mt. St. Joseph
R.D. 2, Box 101
Newburgh, New York

Convent of Our Lady
189 Howard Avenue
Grymes Hill, Staten Island, New York

St. Colman's Presentation Convent
Watervliet, New York

North Dakota

Sacred Heart Convent
Fargo, North Dakota

South Dakota

Presentation Convent
Aberdeen, South Dakota

Texas

Presentation Convent
8931 Kennedy Road
San Antonio, Texas

SECULAR INSTITUTES

The rise of Secular Institutes is one of the most recent developments that has taken place in the United States. Most of the people of the English-speaking world including those in our own country know little or nothing about the purpose, function, or activity of these groups, even though some of them have been in existence for two centuries.

Secular Institutes are groups of lay persons who live in the world while attempting to live up to the ideals and aspirations followed by the members of religious congregations. Persons who consecrate themselves to God in these institutes strive for perfection through the observance of the evangelical virtues and dedicate their lives according to the apostolate of the institute to which they belong. These counsels are assumed as obligations by vow, promise, oath, or consecration which mutually bind all the members of the group.

Secular Institutes differ from religious communities in three aspects: the members of Secular Institutes take semi-public or social vows, for the most part they do not live a common life, i.e., live together in the same convent as sisters do, and finally, except for some semi-formal uniform or a medal, they do not wear a distinctive habit or dress.

California

Society of Our Lady of the Way
P. O. Box 17396
Los Angeles 4, California

Society Devoted to the Sacred Heart
Motherhouse, 728 S. Hudson Avenue
Los Angeles, California

Illinois

Daughters of the Most Holy and Immaculate Heart of Mary
4541 S. Ashland Avenue
Chicago 9, Illinois

Opus Dei
American Central House
4944 Woodlawn Avenue
Chicago, Illinois

Regnum Christi
c/o Very Rev. Armando Pierini, P.S.S.C.
P.O. Box 447
Chicago 90, Illinois

Caritas Christi
c/o Very Patrick M. J. Clancy, O.P.
700 Division Street
River Forest, Illinois

Massachusetts

Teresian Institute
Directress
312 Dartmouth Street
Boston 16, Massachusetts

Oblate Missionaries of Mary Immaculate
Directress
56 Fairmont Street
Lowell, Massachusetts

Missouri

Rural Parish Workers
Directress
Box 300, Rt. 1
Cadet, Missouri

Washington, D.C.

Missionaries of the Kingship of Christ
c/o Rev. Stephen Hartdegen, O.F.M.
Holy Name College
14th and Shepherd Streets, N.E.
Washington 17, D.C.

Company of St. Paul
1601 Hobart Street, N.W.
Washington 9, D.C.

Wisconsin

Schoenstatt Sisters of Mary
3009 Cottage Grove Road
Madison 4, Wisconsin

PIOUS UNIONS

The following organizations have been approved by the ordinaries of their dioceses. They will become Secular Institutes as soon as they receive approbation from the Holy See.

Canada

Domus Dominae
Madonna House
Combermere,
Ontario, Canada

Illinois

Regina Mundi
Directress
10210 S. Walden Parkway
Chicago 43, Illinois

International Catholic Auxiliaries
Directress
1734 Asbury Avenue
Evanston, Illinois

Louisiana

Caritas
Directress
3316 Feliciana Street
New Orleans 17, Louisiana

The Bishop's Helpers
Directress
Box 532
Lafayette, Louisiana

Mississippi

Pax Christi
Central House
708 Avenue I
Greenwood, Mississippi

New York

Jesus Caritas
Directress
185 Claremont Avenue
New York 27, New York

Ohio

The Grail
U.S. National Center
Grailville, Loveland, Ohio

Pennsylvania

Daughters of Our Lady of Fatima
Fatima House
25 N. Highland Avenue
Lansdowne, Pennsylvania

Vermont

Oblates of St. Joseph
Directress, Marydawn
Pittsford, Vermont

GLOSSARY

Abridged Abbreviated Office: The shortened form of the Divine Office.

Apostolate: This refers to the active works undertaken by a community of sisters.

Aspirancy: The pre-postulancy period wherein a young girl who desires to enter a religious community but has not graduated from high school, attends a secondary school operated by a religious congregation.

Bandeau: A white linen cloth worn around the forehead to which the veil is attached.

Cloister: An enclosure for religious retirement.   Certain sections of convents and monasteries are encloistered and are closed to the free entry of outsiders, within the limits of the material enclosure.

Cloistered Nun: A purely contemplative nun, seeking personal perfection by close union with God and remaining within the cloister permanently.

Coif: See Wimple.

Diocesan Community: This refers to a congregation of sisters who are under the jurisdiction of the ordinary (bishop) of the diocese in which they are located.

Dispensation: Releasing of vows.   The bishop (ordinary) of the diocese and certain religious superiors can for a just reason dispense their subjects from all vows except those reserved to the pope.

Divine Office: The book of prayer, composed of psalms, hymns, and lessons, which all priests, deacons, and sub-deacons are bound to recite daily.   It is said or sung in choir by monks, friars, nuns, and sisters.   The Office is composed of eight hours; namely, Matins, Lauds, Prime, Terce, Sext, None, Vespers, and Compline.

Evangelical Virtues or Counsels: These are the well-known virtues of poverty, chastity, and obedience recommended by Christ in the Gospels to be followed voluntarily.   Religious take vows to help them observe these virtues and thus strive for a life of perfection in this world.

Examen: One of the fundamental means of furthering personal sanctification.   It is a form of self-examination in which one takes account of the progress or lack of progress in daily religious life.   Each morning a special resolution is made.   At noon (particular examen) and at night (general examen) an account is taken of the progress made and the resolution is renewed.

Extern Sister: A member of a cloistered order of nuns who lives within the convent but outside the enclosure.   She takes care of the external affairs of the convent, serves as portress, and does the shopping.

Canonical Year of Novitiate: This is the one year and a day (Novitiate Year) required by Canon Law of all religious.   During this year the Novice under the discipline of a Mistress may not be employed in the exterior works of the congregation.   She devotes her time to the study of the vows and to the exercises of virtue.

Chaplet: A general name applied to the rosary or in most cases to a string of beads used for reasons of devotion.   For example: the chaplet of the Seven Dolors, Infant of Prague, and the Franciscan Crown rosary (The Seven Joys of Our Lady).

Cincture: A cord or belt worn about the waist which holds the habit in place and from which the rosary is suspended.   Some cords have three knots symbolizing the three Holy Vows.

Guimpe: A white linen starched rounded cloth which covers the chest.

Home Missionary: A sister who devotes her life to the salvation of the unfortunate in the United States, especially in the South, West, and the slums of our big cities.

Juniorate: This is the time after first vows until profession of perpetual vows in which the sister is trained in the works of the apostolate either actively or as a college student.

Lay Sister: This is a sister who is similar to the choir religious. She is cloistered, has the privilege of pronouncing solemn vows, but does not recite the Divine Office in choir.

Little Office of the Blessed Virgin: This is a shorter form of the Divine Office which consists of psalms, lessons, and hymns in honor of the Blessed Virgin. It is divided into eight hours as is the Breviary.

Major Papal Enclosure: An order of nuns who are strictly cloistered. They may not leave the convent except for extraordinary reasons, i.e., sickness requiring hospitalization.

Meditation or mental prayer: Usually a period of one half-hour to one hour in which a religious occupies herself in reflecting on a supernatural truth and in prayer with a view to more intensive union with God and growth in the spiritual life.

Minor Papal Enclosure: A group of nuns who are cloistered but who may leave the cloister to perform their works, such as teaching, attending teachers' institutes, or to complete their studies at a college or university.

Novice: This is a person who undergoes a period of formation or probation for not less than one year, for the purpose of determining fitness for profession into a religious community. A young girl who has satisfactorily completed the period of postulancy becomes a novice upon investure of the habit.

Novitiate: It may be a building or separate quarters used exclusively for the novices, since they must be entirely separated from the professed religious. Or it may refer to the time of probation spent by a candidate for the religious life in a certain convent, under the direction of a specially appointed Mistress of Novices, before the candidate is admitted to religious profession.

Nun: She is a religious belonging to an institute of religious who take solemn vows, whereas a sister is one who takes simple vows. In the United States these two terms are often used interchangeably.

Perpetual Vows: Vows which a religious sister makes for the rest of her life.

Pontifical Community: A congregation of sisters who, while they work in one or more dioceses, fall under the jurisdiction of the Holy Father.

Postulancy: A specified time of probation in which a young girl receives the postulant habit and prepares to enter the novitiate. While the postulancy is usually six months, many communities have extended it for a longer period to enable the postulant to acquire one year of college training before entering the novitiate.

Postulant: One who is being prepared to enter the novitiate.

Prayers in Common: The prayers and devotions which sisters say together as a group.

Professed: Professed sisters are members of religious congregations who have been admitted into vows.

Profession of Vows: An oral contract made publicly in the presence of an authorized person, usually the bishop of the diocese or his representative, and by which a novice after completing the novitiate becomes a simple professed religious.

Religious: One who has made her profession of vows in a religious community.

Roman Collar: A circular collar worn about the neck by some congregations of sisters. It is similar to the collar worn by priests.

Sister: A member of a religious community who makes simple vows.

Spiritual Reading: A community devotion by which the members, either privately or in common, read certain approved books to bring the soul closer to God.

Temporary Vows: The three years of preliminary profession of simple vows which most religious make upon the completion of the novitiate. At the end of three years, these vows may be renewed for three years or the sisters may be permitted to make final vows. They lapse after this three year period unless renewed or made perpetual.

Tertianship: This is a designated period for spiritual renovation in a religious institute to give the religious time to renew the vigor of her spiritual life. Similar to the novitiate, it is made after the religious has passed several years in final vows.

Wimple: This is a linen covering, usually starched, which fits a sister closely about the neck, throat, face, and head. It was once common attire for women. It is also known as a barbette.

APPENDIX

INSTITUTE OF THE SISTERS OF OUR LADY OF MT. CARMEL

Works: Domestic

Write to: Mother Superior, Carmelite Junior Seminary, Hamilton, Massachusetts

SISTERS OF CHARITY (GREY NUNS)

Works: Teaching—Nursing—Social Work

Write to: Provincial House, 10 Pelham Road, Lexington 73, Massachusetts

SISTERS OF CHARITY OF OUR LADY, MOTHER OF MERCY

Works: Teaching—Nursing—Social Work

Write to: Convent of the Holy Family, Baltic, Connecticut

CISTERCIAN NUNS OF THE STRICT OBSERVANCE

Works: Cloistered

Write to: Mount St. Mary's Abbey, Arnold Street, RFD, Box 500, Wrentham, Massachusetts

CONGREGATION OF OUR LADY OF THE ROSARY

Works: Teaching—Social Work—Missions

Write to: St. Agnes Convent, Sparkhill, New York

CONGREGATION OF ST. CATHERINE OF SIENA, OAKFORD, UNION OF SOUTH AFRICA

Works: Teaching

Write to: St. Albert's College, 6172 Chabot Road, Oakland, California

DOMINICAN SISTERS OF THE IMMACULATE CONCEPTION

Works: Nursing

Write to: Provincial House, 9000 81st Street, Justice, Illinois

CONGREGATION OF ST. MARY

Works: Teaching

Write to: St. Mary's Dominican Convent, 7214 St. Charles Avenue, New Orleans 18, Louisiana

DOMINICAN SISTERS OF ST. DOMINIC OF THE ROMAN CONGREGATION

Works: Teaching

Write to: St. Dominic's Institute, 200 Ivy Street, Brookline 46, Massachusetts

FRANCISCAN HANDMAIDS OF THE MOST PURE HEART OF MARY

Works: Teaching—Social Work

Write to: Novitiate, 444 Woodvale Avenue, Pleasant Plains, S.I., New York

FRANCISCAN MISSIONARY SISTERS OF THE IMMACULATE CONCEPTION

Works: Home Missions

Write to: Novitiate, 1579 Woodworth Street, San Fernando, California

FRANCISCAN MISSIONARIES OF ST. JOSEPH

Works: Domestic

Write to: Mount St. Joseph, Slingerlands, New York

FRANCISCAN SISTERS OF CALAIS

Works: Nursing

Write to: St. Francis Hospital, Monroe, Louisiana

GREY SISTERS OF ST. ELIZABETH

Works: Domestic

Write to: Mother Superior, Mount St. Alphonsus, Esopus, New York

SERVANTS OF THE HOLY INFANCY OF JESUS

Works: Domestic—Nursing

Write to: Villa Marie, P.O. Box 708, Plainfield, New Jersey

SISTERS OF THE HOLY INFANT JESUS

Works: Teaching

Write to: Holy Angels School, Colma, California

MOTHERS OF THE HELPLESS

Works: Social Work

Write to: St. Joseph Novitiate, 157 Piermont Avenue, Nyack, New York

LITTLE SISTERS OF THE HOLY FAMILY

Works: Domestic

Write to: Mont Sainte-Famille, 1820 Ouest, Rue Galt, Sherbrooke, P. Q., Canada

DAUGHTERS OF JESUS

Works: Teaching

Write to: St. Egbert's Convent, Morehead City, North Carolina

Society of the Sisters Faithful Companions of Jesus

Write to: St. Joseph's Convent, Columbus Street, Fitchburg, Massachusetts
Blessed Sacrament Convent, 20 Atkins Street, Provindence 8, Rhode Island
St. Philomena's Convent, Corys Lane, Portsmouth, Rhode Island

Mantellate Sisters, Servants of Mary

Works: Teaching—Nursing—Social Work
Write to: Villa Santa Maria, 167th and Oak Forest Avenue, Tinley Park, Illinois

Servants of Mary

Works: Teaching
Write to: Convent of Our Lady of Sorrows, 74th and Military Avenue, Omaha, Nebraska

Daughters of Charity of the Most Precious Blood

Works: Domestic—Nursing
Write to: Day Nursery, 1482 North Avenue, Bridgeport, Connecticut

Servants of Our Lady, Queen of the Clergy

Works: Domestic
Write to: Mother Superior, Lac-au-Saumon, P.Q., Canada

Sisters of Divine Providence of Kentucky

Works: Teaching—Nursing—Social Work
Write to: St. Anne Convent, Melbourne, Kentucky

Sisters of Reparation of the Congregation of Mary

Works: Social Work
Write to: St. Zita's Villa, Monsey, New York

Institute of St. Joan of Arc of Ottawa

Works: Teaching
Write to: St. Aloysius School, Newburyport, Massachusetts

Sisters of Ste. Jeanne D'Arc

Works: Domestic
Write to: "Jeanne D'Arc," 1681 Chemin St. Louis, Quebec 6, Canada

Religious Hospitallers of Saint Joseph

Works: Teaching—Nursing—Missions
Write to: Motherhouse, 251 Pine Avenue W., Montreal, P.Q., Canada

Sisters of St. Joseph of St. Augustine, Florida

Works: Teaching—Nursing—Social Work
Write to: St. Joseph Convent, 241 George Street, St. Augustine, Florida

Sisters of St. Joseph (Le Puy, France)

Works: Teaching
Write to: St. Teresa's Convent, 2510 S. Main Street, Fall River, Massachusetts

Sisters of St. Joseph (Lyons, France)

Works: Teaching—Nursing
Write to: Mother Superior, 277 Minot Avenue, Auburn, Maine

Vincentian Sisters of Charity

Works: Teaching
Write to: Mother Superior, Villa San Bernardo, 1160 Broadway, Bedford, Ohio

Congregation of the Religious of Nazareth

Works: Teaching—Nursing
Write to: La Purisima Convent, 213 W. Olive Avenue, Lampoc, California

Pious Disciples of the Divine Master

Works: Domestic
Write to: Mother Superior, St. Paul's Seminary, 42 Sunset Avenue, Port Richmond, S.I., New York

Institute of Our Lady of Sorrows

Works: Teaching
Write to: Mother Superior, Sacred Heart Mission House, Moreauville, Louisiana

White Sisters of Charity of St. Vincent de Paul

Write to: Mother Superior, Our Lady of Carey Seminary, Carey, Ohio

Sisters Servants of Christ the King

Works: Domestic
Write to: Loretto Convent, Mt. Calvary, Wisconsin

Congregation of the Handmaids of the Precious Blood

Write to: Novitiate, Jemez Springs, New Mexico

HERMANAS CATEQUISTAS GUADALUPANAS
Write to: Mother Superior, 7815 Somerset Road, San Antonio, Texas

MISSIONARIES OF JESUS, MARY, AND JOSEPH
Works: Social Work
Write to: Provincial House, 810 Antelope Street, Corpus Christi, Texas

OBLATES OF THE MOST HOLY REDEEMER
Works: Teaching–Social Work
Write to: Mother Superior, Divine Word Seminary, Duxbury, Massachusetts

RELIGIOUS DAUGHTERS OF ST. JOSEPH
Works: Teaching
Write to: St. Julia School, 3100 Lyons Road, Austin 2, Texas

BENEDICTINE SISTERS
Write to: Mother Superior, 420 S. San Joaquin Street, Stockton, California

DAUGHTERS OF THE MOST HOLY SAVIOUR
Write to: Mother Superior, Holy Redeemer College, 8555 Golf Links Road, Oakland 5, California

DAUGHTERS OF ST. MARY OF LEUCA
Write to: Oblate College, 391 Michigan Avenue, N.E., Washington 17, D.C.

SERVANTS OF ST. JOSEPH
Works: Social Work–Domestic
Write to: St. Joseph Nursery School, 201 S. Spring Street, Falls Church, Virginia

SISTERS OF MERCY
Write to: St. John's Convent, 11154 San Pablo Avenue, El Cerrito, California

SISTERS OF MERCY
Works: Teaching
Write to: Holy Infant School, 324 New Ballwin Road, Ballwin, Missouri

MISSIONARY SISTERS OF OUR LADY OF LA SALETTE
Write to: Shrine of Our Lady of La Salette, Attleboro, Massachusetts

SISTERS OF GUADALUPE
Works: Domestic
Write to: St. Mary College, Winona, Minnesota

CONGREGATION OF CONSOLERS OF THE SACRED HEART
Write to: Mother Superior, 237 W. Magnolia Street, San Antonio, Texas

DAUGHTERS OF OUR LADY OF THE SACRED HEART
Works: Domestic
Write to: St. Francis De Sales Convent, 424 E. Browning Road, Bellmawr, New Jersey

DAUGHTERS OF THE SACRED HEART OF MALTA
Works: Domestic
Write to: SS. Peter and Paul Mission Seminary, Newark, Ohio

LITTLE MISSIONARIES OF THE EUCHARIST
Write to: St. Therese House, 50 Brown Avenue, Roslindale, Massachusetts

MISSIONARY SISTERS OF NOTRE DAME DE AGNES
Works: Teaching–Nursing
Write to: St. Mary's Convent, 338 N. Main Street, Union City, Connecticut

SERVANTS OF THE MOST SACRED HEART OF JESUS
Write to: Visitatrice, 3840 Shannon Road, Erie, Pennsylvania

TEACHING SISTERS OF MARY IMMACULATE
Write to: Mother Superior, 714 Monroe Street N.E., Washington 17, D.C.

SISTERS OF MERCY
Works: Teaching
Write to: Immaculate Conception School, 4501 W. 2nd Avenue, Hialeah, Florida

GEOGRAPHICAL INDEX

* This index lists the communities of sisters in the United States according to their key words, popular names, or geographical locations.